Marxism and Criminology

Studies in Critical Social Sciences Book Series

Haymarket Books is proud to be working with Brill Academic Publishers (www.brill.nl) to republish the *Studies in Critical Social Sciences* book series in paperback editions. This peer-reviewed book series offers insights into our current reality by exploring the content and consequences of power relationships under capitalism, and by considering the spaces of opposition and resistance to these changes that have been defining our new age. Our full catalog of *SCSS* volumes can be viewed at https://www.haymarketbooks .org/series_collections/4-studies-in-critical-social-sciences.

MARXISM AND CRIMINOLOGY

A History of Criminal Selectivity

VALERIA VEGH WEIS

Haymarket Books
Chicago, IL

First published in 2017 by Brill Academic Publishers, The Netherlands.
© 2017 Koninklijke Brill NV, Leiden, The Netherlands

Published in paperback in 2018 by
Haymarket Books
P.O. Box 180165
Chicago, IL 60618
773-583-7884
www.haymarketbooks.org

ISBN: 978-1-60846-930-7

Trade distribution:
In the U.S. through Consortium Book Sales, www.cbsd.com
In the UK, Turnaround Publisher Services, www.turnaround-uk.com
In Canada, Publishers Group Canada, www.pgcbooks.ca
All other countries, Ingram Publisher Services International, ips_intlsales@
ingramcontent.com

Cover design by Jamie Kerry and Ragina Johnson.

This book was published with the generous support of Lannan Foundation
and the Wallace Action Fund.

Printed in Canada.

10 9 8 7 6 5 4 3 2 1

Library of Congress Cataloging-in-Publication Data is available.

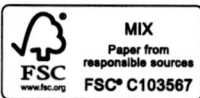

To Enzo, Dolly, Samy, Diana and Carlos

∴

Bullets kill and bars constrain, but the practice of supervision inevitably involves the construction of a set of narratives which allows the kept, the keepers, and the public to believe in a capacity to control [crime] that cannot afford to be tested too frequently.

SIMON 1993

Contents

Foreword

It is very rare these days to find a book that combines a critical, historical and structural account of crime, punishment, and social control. *Marxism and Criminology: A History of Criminal Selectivity* achieves those goals by doing for crime and crime control what Rusche and Kirchheimer – in their path breaking text *Punishment and Social Structure* – did for the analysis of punishment and incarceration. Valeria Vegh Weis offers a form of periodization that echoes *Punishment and Social Structure*'s claims that the dominant forms of punishment in any period will correspond with the main form of production relations. However, Vegh Weis goes beyond that framework and does not limit the analysis to the category of 'labour market' – as Rusche and Kirchheimer did – but she analyses the complex socio-economic conditions underpinning crime and crime control.

To do so, Vegh Weis develops a typology aiming to identify three modalities of 'criminal selectivity' starting from the late 15th century to the present. Within each of these modalities, she analyses the process and discourses associated with the changing forms of selectivity and, in particular, those activities that were 'under-criminalized' and those that were 'over-criminalized.' In the first mode, *original criminal selectivity*, she argues that activities such as the expulsion of farmers and the appropriation of their land were considered legitimate, while vagrancy, begging and prostitution were considered to be serious crimes in need of strict regulation. The second mode, which is referred to as 'disciplinary,' involves the growth of the modern state that introduced new forms of control to discipline the poor and the working class. The third mode is identified as 'bulimic,' in which the poor are culturally included but economically expelled. Drawing on Marx's *Capital* and *Theories of Surplus Value*, it is suggested that the attempts of the previous period to incorporate the working class into the socio-economic structure is reversed.

By this logic, this book moves beyond the limited discourse of much conventional criminology and adopts a broader perspective firmly located within a Marxian tradition. Rather than adopting the classic conservative perspective of seeing crime as a function of the motivation of offenders or alternatively the liberal perspective that sees crime simply as a response to deprivation, Vegh Weis locates the social construction of crime in a historical context. Is in this way that she poses the question of selectivity and why certain groups have come to be conceived as 'criminals' while others are not. This, in turn, raises the question of social categories and their application. It is now commonplace in criminology to point out that the conception of crime and the criminal are structured by class, age, gender and race. Hundreds of studies have discussed the interaction between these 'variables,' but they rarely ask questions about how crime and crime control became associated with the specific combination of these attributes. Understanding the historical development of social categories is a critical, if neglected task, as Vegh Weis suggests.

Moreover, the book does not restrict the analysis to a narrow Marxist framework, but also incorporates a range of sources, including Michel Foucault's analysis of discipline. When describing the emergence of what it is referred as a 'legally-disciplining criminal selectivity' (late 18th century) – the first phase of the *disciplining criminal selectivity* -, Vegh Weis takes into account the lessons of *Discipline and Punish*. There, Foucault notes that, in the transformation from the *Ancien Régime* to industrial capitalism, the notion of crime was distorted, involving a shift from the attack of the body (murder, assault) to theft, and from 'mass cruelty' towards more marginalized forms of professional criminality. This, in turn, required for more efficient, continuous and dedicated forms of policing. Activities that were once considered rights, like the collection of wood were now to be seen as theft, as Marx pointed out in his early writings. As VeghWeis clearly states, with the changing relations of production, a range of practices that were once tolerated became outlawed. At the same time, the bourgeoisie was careful to protect and play down its own transgressions, focusing regulation almost entirely on the activities of the poor. Thus, the aim was not so much to remove illegalities but rather to redistribute and redefine them. Criminal activity was held to be an infringement of the 'social contract' and the criminal becomes the enemy of society as a whole. Crime itself was re-categorized and reconstructed on a continuum of 'seriousness' and assesses, not only in terms of its immediate impact on the victim, but also in terms of its consequences for future disorder. Arriving to the 19th century, Vegh Weis, also following Foucault, refers to the emergence of a 'police-medically disciplining criminal selectivity' – the second phase of the *disciplining criminal selectivity* -, which traces the transition from crime as an 'act' to a situation in which the criminal becomes a specific type of person and the object of a new set of knowledges.

It is no accident that this book and the powerful works of Rusche and Kirchheimer, and Michel Foucault that inspire it, are drawn on the work of Marx and Engels, and are located in the Marxist tradition. Indeed, Marxism provides a critical examination of social phenomena that, unlike the traditional forms of positivism, is able to go beyond appearances and identify the underlying mechanisms in play. Marxism is a body of work that takes the nature of crime, justice and legality seriously, while providing the tools for understanding the mechanisms that sustain and perpetuate them. It is an historically informed approach that aims to understand the issues of our time as function of the changing social relations of production. It aims to link theory to practice, agency and structure. Contrary to both liberal and orthodox interpretations of crime and punishment, Marxism allows us to develop a deeper understanding of these issues within an emancipatory framework.

It is true that some critics discourage a Marxist analysis of crime and punishment by expressing that Marx was critical of the advent of private property seeing it as a form of theft, and that he was at times scathing about the so called 'dangerous classes,' seeing them as parasitic and a potentially reactionary force. However, as Vegh Weis points out, it was also recognized by Marx that, in the dawn of capitalism, the enclosure movement and the forceful evictions from the land separated the worker from the means of production and that many had little option but to become thieves, beggars or bandits. Thus, Marx was sensitive to the conditions that produced criminality and which filled the ranks of the criminal classes with recruits. Marx and Engels demonstrated that it was the very capitalist system, which the bourgeoisie put forward as the model of a just and virtuous society, that produced these threats to its own sense of respectability and order. In this account, Marx and Engels' aim wss not to romanticize the deviant or promulgate illusions about his or her 'freedom' or 'spontaneity,' but rather to point out that the deviants' existence, however authentic, does not transcend the limits of the larger social order. Concerning the analysis of the law, as Vegh Weis suggests, Marx and Engels were not averse to using it to promote or defend working class interests. On the contrary, their aim was to use the legal freedoms available in the bourgeois State to the full in order to develop the workers' movement and to maximize political freedom. Indeed, Marx and Engels constantly promoted demands for universal suffrage, a free press, freedom for trade unions and the abolition of arbitrary and repressive laws.

In sum, this book strives towards a theoretical perspective that connects with the liberative dimension of Marxism and utilizes the critique of crime and social control that allows us to better understand the past while encouraging us to work towards an alternative future.

Roger Matthews
University of Kent
United Kingdom

Preface

"I can't breathe." These were the last words of Eric Gardner, an unarmed Black-American man who died while being arrested in July 2015. Mr. Gardner was committing a low-level offense: selling loose cigarettes in the streets of Staten Island, New York. A neighbor called 911 to complain about Mr. Gardner's familiar presence in front of a local store. Two police officers arrived and, during the arrest, put him in a chokehold – a technique that had been banned by the Police Department as a legal form of restraint. According to videotapes, Mr. Gardner did not resist the arrest. Despite pleading eleven times for help, he was left in the ground, handcuffed and motionless, without immediate aid. The practitioners and paramedics who arrived to attend to him did not follow expected protocol. Videos of Mr. Gardner's death quickly became viral. None of these documented facts were enough to convince the grand jury to bring charges against the police officers responsible for his death (Al Baker 2015).

What struck many social justice advocates about the case was its unfairness. Does the unfairness that plagued Garner's case (social inequality, police brutality, lack of accountability) represent an isolated incident or is it part of a systematic bias in criminal justice systems? Is this punitive and biased legal response to a social conflict a local phenomenon, exclusive to urban areas like New York City, or a national one? Could it even be global? To what extent does the heartbreaking experience of Mr. Gardner describe the current function of criminal justice? Can we track this legal path along modern history? This book thinks through these complex questions lurking beneath Gardner's case as a striking sample of how criminal justice systems have been resting on a complex paradox: a promise of justice mixed with practical unfairness. As a result, it seems that entire communities 'can't breathe' when facing the criminal justice system.[1]

Consider the United States: as of the writing of this book, more than 2 million people are currently in prison serving an average sentence of 1.5 to 2.5 years; more than 7 million are on probation; and more than 3 million are on parole (Garland 2016). This means that 12 million people are part of the U.S.

---

1 'I can't breathe' is now a song written by Mr. Gardner's siblings (Sacks 2016) and a t-shirt wore by famous basket players (The Washington Times 2014; Scott 2014).

system of mass penal control. Most of them are unemployed[2] under-educated[3] young[4] Black-American and Latino males.[5] The ethnic composition of the U.S. prison population has *reversed* over the past 50 years, turning over from 70% white at the mid-century point to nearly 70% Black and Latino today. As a result, more Black-Americans are under correctional control today than were enslaved in 1850, a decade before the civil war started (Alexander 2010, 175). However, ethnic patterns of criminal activity have not been fundamentally altered during the last half of the century (Wacquant 2001, 97).

These biases are present from the start, during the creation of the statutes and during the enforcement of laws. In the first eight months of 2014, for example, Black-American and Latino communities accounted for 86% of those arrested for marijuana possession in New York City (Goldstein 2014). On a national level, 1,100 people are killed by police officers each year: 95% of the victims are male, 50% are 34-years-old or younger, and Black-Americans are heavily over-represented in these numbers, accounting for one in four of these deaths (The Counted 2016). Bias also seems to be an intrinsic aspect of the judicial system. Few of these arrests go to trial: 97% of such cases are closed through plea bargain, where the stigmatized minority population faces a lack of adequate legal defense, as well as implicit and explicit bias from public

---

2 The unemployment rate for Black-Americans averaged 11.6% between 1963 and 2012, more than double the white jobless rate over that time (Fletcher 2013). Black and Latinos families headed by single mothers are likely to live below the poverty line (McKernan et al., 2009).

3 A quarter of Black-American students attend 'drop out factories,' high schools where close to half (or more) of the students aren't graduating in four years. And numerous studies document how even high-achieving poor students rarely apply to top colleges (Building a Grad Nation Report 2016).

4 Black-Americans are not significantly more likely than whites to be stopped for clear traffic safety law violations. But in investigatory stops, a Black-American man age twenty-five or younger has a 28% chance of being stopped for an investigatory reason over the course of a year; a similar young white man has a 12.5% chance. As people grow older they are less likely to be stopped in this way, but a Black-American man must reach fifty – well into the graying years – before his risk of an investigatory stop drops below that of a white man under age twenty-five (Epp and Maynard-Moody 2014).

5 A white woman has only a 7% chance of being stopped by police officers for an investigatory reason over the course of a year (Epp and Maynard-Moody 2014). When discussing sentencing, the average sentence for males is 278.4% greater than that of females (51.5 versus 18.5 months) (Mustard 2001, 296). Females receive even shorter sentences relative to men than White-Americans relative to Black-Americans (302). On the other hand, when combining gender with class and race, studies show that women of color and low income women are disproportionately affected by mandatory arrest policies for domestic violence (INCITE-NATIONAL 2016, 38).

servants (Gleeson 2016). Even when the accused are granted a trial, they confront mostly white juries. Overall, Latinos and Black-Americans are incarcerated at a much higher rate than whites: in a sample of 100,000 U.S. residents, more than 4,000 would be people of color, in comparison with less than 700 White-Americans.[6] Unfairness does not end when people are released from prison. After serving time, they can lose the franchise to vote, face removal from public housing, have their parental rights withdrawn, be prohibited against becoming foster or adoptive parents, confront restrictions to holding public office, and be rejected from welfare assistance. These are only a few of several collateral consequences of convictions (Jacobs 2015).

This problem is not exclusive to the United States. In Europe, criminal justice is not quite as demographically homogenous as in the United States, but it still disproportionately targets immigrants and minorities (Antunes 2003). Currently, Europe is rethinking the operation of its criminal justice systems in face of mass, often forced, migrations and their unknown impact on European cultural identity. These debates have been intensified by backlashes of local populations against immigrants. Recently, immigration policies have been cited as a key factor in Great Britain's decision to leave the European Union. Similarly, the United States is in a critical moment of national rethinking about class and racial inequality. Data increasingly provides evidence that those targeted by a system of mass penal control are often racial minorities and the poor. These discussions have been exacerbated by high tensions between law enforcement and communities of color,[7] and by the emergence, in the United States, of the Black Lives Matter movement. The relevance of these debates in the public arena is so important that the last U.S. presidential candidates, from both conservative and liberal sides, have offered radical agendas for rethinking the criminal justice system.

The unfairness of criminal justice systems is currently in the spotlight. This illumination is already a victory if we acknowledge that such unfairness has

---

6 Latinos and Black-Americans are incarcerated at a rate of 4,347 people per 100,000 U.S. residents of the same race and gender, while white men were imprisoned at a rate of 678 prisoners per 100,000 inhabitants (Bureau of Justice Statistics 2010).

7 One of the outcomes was the recent resign of Bratton, who was the leader of the broken windows policing model. This happened after communities of color' organizations protested against him in City Hall. The New York-based Communities United for Police Reform asserted that Bratton "was no reformer to communities impacted by abusive and discriminatory policing." Civil Rights Attorney Darius Charney, who sued the N.Y.P.D. over its stop-and-frisk practices, expressed his concern about Bratton's legacy (Weichselbaum 2016).

been hidden under the name of idealized justice. This idealization proclaims that if a subset of the population had been targeted more intensively by the criminal justice system, it is just the reasonable and unbiased response to the fact that the real offenders were among those people. Historically, criminal justice systems often punish people as a mode of social control and not just as a response to their crimes. This distortion is the core of legal unfairness. The manipulation of crime control as a tool to intervene in social unrest neglects the corollary that punishment ought to be used as a last resort and only for those behaviors that cause real social harm.

We must then look at how this unfairness is not only a clear feature in the operation of criminal justice systems, but that it is also not a recent event. In fact, this unfairness has been with us since the 15th century at least. It is not an accident, but a mandated feature of a criminal justice system. This book is committed to challenging existing narratives that analyze crime and punishment purely from a normative-legal perspective. Instead, it conceives of them as part of the socio-economic environment, plagued by legal discretion and bias. The book discusses the persistence of unfairness in crime control through a critical, holistic and historical analysis. This focus is not just a personal and impassioned response to bias. Instead, this book sutures the idea of unfairness to a critical and theoretical perspective. Such unfairness in all the spheres of a criminal justice system, plagued by stigmatizing patterns of class, race, ethnicity, gender, and religious bias, will be referred to as 'criminal selectivity.'

Criminal selectivity is much more pervasive in society rather than being limited to criminal justice systems. It begins in the context of unequal economic distribution. As Thomas Piketty (2013) notes in his widely read and discussed book, 10% of the most economically advantaged people in the world own between 80% and 90% of global wealth, while 50% of the poorest population combined own less than 5% of the world's wealth. 921 million people worldwide live in slums, well below the poverty line (Davis 2006). In the United States alone, 1.5 million families (with three million children overall) live on less than $2.00 per person per day (Kathryn and Luke 2015). The situation is even more striking for the racial minorities. Young Black-American men are more likely to go to prison than to college. Just to give an example, while 992 Black-American men received a bachelor's degree from the Illinois State Universities in 1999, roughly 7,000 Black-American men were released from Illinois state prison system in 2000 for low-level drug offenses (Alexander 2010, 184–185). Criminal selectivity seems to be working as a means to fulfill social control functions over racial minorities and impoverished populations, and not as an exclusive means of crime control.

The scope of this book is the criminal justice system, and it will comprehensively analyze criminal selectivity from looking at how it operates throughout the penal process. The first stage takes place through the drafting of statutes, when selectivity generates 'inequality under the law.' The second stage in this process may be called 'law enforcement profiling,' which can be defined as the biased discretional and selective activity of law enforcement agents (including border patrol and special teams).[8] This is not just 'racial profiling' – as it is commonly referred to – but also includes class, ethnicity, gender, and religion bias. The third stage involves judicial and prosecutorial activity. We might call the third stage 'courts' discretion,' to make it clear that it does not only refer to the so-called 'prosecutorial discretion,' but also includes judges', defense attorneys', and juries' biased performance. The fourth stage, which we will call 'differential penalization,' relates to imbalanced punishments and, in particular, to prison management. It includes the administration of the collateral consequences of convictions that help re-start the cycle of economic and social exclusion.

The book will also be analyzing this holistic analysis of the selective operation of the criminal justice system from a historical perspective to show that unfairness has been a standard pattern of the capitalist system of production. Examining the continuities and discontinuities of this long historical process may help us understand criminal selectivity as it relates to the complex socio-economic structure, with its cultural, political, religious, ethnic and gender-specific features. The book takes its readers on a path through the capitalist system of production, focusing on those behaviors that have been systematically criminalized and those that have been consistently ignored by crime control agencies since the 15th century to today. The book also proposes who were the social actors that perform both kinds of behaviors. Finally, the book points out which were the discourses that have made this unfair operation of the criminal justice system possible, as well as the underlying material goals of punishment within those ideological discourses.

In order to understand how unfairness have been plaguing each stage of the criminal justice system through capitalism it was necessary to go beyond legal analyses. This history of criminal selectivity is inextricably tied to the socio-economic spheres in which it takes place. Marx and Engels are called to bring to the table the methodology of historical materialism while their theoretical contributions are used as sources for reflection. This double approach is the one that allows us to situate crime and punishment in the development of the

---

8 While writing this lines, a s.w.a.t. team – a special group designed to confront particularly complex crimes- entered in the house of a black mother to enforce a traffic ticket. While doing so, they killed her, while also injuring her five-years old son (Lowery 2016).

capitalist system of production, and to analyze in-depth the interaction of the legal sphere with its economic, political, social, cultural, religious, ethnic and gender implications. This materialistic perspective is the one that helps prove that, far from being a circumstantial phenomenon, the selective functioning of the criminal justice system has been present since the origins of capitalism because it has been a necessary tool for the foundation and reproduction of this mode of production.

Although this book does not suggest concrete public policies, it is hoped that the analysis provided here would serve as an impetus to ask deeper questions in more comprehensive ways to frame the discussion of how to deal with and overcome unfairness in criminal justice systems. When analyzing the history of modern crime and punishment, evidence suggests that the most outrageous crime is the drastic inequality within the operation of criminal justice. The contemporary system that has been born in the name of 'justice' has been operating in a biased manner in terms of class, race, ethnicity, religion, gender, and age. After more than half a millennium of unfairness, the time is very ripe to think radically about how to overturn this feature. The proposed concept of criminal selectivity is meant to illuminate the intrinsic unfairness in the application of and punishment that thrives alongside capitalism. My desire is that this clarification might make the all too distant idea of 'change' became a much more feasible goal.

Acknowledgements

I write these lines with deep gratitude because I have a lot for which to be thankful. This book would not have been possible without the academic and emotional collaboration, support, and inspiration of a great number of people.

Martin O'Reagan and Brittany Magnin undertook the copyediting process. They have enthusiastically helped me in nourishing the book with a bright tone, polishing lines that I have thought in a non-native language. Martin has been the principal responsible for the editing process and has accompanied me during long days of reviewing and editing. Brittany has played the role of a magician in helping to assure that my voice comes through clearly and powerfully. I want to express my profound gratitude to Hanna Zemichael who helped me to polish and improve the final version of the manuscript.

The cover of the book is the result of countless days and nights of effort put forth by my partner, Enzo Leone. Enzo did not leave my side for even one single minute; he was always here to read each and every line, give comments and express his support and encouragement which are responsible for making this book come to light. Many thanks to my amazing friend Noelia Langle who kindly offered her artistic support.

I would also like to extend my thanks to all the great friends and colleagues I have encountered at New York University School of Law who accompanied me on this journey. I am particularly grateful to Gabe Chipkin who helped me prepare the first draft, and to Samantha Wayne and Giuseppe Bianco who gave me critical inputs in key sections of the book. A very special thanks to Christopher Stahl, a star consultant from the NYU Writing Center, who helped me to think and write better in our inspiring weekly meetings. Thanks to Professors Anthony Thompson, Kim Taylor-Thompson, Thane Rosenbaum, and Peggy Cooper Davis for their invaluable support and encouragement.

My sincere gratitude crosses the equator all the way back to Argentina, my homeland. I remember going to visit Atilio Boron, with this project in hand and a deep admiration, at the very beginning of this process. I was greeted warmly with his human quality that comes to overshadow his theoretical grandeur. He introduced me to the person that would be my Ph.D. director, Fernando Lizárraga, a privileged guide through the process of creating and writing, and the most detailed and keen critic of my work. Fernando has accompanied me since this book was just an idea, throughout the process of thinking, writing and revising it. Atilio also introduced me to Mariano Ciafardini, a prominent academic and activist in whom I found my passion for teaching. I also want to thank Roberto Gargarella, who has encouraged my project since the moment it was a proposal presented to the Buenos Aires University Ph.D. Committee.

No less significant was the support of my Argentinean peers who sustained me emotionally and academically in moments of hesitation and uncertainty, typical of any writing process. Here, the big thanks goes to Betina Riva, who made the extensive effort to empathize with Marxism from its intransigent liberal stance to help me read, edit, re-read and re-correct the thesis as many times as necessary. I also want to thank Tamara Rotundo, who helped me incorporate the subjective perspective in the macro-social analysis and to Antonella Comba, who played a fundamental role in the final and critical moments of the writing process.

Institutionally, I feel extremely grateful to Brill for giving me the opportunity to publish this book. Particularly, I want to express my gratitude to David Fasenfest, Rosanna Woensdregt and Maria Baluch for their priceless patience and support. I thank the CONICET and BECAR scholarships which allowed me to start this work process, and to FULBRIGHT and GLOBAL HAUSER scholarships that made the enrichment of this work, during my studies at New York University, possible. Many thanks to the Defense Attorney Office of Buenos Aires City, and particularly to the interdisciplinary team for which I have been working for the last four years. Thanks to my fellows and students at Buenos Aires University, IUPFA and UNQ, who allowed me to think and discuss many of the topics that are displayed in this book.

My last and most profound thanks are for my mom Dolly, my father Carlos, my sisters Diana and Samy, and my partner Enzo.

List of Illustrations

Figure

Tables

CHAPTER 1

Introduction

This book explores the historical and socio-economic conditions underpinning inequality throughout all the stages of the criminal process, based on criteria such as class, race, ethnicity, religion, gender, and age. As it was mentioned in the Preface, those stages include the unequal legal treatment in statutes and common law, law enforcement profiling, courts' discretion, and differential penalization. The systematic and comprehensive inequality throughout all those instances will be termed 'criminal selectivity.' The book relies on the theoretical contributions of Karl Marx, Friedrich Engels, and contemporary Marxist thought to approach the phenomenon of criminal selectivity coupled with the historical development of the capitalist system of production and its productivity ideals from the 15th century to today.

The unfairness of criminal justice systems has been widely recognized today as a key concept for analyzing the relationship between crime and its control. However, the selectivity phenomenon has not been sufficiently acknowledged or widely discussed. Moreover, there is a dearth of studies that address the development of selectivity throughout modern history by identifying the specific mechanisms through which it materially unfolds. Conversely, abstract, fragmentary and biased analysis of inequality in the criminal justice systems have prevailed. This research looks to correct this oversight and seeks to outline the groundwork to build a more accurate analysis of the ever-evolving criminal justice system.

Against this backdrop, this book proposes a typology of criminal selectivity that evolves alongside the emerging socio-economic structure, through three successive forms: *original criminal selectivity* (late 15th to 18th century), *disciplining criminal selectivity* (late 18th to 20th century) and *bulimic criminal selectivity* (late 20th century to the present).[1] This approach corresponds to the

---

1   While a periodization may contain some level of arbitrariness, it is also a useful tool to deepen the understanding of the historical development of criminal selectivity. The identified modalities do not override the previous ones, but they incorporate them, deploying in a predominantly new form.

From the vastness of the work of Marx and Engels, this book focuses on those texts that have addressed explicitly or tangentially some dimension of criminal selectivity. Many of these run throughout the book, but as particularized for the construction of original criminal selectivity, the book draws on Chapter XXIV of Volume I of *Capital* (1867) by Marx, where the German philosopher explores the characterization of primitive accumulation. In disciplining

two cores of Marxist analysis: the study of the forces of production and the social relations of production.[2]

---

criminal selectivity, this incorporates a wide variety of texts: *On the Jewish Question* (1844) and *Critique of the Gotha Program* (1875), both by Marx, and *The German Ideology* (1845) by Marx and Engels, to characterize legal-disciplining selectivity and the regulatory system forged by the bourgeoisie in its rise to political power. Chapters I, VII and XXIII of Volume I of *Capital* (1867) by Marx and *The Condition of the Working Class in England* (1845) by Engels have been used for the analysis of police-disciplining medical selectivity, while they deploy there a rigorous analysis of policing and positivist discourse oriented to the disciplining of the working class. *Theories of Surplus Value* (1867b) by Marx have been used to study the socio-criminal disciplining selectivity, where Marx ironically faces the functionalist ideologies that seek to postulate a rationale to understand the persistence offenses in the framework of capitalism. Finally, in the development of the bulimic criminal selectivity, Chapters I and II of Volume III of *Capital* (1867) and *Theories of Surplus Value* (1867b), both by Marx, have provided illuminating concepts for the study of the financial capitalism and the characters that conflict and control adopted in this framework.

Throughout the book, other important works of Marx will be considered, namely: *Critique of Hegel's Philosophy of Right* (1844b); *Economic and Philosophic Manuscripts of 1844* (1844c); *The Poverty of Philosophy* (1847); *Struggle Class in France 1848–1850* (1850), *The 18th Brumaire of Louis Bonaparte* (1852), fundamental elements for the critique of political economy (1857/8b), *Preface to A Contribution to the Critique of Political Economy* (1859b), *The Civil War in France* (1871), and a large number of newspaper articles: "Debates on the Law on the Theft of Wood" (1842), "From the Mosel" (1843), "Speech in defense" (1849), "A Bourgeois Document" (1849b), "Revelations Concerning the Communist Trial in Cologne" (1852b), "Capital Punishment" (1853), "Imprisonment of Lady Bulwer-Lytton" (1858) and "Population, Crime and Pauperism" (1859). Concerning colonialism, the book addresses a variety of articles published in New-York Daily Tribune, Rheinische Zeitung (the Rheinische Zeitung) and the Neue Rheinische Zeitung (The Neue Rheinische Zeitung).

Among Engels' works, the following will be considered: *Principles of Communism* (1847), *The Peasants War in Germany* (1850), *Her Eugen Duhring's Revolution in Science (Anti-Dühring)* (1878), *Socialism: Utopian and Scientific* (1880) and *The Origin of the Family* (1884b). Among his articles are included: "The Latest Feat of the House of Bourbon" (1848) and "Marx and the Neue Rheinische Zeitung" (1884).

Regarding the work that Marx and Engels wrote together, the following will be analyzed: *The Communist Manifesto* (1848), *The Holy Family* (1848b), *The Revolutions of 1848* (1848c), along with their correspondence and other thinkers and activists systematized by Enzensberger (1974), as well as in Selected Works (1963, 1974) and the Marxists Internet Archive (2000).

2   Marx explains that in each mode of production, the forces of production correspond to a type of relation of production that constitutes the social structure. The economic structure relates to a superstructure composed of, social, cultural, legal and political institutions, class struggle, political and social actions of individuals, daily life and others. Marxism is understood here as a space for open dialogue between structure and superstructure.

Each chapter of the book will focus on a different modality of criminal selectivity. The first section of each chapter will analyze the contextual setting of that mode of criminal selectivity. The second sections will explore how criminal selectivity is expressed in two mechanisms referred to as *under-criminalization* and *over-criminalization*. The third sections will dig in who were the social sectors that have suffered persecution inflicted by criminal selectivity and who were those in power of this selectivity process. Finally, the fourth sections of each chapter will discuss the discourses that have legitimized the application of punishment in each mode of criminal selectivity (theories of punishment), as well as the latent explanations underpinning those theories. Using this logic, the book contributes and delves into the question raised by Becker (1962) – founding father of the labeling approach – and ratified by Taylor, Walton and Young (1973) – major exponents of the critical criminology – as a challenge to the criminological thought: *who enforces the rules and why?*

With a view to answer this question, this book intends to build new categories of analysis that redefine central criminal concepts from a socio-economic perspective based on the Marxist conceptual framework. This relies on the conviction that "some Marxist concepts help us in the process of destroying the criminology we do not need (or want) and build the set of notions (criminal, punishment, prisons, etc.) that we need here and now" (Melossi 2012, 138). This discussion proposes to reframe the dominant narratives of crime and punishment with the goal of re-conceptualizing the current unfairness of the criminal justice system from a historical and comprehensive perspective. The fundamental purpose is to clarify that inequality and punishment are inherently related and that only a thorough understanding of their historical and structural roots can open a path for change.

Regarding the timeline, this research focuses on the historical development of criminal selectivity from the 15th century – described by Marx as the dawn of the capitalist system of production – up to today. Concerning the geographical scope, the focus is on the events that took place in Western Europe because, generally speaking, the historical trends of the criminal justice systems were first developed, defined and shaped there. Also, classical Marxist studies have predominantly centered on Europe. From the 20th century to today,

---

Following the concepts of 'hegemony' and 'historical bloc' of Gramsci (1948, 1949), 'over-determination' of Althusser (1965) and 'relative autonomy' of Poulantzas (1969), it is possible to affirm that the structure conditions (not determines) the superstructure. The latter has an autonomous capacity to influence the material processes, creating an ongoing dialogue. Superstructural instances, including the law, can be studied and analyzed in a timely and precise manner, given their relative independence from the economic base.

the book emphases mainly on the United States. This is the time-period when the country became an economic and political superpower, as well as a center for criminological theories.

This investigation relies on the dialogue of three different frameworks: the theoretical and methodological legacy of Marx and Engels; contemporary Marxist thought; and criminology theories which utilize interdisciplinary studies. The first ones liberate the research from the risk of relying on a norm-based legalistic analysis removed from empirical reality. The contributions of criminology (and other disciplinary fields) help to avoid those studies that oversimplify the connection between criminal selectivity to the needs of capitalism.

Finally, this research is situated in the fields of criminal law and criminology,[3] understanding them as part of the broader field of social sciences. This means neglecting the most orthodox views that conceive criminology as just an auxiliary tool to analyze criminal law.[4] This book maintains that a critical analysis cannot circumscribe the criminal field only to the punitive actors (the offender, the victim, law enforcement, judges, etc.) and separate it from its socioeconomic context.

Criminological Theories and the Notion of 'Criminal Selectivity'

The history of criminological thoughts (and its lack of attention to the criminal selective process) can be divided into two separate periods: before and after the mid-20th century. Before the mid-20th-century, criminological schools

---

3   Authors identified with critical criminology, including Baratta and Bergalli, explain that the word 'criminology' refers to a 'science about crime' committed to the positivist approach. Therefore, they proposed replacing it with the concept of 'legal and criminal sociology' or 'sociology of penal control' (Anitua 2005, 4). In Bergalli's own words, "the noun 'criminology' belongs and is anchored to the etiological paradigm on individual causes of crime" (1987, 783).

4   While criminology forms a separate field with a defined object of study, in practice it has been developed as an auxiliary discipline of the interests of criminal law, and more specifically, of law and order. This, as "criminologists do not challenge traditional moral and political assumptions contained in the legal definitions of their subject" (Van Swaaningen 1997, 8). Nevertheless, critical criminologists "refused to practice criminology as an auxiliary discipline to criminal law coercion and devoted themselves to the study of the functioning of the criminal justice system as a state instrument to maintain unchanged power relations" (129). Moreover, sustaining criminology as an auxiliary field narrows the horizons of analysis for criminal law: indeed, "criminology emerged in the second half of the nineteenth century to save the criminal law of certain death as a doctrine that has lost touch with social reality" (397).

concentrated only on the crime itself (classical school), only on the criminal (inquisition and positivism), or only on the social and geographic environment of the offender (sociological schools). The explanation of crime relied on behavioral problems, biological shortcomings, and individual socialization, respectively. All of them ignored references to the social context that encompasses the crime conflict. As Young expressed: "[t]he correctional criminology had achieved a feat. It had gotten run over the offense for nearly a century without recourse to state theory" (1976, 11). With variants, these conceptions remain in force: Criminology "is not a paleontological museum, but a real zoo in which all species are alive" (Zaffaroni 2011, 8).

In the mid-20th century, Sutherland (1940, 1949), an exponent of one of the sociological theories, the Chicago school, noted the existence of a 'dark figure of crime' in statistics: not all criminal behaviors were effectively criminalized. He named these unnoticed actions as white-collar crimes and described them as crimes committed by professional traders and people of good social reputation – this means people far away from traditional criminal stereotypes. Sellin (1944), an exponent of the theories of conflict, anticipated the concept of criminal selectivity through the distinction between 'real' and 'apparent' criminality. Notwithstanding the relevance of Sutherland and Sellin's contributions, they have concentrated their efforts on the study of their specific historical context. Thus, they have neither delved into the phenomenon of selectivity from a long-term historical perspective nor have they linked the selectivity phenomenon to its socio-economic context.

Bonger, Pashukanis, and Rusche and Kirchheimer provide the first Marxist approaches to crime and its control. Bonger (1905) points out the link between crime and capitalism. He highlights the role of economic hardship and disruption of humanitarian ties as determinants of crime. Bonger identifies harmful behaviors that are not classified as 'crimes' in the statistics. Even before Sutherland (1940, 1949), he identifies the existence of offences committed by bankers, brokers and traders while doing business. These actions were unrepresented in crime statistics (1940, 599–607). Pashukanis (1924), despite failing to identify the selective phenomenon, utilizes Chapter 2 of *Capital*[5] to explain that fetishism permeates the entire law. Law offers a false perception of men and women, and legal transactions as equal and fair. This distortion reinforces capitalist relations under the wing of a false 'general interest.' Pashukanis also introduces the notion of 'social order' – as opposed to the concept of

---

5   In Chapter 11 of *Capital*, Marx (1867) develops the concept of fetishism as an outstanding feature of capitalism. This is a process of alienation, whereby the labor force – the most important of all merchandise, as notable for its ability to produce more goods – becomes an object.

'society' – to characterize the conflicting nature of social reality. Rusche, in his own work (1930, 1933), and in conjunction with Kirchheimer (1938), addresses a historical analysis of changes in the punitive system relating to the labor market. Despite the great contribution of the latter work, Greenberg (1976), Pavarini and Melossi (1980), and Garland (1990) note that the category 'labor market' is very restrictive and does not include the broader socio-economic conditions underpinning punishment.

In the 1960s, the u.s. sociologists developed the labeling approach. This theory focused on the criminal agencies and their unequal practices. With this theory, "punitive power actually enters the universe of the criminological horizon as partially independent investigation of the crime" (De Giorgi 2002, 54). Becker, the author of *Outsiders*, one the most relevant book of this theory, explains: "It is very interesting that most of the scientific research and speculation about diversion deal more with the people who break the rules than with those who produce or apply it" (1962, 182). Since the labeling approach, the criminological thought stopped asking 'who is the criminal?' and started asking 'who is considered the target?' (Anitua 2005, 363).

Tannenbaum (1938), Lemert (1951), and notably Becker (1962) propose the concept of 'deviant' - the individual who does not follow social expectations -, as opposed to the notion of 'criminal' – that has to do with the label imposed by penal agencies -. Becker also created the concept of 'moral entrepreneurs' to refer to those individuals or groups that directly or indirectly help to build standards regarding what gets considered as 'criminal' (182). This concept may be combined with the notion of moral panics – formulated by Cohen (1974) – that refers to the mechanisms that are used to create a favorable social environment for the enactment and enforcement of criminal laws.

Despite these significant contributions, the labeling approach does not exceed the limits of the 'middle-range theory' (Merton 1949):[6] It studies crime control but it does not question the broader issues (social control) in which the former takes place. Thus, the key issues remain unanswered: Who defines what is 'criminal' and what is not? What interests do they defend? How do their acts further entrench the capitalist system of production? (Taylor et al. 1973, 196). Also, this theory does not analyze the actual fact behind the label – the 'crime conflict' (i.e. the fact that behind the label of 'theft' someone has actually taken something from another person)-.

---

6 Merton created the concept of 'middle-range theory' to describe those approaches that focus on the intermediate stages between those minor assumptions that are abundantly produced during daily routine research, and those systematic efforts to develop a unified theory to explain all observed uniformities of behavior, organization and social change (1949, 56).

In Becker-Gouldner's discussion (1973), Gouldner takes a Marxist perspective to criticize the labeling approach. He says that this theory considers the deviants as passive actors that 'receive' a label. However, those considered deviants may have a conscious political motive to deviate from the norm, or they can refuse the label as illegitimate. So far, the labeling approach remains "within the narrow confines of a micro-sociological perspective [as] it is not founded on general assumptions concerning the material foundation of the power of labeling" (De Giorgi 2002, 54). Taylor, Walton and Young add in the same vein:

> Of course, there are those who define and are defined, but who represent the first? What interests do they defend? How do they entrench their actions [in] the current character of capitalist society? It gives no answer to these questions: who are defined as a group of villains who are self-employed? (1973, 196).

Because of these critiques, Sparks urges that the questions raised by the labeling approach from a historical and macro-social perspective should be reformulated. Instead of focusing on the process of criminalization, we should ask why these forms of behavior are qualified as criminal and why there are certain activities that are demonstrably harmful but not criminalized (1980, 175).

Although he does not use the term criminal selectivity, Foucault (1964, 1972, 1977/8, 1978/9) refers to the 'differential administration of illegalities' as an axial element of modern criminal law. Even though some academic positions place Foucault as opposed to the Marxist theoretical perspective, it is possible to draw a confluence between the two. This is particularly pronounced in Foucault's *Discipline and Punish* (1975), where he focuses on the political economy of punishment.[7]

---

7 As Said states: "[with] a rapid and comprehensive review of the work of Foucault, we are obliged to accept that if there is a microphysics of power, the power is everywhere, and the reproduction of power relations and correlative struggles is infinite. That is, there are power relations in school, clinic, in prison, in the family, in sexuality, etc. Now, from this, a questionable procedure, argue that these findings cannot be brought within the scope of society as a whole. Well, if society is composed of individuals involved in the gears of the power that is exercised in different institutions, it is evident that these power relations manifest themselves in society in general. It would be unwise to suggest that, on the one hand, there are connections subjected to a 'non-political' rule, which would be the above, and, on the contrary, the ratio of 'political power' would be the one between 'governors and the governed,' between 'state and society'" (1996, 428).

In the 1970s, critical criminology took one step further from the labelling approach theory. It researched the connection between the function of the criminal agencies and the characteristics of the capitalist system of production. From a materialist analysis, critical criminologists successfully studied the unequal role of the penal institutions without splitting them from the study of social control.

Taylor, Walton and Young are the co-authors of the most important work in this trend, *The New Criminology: For a Social Theory of Deviance* (1973), and its sequel, *Critical Criminology* (1975). They develop an outstanding review of previous criminological thought, from a materialistic perspective. Through it, they enable a critical reflection of the (non-) treatment of criminal selectivity by the criminological thought before the 1970s. They underline how 500 years of criminological reflection lacks an actual analysis of the inequality of the criminal justice system and its relation to the social structure. Conversely, these authors highlight:

> [t]he importance of inquiring how far a particular form of political economy, speaking crudely, the Western industrial capitalism, [...] – has influenced the way of criminal law as we know it, and (more generally) ask what are the relations between capitalism and the trappings of 'criminal justice' (1973, 176).

In this line of questioning, critical criminologists resort to Marx, contending that he "offers such insight into the links between law and economics" like no other researcher (Renner 1975, 76). Marxism helps them visualize and denounce the class character of criminal law and criminal behavior as an expression of a class society:

> The criminal law is not the reflection of customs (as some theorists argue), but are rules imposed by the state in the interests of the ruling class and which are in inherent conflict with the class society. Criminal behavior is, then, the inevitable expression of class conflict resulting from the explosive nature of economic relations.
>
> CHAMBLISS 1975, 151

A materialist theory should critically contemplate the phenomena of crime and criminalization:

> A critical theory of crime control in capitalist society now faces the criminal law as a coercive instrument of the state, used by the state and its

ruling class to preserve the existing economic and social order. Therefore, in developing a critical Marxist theory of crime control, we must consider the following issues: (1) the offense and the ruling class, (2) crime control in the capitalist state, and (3) the demystification of the law. The goal is a critical understanding of the modern legal regime.

QUINNEY 1975, 241–242

Among critical criminologists, Baratta (1974, 1985, 1986, 1995) proposes to develop a criminological position from the perspective of the 'working class.' Melossi (1980b, 1984, 1990, 1991, 1997, 2012) and Pavarini (1975, 1980b, 1995, 2006) in their joint work, *The Prison and the Factory* (1980), seek to link the origins of prisons with the development of factories. Avoiding a purely economic view, they highlight how punishment has been deployed by the requirements of the system of production. Bales (1984) studies the intersection between legal and illegal businesses in the capitalist system. Quinney (1982) advocates for the development of a Marxist theory to critically understand the modern legal system. Chambliss (1964, 1975, 1976, 1978) raises the possibility of a political-economic theory of crime. He visualizes the class character of criminal law and characterizes criminal behaviors as an expression of a class society. Chambliss also focuses his attention on the application of penal control in U.S. ghettos, in contrast with the lack of monitoring of the crimes committed by influential individuals. Spitzer (1975) proposes to develop a Marxist criminological theory that differentiates the categories of people on which crime control rests. Bergalli (1980, 1982, 1987, 1996, 1997, 2003, 2012), an exponent of the Latin-American critical criminology, studies the intersection between social control and the penal system. He calls for a reflection on the complexity of socially harmful acts that are not criminalized.

In short, critical criminology proposes a theoretical perspective that includes the criminal institutions and their interaction with the socio-economic system. However, several authors have formulated serious objections to this approach: the difficulties of bringing together Marxism and criminology; the absence of proactive proposals to address crime; the diversity of the various theoretical positions; the idealization of the offender; and the lack of empirical work (Anitua 2005, 426). Van Swaaningen notes that:

Sectarianism, different theories describing the crime as a mere example of deviation, the unwillingness to treat positivist and statistical issues, and the message that, regarding penal reform, nothing will work, are the factors that make an internal crisis, in analyzing critical criminology (1997, 9).

Melossi (1984) explains that to overcome these problems, critical criminology should bet on a combination of the micro-sociological interactionism approach and the macro-sociological perspective of Marxism. As a result of its desire to progress in the second area, critical criminology neglected the first one. It also failed to pay sufficient attention to white-collar crimes and did not delve into the historical development and particular mechanisms of the selective phenomenon.

Abolitionism was then developed in the 1970s and 1980s. It distinguishes between 'criminalization' and 'decriminalization,' a counterpoint to the concept of criminal selectivity. One of its exponents, Christie (1993), warns about the link between the increasing criminalization and crime control as an 'industry.'

In the 1980s, the right realism theory sought to develop a criminological approach centered on the return to a biological etiology (Murray and Herrnstein 1994) or a rationalist one (G. Becker 1968). Both ignore the economic and social context in which crime unfolds. Conversely, they focus on crime control through a law and order logic as the only viable option for resolving crime conflicts. They state that the failure to reduce crime was not a sign of the inaccuracy of law and order policies, but of their faulty implementation, in a self-validating reasoning. This approach has exponentially increased criminalization, ignoring the socio-economic factors behind the crime conflict, as well as the selective phenomenon.

Also in the 1980s, the school of left realism tried to answer the crisis surrounding the Marxist approach. It acknowledges that the crimes committed by the most disadvantaged people mostly affect those of the same social status. Therefore, a Marxist proposal had to address concrete responses to crime, in defense of the disadvantaged. The strategy was to concentrate on the advancement of criminal policies from a leftist perspective to compete with the proposals of law and order. Left realism faced the difficult challenge of not falling into legitimizing or merely reforming solutions, but also of not embracing idealism and rejection (Lea and Young 1984). Despite these efforts, this approach ended up giving excessive importance to the communal voice in political, criminal and security decisions (Zaffaroni et al. 2000, 314). This strategy confused community fear rooted in real violence with moral panics induced by manipulation of the population (315). By focusing on the design of criminal policy, this approach also neglected wider theoretical research and, notably, it did not conduct any research on criminal selectivity.

At the beginning of the 21st century, cultural criminology provided insight into the cultural transformations that underlie changes in criminal policies. This school concentrates on the socio-cultural processes configured after the advent of neoliberal governments. As one of its exponents, Young

(1999, 2000, 2007, 2008, 2012) disputed the Manichean division between 'included' and 'excluded' populations. He offers the concepts of 'bulimia' and 'inclusion-exclusion' as a sophisticated perspective that puts those categories in dialogue. Highly relevant is the work of thinkers such as Simon, Wacquant, Garland, De Giorgi, Alexander, Bourgois, Tonry, Harcourt and Greenberg, among many others. They have been studying the law and order phenomenon of recent decades. Their contributions are indispensable for the study of the selectivity phenomenon, and some of them have even called for further investigations on the historical interrelation between crime and social control. Simon in particular invited us to "look across the many historical examples in which crime and government have been in some deep sense intertwined" (2007, 15).

This brief summary of the criminological thoughts shows that even though some theories attempted to clarify the inequality within the criminal justice system, they did not develop studies of the particular phenomenon of criminal selectivity. It has only been considered collaterally (critical criminology and left realism) and from an abstract perspective (labelling approach). Furthermore, these theories have neither identified the specific mechanisms through which criminal selectivity has manifested, nor did they trace its development in earlier historical moments. Therefore, criminal selectivity has not yet been explored in its own right within a historical and socio-economic context.

Criminal Selectivity through the Work of Marx and Engels

To develop a consistent analysis of criminal selectivity from Marx and Engels' perspective, it is imperative to first analyze the objections to this approach. For analytical purposes, it is possible to structure the different objections in three categories. First, Marx and Engels did not study the criminal field in depth. Thus, any inferences drawn from their works would be insufficient. Second, crime and its control are superstructural phenomena determined by the economic structure and, hence, Marx and Engels did not offer a separate analysis of them. Third, the Marxist approach led to the experience of the so-called 'real socialism.' Thus, this approach may result in new abuses as the ones committed in that context. Let us analyze each of these in detail.

Marx and Engels' Contributions Did Not Analyze Crime and Crime Control in Depth

Gouldner (1973) argues that Marx and Engels did not make significant contributions to the criminological field. He also states that they conceived offenders as part of the lumpen-proletariat, a social sector that intervenes in the class struggle against the interest of the working class. According to this view, Marx and Engels would reject offenders as counter-revolutionary figures that do not deserve attention. Ramirez (1983) also notes that the founding fathers of Marxism made few specific references about the criminal field. Similarly, Tittle agrees that they mentioned very little about crime and therefore did not provide a sufficient basis for a theory of criminal behavior (1983, 345). Zaffaroni also points out that Marx had very few direct references to the criminal field (2011, 157).

These concerns about a lack of systematic development of the criminal topic in Marx and Engels's work seems to refer to an exegetical analysis. However, we must note that a Marxist legal theory is in no way limited to a mere compilation of the thoughts of Marx on the topic. It is rather a critical discourse about the role of law in society based on the foundational tenets of Marxist thought and on its methodology (historical materialism). This means a similar approach to what Marx did with political economy in *Capital* (Cerroni 1973). Following this logic, this book proposes that it is possible and desirable to sieve enriching positions about crime and crime control from the Marxist thought. This process is two-fold: studying Marx and Engels's passages that strictly address this topic; and digging into the macro-analysis of the authors that contribute to a holistic analysis of the criminal phenomenon, as well as applying the historical materialist analysis to the criminal field. Following this logic, Baratta comments:

> [Although] Marx did not develop a systematic theory of law in the traditional sense; this does not mean that Marx considered the issue of law irrelevant. By contrast, he addressed the issue in all his major writings from both periods, although, true, it was not treated autonomously and systematically, but in the field of philosophy, economic and social theory (1974, 25).

The conceptual tools and the theoretical hypotheses of Marx's work can be of great importance to analyze the criminal phenomenon by applying them without dogmatism. That is, considering Marxism as an open building, which, like any other, can and should be continuously reformulated through its confrontation with arguments and different theoretical approaches (217). Thus, one may, in fact, find substantive elements in the writings of the founding fathers of Marxism to clarify the functionality of law in general and of the criminal field in particular, with regard to the existing social relationships and the underlying economic structure.

Marx and Engels' Contributions Understood Crime and Crime Control as Superstructural Aspects

Zaffaroni says that "the risk of Marxist analysis is its proclivity to a deterministic analysis, which can lead to an economic reductionism" (2000, 309). Thus, he argues, Marx's analysis explains the criminal phenomenon exclusively in relation to the economic sphere. Ferrajoli and Zolo argue that the difficulty of using a Marxist framework to analyze the criminal field is that the latter does not respond to an economic-social causation, i.e., that the theory of Marx and Engels reduces social explanations to an economic account (1977, 63). Sutherland and Cressey claim that the socialist school of criminology – which was based on the works of Marx and Engels and began around 1850 – was characterized by its emphasis on economic determinism (Taylor et al. 1973, 247). Radzinowicz in *History of the English Criminal Law* (1987) analyzes one article of Marx, in which he identifies the alleged reduction of broader phenomena to an economic explanation. Schafer (1969), Schur (1971) and Coser (1956) also follow this line of thought (Taylor et al. 1973, 247, n 94). Hirst (1975) explains that the work of Marx and Engels neglects what he refers to as 'individual aspects' of the superstructure and, on the contrary, emphasizes the superstructure as a whole.

In response to these critics, Taylor and Walton claim that what the Marxist framework offers is the logic of halting focus on the offender. Instead, it focuses on how crime is represented in the ideologies of the ruling class. This challenge includes moving towards a vision that takes into account crimes committed by all sectors of the population (1975, 286–287). Melossi objects that the accusations of economic determinism are heavily influenced by the ideology of the bourgeoisie (1980, 199). Contrariwise, Marx and Engels do not understand the criminal field as a passive superstructural phenomenon that responds automatically to economic factors. Engels himself states in his letter to Bloch (1890) that:

> According to the materialist conception of history, the factor which ultimately determines history is the production and reproduction of real life. Neither Marx nor I have ever asserted more than this. If somebody twists this into saying that the economic element is the only determining one, he transforms that proposition into an empty, abstract, senseless phrase.

Boron (2006) explains that the misunderstanding of economic determinism comes from a confusion of German words. Those who defend the 'deterministic' view mistranslated the word 'bedingen' as 'to determine' when in fact, it should be translated as 'to be mutually dependent, or conditional.' Greenberg

(1976) explains that, indeed, Marxism invites us to avoid determinism and to use intermediate concepts that can account for a sociology of law. Reducing Marx's theories to the simple idea of economic determinism undermines the fact that he spent many years in the detailed study of legal theory. Needless to say, Marx was a jurist, Doctor in Law, and until mid-1840s was devoted to the study of the philosophy of law. His training was in the legal field and only later did he become interested in political economy. Moreover, he developed his analytical method through a critical review of the *Hegelian Philosophy of Law* (Engels 1884, 464). All this reaffirms the thought of Gramsci (1948, 1949), Althusser (1968) and Poulantzas (1969), who argue that superstructural instances, including the law, can be studied and analyzed in a timely and precise manner, given their relative independence from the economic base. Overall, it is possible to reject the narrow positions that conceive Marx and Engels' analysis from a determinist perspective. A more sophisticated Marxist approach to the criminal phenomenon exceeds its understanding as a mere reflection of the economic structure.

Marx and Engels' Contributions Lead to the Failure of 'Real Socialism'

The experience of 'real socialism,' specifically as it relates to the abuses committed by the criminal system agents, caused significant resentment among critical thinkers. Many of them assimilate Marx and Engels' contributions with the experience of the U.R.S.S. and reject them to avoid the risk of repeating the abuses of that historical period. As an example, Foucault, in the debate with the Maoist Pierre Victor, expresses his fear that forms of class justice reproduce the oppression that is inherent to the structure of the state (1972, 185). Also Zolo and Ferrajoli (1977) point out that a Marxist approach implies the risk of falling back into what they call a 'criminological holism.' They base this assumption on a passage in which V.I. Lenin expresses his hope that, within socialism, interpersonal conflicts may disappear as a consequence of the equality in socio-economic relations. Zolo and Ferrajoli state that, from that assumption, any crime committed in the context of a socialist regime would be treated as a social pathology and, therefore, subjected to paternalistic interventions.

However, as Marx and Engels say in *The Holy Family* (1848b), socialism is a social space that is created collectively and where everyone can freely assert their individuality. It was under that conception that Lenin, in the referred passage, explains that socialism aims to eliminate *class* antagonism. Lenin does not state that personal, aesthetic, organizational and other kinds of conflicts would disappear. In other words, socialism is not intended to over-come *all forms* of antagonism, but mainly the class one:

> We are not utopians, and we do not exclude all that are possible and inevitable individual excesses, as we do not exclude the need to suppress such excesses. But first, this does not require any particular machine, any special apparatus of repression; the armed people themselves will handle this matter with the same simplicity, with the same ease with which any crowd of civilians, even in today's society, which separates people who fight or oppose the use of violence against a woman. We also know that the leading social cause of excesses that constitute violations of the rules of social coexistence is the exploitation of the masses, their poverty, their misery. Eliminating the main cause, excesses will inevitably begin to 'die.'
>
>   LENIN 1916, 101–102

Socialism would then refer to the advent of a society without conflict be-tween classes and without exploitation. It does not promise the end of poten-tial interpersonal disagreements typical in the life of society. In the words of Greenberg: "From Socialism [one] can safely expect the elimination of many crimes. Is not that enough?" (1976, 613). Overall, the fear of repeating the ex-periences of 'real socialism' is a shared concern. Although this concern should not lead to the rejection of Marx and Engels's proposals, because they cannot be assimilated to those critical historical processes.

Marx and Engels' Contributions Are Necessary to Analyze Crime and Crime Control

In contrast to these readings, multiple voices assert that it is possible and neces-sary to use the work of Marx and Engels to analyze crime and punishment. Me-lossi notes that there is a lack of studies done on the contributions of the fathers of historical materialism in relation to the criminal field (1980, 187). Colvin and Pauly (1983) propose a structural approach under classic Marxism to under-stand that social relationships are built on the process of material production. Horton and Platt affirm that Marxist thought proposes a promising alternative to identify worldwide continuities in crime patterns (1986, 126). Werkentin, Bauermann and Budge (1974) advocate for a Marxist Criminology that, in con-trast with the 'bourgeois criminology,' links economic analysis and criminal process. Bales, Gordon, Quinney and Spitzer credit the possibility of this ap-proach (Tittle 1983, 345). Chambliss (1975) argues that, although Marx did not systematically work in the field, there are various places in his study of capital-ism where he pays attention to crime and law.

These positions assert that the criticisms discussed above have focused more on the hermeneutics of Marx's texts or on individual political experienc-es rather than on Marxist analytical matrix. Indeed, we should not disregard the hermeneutical methodology to screen Marx and Engels' contributions to re-think those passages that address criminological topics. However, it is also relevant to dive deeper into their theoretical and methodological analysis of the socio-economic structure that conditions the criminal phenomenon. Fol-lowing this logic, Taylor, Walton and Young claim that it is necessary to explore not only the theoretical work of Marx and Engels but also their materialistic methodology:

> The only radical approach that does not degenerate into mere moralizing is one materialistic [...] What is a materialistic approach? And how is it radical? [...] A criminology that is normatively committed to the aboli-tion of inequalities in wealth and power, [while] any theoretical position that is not minimally engaged with this look will fall into correctional-ism (i.e., individual rehabilitation or partial social reform) [...] which are inevitably linked to identifying deviation with pathology (1974, 461).

In other words, while it is true that Marx and Engels did not specifically delve into crime and crime control, they laid the foundation for a complex analysis from the point of view of historical materialism. This methodological approach allows us to clarify the functionality of law as it relates to social relationships and the underlying economic structure. Marxist theory of law does not just reiterate the exact thoughts of Marx on legal topics. Instead, it builds a critical and unique discourse surrounding the role of law in our society, just as the thinker of Trier did regarding the political economy in *Capital* (Cerroni 1973).

This book proposes that the desirable double track is as follows. On the one hand, we should focus on the writings where Marx and Engels directly address criminological issues. On the other, we should deepen in the study of their macro-sociological analysis and in the application of their methodology – historical materialism – to the study of crime and crime control. This should be done avoiding dogmatism and economist reductionism, to prevent falling into the errors of 'real socialism.' On the contrary, the path should seek to nurture the contributions of vast theoretical and disciplinary fields and, from them, recast the words and methodology of Marx and Engels to develop a richer criti-cal perspective.

A Conceptualization of Criminal Selectivity from
a Marxist Perspective

The recovery of criminal selectivity from a complex, historical and totalizing setting, is sought through the theoretical and methodological contributions of Marx and Engels, combined with contributions from multiple disciplines and contemporary Marxist-based thought. Criminal selectivity mediates between 'crime conflict' and 'crime control,' evidencing how they are socio-economically conditioned. Analyzing criminal selectivity then demands to study the historical continuities and disruptions of those two phenomena. This means understanding 'conflict' and 'control' in their criminal specificity ('crime conflict' and 'crime control') but always in relation to the social context in which they take place ('social conflict' and 'social control').

Looking deeper into 'conflict,' we understand 'social conflict' as the problematic economic and social situation (including cultural, ethnic and religious factors) in which 'crime conflict' occurs. 'Crime conflict' refers to 'negative social behaviors' (Baratta 1986)[8] or events that cause 'social harm' (Schwendinger and Schwendinger 1970), regardless of whether or not they qualify as crimes by today's legal standards. 'Negative social behaviors' describe "harmful behaviors which warrant guardianship of the most significant individual and collective needs" (Baratta 1986, 99). This perspective argues that it is not necessary to accept an ontological conception of crime to effectively address crime conflict. Social harm problematizes what is conceived as criminal. It evaluates the possibility of conceiving as criminal "[the] practices of those in power who are seriously harmful to most of humanity and are not defined and sanctioned by civil or criminal laws, such as genocide and economic exploitation" (Schwendinger and Schwendinger 1970, 168–169). Several academics propose to replace the notion of 'crime' with the broader concept of social harm (Hillyard and Tombs 2013).

This book seeks to understand 'crime conflict' from a conflicting factual basis and from the interests of the working classes (Baratta 1986) which represent the "most part of humanity" (Schwendinger and Schwendinger 1970). 'Working class' is interpreted in the broad sense, that is, anyone who sets out to

---

8   The 'negative social' character emerges from contrasting the behavior with the needs and important interests of individuals or the community, based on endpoints counted as valid. With Marx as an input and from a non-mechanical but dialectical conception of social conflict, it is possible to suggest identification criteria of general needs and interests that are carriers of the subordinate classes in a particular historical situation (Baratta 1986, 99, n 28).

sell their labor to live, notwithstanding that each individual may or may not do so effectively. This means looking at the employed and unemployed workers as a whole (cf. Marx 1867, 517).

'Control' encompasses 'social control' and 'crime control.' 'Social control'[9] refers to crime control and the 'ideological state apparatuses' (Althusser 1968). The latter describes the additional punitive mechanisms, namely employment,

---

9   The discussion of the concept of 'social control' is profound. Only for the purpose of introducing it, it is here highlighted that its original use is attributed to Ross (1896), in the framework of the Chicago school in the United States in the late 19th century and early 20th century. However, Spencer (1879) had used the term even before then (Anitua 2005). Afterwards, the structural-functionalism theory conceived law as the main mechanism for social control.

Because of the multiple uses of the term social control, Cohen calls it a 'Mickey Mouse concept' which has been used to describe "all social processes that lead to conformity, from the childhood socialization to public execution" (1985, 5). Similarly, Van Swaaningen explains that the characterization of social control "as an Orwellian conspiracy of the State and their accomplices is too negative and [...] does not reflect forms of social control that are currently fragmented and partially privatized at the national level" (1997, 38). Cohen, as opposed to the loose and indefinite use of social control, proposes that it should be limited to characterize the "organized ways in which society responds to behavior and people it regards as deviant, problematic, worrying, threatening, troublesome or undesirable in some way or another" (1985, 1).

Bergalli (2012) defines social control as "the mechanisms of transmission and imposition of values and models of behavior aimed at producing cohesion or expression of an organizing ability of the groups, but always from a position of power crowning when the diverted behave as such, and not always exerted from the state level." Bergalli rejects the use of the notion of 'social control' to refer to the role of modern penal systems. He explains that social control implies that those that are controlled accept the correction, while in the penal system the control is imposed in the form of punishment and in response to a violation of the norms (1996, 1.5). However, it is at least problematic to affirm that social control has to do with an acceptance of the situation by the individuals that are controlled (Does the worker choose to undergo labor discipline? Does the student agree with school discipline? Or going further, does the child accept familial social control?).

Pavarini proposes dividing the concept of social control into 'formal social control' and 'informal social control.' The former is applied by institutional agencies that are in charge of the discipline of social behaviors defined as deserving social control through formalized procedures and forms of intervention. On the other hand, "everything that does not come into that notion is informal social control" (1980b, 109). This contribution blurs the relevance of crime control as a critical tool, and is therefore worthy of a categorical distinction within (formal) social control.

Melossi (1990) distinguishes between 'social action control' in reference to the internalization of values and rules, and 'social control of the reaction' which represses behaviors that are contrary to the established order. The latter is subdivided into two categories. First, 'informal and diffuse social control' (family, religious groups, media, work, school, sports club)

the media (which includes the media criminology[10]), the remaining areas of law outside of penal control, religion, social reaction, family and school, among others. Social control aims at acting on the social conflict, and needs to be analyzed within the economic and social system in which it is framed.

'Crime control'(or criminal tool, or penal control, or criminal justice system) refers to the exercise of state coercion specifically oriented to treat the 'crime conflict' (although its effects exceed it).'[11] As it has been argued, crime control is sifted through criminal selectivity and is manifested in the unequal legal treatment (statutes and common law), law enforcement profiling (activity of police officers, border patrol, military officers in police roles, and special police units), courts' discretion (biased performance of prosecutors, judges, defense attorneys and juries), and differential penalization (unequal imposition of prison time, parole, probation, fines, collateral consequences of convictions).

Thus, criminal selectivity must be understood in the historical interrelation between social/crime conflict and social/crime control. Delving into the selectivity phenomenon, it operates at two different levels: 'primary criminalization' and 'secondary criminalization.'[12] These concepts are essential to identify the agencies that embody this unequal crime control.

---

that do not belong to the government sphere and that address social norms. Second, a 'formal or institutionalized social control' which operates through non-punitive state institutions (ministries and agencies), and punitive institutions (criminalization agencies). Melossi also highlights differences between 'active social control' – that produces behavior – and the 'reagent social control,' the inhibition of behaviors (17). In another text, Melossi (1991) also differentiates between a model of 'oriented state- social control' that takes place in the western world, in contrast to a model of dispersed and entrepreneurial state typical of the Mediterranean countries with a more centralized and indifferent state.

10   *See* Zaffaroni (2011).

11   Bergalli describes crime control as the one that is defined and established by and from the rules of law (2012). He also calls it 'legal and criminal state control' and defines it as the one which is exercised in primarily legal-coercive terms through punitive control agencies, such as the police, judiciary, criminal authorities and penal institutions (1996, 15).

12   These two notions were first outlined by Becker (1962) and critical criminologists, and recently defined by Zaffaroni, Alagia and Slokar (2000, 8).
     The notion of 'primary criminalization' was delineated by the conflict theory as "the process in which powerful groups manage to influence legislation, using penal institutions as a weapon to combat and neutralize behaviors of opposing groups" (Vold 1958, quoted in Baratta 1986, 133–134). Afterwards, Becker noted that "the rules that these labels [referring to the process of labeling by penal agencies] generate and sustain do not respond to everyone's opinion. On the contrary, they are subjected to conflicts and disagreements, they are part of the political process of society" (1962, 37). Baratta argues

'Primary criminalization' refers to the primary filtering process where only certain types of 'social negative behaviors' are legislated. In other words, it describes the filter which is in place on the set of harmful conducts for the purpose of qualifying as criminals only some of them. The cut is twofold. First, only certain harmful behaviors are subjected to criminal sanction. They are the grosser offenses, committed with simple or primitive resources, that demand easier evidence gathering, produce low social-political conflict and are typically perpetrated by the most vulnerable people. In contrast, those behaviors that are more complex, that demand higher levels of know-how to conduct the investigation, that do not produce social unrest, and that are usually committed by individuals from the upper social classes, are not the core of the legislative process, in spite of producing high levels of social harm. Second, some of the behaviors that are legislated – the ones that represent a more severe threat to social order- are attached to more serious punitive consequences. The result of the process of primary criminalization is the 'unequal legal treatment' of negative social behaviors or, shortly, inequality under the law.

It is pragmatically impossible to prosecute each and every offense perpetrated everyday in a given jurisdiction. 'Secondary criminalization' consists

---

that primary criminalization refers to the rules that define the 'criminalization and de-criminalization' processes (1986, 95), i.e. 'production rules' tending to preserve 'antisocial actions' (168). These rules are made by those belonging to the hegemonic social class, and are functional to the demands of capitalist accumulation (185). Zaffaroni, Alagia and Slokar define primary criminalization as "the act and the effect of a criminal law sanction that materially incriminates or permits the punishment of certain persons [by the] political agencies (parliament and executive branch)" (2000, 7).

The notion of 'secondary criminalization' was outlined by Becker when he explained that deviation is caused by the response of people to certain types of conduct, which are labelled as deviant (1962, 37). He added that, once the rule exists, it is applied to certain people of the underclass to increase the population that the norm has created (181–182). Baratta defines the process of secondary criminalization as "the criminal process involving the action of the bodies of inquiry and culminating in the judgment" (1986, 168). Zaffaroni, Alagia and Slokar identify that this process is executed by policemen, judges and prison officers. They define secondary criminalization as a punitive action exerted on specific individuals, and that occurs when law enforcement agencies detect a person – whom performing is attributed to some primarily criminalized act – investigate him/ her – in some cases depriving him/her of his/her freedom of movement – and subjects him/her to the judicial agency. The judiciary legitimizes the past proceedings, supports a process – namely the progress of series of secret or public events to establish whether he/she has actually performed the criminalized action – publicly discusses whether he/ she has done it and, if so, allows the imposition of a punishment of a certain magnitude. When that punishment consists on deprivation of freedom of movement, it is executed by a correctional agency, in a process that can be called 'prisonization' (2000, 7).

then of a secondary filtering process that is responsible for selecting which of the universe of behaviors are going to be effectively criminalized or, in other words, when the law will actually be enforced. It expresses in law enforcement profiling, courts' discretion, and differential penalization. In these three instances, this secondary filtering process is conditioned by the class and racial characteristics of the offenders, as well as by their age, gender, ethnicity and religion. The targeted individuals are those who respond to "the aesthetic public image of the offender, with classist, racist, age and gender components" (Zaffaroni et al. 2000, 9). Conversely, in the other extreme of the selective process, the authors of white-collar crimes, organized crime, or war crimes, who do not respond to the threatening image of the offender, are rarely targeted. This second filter has also been conceptualized as 'selective enforcement.'

Existing research in this area explains that the concepts of primary and secondary criminalization are highly relevant to understand the screening by state agencies. However, they do not explain *how* such screening takes place. Therefore, this book develops the concepts of *over-criminalization* and *under-criminalization*, which intersect with the concepts of primary and secondary criminalization.

The notion of *under-criminalization* explains *how* certain types of conduct are minimally legislated (*primary over-criminalization*) and rarely enforced (*secondary over-criminalization*) even though they produce social harm. Then, *under-criminalization* is not connected with the harmfulness of the behavior but with the demographic features of the subset of the population that perpetrates it. On the other hand, *over-criminalization* explains how other types of ordinary activities are subjected to an over-inclusive legislation (*primary over-criminalization*) and over-dimensioned targeting (*secondary over-criminalization*) despite the scarce social harm that they produce.

Concerning crimes that are usually over-criminalized, it is worth proposing a final distinction between *coarse crimes* and *criminalized survival strategies*. *Coarse crimes* refer to those behaviors that are perpetrated in a rudimentary manner, without much planning and that usually affect property. These conducts are disproportionately criminalized (over-criminalized) in relation to the social harm that they produce (a reparable effect on property). *Criminalized survival strategies* refer to activities designed to ensure revenue outside of formal employment. Although they do not directly affect other individuals,[13] they are strongly over-criminalized (panhandling and vagrancy as their main exponents).

---

13   Modern doctrine justifies the punishment of these kind of behaviors through the allegation of harm to supra-individual interests – such as public order – or through the characterization of these behaviors as a spearhead of more severe crimes.

Finally, to dig into the concept of *over-criminalization*, this book recovers the notion of 'less eligibility' to account for the modifications in the conditions of punishment in each historical period. Marx outlines the notion of less eligibility in *Capital* (1867, 896–904). He states that the general situation of the marginal classes tends to improve when a stable dynamic of capitalist valorization ensures long periods of economic growth and social stability. Meanwhile, the general situation of the marginal classes tends to deteriorate when the crisis of a specific mode of capitalist social formation urges the revolution of the production system and causes the development of a new regime of accumulation. The concept was further developed in an article by Rusche (1933) and disseminated in the work *Punishment and Social Structure* (1938), co-written with Kirchheimer. The authors suggest that, to serve as a deterrent, punishment must offer worse conditions than those that the labor market offers to the lowest stratum of the working class (1938, 4).[14]

'Less eligibility' is used here in a broader sense, not reducing it to the assessment of the labor market but extending it to the complexity of the socio-economic context of each mode of criminal selectivity. Social policies are considered in relation to crime control, suggesting that the worst stratum of the employed working class marks the limit of social assistance. That is, social policies must offer worse conditions and remain 'less eligible' than the conditions of the occupied working class to ensure that the workers accept the conditions of the labor market. Meanwhile, crime control must offer worse conditions than social policies to serve deterrence.

Based on this framework, criminal selectivity (see Figure 1) may be described as the mode under which the criminal justice system operates in its different instances of criminalization (primary and secondary) and which is embodied in two mechanisms. The first one refers to the overly-punitive treatment of those behaviors committed by individuals that are in a vulnerable position

---

14   The conditions imposed by punishment, then, should leave the offender in worse conditions than those experienced by the least privileged stratum of the free working class. While the conditions of this class depend on selling their labor force – the only good that they possess – punishments should be compared with the conditions granted by the labor market in each historical moment, and be worse than them. It is then that this negative condition finds concrete forms throughout the transformation of social structure (Rusche and Kirchheimer 1938, 4). Thus, when there is an overabundance of work force, punishment assumes forms that may constitute cruel humiliations. By contrast, in situations of workforce scarcity, punishment acquires forms oriented to use the workforce of the criminal population in the labor market; or, at least, to discipline it to make it functional for labor.

because of their class, gender, cultural, ethnic and religious membership (over-criminalization). The second mechanism refers to absence or minimization of the punitive treatment of behaviors committed by those individuals who bear a socially advantageous position in relation to their class, gender, cultural, ethnic and religious membership (under-criminalization).[15]

Before going into Chapter 2 and for the purpose of clarifying the explanatory variables in analysis, Figure 1 serves to clarify and summarize the various forms of criminal selectivity.

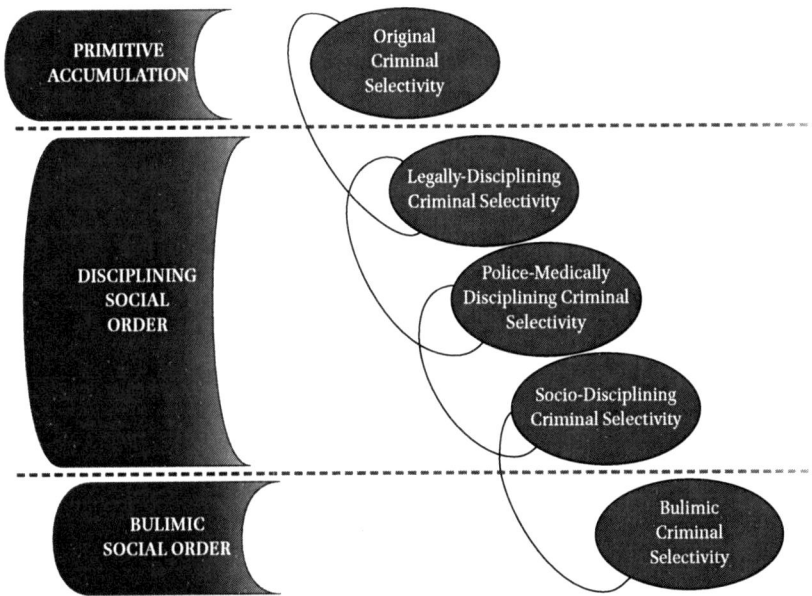

FIGURE 1   *Development of criminal selectivity*

15   As it was mentioned, the notions of primary criminalization and secondary criminalization were coined as such in the second half of the 20th century. However, it is analytically possible and desirable to apply them to previous historical periods. This responds to the fact that the motivation of this book is precisely to show how these phenomena, far from being exclusive to late modernity in which they were theoretically defined, are inherent to the historical function of the criminal justice system. Even during original criminal selectivity, criminalization agencies were already present through the figures of the count, the sovereigns and their local representatives, the nascent judiciary, king guards and other coercive structures. This retrospective analysis should not withdraw the specificities of the context and does not represent an indiscriminate use of analogy.

CHAPTER 2

Original Criminal Selectivity

In assessing the origins and scope of today's punitive system, it is necessary to examine the foundations of capitalist production. To do this, the book will review that initial process based on Marx's principal work, *Capital* (1867). Although this work does not mention crime conflict and crime control expressly, "his analysis provides us with the means of understanding the intervention of the repressive, or preventive actions of the state. It is with this tool we can analyze the historical and present problem of crime and punishment" (Melossi 1976, 26).

This framework allows us to explore the origins and early development of the practice of criminal selectivity imposed as an unequivocal mode of operation of the punitive system – with some variation – until the present. This means that criminal selectivity was present from the very beginning of modern criminal law.

This chapter develops two central theses. First, that the origin of criminal selectivity can be traced to the very process of the primitive accumulation described by Marx in the famous Chapter 24 of *Capital*. From here, this first form of criminal selectivity is understood as *original criminal selectivity* (late 15th to early 18th century). Second, this chapter focuses on how criminal selectivity was necessary to establish the capitalist system of production. It shows how crime control, in the framework of the primitive accumulation, acted as a mechanism of social control. This means that crime control was not exclusively focused on the resolution of merely crime conflicts. Crime control intensively contributed to the process of creating a working class and accumulating the original capital.

From this, the chapter develops how *original criminal selectivity* operated through the mechanisms of *original under-criminalization* and *original over-criminalization*. *Original under-criminalization* operated on the acts committed by the feudal estates, the emerging mercantile bourgeoisie and the absolute monarchies. Original over-criminalization operated on the acts committed by the emerging working class[1] that was immersed in an absolute deprivation, as a result of the dismemberment of the feudal social networks.

---

1   The notion of 'class' is understood in a classic sense, as the objective position in the societal productive structure, but enriched by the cultural view; i.e. understanding class as "a historical phenomenon unifying a number of disparate and seemingly unconnected events, both

For the purpose of introducing the variables involved in the framework of original criminal selectivity, the following incorporates an explanatory table:

TABLE 1   *Original criminal selectivity*

Characteristics				Chapter 2 Original criminal selectivity
Section 1 Contextual settings: Where, When and How				Primitive Accumulation – late 15th to early 18th century
Section 2 Conflict-Control	Conflict	Social		Working class formation, intern struggles among nobles and with the monarchy, emergence of the bourgeoisie as a social class, struggle between colonized and colonizers.
		Criminal		Urban marginality and Peasants' resistance.
	Control	Social		It tends to coincide with criminal control.
		Criminal	Under-criminalization	Acts of conquest (death, enslavement, fire, torture) and illegal expropriations in European rural lands.
			Over-criminalization	Criminalized survival strategies (vagrancy, begging, prostitution), coarse crimes (rough crimes against property), religious crimes (heresy, witchcraft, contraception, infanticide), and resistance to land expropriation.
Section 3 Who Were Prosecuted?	Under-criminalized social sectors			Monarchy, feudal lords, and mercantile bourgeoisie.
	Over-criminalized social sectors			Proto-Lumpen-proletariat and proto-proletariat.
Section 4 Punishment	Manifest Functions			Emergency discourses (witchcraft, leisure, peasant rebellion, games, begging as threatens).
	Latent Functions			To contribute to the formation of the working class; to impose the power of general obedience to the sovereign; to fragment the impoverished sectors.

in the raw material of experience and in consciousness. I emphasize that it is a historical phenomenon. I do not see class as a 'structure,' nor even as a 'category,' but as something which in fact happens (and can be shown to have happened) in human relationships" (Thompson 1963, 9).

Where, How and When of the Primitive Accumulation (Late 15th to Early 18th Century)

In Chapter 24 of *Capital*, Marx reveals to us the essence of the primitive accumulation of capital in Western Europe: the historical process of divorcing the producers from their means of production. This phenomenon led to a double-transformation: on the one hand, the social means of subsistence and the social means of production became capital. On the other, the immediate producers were transformed into wage laborers (1867, 786).

Marx then shows *how* this double-transformation was attributable to three main processes: (a) the breaking-up of the bands of feudal retainers throwing a mass of free and disadvantaged workers to the labor market; (b) the violent expulsion of peasants from their land by the feudal lords thereby creating an incomparably larger number of free and dispossessed workers; (c) the flowering of Flemish wool manufactures and the consequent rise in wool prices which then justified the transformation of farmland to pasture land for sheep grazing (789). In other words, primitive accumulation was attributable to the appropriation of communal property, the expulsion of the peasants to the cities, and their modeling as a future working class. All this happened concurrent with the dissolution of feudal armies and the remnants of feudal structures. As a whole, this process of expropriation-accumulation proportioned the necessary capital for the development of the Industrial Revolution, as well as the free workers that capitalism needed.

Concerning *where*, Marx illustrates that the process of primitive accumulation was a global one conducted for the benefit of the European powers (particularly, Spain, Portugal, Holland, France and England, in chronological order). In the European colonies, the plundering of natural resources and violent subjugation of the local population was fundamental to ensure the primitive accumulation of capital. In this context, large commercial cities emerged (Genoa, Florence, Venice, Milan, Flanders, Ghent, Bruges, Antwerp, Amsterdam, Madrid, Paris, London), and modern states developed. The rising bourgeoisie (mostly merchants and bankers) and the decomposing feudal structure dealt with alliances and confrontations (Geremek 1989, Pirenne1961). Marx prioritizes the English model as the 'classic form' of capitalism (1867, 787), but without neglecting the specific features of the other European countries.[2]

---

2 Campagne emphasizes: "The English route was not the only variant from which preindustrial societies qualitatively transformed their economic and social structures in the capitalist ones. However, it was the first to be deployed in historical time. Although this does not lead to a historical necessity of chronological primacy, or to convert the English model in the

In discussing when primitive accumulation took place, and putting aside the great historiographical debates on this crucial juncture,[3] Marx envisioned that the onset of capitalism took place along with the decline of feudalism. In his own words: "Although we come across the first beginnings of capitalist production as early as the 14th or 15th century, sporadically, in certain towns of the Mediterranean, the capitalistic era dates from the 16th century" (787). In the case of England, this process may be detected even earlier:

> [...] *serfdom had practically disappeared in the last part of the 14th century. The immense majority of the population consisted then, and to a still larger extent, in the 15th century*, of free peasant proprietors, whatever was the feudal title under which their right of property was hidden. in the larger seigniorial domains, the old bailiff, himself a serf, was displaced by the free farmer. The wage-laborers of agriculture consisted partly of

standard by which all other transitions should be measured, but it imposes a comparative perspective to study the origins of our contemporary society. The English road to agrarian capitalism remains as the 'classic' one" (2005, 163). Meanwhile, Spain, Portugal, and France participated in overseas conquest, but they did not respond to the same industrial economic model adopted by England. They were undergoing a commercial development, and industrialization was developed there only after the first colonial conquests.

3   Among the most prominent authors that study these processes, Bois (1989) understands that feudalism and capitalism do not represent two separate logics. He argues that as a result of feudal overpopulation, peasant holdings were divided, forcing laborers to offer themselves as a labor force (phase A). Then, in a second phase (phase B) farmers achieved an improved condition and become able to better negotiate the terms of access to land, until the pressure on land makes the process repeat phase A. Between the 14th and 16th centuries, phase B occurs, and wage labor slowly increases. Thus, phase A generates waves of employees, which are interrupted in phase B, but that reappear in the next phase A with a growing wave until the secondary momentum becomes principal and the transition to capitalism starts.

Brenner (1988) rejects this model and explains the process from feudalism to capitalism through class, property relations and exploitation. He notes that where the farmer loses social relevance and intermediate sectors become more relevant, as it happened in England, capitalism appeared. Conversely, i France, feudalism was perpetuated in the form of small extensions of land held by peasants. Brenner does not take into account the demographic variables, because he understands that the generalization of capitalist relations mostly arises from two processes: the abolition of serfdom and the expropriation of small direct producers.

Astarita (2005) criticizes Marx and suggests that the impoverished populations that arise from the process of communal enclosures were critical and poorly disciplined, which means that they constituted a problem rather than a prerequisite for capitalism. Astarita adds that feudalism did not end in that context, but persisted within the Ancient Régime, so the transition to capitalism was resolved within the same feudal logic, as a response to the demographic crisis and the transformation of social relations.

peasants, who utilized their leisure time by working on the large estates, partly of a special independent class of wage-laborers, relatively and absolutely few in numbers (788; emphasis added).

To conclude: "The prelude of the revolution that laid the foundation of the capitalist mode of production played out in the last third quarter of the 15th century, and the first decade of the 16th century" (789). From there, the primitive accumulation extended over time until the 18th century (792).

Conflict-control is analyzed within this historical framework in order to explore how this process of accumulation, which gave rise to original criminal selectivity, was conducted.

Original Conflict-Control

The social conflict that marked the birth of capitalism was the need of the commercial bourgeoisie, in tensioned alliance with the feudal and monarchical sectors,[4] to establish and train the future proletariat, clamping down any resistance or dissent. In the rural areas, the utilized mechanisms were land expropriation and repression of peasant resistance. In the cities, the hegemonic mechanisms were work regulations and massive impoverishment. Thus, in both, rural and urban areas, the result was the absolute impoverishment of entire populations, left with no other recourse than to sell their labor (Geremek 1986, 20).[5] This social conflict was inserted into a broader context: the internal struggles among lords, the disputes between lords and monarchies, the emergence of the bourgeoisie as a new class, the confrontations between unions and

---

4   Tomas y Valiente (1969) places the appearance of absolute monarchies between the 16th and 18th centuries, at the beginning of the modern history. Anderson (1979), Moore (1987) and Astarita (1998) highlight the presence of a proto-absolutism that started to develop in 1250 and was fully in force during the 14th and 15th centuries.

5   During feudalism, subsistence difficulties – caused by crop failures or reduced performance of medieval agriculture – made indigence an endemic phenomenon in rural areas. However, it was muffled by existing social bonds between farmers, as well as by the possibility of serving feudal lords. These solidarity connections absorbed those who did not have enough, or any, land to fulfill their basic needs (Geremek 1989, 22). With the crises of 1513 and 1515, and then the one held between 1526 and 1535, vagrancy became a mass phenomenon: agriculture products were not enough to cover the population growth and the poor harvest, demand increased the price of grain, and the result was a major crisis at the European level. The effects include migrations to urban centers that became overwhelmed and the fact that the poor became dysfunctional (138).

independent artisans, the destruction of community ties in the cities, and an increasing cultural and social exchange among people who, up until then, had lived attached to a particular place and to rigorous customs (Ciafardini 2012b). In *The Origins of the Family, Private Property and the State*, Engels affirms: "By way of exception, however, periods occur in which the warring classes balance each other so nearly that the state power, as ostensible mediator, acquires, for the moment, a certain degree of independence of both" (1884b, 159). This is exemplified by the absolute monarchies of the 17th and 18th centuries, which held the balance between the nobility and the bourgeoisie. Still far from the domain of political power, the commercial bourgeoisie's role increased in importance alongside primitive accumulation. Thus, in *The Eighteenth Brumaire of Louis Bonaparte*, Marx says that "under the absolute monarchy, during the first revolution, and under Napoleon, the bureaucracy was only the means to prepare the class rule of the bourgeoisie" (1852, 104). With Engels, in *The Communist Manifesto* (1848), Marx explains that the bourgeoisie developed within this constant tension with the feudal and monarchic powers:

> Each of these evolutionary stages of the bourgeoisie was accompanied by a corresponding political advance. Oppressed class under the sway of the feudal lords; armed and self-governing association in the commune; in parts independent urban republic; in other third tributary state of the monarchy; then the counterweight manufacturing time of the nobility in the feudal or the absolute monarchy, the foundation of the great monarchies in general.

Beyond Europe, the social conflict involved struggles between colonized peoples and colonial powers, and among conquerors in the fight for territorial expansion.

Crime conflict focused particularly on the marginalized masses accused of perpetrating criminalized survival strategies (mainly panhandling, vagrancy and prostitution) and coarse crime (especially petty property offenses). Criminal prosecution of these sectors also applied to the riots that took place in times of crisis. The internal organization of crime was based on "the great gangs of malefactors (looters working in small, armed units; groups of smugglers firing on the agents of the tax authorities; disbanded soldiers or deserters who roamed the countryside together)" (Foucault 1975, 75).

Against this backdrop, crime control and social control tended to coincide, without these two phenomena being clearly separated. Primitive accumulation, as a foundational process of capitalism, needed to entirely subsume the former mode of production. For this, it had to collect a foundational amount of capital, overcome – or make alliances with- the remaining feudal lords and subjugate the popular sectors. A process with these characteristics – involving dispossession and subjugation on a global scale – necessitated a resort to violence for it to be achievable. The principal mechanism of force relied on was the use of crime control, selectively applied. This means that *crime control acquired a foundational selective profile that helped to lay the foundations of the capitalist system of production.* The expected outcome of this process – marked by laws, customs, education, and violence – was to create a docile working class (Marx 1867, 799).[6] Although violence cannot by itself create a new economic formation, when a particular economic base is unleashed, violence accelerates the processes that gave life to it and encourage its employment (Mansilla 1965, 50). This means that, even though the process of dispossession of the primitive accumulation was the one that sowed the foundations of the capitalist system of production, crime control was an essential tool for the pursuit of that end.

Original criminal selectivity operated through two mechanisms: on the one hand, the minimum application of crime control over the acts committed by advantaged sectors linked to rising capital (original under-criminalization); on the other, the over-dimensioned criminal treatment of the actions of resistance, or mere subsistence, of economically disadvantaged sectors (original over-criminalization). Let us analyze them.

Original Under-Criminalization

Marx describes the process of primitive accumulation as enacted through atrocious events perpetrated upon entire populations.[7] However, these acts were not perceived as criminal, but as necessary evils in carrying out capitalist development. Original under-criminalization was deployed at two level. First, it operated through the limited and narrow legislation of the native populations and enslaved men's domination committed by the nascent mercantile bourgeoisie in alliance with the feudal and monarchic powers (primary under-criminalization). Second, original under-criminalization functioned through the rare prosecution of those already restricted regulations (secondary under-criminalization). Original under-criminalization found its legitimacy in the conception of those negative social behaviors as necessary for the territorial expansion (in relation to the offenses committed in the colonies) and the development of farm production (in relation to the crimes committed in the

---

6   *See also* Thompson (1963).

7   Coinciding, Hobsbawm suggests that in the colonial system of the 16th century, the Spanish and Portuguese expansion was based on theft and monopoly. He describes this initial process as a 'looting' (1971, 80).

rural areas of Europe). This means that, despite their high physical violence, these actions were regarded as necessary for the founding and developing of the commercial basis for capitalism.

These under-criminalized behaviors had a precise geographical division that requires a separate analysis. (a) On the one hand, original under-criminalization took place in the colonies at the expense of their native populations and enslaved Africans in the context of colonialism. (b) On the other hand, original under-criminalization operated in Europe over the expropriation of peasants, the occupation of common lands, and the destruction of customary rights. (c) Finally, even though both processes involved behaviors that were not criminalized at the moment of their perpetration, the last part of the analysis suggests the need to characterize these historical events as criminal offenses.

a   Original Under-Criminalization of Native Population and
          Enslaved-Men's Oppression

In the colonies, we find a range of heinous acts committed against the native population. Conquerors kidnapped and sold them as slaves, dispossessed them of their belongings, and burnt their homes, under a widespread violence. These acts were carried out by individuals under state control and gangs. Marx recounts how, in America, there were daily executions and subjections of men in the silver, gold and mercury mines, as well as mass destruction for land occupation. In Eastern Europe, the imposition of serfdom, the beginning of the conquest and the looting of the East Indies prevailed (1867, 823). During the first fifty years of conquest alone, the American native population was reduced to 25% of its pre-conquest size. For example, the inhabitants of Central Mexico were 25,200,000 in 1519, but by 1605 only 1,075,000 remained (4.25% of the initial population); of the 6,000,000 inhabitants of Peru in 1532, only 1,090,000 remained in 1628 (Colombres 1989, 14–15). The author of *Capital* states:

> [...] the Puritans of New England, in 1703, by decrees of their assembly set a premium of £40 on every Indian scalp and every captured red-skin: in 1720 a premium of £100 on every scalp; in 1744, after Massachusetts-Bay had proclaimed a certain tribe as rebels, the following prices: for a male scalp of 12 years and upwards £100 (new currency), for a male prisoner £105, for women and children prisoners £50, for scalps of women and children £50. Some decades later, the colonial system took its revenge on the descendants of the pious pilgrim fathers, who had grown seditious in the meantime. At English instigation and for English pay they were tomahawked by red-skins. The British Parliament proclaimed blood-hounds and scalping as 'means that God and Nature had given into its hand.' (1867, 825–826).

The extermination of the native population was complemented with widespread slavery. In the mid-19th century, gangs of kidnappers, especially in port cities, abducted children, usually from the poorest families, and sold them as slaves in the colonies (Rusche and Kirchheimer 1938, 70). Trafficking from Africa to America involved more than 60,000,000 people, with only one in six reaching their destination (Colombres 1989, 25). This was translated in an unprecedented economic wealth for the colonizers: between 1757 and 1766 alone, England received 6 million pounds exclusively from the East Indies. "Between 1769 and 1770, the English manufactured a famine by buying up all the rice and refusing to sell it again, except at fabulous prices" (Marx 1867, 825). In relation to slavery in Holland (the model capitalist nation of the 17th century),[8] Marx states:

> Nothing is more characteristic than their system of stealing men, to get slaves for Java. The men stealers were trained for this purpose. The thief, the interpreter, and the seller were the chief agents in this trade, native princes the chief dealers. The young people were stolen, were thrown into the secret dungeons of Celebes until they were ready for sending to the slave-ships (824).

The colonial powers also benefited from slavery committed in the United States, where the blood of Black-Americans helped spur capitalist development in Europe:

> Cotton, like oil, later on, was the world's most widely traded commodity, but that analogy doesn't even begin to explain how crucial the ever-growing efficiency of cotton-picking was to the modernizing global economy. Neither Britain nor any other country that followed it down the path of textile-based industrialization could have accomplished this economic transformation without the millions of acres of cotton fields of the expanding American South. To replace the fiber, it imported from American slave labor camps with an equivalent amount of wool, Britain in 1830 would have had to devote 23 million acres to sheep pasture – more than the sum total of the island's agricultural land.
> BAPTIST 2014, 244

From 1660 to 1775, the number of unfree men and women increased from only a few to one-fifth of the population of the United States, as the result of the

---

8 The Netherlands was the first major competitor, with more capital than its rivals, thanks in large part to its control of the Baltic trade since the 16th century. A Company of the Dutch East Indies created in 1602 held the power to make war and negotiate treaties (Chomsky 1992, 16).

forced migration and the imposed notion that children of slaves were also slaves (43). Those millions of slaves became the core of the cotton industry that transformed the United States into "the fastest-growing economy in the world" (221). Between the 1790s and 1820s, the country acquired a near-monopoly on the world's most widely traded commodity and, after 1820, cotton accounted for the majority of all U.S. exports. The cotton industry continued its expansion during the 19th century. By way of illustration, the cotton produced in the south of the United States increased from 1.4 million in 1800 to almost 2 billion pounds by 1860 (220).

Contrary to many claims, this high productivity was not based on mechanical innovations, as they did not appear until the 1930s (245). Conversely, between the arrival of the first Africans in 1619 and the outbreak of revolution in 1775, slavery had been one of the engines of colonial economic growth. (42). The increasing productivity responded to the greatness of the 'pushing system,' the label for the ever-increasing daily picking quotas that enslavers set for slaves. This system shows how slavery and torture were a more 'efficient' system than free labor.[9] The subjugation of the enslaved involved sexual humiliation, mutilation, electric shocks, solitary confinement in stress positions, burning and waterboarding (266).

While most of the behaviors mentioned above were considered crimes in the existing criminal legislation, they were not pondered as such when the victim was an enslaved man or woman, or a Native-American. These subsets of the population did not receive any legal recognition.[10] However, this was

---

9   There had been a few historical examples of payment or free time being given as compensation if higher quotas were achieved. On the contrary, the aim of avoiding being tortured was what forced slaves to invent ways to make their labor more efficient and profitable for their owners. In Baptist words: "Picking all day long until late at night, even by candlelight, they had to dissociate their minds from pain that racked stooping backs; from blood running down pricked fingertips; from hands that gnarled into claws over a few short years; from thirst, hunger, blurred vision, and anxiety about the whip behind and before them. One had to separate mind from hand – to become, for a time, little more than a hand" (2014, 259). Baptist adds that enslavers tortured the fastest slaves even more to find out "new efficiencies that they could not imagine." The consequences were high levels of disease, malnourishment, infant mortality (one in every four children would not reach his or her first birthday), low average life expectancy and, of course, grief (265).

10   The conquest of America was pursued under an ethnocentric line that characterized the indigenous communities as 'others,' under the conviction of the cultural superiority of Europe. These presumptions laid the foundation for the justification of slavery and the assimilation of indigenous peoples, who were considered part of the landscape, like animals and plants, and capable of being apprehended by the conquerors (Todorov 1939, 76).

not an unequivocal conviction: mainly since the 16th century,[11] rising criticism prompted the enactment of protective legislation for Native-American peoples (although it did not apply to enslaved men, whose emancipation did not arrive until the 19th century). The Laws of Burgos (1512–1513) established the institute of the 'encomienda,' which excluded Native populations from the enslaved-category and cataloged them as 'vassals of the king.' In 1542, and under the impulse of Las Casas, the New Laws decreed the absolute prohibition of the enslavement of indigenous people, who would then enjoy the same rights and obligations of any other vassal.

Nevertheless, these regulations were violently rejected by the conquerors, who needed to subdue the local workforce to quickly profit from domestic production and pay off the debts they had undertaken for the conquest. This led to the practical failure and repeal of the New Laws in 1545. Later on, the Laws of the Indies (1680) restored the rights of indigenous people and impose the obligation of Spaniards to respect these regulations, avoiding any excess or violent treatment.[12] Even then, compliance was inconsistent (Ayala 1945, Levene 1924).

Despite their weak enforcement, protective laws made it clear that, even in this remote historical period, there were voices that conceived native peoples as right-bearers and the actions of the conquest as right-violations. This means that the actions perpetrated in the colonies could have been conceived from a criminal perspective, even in the 16th century. The perception of these actions as crimes was part of the consciousness of relevant actors of the period such as Las Casas. It was the mechanism of original under-criminalization which hid this character. Original under-criminalization manifested in a restricted legislation of the negative social behaviors perpetrated by conquerors (primary under-criminalization) and in its minimum and inconsistent application (secondary under-criminalization). Thus, despite the excessive violence that

---

11   The two extreme positions in the framework of the conquest were supported by Sepulveda and Cortes, on the one hand, and Las Casas, on the other. The formers claimed that the Native peoples were savages and beasts, whose tyranny justified the right to intervene and enslave them. Their enslavement, and even their extermination, not only should not be persecuted but was consistent with the desirable natural order. Meanwhile, Las Casas argued that Europe was an advanced version of the indigenous world, but felt that they were noble, obedient, peaceful and selfless about material resources. These reasons pushed Las Casas to argue against their enslavement (Todorov 1982, 155–171).

12   The Book VI, Title XV, Law VII of the Law of Indians (1680) established "we command the Viceroys and Audiences to proceed against those who are thus delinquent: and not only shall they be deprived of the Indians, but they shall be condemned to the corporal and pecuniary punishment which shall appear just. And we command that it be a cause of accusation [...] if they cloak or consent to such excess" (Halleck 1859, 155).

ruled in the colonies, crime control operated limitedly. The reasons behind this scarce implementation were, on the one hand, that part of the victims (enslaved population) were not considered 'persons,' and therefore not entitled to legal protection. On the other, it responded to the lax implementation of the legal protections for Native-American peoples. The civilizing project legitimized original under-criminalization by interpreting the harmful events that took place in the colonies not as crimes, but as necessary actions against wild populations who were delaying the progress of history.[13]

Other criminally under-detected behavior of the primitive accumulation was the maritime attacks committed by pirates and corsairs. The particularity of this behavior was that it took place on the seas, and that affected the proper ruling sectors: pirates and corsairs forcibly took the spoils of competing nations. These were not small or irrelevant acts, but great raids sponsored and promoted by the Crown and the emerging entrepreneurs of the conquest. "Just to give an example, the spoils of Francis Drake, can be considered rightly as the source and origin of British foreign investment" (Keynes quoted in Chomsky 1992, 17). In this way, England used that booty to pay off all its external debt and invested in the East India Company Levant Company. Drake's spoils set the foundations of England foreign relations (18). These resources, obtained by acts of piracy, brought the first spoils with which England laid the basis of the capitalist system. While it was not an inter-class sabotage act but an intra-class dispossession among colonial powers, it clarified the ransacking character of the behaviors that were necessary to achieve the primitive capital accumulation.

b   Original Under-Criminalization of Peasants' Expropriation

Parallel to this process of conquest and subjugation, primitive accumulation in the European territory was deployed through enclosures:[14] a process of violent appropriation of peasants' lands and communal property. It began in the late 15th century and continued through the 16th century;

---

13   Paradoxically, the revolts conducted by the enslaved people against oppression had been the ones to be prosecuted. Baptist brings an interesting example from the Haitian history. In 1804, the local population rebelled and, after decades of genocide and oppression, installed a basis for citizenship that was the renunciation of white privilege (2014, 116). The previous genocide had not been treated as a crime, but this revolt was prosecuted as the most terrible offense: "Each convicted rebel was to be taken to his respective home plantation, to be executed in the face of all the gathered slaves" (140).

14   In the 16th century, 'enclosure' was a technical term indicating the set of strategies used by the British lords and rich peasants to eliminate communal land ownership and expand its properties (Federici 2004, 102).

and it has its principal expression in Western Europe (Marx 1867, 788).[15] Such was the extension of this process that it was described as "the revolution of the rich against the poor" (Polanyi 1944, 69–82). Where the Protestant Reformation was imposed, even the lands of the Catholic Church were sold to speculators for ridiculous prices, leading to the expulsion of large masses of peasants that worked them:

> The process of forcible expropriation of the people received in the 16th century a new and frightful impulse from the Reformation, and from the consequent colossal spoliation of the church property. The Catholic church was, at the time of the Reformation, feudal proprietor of a great part of the English land. The suppression of the monasteries, &c., hurled their inmates into the proletariat.[16]
>
> MARX 1867, 792

This plundering of Church land deepened the social metamorphosis – already begun by the fraudulent sale and looting of communal land – from feudal property and clan heritage into a modern private property. This process 'liberated' the fields to ensure capital progress, and divorced the peasants from their means of production to aid their transformation into the future proletariat. By the 17th century, three-quarters of the land belonged to large landowners, who offered to sharecrop to the expropriated peasants, or even hired them as wage laborers in their former land (795).

---

15   Dispossession occurred particularly in France, Germany, Scotland, Spain, Normandy, Burgundy and, in its most dramatic form, in England. The intensity with which they operated in each region depended on the strength of the rights of land ownership of farmers (for instance, in France they were stronger), government policies (e.g. in Germany the peasant proprietorship defended enclosures) and the level of peasant resistance (Geremek 1986, 120–121; Campagne 2005, 166). Conversely, in Eastern Europe expropriation was implemented through exorbitant rises in rents, which produced a slow transfer of land to the detriment of small farmers who could not pay them (Marx 1881 quoted in Levrero 1979, 54; Geremek 1986, 122). This process produced endemic poverty in the fields (Geremek 1986, 115).

16   Marx explains that the decline of the Church changed the conditions of land property to the detriment of the farmers that worked in the Church's lands (1867, 793–794). It is noteworthy that this situation, however, was not straightforward, as farmers who worked the church lands did it in extremely harsh conditions. Moreover, some of the expropriation of such lands included the workers who were absorbed by the new owner (Campagne 2005, 170).

The objectives of this process were, first, the transformation of farmland into pastures for extensive sheep breeding to supply wool for manufacturing.[17] It is this logic that Moro (1516) uses in his *Utopia*, referring to an amazing country where sheep devour men – signifying how the value of the wool was imposed over the rights of the farmers to preserve their land.[18] Second, this process ingrained capitalist social relations in rural areas. That is, it normalized the consolidation of private property at the expense of communal property. It crystallized the appropriation of the common space and destroyed the efficient capacity of the farmers to own property (Luchia 2004, 3). Third, these dispossessions created a mass of 'free' workers – a term that understood 'free' to mean an absence of ties to the land – ready to sell their labor. Peasants were conducted to work in the emerging boroughs and even in the field, working both on the land and in the incipient wool markets. In the words

---

17   Wool production – particularly in Flanders – was rapidly growing, increasing the price of wool and the requirements for grazing sheep. The aim was to unite the separate individual properties and constitute a continuous undivided and fenced property owned by large landowners (closed fields). Even when the wool trade declined in 1550, the enclosures did not stop; producers diverted their efforts towards selling meat and dairy production, which were demanded by the growing urban population. The breakdown of the trend occurred only in the last decade of the 16th century when a succession of bad harvests and possible famine derived livestock to grain production. Even then the movement of enclosures did not stop; although the reversion of farmland to grassland no longer had the same impulse (Campagne 2005, 172).

18   Moro (1516) claims: "'But I do not think that this necessity of stealing arises only from hence; there is another causes of it, more peculiar to England.' 'What is that?' said the Cardinal: 'The increase of pasture,' said I, 'by which your sheep, which are naturally mild, and easily kept in order, may be said now to devour men and unpeople, not only villages, but towns; for wherever it is found that the sheep of any soil yield a softer and richer wool than ordinary, there the nobility and gentry, and even those holy men, the devout! Not contented with the old rents which their farms yielded, nor thinking it enough that they, living at their ease, do no good to the public, resolve to do it hurt instead of good. They stop the course of agriculture, destroying houses and towns, reserving only the churches, and enclose grounds that they may lodge their sheep in them. As if forests and parks had swallowed up too little of the land, those worthy countrymen turn the best-inhabited places into solitudes; for when an insatiable wretch, who is a plague to his country, resolves to enclose many thousand acres of ground, the owners, as well as tenants, are turned out of their possessions by trick or by main force, or, being wearied out by ill usage, they are compelled to sell them; by which means those miserable people, both men and women, married and unmarried, old and young, with their poor but numerous families (since country business requires many hands), are all forced to change their seats, not knowing whither to go; and they must sell, almost for nothing, their household stuff, which could not bring them much money, even though they might stay for a buyer.'"

of Marx, these "idyllic methods of primitive accumulation [...] conquered the field for capitalistic agriculture, made the soil part and parcel of capital, and created for the town industries the necessary supply of a 'free' and outlawed proletariat" (1867, 805). Thus, far from producing 'free men' – in contrast with the social subjection of men and women in feudalism – "what was 'freed' was the capital. The earth was now 'free' to function as a means of accumulation and exploitation, and no longer as a means of subsistence" (Federici 2004, 113).

This original dispossession was carried out through individual and violent actions, in which the "dwellings of the peasants and the cottages of the laborers were razed to the ground or doomed to decay" (Marx 1867, 790), without legal repercussion. That is, expropriations and usurpations without fair compensation, destruction of homesteads and attacks against the physical integrity of the peasants, were all perpetrated without any legal grounding within the existing regulations.

The monarchical legislation sought to counter the expropriation, both to appease the resistance of the peasants and to keep the tithes being paid. However, the bills were insufficient and contradictory, and only prescribed financial penalties for non-compliance. Those penalties did not constitute a sufficient deterrence to stop enclosures (primary under-criminalization).[19] Furthermore, the application of the legislation was oscillating, and the expropriators used their power to avoid being prosecuted (Luchia 2004, 9). Only a few cases came to be judged (secondary under-criminalization)[20] and acts of

---

19   England passed the first legislation against enclosures and depopulation of rural areas in
      1488. The legislation initially applied to the particular territory of the Isle of Wight, but,
      after a year, it acquired a general character (Campagne 2005, 174). As Marx points out, a
      decree of Henry VII prohibited the destruction of all households of farmers with more
      than 20 acres of land. As the decree was not enforced, another one carved by Henry VIII
      in 1515 confirmed the order, obliged to restore ruined farms, and established the extension of land that should be kept between the farmland and pasture land. More ahead, an
      order of 1533 limited the number of cattle that an individual could held to 2,400 heads
      and imposed the obligation of payment surplus for each extra animal. The purpose of the
      order was to discourage expropriations of land to be used for sheep breeding. Still, in 1638,
      Charles I appointed a royal commission to enforce payments because the old orders were
      ineffective (1867, 792).

20   As landlords do not cooperate with the implementation of the legislation, the king threatened to punish offenders with financial penalties, or with the expropriation of the actual
      terrain. However, the situation did not change. Finally, in 1607, the king processed and
      fined numerous offenders, but even then the voice of the nascent bourgeoisie began to
      acquire more relevance and sought to legitimize enclosures, challenging royal power, so
      the process did not exceed specific cases (Campagne 2005, 174–180). In Spain, the catholic
      monarchy tried to stop appropriations through the appointment of judges in the Courts

dispossession became widespread, even in violation of the applicable law. The legislation failed to stop the expropriations because these acts were deemed necessary to entrench the capitalist system of production through the consolidation of large farms, and the 'setting free' of the agricultural populations to be proletarians for the burgeoning manufacturing industry (Marx 1867, 796). This highlights the filtering of the legal superstructure through economic dictates: in the face of the advancing capital organization and the need to transform peasants into proletarians, little could be done by the law. On the contrary, any legislation that delayed this process was, in this context, doomed to failure.

c   Original Under-Criminalization Revisionism

The concept of original under-criminalization shows how limited the legislation and prosecution of harmful behaviors committed in rural Europe and the colonies really were, regardless of their criminogenic character. Such was the degree of social harm produced by those behaviors that different contemporary authors posed theoretical proposals, and even regulatory changes, to fully recognize their criminal character.

New theories reassess the object of study of criminology, and propose to analyze the role of the state in colonial conquest, as well as other harmful acts committed in the course of history by the ruling sectors.[21] To avoid the legal constraints of the concept of 'genocide,' these new approaches have suggested other notions such as 'democide' (Rummel), 'one-sided mass killing' (Chalk and Jonassohn), and 'slaughter' (Semelin) (Zaffaroni 2011, 431). Regardless of legal limitations of the concept of 'genocide,'[22] Feierstein chooses to use the term 'constituent genocide' referring to the process by which the configuration of the states lays in the annihilation of the social fractions that were not part of the state pact. He also proposes the concept of 'colonial genocide' to refer to the exploitation and annihilation of indigenous peoples, and the appropriation of

---

of Toledo in 1480. However, lawsuits were mostly decided in favor of the appropriators (Luchia 2004, 9).

21   As it was mentioned in Chapter 1, theories of social harm propose that the field of study of criminology should not be reduced to acts committed on an individual basis, but also, and above all, to those committed by the state and private corporations. This theoretical position intends to demonstrate the criminal nature of wars, massacres and conquests. This will be approach with more detail in Chapter 4.

22   Under international law standards, it is not possible to charge with genocide any act that took place prior to the sanction of the Convention on the Prevention and Punishment of the Crime of Genocide by United Nations in 1948. Notwithstanding this, it is possible to invoke customary law to apply the Convention to those acts committed before its sanction.

their natural resources. He notes that "one of the peculiarities of the genocide as a social practice [is] its ability to destroy and reorganize social relations in societies in which it is implemented" (2007, 99).[23] From the sociology of social control, Pegoraro proposes to qualify the process of primitive accumulation as 'organized economic crime,'[24] as it involved:

> A massive and widespread violence police that was not caused by psychological or pathological deviations of some adventurous; it that was the product of an organized and complex activity that required connections among politicians, businessmen, officials, military, diverse professionals, priests, diplomats that, directly and indirectly, responded to a private enrichment strategy, linked to public officials and to the impunity of their social stratum (2002, 55).

Finally, not to promote a retroactive application of the law, but for purely analytical purposes, the human rights paradigm agreed upon in the international treaties of the 1940s makes the criminogenic nature of the events even clearer.

Centuries prior to the above mentioned theoretical developments, Marx himself denounced the criminogenic nature of primitive accumulation, which he characterized as a global network that involved political, economic, religious and military forces (1867, 785). Then, "[t]he treasures captured outside Europe by undisguised looting, enslavement, and murder, floated back to the mother-country and were there turned into capital" (826). In other words, the colonial system "proclaimed surplus-value making as the sole end and aim of humanity" (827). So, despite its bloody and mischievous nature, the outrages in the colonies and the expropriations in Europe were perpetrated without punitive consequences because they were necessary to establish the capitalist system of production.

---

23   Feierstein proposes to understand genocide as a quirky technology of power, with causes, effects and specific consequences that may be tracked and analyzed throughout history (2007, 13). He describes the actions perpetrated by the Spanish catholic monarchy as a 'modern genocide.' It was the first proto-state that was built on the exclusion of neither non-catholics (mainly Muslims and Jews) nor indigenous peoples (34). European genocides, the conquests, and the witch-hunt are framed, according to Feierstein, in the passage between 'pre-state genocides' and 'modern genocide' or 'modern genocidal practice' (98–99).

24   Pegoraro defines 'organized economic crime' as a "criminal organization dedicated to legal-illegal businesses of a certain legal and political complexity with the necessary participation of institutions & state agents, who obtain significant economic rewards and enjoy impunity and social and criminal 'immunity'" (2002, 52–53).

Following these guidelines and theoretical contributions, it is possible to understand that the primitive accumulation was essentially a 'slaughter' of European peasants and Native-American peoples. It was also an 'economic organized crime' by which the monarchy, feudal lords and rising bourgeoisie, pursuing public and private interests, perpetrated a massive robbery. Additionally, regardless of legal objections, it is also possible to characterize the primitive accumulation as a 'constituent genocide' committed with the purpose of founding capitalism through the elimination of feudal relations and the construction of capitalist social relations.

The perceived legitimacy of original under-criminalization relied on the justification of colonial pillage and the plunder of peasant lands as necessary to achieve progress. Following this logic, the dominant discourses claimed that the civilization of the colonies had to be done even at the cost of native people's lives, and that technical innovations in the field were necessary even at the cost of farmers' subsistence. Deaths and injuries were dismissed as unfortunate side-effects – 'collateral damage' we would say today – to promote 'civilization.' Moreover, this scenario of death and looting was masked by the popular presentation of the settlers and expropriators as good and hardworking entrepreneurs, who fought hard against lazy and wild people:

> The legend of theological original sin tells us certainly how man came to be condemned to eat his bread in the sweat of his brow; but the history of economic original sin reveals to us that there are people to whom this is by no means essential. Never mind! Thus it came to pass that the former sort accumulated wealth, and the latter sort had at last nothing to sell except their own skins. And from this original sin dates the poverty of the great majority that, despite all its labour, has up to now nothing to sell but itself, and the wealth of the few that increases constantly although they have long ceased to work [...] As a matter of fact, the methods of primitive accumulation are anything but idyllic (Marx 1867, 784–785).[25]

---

25   The bourgeois ideologues claim that primitive accumulation was the result of the laborious and thrifty spirit of individuals who stood out from a mass of lazy and ragged people that were ruined and impoverished because of their own fault. They explain that this is the root of the poverty of the working masses and the wealth of the elite. Such explanations serve to justify private property and capitalist profits, and also to define this system of production as harmonious and, therefore, eternal (Mansilla 1965, 44). Following the same logic, in the United States, the well-off claim that they are enjoying the result of the effort of hardworking parents that implemented a successful agricultural system in the beginning of the 19th century. However, far from that romantic and utopian version of u.s. history, slavery was the true key to the national development and the concentration

That is, although they hid a crusade of expropriation that has been "written in the annals of mankind in letters of blood and fire" (786), these harmful acts were presented as stepping stones made by valuable leaders that would give rise to an overall improvement of the world. So if money "comes into the world with a congenital blood-stain on one cheek, capital comes dripping from head to foot, from every pore, with blood and dirt" (834). This primitive extermination was what made possible the birth of capitalism. Its conception as a crime could not be afforded at that stage. The result of this is what we call *original under-criminalization.*

Original Over-Criminalization

Contrary to limitations in the attribution of a criminal character to the acts committed by the dominant sectors, petty crimes were abundantly and broadly legislated and over-dimensionally enforced. Behaviors such as vagrancy, panhandling and resistance to dispossession of peasant land were identified as illegal and subjected to relentless persecution and severe punishment, in a process that can be termed *original over-criminalization.* This notion describes the mechanisms that privileged the legislation (primary over-criminalization) and effective persecution (secondary over-criminalization) of those behaviors committed by impoverished sectors, with the goal of dismembering their communal and independent practices, and compelling them to wage labor. Original over-criminalization operated three-fold: (a) on the acts of resistance

---

of money in some sectors. Slavery has been hidden through metaphors. Slaves were not the main element of the national production but just 'right hands:' "[t]he threat of torture drove enslaved people to inflict this creation and destruction on themselves. Torture walked right behind them. But neither their contemporaries then, nor historians since, have used [the word] 'torture' to describe the violence applied by enslavers [...] No one was willing, in other words, to admit that they lived in an economy whose bottom gear was torture" (Baptist 2014, 263). This refusal to admit the commission of crimes has been analyzed by Sykes and Matza (1957) and named 'techniques of neutralization.' That is, to commit any kind of harm, individuals have to convince themselves that it is justified. One of the most widely spread techniques is denying the condition of the victim and ensure that they deserve this kind of treatment. Conceiving slaves as less than humans, as mere hands, was an extraordinary neutralization technique used by enslavers to ignore the fact that their wealth was built upon torture: "[p]lanter-entrepreneurs conquered a subcontinent in a lifetime, created from nothing the most significant staple-commodity stream in the world economy. They became the richest class of white people in the United States, and perhaps the world" (Baptist 2014, 269). This discourse has not come to an end yet: "[a]s American slavery evolved, an elaborate and enduring mythology about the inferiority of black people was created to legitimate, perpetuate, and defend slavery" (Equal Justice Initiative 2013, 1).

against enclosures by the peasants; (b) on the criminalized survival strategies committed by the excluded urban masses that were forced to find employment in the nascent capitalist industries; and (c) on the organization and reproductive behaviors of women.

a   Original Over-Criminalization on the Peasants' Acts of Resistance
         against Enclosures

The first enclosures in European rural territory took place during the 15th and 16th centuries. As it was described above, these enclosures were subjected to original under-criminalization, and had different levels of success in relation to the particular characteristics of each area. Many rural communities displayed a fierce opposition to enclosures, destroying them, and even sabotaging the work being carried out in the fields. In Germany, a great explosion of urban and rural uprisings, known as 'peasant wars,' took place against the privatization of land (Engels 1850).[26] The Kett rebellion in 1549 and the Newton Ren in 1607, both in England, found hundreds of men, women and children, armed with forks and shovels, destroying the fences erected around the common lands. In France, riots arose in 1563 after the Protestant Reformation absorbed the church lands, dispossessing the peasants that worked them. Between 1593 and 1595 the revolt of the Croquants occurred (Federici 2004, 240). In Spain, the struggle to re-appropriate land was circuitous, with significant peasant confrontation (Astarita 2014).

The resistance of the peasants was based on the belief that certain resources should be enjoyed by all: they broke the law to defend the land that naturally belonged to them in view of the communal character of the good. The process was so complex that the progress of privatization of lands and pauperization of the peasantry, paradoxically, reinforced the need to preserve the commons: grass, firewood, acorns, coal and all kinds of wild resources could no longer be found in individual fields, so they were searched for in common lands (Sanz Rozalen quoted in Luchia 2004, 9). These rebellions led to the open deployment of repressive measures to retrain peasants (Geremek 1986, 139 and 189). This is how, at the time of claiming to exercise those possessory actions (re-occupation of land) that were considered common-law by the weight of years

---

26   Engels is very critical of the sector that constituted the future lumpen-proletariat because
      its actions operated to the detriment of the organized peasants. This criticized sector
      joined the armies of the princes against the peasants, i.e., they served as shock troops in
      the annihilation of the organized peasants, and even managed to get into the groups of
      armed peasants to demoralize them (1850, 35 and 87).

of labor and common understanding, peasants were subjected to original over-criminalization.

b   Original Over-Criminalization on the Criminalized Survival
         Strategies in the Cities

Those expelled peasants that had to move to the nascent cities and the already existing urban poor populations were subjected to the original over-criminalization even more strongly than their peers in the countryside, and for a more extended period of time. As Marx explains, peasants were expelled as a result of the enclosures, and left to sell their labor in the cities where they were needed. However, they could not possibly be absorbed by the nascent manufactures as fast as they were being uprooted from their lands. In other words, the expulsion of peasants occurred at a much faster pace than the developing manufacturing industry could absorb them into the labor force (1867, 806).

Even in the cases where the peasants managed to be employed, it was extremely hard for them to respond to the dissimilar customs of the urban social discipline. Beatings and punishments were applied to inculcate them into the meticulous program of social change (Astarita 1998, 37).[27] Therefore, the difficulties encountered in labor absorption were equally the result of the clumsiness and naivety of those to be included in this work, as well as of the unattractiveness of that potential labor force for the employers (38).

This situation was aggravated in those countries where the Protestant Reformation was embraced. The change in the position of the Catholic Church and the confiscation of their property led to a complete disorganization of the assistance to the poor (Rusche and Kirchheimer 1938, 41–42). The poor who lived in the Church's lands,[28] and even the clergy, had to abandon their houses, while the tithes received by the impoverished farmers were eliminated, increasing the general level of pauperization (Marx 1867, 793). Further, the Protestant Reformation itself introduced work as a religious obligation against the vice of leisure. It noted that the glory of God is not in leisure or enjoyment, but work; therefore, the first and foremost of all sins was time dilation, and the laziness

---

27   Piven and Cloward explain that those populations were used to work in harmony with the solar rhythm and the seasons. The process of human adaptation to the economic changes caused long periods of massive unemployment, unrest and disorganization (quoted in Melossi 1980, 54).

28   This was the largest land transfer in history since the Norman Conquest (Federici 2004, 101). In the case of England, with the dissolution of the monasteries, monks and nuns themselves were reduced to panhandling, while about 80,000 dependents were forced to offer themselves in a collapsed job market (Pound 1971, 16).

of those capable of work was considered a sin against God (Weber 1904). Time was revalued as too-precious a commodity to be wasted (Thompson 1984, 281). Marx (1844b) noted so:

> Luther, to be sure, overcame servitude based on devotion, but by replacing it with servitude based on conviction. He shattered faith in authority by restoring the authority of faith. He transformed the priests into laymen by changing the laymen into priests. He liberated man from external religiosity by making religiosity that which is innermost to man. He freed the body of chains by putting the heart in chains (1844b, 138).[29]

The result of the arrival of masses of peasants to the cities, the change of the Church's position, and the new paradigm imposed by the Protestant Reformation increased the number of idle urban masses. They turned into beggars, robbers, vagabonds, partly from inclination, but in most cases from stress of circumstances (1867, 806). Neither charities nor the churches were ready to meet the demand of the new economic situation, while the fear of riots and epidemics expanded. Poverty became a threat, causing a change of attitude to the deprived population and the principle of mistrusting (and eventually punishment) of the poor was introduced (Geremek 1986, 33–35).[30] This change was reflected in the passage from a private, Church-centralized, universal charity, to a public, secular and standardized charity, nourished by indirect taxes of the general population.[31] These indirect taxes also helped stigmatize the poor,

---

29   Through this process, wealth lost its sinful connotations and the idea of voluntary generosity towards the poor as an absolution of faults lost its meaning. The rising bourgeoisie started to justify its life not by works of charity, but by its everyday conduct (Rusche and Kirchheimer 1938, 43). Particularly the English and Dutch bourgeoisies, who had not benefited as strongly from colonial campaigns as other European nations, found in Calvinism the theoretical foundation of their ascetic activity: to maintain the level of mere economic survival, work and savings became religious obligations (44).

30   In the 12th century, the Church had already introduced divisions to organize assistance to the poor. The first division was between the mendicant clergy (the one that voluntary decided to live in poverty) and the material poverty of the laity that deserved assistance. The Church also distinguished between 'honest' and 'dishonest' mendicants – those who could work but preferred to beg and steal. However, until the 13th century, even robbing was not always considered a crime if it was caused by real poverty, since the poorer, the greater the right to assistance. These considerations responded to the fact that a controlled number of deprived populations allowed idealization of poverty to prevail (Geremek 1986, 34–35).

31   Since the 16th century, Europe began a process of transition from a religious to a secular organization of charity. In 1531, Charles V created a royal a commission to organize

because it confronted them with those currently employed, who were not satisfied with the duty of taking care of the mendicants.

The standardized nature of the new charity emerged as its most striking feature and led to the cessation of 'giving without looking at who.' It began to distinguish between the 'true' poor (the one incapable of working because they were too ill or old, so-called 'impotent' or 'deserving' poor) and the 'fake' or 'false' poor (the one capable of working, and so-called 'idle' or 'able-bodied' poor). The 'true' poor were required not only to be incapable of working because of age or illness to deserve charity but also had to meet further standards. They could not have a family able to feed him (principle of family responsibility), they had to be from the region where he was panhandling – if not, each region could return them to their hometown (principle of residence or settlement), and, eventually, they had to be recorded in a register and carry a permit. With all these requirements, the extent of protection excluded even part of those unable to work. Middle and upper classes that had fallen with the loss of feudalism also received help; a highborn background legitimated them to receive charity, regardless of their ability to work (Geremek 1986, 49).

Far from this situation was the 'false' poor, who were defined as those who chose poverty, panhandling or vagrancy as a means to escape work. To discourage these fake poor and to delegitimize leisure, new laws interpreted their behavior as close to sin and crime, demonizing leisure, labor indiscipline and aversion to work. The new legislation sought to settle that their situation was no longer a matter of charity, but a criminal problem that necessitated legal intervention (Rusche and Kirchheimer 1938, 46). Being poor while preserving the physical ability to work was considered a deliberate decision that should be tried criminally. It was the beginning of a path of transition to the principles of Contractualism, and its vision of the offender as a rational being who voluntarily decides to break the social contract. This means that from a religious conception that secures salvation for those that help the poor, poverty becomes a negative and 'volunteer' attitude (Betran 2000, 106). Marx denounces this characterization as false: the law treated them as 'volunteer' criminals, under the assumption "that it depended on their own goodwill to go on working under the old conditions that no longer existed" (1867, 806). However, "[t]he

---

charity in secular terms but that still contemplated the collaboration of the clergy. In 1601, England passed the Act for the Relief of the Poor, which imposed a system of relief that lasted until 1834 and established that the inhabitants of each parish had to pay a tax for the assistance of the poor people. This legal instrument crystallized the spirit of the Old Poor Laws and marked the passing from the traditional voluntary charity to a charity supported by mandatory taxes under secular administration (Lopez Castellano 2004).

fathers of the present working-class were chastised for their enforced transformation into vagabonds and paupers" (806), resulting in stigmatization, criminalization, and widespread marginalization of all the poor (Betrán 2000, 113).

This distinction between 'true' and 'false' poor was established not as a mere classification of poverty, but the result of a control strategy developed over less economically skilled sectors (106). It was aimed at reaffirming the role that each person had in society, to put each one in its place and to foster a sense of security as integral to the process of primitive accumulation (125). The need to distinguish true and false poor reflected the concerns of a capitalist bourgeoisie, which, to develop their manufacturing companies, needed cheap (i.e., abundant) labor (107, n 8). Characterizing the idle as a problem of public order (111), and framing them as social despicable (113, n 30) was a way to ensure the availability of the labor force. Original over-criminalization helped impose such a dramatic shift in the social conception of poverty. Its most notorious profile was reflected in the so-called Poor Laws, a name strictly referring to the English legislation of the period, but has been extended to characterize the broader regulations all over Western Europe.[32]

The first element that stands out in these laws is the stipulation of severe penalties with no proportion to the low social harm involved in the prosecuted conduct (mostly mere panhandling or vagrancy). In the English case, the Tudor Dynasty (1485–1603) was the one that began the first period of the Poor Laws (the Old Poor Laws).[33] At this time, some of the cruelest regulations regarding the lack of employment were promulgated and implemented; the scope extended to those predisposed to work but who could not be inserted into the market. This resulted in an increasingly disproportional number of executions and corporal punishments (Rusche and Kirchheimer 1938, 42). In 1494, Henry VII (King of England from 1485 to 1509) established compulsory labor for the unemployed, under penalty of stocks for three days and nights, with only bread and water, and subsequent banishment. In the case of recidivism,

---

32   Even though the English model was the most eloquent, southern German cities were the main model for this widespread reform of charity (Geremek 1986, 57–58). The general character of this transformative process is expressed in the fact that even the United States passed Poor Laws in the 18th and 19th centuries to control 'suspicious' or 'undesirable' population (Chambliss 1964, 74–75).

33   Although there were previous laws about poverty, such as the Roasters Ordinance of 1349 and the Statute of Cambridge of 1388, they were not effectively applied. These laws were intended to make a workforce available, as the Black Death had crippled a large part of the population and wars and crusades had absorbed the servants. This makes clear that even those first laws against vagrancy had a clear intention of establishing a labor force and stabilizing wages.

the punishment was extended to six days (Dobb 1969, 233–234). In 1524, Henry VIII (1509–1547) described idleness as the 'mother and root of all vices' and ordered that the homeless be '"tayed at a carl's tayle' and 'betcn by the Sheriff's officers with whippes' and have 'round colers of orion' affixed to their necks" (234). In 1530 it was established that, in case of recidivism, "the whipping is to be repeated and half the ear sliced off; but for the third relapse the offender is to be executed as a hardened criminal and enemy" (Marx 1867, 806). Finally, the rules of 1547 imposed not only atrocious corporal punishment, but even enslavement and death if the 'false' poor resisted (625).[34] As a result of these laws, out of a population of three million, 72,000 thieves were hanged during the reign of Henry VIII.[35] Closing the Tudor period, Elizabeth I (Queen from 1558 to 1603)[36] imposed flogging and burning the right ear with a hot iron as the punishment for vagrancy (Dobb 1969, 234).[37]

---

34   This refers to the statues sanctioned by Edward VI (1547–1553) which "decreed that any-
     one refusing to work 'should be branded with a red-hot iron on the breast' and 'should be
     adjudged the slaves for two years of any person who should inform against such idler,' the
     master being entitled to drive his slave to work by beating, chaining or otherwise in such
     labour, however vile so ever it be 'and to make him a slave for life and brand him on cheek
     or forehead if he should run away'" (Dobb 1969, 234). The statue also established that if
     the slaves disappeared for two weeks, they should be condemn to slavery for lifetime,
     marking him/her with an S (for 'slave') on the forehead or on one cheek. If they escaped
     a third time, they had to be hanged (Marx 1867, 806). If beggars give a false birthplace,
     they were punished with lifetime slavery. If slaves attempted anything against their mas-
     ters, they were executed. If vagabonds idled outside their hometown, they were branded
     with a red hot iron with the letter V on their breast and they were chained and sent to
     work (807). The last part of the statue required the unemployed poor to work for whoever
     demanded them (Moulier-Boutang 1998, 410). Anyone who wanted the children of the
     vagrants, could teach them a job and use their workforces until the age of 24 for men and
     20 for women. If they escaped before that age, they could be kept in slavery for the rest of
     the training course. If their parents claimed mercy for them, they could also be enslaved.
     It was lawful to flog and chain the children, and even to put an iron ring on their necks,
     arms or legs to identify them better and have them at hand. "This kind of parish-slaves
     was kept up in England until far into the 19th century under the name of 'roundsmen'"
     (Marx 1867, 807).

35   Moro reacts precisely against these laws in his book *Utopia* (1516) which is basically a
     denunciation of the criminalization of poverty under the reign of Henry VIII Tudor.

36   Elizabeth I arrived to the throne after the brief reigns of Juana I (Queen of England in
     1553, deposed and executed) and Mary I (Queen of England 1553–1558).

37   In case of a second offense, they received the label of 'criminal,' unless someone agreed
     to take the vagrant away for two-years of service. For the third offense, the vagrant would
     be assumed as a felon without benefit of clergy, although this was only applicable to
     the 'professional beggars,' and not those unemployed for reasons beyond their control.

In Paris, in 1516, the authorities set the general punishment of deportation, by ordering all vagrants to leave the city, under threat of being submitted to forced labor during the day and imprisonment in chains during the night (Geremek 1986, 141–142). The judgment of the Parliament of Paris established, on February 5, 1535, the death penalty for mendicants who refused to perform useful work, and the non-natives who declined to leave the city after being ordered. It also established flogging or banishment for mendicants who pretended to be incapable of work and, in cases of recidivism, additional punishment to be decided by the judge (164). Even in some French cities, gallows were erected during food distributions to punish those who undeservedly claimed entitlement (Federici 2004, 136). For the entire French territory, the penalties consisted of marking a fleur-de-lis on the bodies of the vagrants with a hot iron, wresting their eyes, cutting off their tongue, flogging, and scarring their bodies with hot irons (Anitua 2005, 59).

In Spain, in 1530, Charles V enacted a provision in Augsburg that stated that the mendicants must be arrested and punished in a severe and exemplary manner. In 1531, he established that local authorities could impose discretional punishments such as flogging, forced labor and banishment to galleys (Geremek 1989, 160–161). In 1734, Felipe V promulgated a regulation concerning thefts committed in the court or in the roads that led to it: if the person was under 17 years-old and more than 15, they would receive two hundred lashes and ten years in the galleys, as well as their abettors. However, this policy failed to reduce the number of burglaries and it was abolished in 1745. It reentered into force in 1764 by decree of Charles III, a sign that an insistence on increasingly brutal punishment despite proven ineffectiveness is not peculiar to our historical period. The General Army Ordinances of 1768 still contained sentences like crossing the tongue with a hot iron, or mutilating the right hand (Zambrana Moral 2005, 224–225).

In the Holy Roman Emperor, Charles V promulgated the *Constitutio Carolina Criminalis* in 1532, which established the wresting of flesh with hot tongs as a punishment for beggars. The regulations considered that beggars not only committed the crime of resisting work, but that such behavior also implicated the crime of fraud (Rodriguez Giles 2011, 194).

The second element that can be traced in the Poor Laws has a strict connection with the above: corporal punishment served as a crude and cruel system

---

The Law on Suppression of Vagrancy of 1597 imposed a new punishment: being stripped to the waist and whipped until they bleed, and then be transferred to their place of birth or last residence (Dobb 1969, 234).

of identifying those who had already committed an offense (and for whom higher penalties applied), favoring their particularized control. Mutilation – amputation of hands, fingers and phalanges, castrations, cutting and removal of the tongue, eyes, ears – was used, especially in the case of the poorest offenders, regardless of what they had done. The reasoning behind these heinous acts was that mutilations possessed an extra feature: they served both as punishment and thereafter lifelong identification as one with a criminal record (Rusche and Kirchheimer 1938, 199). This was combined with the rules of dress: between 1572 and 1672 dress codes were imposed, and everyone was obliged to wear clothes 'according to their status, honor and wealth.' If the code was not respected, fines were applied (Boes 1996, 259). Thus, corporal punishment and dress codes remained present until the end of the 17th century as a crude and cruel criminal database, based on the physical characteristics of offenders.

As a result of this system that made so evident the identification of former offenders – through a lack of a body part, burns, or distinct clothing – it was particularly difficult for those who had received a punishment to find a job again. Thus, they were forced to relapse into crime, and eventually to fall victim to the harshest measures of the law (21). This stigmatization process exposes a striking parallel with the ongoing consequences of recidivism for those who carry out criminal records and attempt to reenter the job market. Moreover, it evinces how the application of punishment initiated a process of selectivity that was irreversible: the brand and 'stigma' (a Greek word for 'tattoo') transformed the offender into a perpetually excluded target of over-criminalization, excluded ever further with each new conviction.

These mechanisms of identification also informed the logic of rooting individuals to specific areas. This is the historical emergence of fixed names, passports and identification papers, which were used to control the flow of populations. Those who did not carry documents had to wear clothes, hairstyles and other signs that would allow their identification. Tattoos and mutilations were part of this process (Anitua 2005, 57). By the same logic, these corporal signs helped control which poor corresponded to which jurisdiction. The goal was to identify – and subject to over-criminalization – those who were found panhandling outside their jurisdiction.

The third element that can be identified in the Poor Laws is their use to compel the impoverished to perform those unattractive jobs that were seen as too risky to be freely chosen. Thus, original over-criminalization served this point, for the purposes of efficient distribution of work in those areas that needed force labor. In France, during the reign of Louis XVI, the Ordinance of July 13, 1777, stated the punishment of galleys – an activity that workers were reluctant to perform – for all persons from 16 to 60 years-old who, enjoying health, did not possess livelihoods and were not engaged in any profession (Marx 1867, 808). The government organized 'homeless hunts' to recruit sailors for the galleys, and it pressed the courts to impose this form of punishment even for minor offenses. Additionally, the government threatened with fines those parents who did not surrender their children to be employed in galleys (Dobb 1969, 279). The legislation also sought to force offenders to work in mines, to compensate the shortage of workers who died after voluntarily accepting this type of work (Anitua 2005, 68).

Also in Spain, crime control was used for the purpose of compelling offenders to work in unattractive and risky activities. The Courts of Madrid (1551) gave numerous orders and royal decrees ordering the gathering of the poor and homeless to "fix them in the Army, in mines, in public works, in arsenals, in mercy houses, in hospices and in hospitals" (Betran 2000, 128).

In Brussels, a decree of 1599 established penalties not only for beggars but also for domestic servants who abandoned their employers, and for workers that left their jobs to beg (Rusche and Kirchheimer 1938, 48). In Venice in 1529, laws ordered the arrest of all foreign beggars, and their conscription into forced labor in the Navy (Geremel 1986, 150–152). The first Italian legislation included repressive wage controls, obedience to the masters, and proscription for those who were employed. The law did not distinguish between genuine and false poor, but between 'good' and 'bad' poor. The latter referred to those who were reluctant to accept the imposed work conditions (Melossi 1980, 95–96).

Spain, Portugal, and England imposed the punishment of deportation to provide labor force to the colonies. Free workers were reluctant to move voluntarily to the uncertain fate of the colonized territories. Also, as a consequence of the extermination of the indigenous populations through war and disease, there were not enough local workers to be used to exploit natural resources. The Spanish Laws for Vagrancy Suppression (1597) legalized deportations stating that those 'rascals' that do not deserve to be released must be banished from the kingdom and its dominions, and sent to the assigned overseas regions (Rusche and Kirchheimer 1938, 19). Sending unwanted populations to remote areas is a mechanism that was still present in the 20th century and that, even today, influences the location of prisons in the countryside, far away from residential and commercial areas.

A fourth and final striking element of the Poor Laws is that, while focused on the working poor, in most cases they far exceeded that sector. Original over-criminalization spanned almost all the impoverished population that did not consent to the existing working conditions. In England, Elizabeth I expanded the scope of persecution to all people on the margins of society, particularly those outside of the wage labor market. She no longer restricted the application of the Poor Laws to vagrants and mendicants, but included also counter-morality behaviors, employment disobedience and poverty in general. Those who practiced illegal games; those who pretended to have knowledge of pseudoscience; those who forged document and licenses or used them; frequent players, jugglers, hawkers and boilermakers became target of over-criminalization. In 1573, the government expanded the definitions again to include men who left their wives and children. These new offenses extended crime control to everything and everyone that opposed the morality that was trying to be imposed. The entire legislation could be reduced to the phrase 'family and obedience' as it was aimed at establishing a new social and moral order under the fierce subjugation of the dispossessed sectors.

In England, James I (King from 1603 to 1625) used the accusation of idleness to legitimize the imposition of the most atrocious punishments for a variety of behaviors. When in 1622 the monarch ordered to investigate the causes of the economic crisis that was hitting the country, the final report blame the idleness of the British workers. It referred in particular to the widespread idle talk and the time lost in leisure and pleasure that put England at a commercial disadvantage in its competition with the industrious Dutch. To address this situation, games became banned, especially those that weakened the sense of individual responsibility and work ethic; taverns and public restrooms were closed; and punishment for nudity and other forms of non-productive sexuality and sociability were settled. Drinking, swearing and insulting were also banned (Federici 2004, 213). The prescribed penalties were public floggings and imprisonment for 6 months for the first offence, and 2 years for the second offence. During detention, offenders could be flogged as many times as the judges decided. Dangerous and incorrigible vagabonds were marked with an R on the left shoulder and subjected to forced labor; and if they were caught panhandling again, they were hanged without mercy (Marx 1867, 808).

In Spain, the Order of 1745 punished those who have no other job other than playing instruments, acting or dancing (artists), or those who sell marshmallows, candy canes and other treats (street vendors). The Ordinance of 1775 proscribed that vagrancy also includes those without an income, particularly gamblers, those often found in taverns, and the ones that walked without purpose (Betran 2000, 128–129). In 1750, the national population was 7 million people, with 2 millions of these unemployed. Among those, only 50,000 were authorized to beg (126). These numbers are evidence that the vast majority of poor people were banned from panhandling and had no access to charity, despite being unable to find a job. These were the ones characterized (and over-criminalized) as 'false' poor.

Following the principle of less eligibility,[38] the punishment applied to the 'false' poor, via the Poor Laws, acquired fearsome characteristics that configured it as 'less eligible' than the social assistance provided to the 'true' poor. In turn, the latter marked the level of less eligibility in relation to those employed in the labor market. The less eligibility of the social assistance in relation to the employed population was three-fold: the meager character of the aid, the multiple requirements to obtain it (registration, authorization, lack of family, remaining in one's hometown) and the fact that asking for assistance when capable of working was severely over-criminalized. Even then, despite employment conditions being extremely hostile, they constituted a better scenario in comparison with welfare.

c   Original Over-Criminalization on the Resistance and
         Reproductive Behaviors of Women

Original over-criminalization of working women along primitive accumulation operated under the widespread accusations of witchcraft. The accusation of being a witch referred to an undisciplined woman who handled contacts that were not sponsored by the new social patterns. Witches were another kind of marginalized category that threatened the social ideal of a docile work force. Witchcraft and Poor Laws worked together to ensure the necessary conditions for the foundation of the capitalist system of production. In fact, the decisive features used to propel an accusation of witchcraft were the same that the ones prescribed in the Poor Laws: panhandling, grumbling, swearing and quarreling (Russell 1980, 141).

Essentially, original over-criminalization of women served to break cultural patterns and create new social bases outside the matriarchal tradition, which was exercising a function of resistance against the new relations of domination. Until then, women were the main transmitters of a culture that the new

---

38   Recalling, the less eligibility principle was based on Marx's analysis and further developed by Rusche and Kirchheimer (1938) to indicate that punishment is not an abstract phenomenon that preserves the same characteristics throughout history. Consequently, punishment must be analyzed through its particular manifestations and its historical development. From this framework, Rusche and Kirchheimer propose that, to be a deterrent, punishment has to offer worse conditions than those offered to the less privileged social strata in the labor market (1938, 4). Broadening this perspective, the book proposes to analyze the less eligibility principle not only in relation to the labor market but also to social policies and their correlation to criminal policies.

ruling class was trying to banish. Particularly, matriarchal tradition resisted the appropriation of private conflicts by the newly created bureaucracies (Zaffaroni 2011, Anitua 2005). In addition, the misogynist nature of the Catholic Church and its divine claims, together with material reasons that supported the subjection of women's bodies for population control, helped to reinforce the persecution of women (Federici 2004, 222). The over-criminalization of the undisciplined women, under the accusation of witchcraft, shows that primitive accumulation was not just an accumulation and concentration of capital and exploitable workers but also an accumulation of differences and divisions within the working class. Different hierarchies – such as genre, race, and age – were also constructed in this framework (223).

The first mechanisms of witchcraft criminalization occurred in the Middle Ages and spread over the 14th to 16th centuries, in parallel with the Old Poor Laws (225). Indeed, the modern idea that witch-hunting is a phenomenon of the Middle Ages is the result of a false preconception, according to which all evils are attributable to the 'Dark Ages.' Actually, witch-hunting was the product of the Renaissance and the Reformation that went from the 14th to the 17th centuries (91). Between 1435 and 1487, 20 treatises on witchcraft were written, Kramer and Sprenger (1486) wrote the *Malleus Maleficarum* (The Hammer of Witches), and Pope Innocent VIII wrote the bull *Summis Desiderantes* (1484) framing witchcraft as an 'emergency.' In southeastern Germany at least 3,200 witches were burned between 1560 and 1670, and 4,500 were burned in Scotland between 1590 and 1650 (Federici 2004, 222). In the mid-16th century, persecution increased and moved from ecclesiastical jurisdiction to secular courts, which introduced the punishment of hanging in the gallows instead of the order to be burned at the stake (Russell 1980, 118–119). The highest levels of persecution occurred between 1580 and 1630, in parallel with the establishment of the economic and political institutions of the mercantile capitalism. It was then that the atmosphere of oppression, envy, irritation, hatred and despair spread superstition, and witch-hunting reached epidemic proportions (Rusche and Kirchheimer 1938, 22). To exemplify, in the German cities of Cologne and Bamberg, Bishop Johann Georg II burned at least 600 women between 1623 and 1633 (Russell 1980, 105–108).[39]

Witch-hunts involved both catholic and protestant countries. In the *Constitutio Criminalis Carolina,* witchcraft was punished with death. Protestant England passed three acts in 1542, 1563 and 1604, introducing the death penalty even in the absence of harm to third persons or destruction of property

---

39   During the 18th century, witch-hunt declined. To exemplify, in 1736, England ordered
       that "no prosecution, suit or proceeding is initiated or will be held against any person or
       persons for witchcraft, sorcery, enchantment or spell" (Russell 1980, 159).

(Federici 2004, 225–226). Witch-hunting also occurred in Spain and Portugal, especially in the 15th century, and after 1550, Scotland, Switzerland, France and the Netherlands also passed similar laws (226). Germany and Scandinavia approved similar laws much later, during the 16th and 17th centuries, as well as the American colonies (Russell 1980, 95–96 and 121).

Witch-hunting occurred along with the persecution of other dissidents such as Jews, converts, Arabs, homosexuals, and critics of orthodoxy. The particularity of witch-hunting was its gender orientation. Women were also over-criminalized if they did not follow the imposed patterns of biological reproduction: European governments began to impose the most severe punishment on those who practiced contraception, abortion and infanticide (Federici 2004, 135).[40] Similarly, in the 16th century, prostitution was, first, subjected to new restrictions and harsh corporal punishment (144).[41] As Marx (1858) illustrates, women were the biggest losers in a society of unemployment, workhouses, and social discipline.

The Different Application of Penalization and the Transit from Physical Punishment to Workhouses

So far we have seen how original under-criminalization enabled that those behaviors connected to the interests of the mercantile bourgeoisie, the monarchists and the feudal lords were scarcely and narrowly legislated in statutes and rarely prosecuted. Among these behaviors, we described how slavery, murder and robbery were rampant in the colonies, while expropriations and repression arose across Western Europe. It has also been shown how original over-criminalization made behaviors committed by impoverished and dispossessed sectors abundantly and broadly legislated in statutes and severely

---

40   In Nuremberg in the 16th century drowning was the punishment for maternal infanticide. In France, a royal edict of 1556 required women to register each pregnancy, and they were sentenced to death if their babies died before baptism in case of a secret childbirth. Similar statutes were passed in England and Scotland in 1624 and 1690. Even a spy system was established to monitor and deprive single mothers of support. Hosting a pregnant unmarried women was illegal because it could help them to escape from public scrutiny (Federici 2004, 136).

41   Between 1530 and 1560, brothels were closed and prostitutes were severely punished with flogging and other cruel forms of punishment, such as the 'chair dip' (ducking stool) or the 'acabussade' (people were tied, sometimes stuck in a cage, and immersed several times in rivers or lakes, until they were nearly drowned). In France, during the 16th century, the rape of a prostitute ceased to be a crime and, in Madrid, they were not allowed to sleep in the streets under penalty of 100 lashes and expulsion from the city for 6 years, plus their head and eyebrows were shaved (Federici 2004, 144–145).

prosecuted, despite the minimum harm that they caused. These behaviors included criminalized survival strategies (resistance to expropriations, vagrancy, panhandling, prostitution), coarse crimes and heresy.

However, original criminal selectivity was not limited to this 'crime distribution' where impoverished classes tended to commit petty crimes against property, and the ruling classes tended to commit serious crimes against life and property. Original criminal selectivity also operated through the harsher treatment of offenders that committed *the same crimes*, but came from different socio-economic status. The dominant classes demanded more guarantees in the procedures carried out against their members, while doling out tougher penalties for the most disadvantaged people. The rising urban bourgeoisie in particular had a practical interest in achieving high levels of efficiency in the prosecution of property crimes committed by the destitute (Rusche and Kirchheimer 1938, 16–17). The result was a rigidly segregated society, where far from bringing equality, the law reinforced the existing social divisions (Emsley 2007, 20).

This dissimilar punitive treatment when committing the same crime operated through two mechanisms. On the one hand, *selectivity affected the fact of criminalization itself.* This means that some behaviors were considered crimes only for people from a low socio-economic status, while upper classes retained the power to privately settle their disputes. In Flanders, North of Italy, Tuscany and Northern Germany, between the 14th and 15th centuries, the legislations provided a broad zone of immunity for acts that were severely punished when perpetrated by the lower classes (Rusche and Kirchheimer 1938, 15). Throughout the German territory in the 16th century, the regulation of robbery specified that if the offender was 'honest' – character that was extremely related to his socio-economic condition – he deserved a differential application of the law (18). Bloody feuds or duels were practiced by the richest sectors as a way of solving their disputes, even though the royalty had outlawed them in England and France in the 16th century (Ellet 2004, 59–60). Indeed, duels were very much alive even in the 19th century: the 1836 manual *The Art of Duelling* expresses: "I should consider it very unwise in the members of government, to adopt any measures that would enforce the prohibition of dueling." Only in the late 19th century, when duel was not a common way of solve disputes anymore, stricter anti-dueling laws were passed and eventually enforced in Europe and the United States (Holland 2004).

On the other hand, *selectivity also affected the type of punishment, the jurisdiction and the criminal procedure to be applied.* People from the upper classes did not receive infamous or corporal punishment, but imprisonment or economic sanctions (Zambrana Moral 2005, 224). To exemplify, in those crimes related to magic that did not constitute heresy, recidivism was punished with life imprisonment or exile for the upper classes, and public flogging for the poor. This different penalization made it possible for the wealthy to avoid the stigma of being exposed in public. However, the legislation did not recognize this discretion as a privilege to the well-off, but as a sample of the benign nature of the law. The explanation was that for the upper classes it was more painful to be penalized through their property; in contrast, as the lower classes did not value their honor so intensely, it was necessary to apply corporal punishment to them. Then, corporal punishment was a benefit for the poor because it helped them to hate vice and embrace virtue, as they would only obey the stick (249, n 173). A clear case was the legislation of Las Siete Partidas in Spain, which stated that the greatest punishment corresponded more to the servant than to the free man, to the villain than to the gentleman, to the young than the old. Even the death penalty was applied selectively: beheading for the distinguished people, hanging for lower class-men, cudgel for the nobles, and the 'arcabuceo' for the military. Following the same logic, the Halsgerichtsordnung Peinliche legislation in Schwarzenberg distinctly applied capital punishment according to social status (Rusche and Kirchheimer 1938, 18).

About jurisdiction, the social status determined the type of court through which people were judged. In the General States of Blois in 1576, members of the respectable classes that were accused of common crimes were presented before a 'bailiwick' or 's'en'echauss'e' court, while poor criminals, especially those without a fixed residence, were judged by the 'pr'evot'e' courts, which were allowed to apply the death penalty. Also, while resolutions in the first two courts could be appealed in the local parliament, there was no appeal against the decision of the third one (Merriman 2006, 23). Regarding the applicable procedure, settlement systems and private agreements applied to the favored classes, including cases expressly found in the criminal law and even in those that entailed the death penalty. The result was legal coverage offered to members of the upper classes for breaches of the peace and all kinds of thefts. In Southern Germany, even when the law imposed restrictions on the possibility of private agreement to resolve conflicts, the upper classes managed to avoid them and continued receiving preferential treatment. On the contrary, in cases of property crimes committed by the lower classes, the law was strictly enforced in ordinary courts and, in most of the cases, decided for the imposition of corporal punishment (Rusche and Kirchheimer 1938, 16). In relation to evidence-gathering, torture was used as a mechanism for obtaining confession, but excluded from this were people under 14-years old, soldiers, professors, King's counselors and their sons (if they had a good reputation), pregnant women and nobles (Real Academia de la Historia 1807).

Even when the same type of punishment was applied, the practical consequences – the *original* collateral consequences of convictions – differed according to the socio-economic status of the offender. Deportation for people from lower classes implied that they would be hanged when seeking refuge. For the wealthy, deportation was not really a rigorous punishment, but a possibility for travelling, establishing a business overseas, and even developing diplomatic relations while representing their city or country, with the prospect of an early and glorious return (Rusche and Kirchheimer 1938, 21).

This analysis leads to another fundamental point regarding the origins of the criminal justice system: during the late 16th and early 17th centuries, the transition between original criminal selectivity and its successor, disciplining criminal selectivity, took place.

The main change in terms of punishment had to do with the appearance of confinement[42] and forced labor as supplements to corporal punishment. First, imprisonment and forced labor coexisted with corporal punishment, fines, deportation, exile and the death penalty (38). Gradually, corporal punishment remained as an auxiliary tool to discipline offenders and oblige them to perform forced work in workhouses that were built in all the developed countries of the Western world during the 17th and 18th centuries. The origins of the workhouses can be traced to 1596, when Amsterdam created a great center of forced labor in a former convent (the Rasp-huis) (Anitua 2005, 66). The reason for it was that, even though Holland was the most advanced European center of the 16th century, it lacked a labor force (Rusche and Kirchheimer 1938, 49). The economic system required these new punitive forms to coerce mendicants to labor. In this regard, it is evident how changes in the mode of punishment, far from being explained in terms of endogenous legal criteria, are closely linked to the prevailing socio-economic needs. Indeed, this new system of punishment ensured almost zero production costs and high profit rates.

The conditions in workhouses were worse than those that corresponded to the free workers (less eligibility). Historical documents show that they were overcrowded (twelve people slept together in each cell, and each bed was shared by two or three people), only basic and monotonous food was provided, uniforms were mandatory, and there was little contact with family, even if all lived in the same building. The principal work that was performed in the Rasp-huis model was scraping wood with a saw to make the fine powder, from which the workers extracted a pigment that was used in the textile industry.

---

42   Confinement was in force since the initial moments of the primitive accumulation but until the 16th century it was used mostly as an instrument to enforce social policies against mendicants (Geremek 1986, 224).

Unlike the mill that was used by free workers in the market, people in the workhouses did this manually, with such a level of physical effort that many men broke their back while doing it (40).

Following the Amsterdam model, British King Edward VI donated his Bridewell house to the city of London to be refurbished as a workhouse (Brewster 1894, 88). All the continent's houses of correction subsequently took this castle's name and were called 'Bridewell' as well. These Bridewells picked up vagrants, idlers, thieves and perpetrators of minor offenses, and they sought their reform through force labor, while discouraging marginalized people to remain circulating in the towns and cities (Melossi 1980, 32). In 1525, Queen Elizabeth I established that each county should be provided with a house of correction to punish and employ rogues, orphans and disreputable women (Brewster 1894, 88). In 1614, the Mayor of London ruled that "one should not punish any beggar but send them to work, which is worse than death for them" (89). Later on, in 1722/3, the Law of Knatchbull allowed parishes to rent houses for the accommodation of poor people and make them work. This law increased the number of workhouses from 700 to 2,000 in three years (Moulier – Boutang 1998, 410). In Spain, the most common institutions for poor people were hospitals, general and specific centers, houses of mercy and hostels (Lopez Castellano 2004). King Carlos II created the first proper workhouses in 1670, ordering the officers of justice to audit the collected taxes and manage the funds required for their functioning (Foucault 1964b, 53). In France, the 'hospital general' or 'maison de force' was created thanks to initiatives that the Jesuits brought to the industrial bourgeoisie of Paris and Lyon (Anitua 2005, 67). Italy, Switzerland, Germany and Norway also established workhouses between the 17th and 18th centuries, producing a drop in capital and physical punishment (Melossi 1980, 12; Mathiessen 1987, 48).

There are different analytical positions regarding the reasons for the emergence of these institutions and the objectives they pursued. Rusche and Kirchheimer claim that the workhouses acted as a labor-market control. There was an increasing demand for workers in the cities, levies in the army and galleys in the maritime activity, which increased the price of salaries. Workhouses were intended to subdue the mass of idle workers and employ them, reducing that general level of wages (1938, 30). To enforce this goal, governments also reduced the economic aid for the poor to oblige them to work. They also encouraged the recruitment of women and children for long working hours (Dobb 1969, 90).

Foucault, Sellin, Melossi and Pavarini argue that the function of the workhouses was undoubtedly more complicated than just controlling salaries. Their aim was to break the resistance of the workers and make them accept working conditions with the maximum degree of exploitation to introduce them to the eminent factory discipline (Melossi 1980, 195). Workhouses involved the control of the labor force, their education and their domestication (36). Sellin reinforces that workhouses emerged to replace the futile corporal punishment that had failed to meet the goals of disciplining workers and deterring criminal behavior (1940, 68). Pavarini also claims that the aim of these institutions was to educate former peasants and artisans, accustomed to live with the seasons' schedule, to turn them into a working class, to make them accept the logic of wage labor, and to make them recognize and embrace the discipline of the factory as a natural condition (1995, 40–41). Foucault (1975) agrees that the role of the workhouses was to install discipline in the souls of this population, replacing the pain in the body caused by physical punishment. These institutions embodied a 'constant micro-punishment' oriented to an 'effective generalization of work,' and to institute a 'microcosm of capitalist population' (Betran 2000, 118). The aim was to vindicate the new meaning of work not so much as an element of redemption (a salvific practice for man on earth) but as a symbolic element that allowed the moral and religious condemnation of the non-working population. Workhouses were the basis upon which disciplinary mechanisms were imposed: a functional device that could improve the exercise of power, making it lighter, more efficient; a design of subtle coercions for a future society (119). To prove this thesis, Melossi explains that the different levels of technique between the workhouses and the free market show that the first ones were not "a place of production itself, but rather a place to learn the discipline of production" (1980, 42). Workhouses were not looking for actual production but for discipline through painful and even futile efforts. For example, the 'scraping technique' continued to be enforced in the workhouses long after it had been surpassed in the outside market for more efficient methods.

The labor market and the disciplining explanations, far from being opposed and contradictory, are likely to be understood from a holistic analysis, based on Marx's perspective. Marx expounds that police methods were typical of the primitive accumulation, when wages and working conditions had to be forced by the coercive power of the state. With the evolution of capitalism, economic coercion gradually displaced the violent and physical mechanisms of oppression. However, state power was still necessary to 'regulate' wages, i.e., to hold workers within the limits that benefit the extraction of surplus value, to lengthen the working day, and to maintain the dependence of the workers (1867, 809). Since the end of the 16th century, workhouses became the new legal instrument, complementary to the Poor Laws, that helped the central goal of primitive accumulation: create an orderly and disciplined proletariat through two additional means. On the one hand, as Rusche and Kirchheimer state, workhouses helped to recruit labor force in those places (the colonies, Holland) and activities (textile work, army, galleys) where it was needed. Also, as they explain, workhouses provided almost free labor that helped reduce wages in the open market. On the other hand, as Sellin, Foucault, Melossi and Pavarini highlight, workhouses sought to impose order and discipline on the errant population that had been expropriated from their hometowns and swarmed in the growing cities. Forced labor in the workhouses was a successful method to transmit to this population its duty to accept wage-labor as the only viable mode to meet their material needs, if they did not want to be criminalized.

In short, force labor in workhouses pursued a threefold purpose: meeting the demand for labor that was not satisfied the market; obliging this work-force to answer the needs of capital in an orderly manner; and controlling the level of wages. All this could be epitomized by a single purpose: creating a disciplined working class. Thus, this original punitive complex was the political-legal 'answer' to the problem of what to do with the poor who did not adapt to the new structure, while sending a clear message about the primacy of discipline to the lower classes in general. *Primary over-criminalization -through the Poor Laws - transformed the poor into criminals, while secondary over-criminalization - through workhouses - transformed criminals into employees.*

Analyzing conflict-control during original criminal selectivity, the following sub-section addresses *who* were the recipients of this mode of selectivity.

Who Were the Social Sectors Targeted by Original Criminal Selectivity?

As is clear from the above, the social sectors favored by original under-criminalization were the monarchy, the feudal lords, and the rising mercantile bourgeoisie. Together, or in conflict with each other, they exercised crime control in Europe and the colonies.

Meanwhile, original over-criminalization was applied with greater intensity against the colonized – whose personhood was not recognized until the 17th century – and against the pauperized populations in Europe. Concerning the latter, Geremek considers that the ones that were targeted by crime control were the expropriated peasants (the 'uprooted peasants') who became tramps or beggars in the cities and in the field. Urban and rural pauperism roots lie in the breakdown of medieval structures, centered in the enclosures (1989, 126).

This mass of working poverty is the one that helped make capitalism, by providing a cheap or free labor force as the emergent working class (136). Astarita
(2005) challenges that argument and argued that the expelled peasants joined
the ranks of the lumpen-proletariat and were targeted by crime control because of their disruptive life-style. The proletariat emerged from what Astarita
called 'marginal workers,' i.e., those who were also subjected to crime control
to foster their subjection to the conditions of capitalist exploitation (44–45).
These masses were impoverished and not supported by the existing social
bonds even prior to the primitive accumulation. To ensure their hold and control, they were employed in temporary jobs inside the villages and, when there
was no work available, they were granted the right to enjoy a small planting
for their subsistence, or the right to graze the common ground (38–40). This
sector was used for long periods of unemployment, and when they could not
produce the minimum required for subsistence, they resorted to "petty theft
[as] a supplementary means of life" (45). Because of this erratic life of seasonal work combined with petty crimes, they were not suitable for disciplined
work. These populations ended up employed in the cities as 'sub-proletarians'
or 'semi-proletarians,' in conditions that favored and fostered their submission
(46). Crime control and the punitive evolution of charity were key elements to
promote that transformation. Finally, Thompson (1984) and Hobsbawm (2001)
state that the over-criminalized population were not the expropriated peasants but the proper urban poor. Those that could no longer enter the guilds
in dissolution (as an effect of accretion of power to the new bourgeoisie) and,
therefore, were also forced to make their living in an unfamiliar system.

From the readings of Marx and Engels, the contributions of Astarita, Geremek, Thompson and Hobsbawn help us understand that original criminal
selectivity – aimed at creating a disciplined working class – operated in different
scenarios and under different modalities. At first, original over-criminalization
targeted peasants that resisted enclosures. When they were evicted – as Geremek proposed – their destinations were varied: some were used as labor force
in the emerging rural industries and even in the land that was once theirs.
Others, particularly the young population without family, roamed through the
margins of the agrarian society (forming the lumpen-proletariat referenced by
Astarita). A third group ended up intensifying the migration to the cities and
become urban workers, or the poor and unemployed population (as characterized by Hobsbawm and Thompson). The situation in the cities was harsh
because they were a mass with little or no skills, finding assimilation in the
production process very difficult. The cities were already filled with an enormous mass of unemployed workers: the craftsmen that were excluded from

the closed system of guilds; the urban poor population without a working trade (who may have been part of the 'marginal worker' defined by Astarita); and the women who were persecuted for their condition on charges of witchcraft, prostitution and abortion.

This means that coming from the field or already settled in the cities, the social sectors targeted by original over-criminalization were both potential lumpen-proletariat (what might be called *proto-lumpen-proletariat*) and potential working class (which might be called *proto-proletariat*). The prefix 'proto' responds to the fact that, from a strict historiographical perspective, it is only possible to identify the masses of proletarians and lumpen-proletarians in the context of the industrial revolution. Thompson (1963) tell us that the working class – and with it, the lumpen-proletariat – was formed between 1790 and 1830, when it merges its labor and political organization. Therefore, in this original context, it is only possible to identify earlier stages of their development.

Referring to what may be called proto-lumpen-proletariat, Engels illustrates that the vagabonds of the 16th century were those who would form the future lumpen-proletariat:

> The *lumpenproletariat* which can be found even in the lowest stages of development of city life. This poor proletariat is, generally speaking, a phenomenon which, in a more or less developed form, can be found in all the phases of society hitherto observed. The number of people without a definite occupation and a stable domicile was at that time gradually being augmented by the decay of feudalism in a society in which every occupation, every realm of life, was entrenched behind some privileges. In no modern country was the number of vagabonds so great as in Germany, in the first half of the Sixteenth Century. One portion of these tramps joined the army in war-time, another begged its way through the country, a third sought to eke out a meager living as day-labourers in those branches of work which were not under guild jurisdiction.

He expresses that "the classes and fractions of classes that betrayed the movement of 1848 and 1849 were those that are also treasonous in 1525, *though at a lower stage of development*" (1850, 24). Engels refers here to different groups that arose during primitive accumulation: those who fought against the peasants and in defense of princes; those who demoralized the farmers' organization; and those who performed unregulated activities in the cities and acted against the workers that were seeking to organize themselves. Rusche and

Kirchheimer confirm Engels' visions and highlight that those foreigners who found difficulties in obtaining citizenship or participating in the guilds offered themselves to princes and other authorities that found in this new and cheap supply of soldiers the means to consolidate and extend their power (1938, 12–13). The lack of labor inclusion of the old and new poor in the cities, especially of the unskilled, configured them as a cheap labor supply for military clashes and the repression of working population; that is, as a proto-lumpen-proletariat. As Marx describes:

> Manufacture begets, in every handicraft that it seizes upon, a class of so-called unskilled laborers, a class which handicraft industry strictly excluded. If it develops a single specialty into a perfection, at the expense of the whole of a man's working capacity it also begins to make a specialty of the absence of all development (1867, 384).

Regarding the other suggested category, the proto-proletariat, Engels explains that in this original context it was possible to identify an 'embryonic proletariat' (1850). As it was mentioned above, peasants' expropriations and forced migrations to the cities took place before the production was able to absorb them. The result was a proletariat that was still in an embryonic stage, the aftermath of this process of 'blocked proletariazation' (Arrighi 1970, 38).

The ruling classes tried to inculcate work discipline and submission to the authority of both, proto-lumpen-proletariats and proto-proletariats, to form the proletariat that capital needed. These masses were the target of original criminal selectivity through the adverse effects of original under-criminalization and through original over-criminalization. Original under-criminalization operated on the illegal expropriation of peasants' land, leaving them without any legal protection. Original over-criminalization targeted those peasants when they tried to defend their communal and customary ownership in the rural areas. It also operated over those who, after being thrown into a developing labor market that was unable to absorb them fully, were accused of laziness and punished with torture, physical mutilation, or death. This shows a contrasting situation to the colonized population that suffered the consequences of original criminal selectivity largely through original under-criminalization of the acts committed against them, which involved such levels of direct violence that, in turn, necessitated resorting to draconian laws to reign them in.

Mixed Insertion in the Primitive Accumulation
The social sectors that have been identified as privileged recipients of the mechanisms of original over-criminalization were excluded from the nascent

productive framework. However, they were not 'full-time' or 'vocational' criminals, as it was said to justify their persecution. On the contrary, since the dawn of capitalism, these over-criminalized sectors were involved in a phenomenon that can be called *mixed insertion*, i.e. they combined illegal activities with discontinued lawful jobs. This concept is likely to be coined from the most recent contributions of sociology[43] and used to understand previous historical periods, and even the very midst of primitive accumulation.

Indeed, the masses that were subject to original over-criminalization came to a cluster of criminalized survival strategies (mostly panhandling and vagrancy) that fell under the purview of crime control. However, they also combine these illegalities with occasional wage labor and, at times, even with the solidarity of their peers – for example, through the use of communal land. That is, this over-criminalized population occupied an ambiguous position: they were absorbed by the labor market through temporary work in the cities or seasonal work in the countryside; and, when their work was not necessary, they suffered absolute exclusion and engaged in what was considered criminal behavior.

Vilar (1964), discussing Spain, supports this analysis when he refers to those who combined temporary jobs with theft and vagrancy. Astarita also describes that the marginal populations combined various criminalized survival strategies with casual wage labor and petty crimes (1998, 36). In rural areas, the 'marginal workers,' who could not be employed in temporary jobs, preyed on the properties of the residents of the village to supplement their income (40). They usually retained a minimum amount of land, which they complemented with seasonal jobs and petty crimes. So they were classless, but not excluded: they came in and out of the formal production (23). Theft was a common practice, done to supplement work or charity (2014). In England, the fact that the expropriated peasants resorted to petty crime to survive was itself used as an argument to reinforce the slowdown of enclosures: the draft of the legislation of the 1515 act exposed the governmental concern about the infinite number of people who, because of the lack of occupation, became vagrants and thieves (Campagne 2005, 175).

Many farmers who could not obtain minimal resources were forced to migrate to urban centers, where anonymity allowed them to combine charity, various criminal activities and temporary unskilled jobs (Rodriguez Giles 2011, 192). Once in the city, the figure of the 'rogue' identified a particular type of marginal person that survived through temporary contracts in domestic

---

43   Modern sociological studies have detected the confluence of legal and illegal activities
       in current marginal populations. This will be explored in more detail in the section Who
       Were the Social Sectors Targeted by Bulimic Criminal Selectivity?.

service, where they were hired by the lower nobility and the urban bourgeoisie. When they could not find work, rogues committed various illicit activities and other ethically questionable unskilled occupations: panhandling, fraud, gambling and theft (128 and 193). They have been described as a border social sector that oscillated between exclusion and integration, from being beggars to the guests of Lords, from sharing intimate spaces with the Lords, to being excluded as criminals (136–137). Another variant of urban marginalized groups were those trainees who had a much more stable employment, but who – to supplement their meagre income – performed petty theft at the home of their teachers, which could lead them to be marginalized as criminals (129).

Mixed insertion is then a conceptual tool that identifies the contemporary phenomenon of combining legal and illegal activities in previous historical periods. Since primitive accumulation, the privileged targets of the mechanism of over-criminalization were not exclusively devoted to crime. When they were offered a chance, they worked in part-time or seasonal jobs that were supplemented with vagrancy, panhandling, robbery or theft.

The following section analyzes *how* punishment was configured in this framework.

Punishment during Original Criminal Selectivity

During primitive accumulation there was no articulated theory about the reasons for punishing, which would be developed only since the 18th century. However, punishment was already accompanied by a legitimating discourse because, since there was crime control, someone has exercised the power of speech on it (Zaffaroni et al. 2000, 157). Legitimating discourses on punishment can be analyzed through their manifest and latent functions. Manifest functions of the original criminal selectivity discourses invoked an 'emergency' that legitimized the immediate exercise of crime control. This 'emergency' was attributed to the 'witches,' the poor, the foreign and the idle, among other individuals who were unaware of the ideal of obedience that was being forged. Meanwhile, the implicit goals behind this emergency discourse (the so-called latent functions of punishment) help show the inconsistences of the manifest functions, while also uncovering why and for what purposes the authorities began to punish in the forms discussed above.

Manifest Functions
The *original* emergency-based discourse was centrally embodied in the *Malleus Maleficarum,* a church-sponsored book that highlighted the containment

and elimination of an evil (heresy and witchcraft) that threatened the existence of humanity and demanded an immediate control (158 and 273). Witches' emergency was not in isolation or as a historical hinge; it was associated with the persecution of heresies, the fear expressed in the invective language directed against heretics, lepers, Jews, prostitutes, vagrants, and homosexuals (Moore 1987, 165).[44] These religious and moral-based risks were inserted into a broader, complex net of other 'emergencies:' colonial populations, rebel peasants, and lazy workers. Aiming to legitimize massacres in foreign lands, the discourse of the colonizers clamored that crime control was necessary to quell the 'emergency' of soulless beings and savages who were a source of delay against the civilized world. Enclosure-leaders use the emergency discourse to legitimize land expropriation and submission of peasants invoking that they were slowing the advance of capital and the modernization of agricultural production. The Protestant Reformation also used the emergency discourse against leisure to legitimize the persecution of unemployed workers and their coercion to work.

This conglomeration of emergency-based discourses served to legitimize a warfare policy that carried on the first major privatization of the operation of the criminal justice system in history: crime conflicts would not be sorted out between victim and offender anymore, but re-conducted through the states' monopoly of violence. It was a complicated process, situated in the transition from feudalism to capitalism, in which the exercise of punishment evolved from the private domain to the state monopoly in its selective specificity. Only after many ups and downs, and after a historic drift with several edges, the definitive expropriation took place and configured itself as an essential act of the criminal justice system's role within capitalism. The construction of an 'other,' who was bad and risky enough to be treated as an emergency and immediately eradicated, legitimized this initially broad and officially-driven crime control. Indeed, the *Malleus* was not just a prescription about the witch emergency, but the first book in formalizing the application of punishment regulated by the state through an integrated model of etiological criminology (causes of crime), criminal law (manifestations of crime), penology (punishment of the offense) and criminology (signs of criminals) (Zaffaroni 2011, 29).

---

44 As a complex process, community-based conflict resolution systems persisted even after the institutionalizing of the states and its monopolistic exercise of crime control. To exemplify, during the Castilian revolution, popular trials took place from 1520 to 1521 and were resolved by public acclamation (Astarita 2014).

Latent Functions

Crime control, operating through original criminal selectivity, cannot be read regarding abstract discourses of emergency. It finds its roots in the needs of the economic and social structure of primitive accumulation. Then, it is possible to ask the following questions. What were the implicit or latent purposes arising from the application of crime control in this original framework? What could be said, without falling into false manifest discourses on 'emergency,' if we seek to explain the material foundation for the legitimate use of state violence? What would be the conclusion if, instead of covering up, we investigate why punishment was applied in this foundational context of capitalism? How would we formulate the aims of the material application of punishment during primitive accumulation?

Actual reasons for the use of crime control in this first stage of capitalism has been described as 'unlimited social defense.' It responded to a conception of society as an organism, and the exercise of power was not discussed, but naturally assumed. Punishment served to defend the social body while the seriousness of the emergency justified an unlimited defense (Zaffaroni et al. 2000, 276). This had already been foreseen by Marx in the article 'Capital Punishment' (1853) when he talks about the aim of punishment and explains that it involves nothing less than a mean by which society defends itself from those events that threaten their material conditions of existence, particularly those committed against property. In his words: "Plainly speaking, and dispensing with all paraphrases, punishment is nothing but a means of society to defend itself against the infraction of its vital conditions, whatever may be their character." Moving away from a conspiratorial reading that detached from a linear or literal reading of this phrase, Marx opens the path to thinking about crime control as a mechanism for securing socio-economic interests. Consequently, crime control orients its application to those who, in any way, undermine the existential conditions of the socio-economic system.

This 'defense' of the new mode of production rested on three concrete latent purposes that original criminal selectivity helped consolidate. The first goal was creating a working class through over-criminalization, while enabling capital accumulation without further questioning through under-criminalization. The second one was affirming the power of the ruling class (represented by the sovereign, who imposed over the remaining groups in conflict, namely the nobility and the bourgeoisie). The other side of this calculation was the duty of submission of the general population, obtained with the help of over-criminalization. The third implicit or latent function of punishment was fragmenting the dispossessed sectors, mostly through over-criminalization. Let us explore them one by one.

Creating a Disciplined Working Class

As shown throughout the chapter, the primary function of crime control was linked to the creation of a disciplined working class. The impoverished sectors were compelled to work under threat of punishment or through the punishment itself. Proof of this is that many of the most torturous corporal punishments were not strictly enforced, but sought to force the poor population to perform undesirable work. It was common that punishment for an offense was replaced for working time in the galleys. The aim was not to disable or destroy potential workers but to force them to work in terrible conditions (Pavarini 1995, 23). On this point, Moro (1516) reflects about punishment and its vicious circle:

> If you do not find a remedy to these evils it is a vain thing to boast of your severity in punishing theft, which, though it may have the appearance of justice, yet in itself is neither just nor convenient; for if you suffer your people to be ill-educated, and their manners to be corrupted from their infancy, and then punish them for those crimes to which their first education disposed them, what else is to be concluded from this but that you first make thieves and then punish them?

Also Foucault, taking up the work of Rusche and Kirchheimer, points out that the use of torture as part of punishment is "the effect of a system of production in which labor force, and therefore the human body, has neither the utility nor the commercial value that are conferred on them in an economy of an industrial type" (1975, 54). That is, the abundance of labor force allowed the ruling class to use extreme violence to transmit the message that the impoverished should abandon their pre-capitalist traditions and accept the new social relations. This message includes the obligation of the poor to take the most terrible works – as galleys or work in the colonies – even though they were extremely risky.

Finally, over-criminalization of these population sectors in response to an 'emergency' helped to obscure the under-criminalization of the acts perpetrated by the well-off in order to enable the foundation of capitalism. Characterizing the over-criminalized as an emergency covered the outrageous character of the acts committed by the upper classes to the detriment of the native populations, enslaved men and women, peasants, and the urban poor.

Imposing the New Social Order

The second latent function of crime control was to subject all the social sectors to the power of the sovereign (from which the rising bourgeoisie would take benefit). All individuals must learn to obey the sovereign. Proof of this was the sanction of Poor Laws across Europe where crime control applied not only to the poor who refused to work but also to those who gave alms to unauthorized beggars (Geremek 1989, 163). The imposition of the new social order was perpetrated by confining each to their expected role, under the strict categories of rulers and ruled:

> Yet, in fact, what had hitherto maintained this practice of torture was not an economy of example, in the sense in which it was to be understood*at the time of the *ideologues* (that the representation of the penalty should be greater than the interest of the crime), but a policy of terror: to make everyone aware, through the body of the criminal, of the unrestrained presence of the sovereign. The public execution did not re-establish justice; it reactivated power.
> FOUCAULT 1975, 49

Foucault shed light on how to understand torture as a political ritual, as one of the ceremonies by which power is manifested. Torture shows that the crime affected not only the victim but also the sovereign that expressed his will through the law. Consequently, the sovereign intervened to defend himself from the ones that had offended him, and not just to mediate between the parties. This is why the punishment could not be identified or even proportionally adjusted to repair the caused damage: punishment had to add an offset for the offense against the sovereign, which consisted of both the disorder introduced in the kingdom and a personal affront towards him. Punishment had to repair the damage and also to ensure the right of the sovereign to make war on anyone who disobeyed his rules: "to punish belongs to that absolute power of life and death which Roman law calls *merum imperium*, a right by virtue of which the prince sees that his law is respected by ordering the punishment of crime" (48). The quality and quantity of the penalty had to overcome the contempt caused to the sovereign, and in that aim it "is carried out in such a way as to give a spectacle not of measure, but of imbalance and excess; in this liturgy of punishment, there must be an over-dimensioned affirmation of power and its intrinsic superiority" (49). It becomes clear that the terror of punishment was not only aimed to intimidate potential offenders. It had a political function that consisted of showing to all the triumph of the law and the sovereign. Any offense was considered a *majestatis crime* and even the least of the offence was a potential regicide (53–54). The power of the sovereign was built by breaking the exercise of justice between peers.

Fragmenting the Dispossessed Sectors

The final implicit function of crime control rested on fostering the fragmentation of the dispossessed sectors, entrenching social divides within the lower classes. This split took its dominant form in the division between true/impotent/deserving poor (the ill and old people) and the false/able bodied poor (the ones capable of working). The 'false' poor were characterized as a source of disturbance and a threat to the social order. This fragmentation was also pursued through the opposition between the witch/prostitute and the good/honest women, as well as between the civilized worker as opposed to the colonized wild men, among other false dichotomies. A clear example of how law tended to reinforce this split and even incite the confrontation between these sectors was the French decree of 1724. It justified sentences imposed on beggars who did not work because they deprived the 'true' poor of their bread by refusing to join the workforce (Rusche and Kirchheimer 1938, 48). Crime control presented the over-criminalized as a disservice to the obedient poor and advocated for the confrontation between them. Far from being a modern phenomenon, this function was present in the very beginning of primitive accumulation.

Moral Entrepreneurs and Moral Panics

The criminalizing discourses were not built in a vacuum. They were supported by special representatives of each of the interest groups – that can be called 'moral entrepreneur' (Becker 1962) – who promoted 'moral panics' (Cohen 1974). The notion of 'moral entrepreneurs' describes those individuals with the power to define and qualify others and are likely to promote and build the sanction and implementation of standards in the proposed sense (Becker 1962, 19). Moral panics condensed political struggles to "control the means of cultural reproduction" (Cohen 1974, 8). Without ignoring the clear late-modern profile of these concepts, it is enriching to apply them to earlier periods to understand the continuities in the selective exercise of crime control, and the participation of different social sectors in their legitimation and promotion. These notions can be traced back to Marx's work, 'Digression: (On Productive Labor)' (1861–1863, 360–361), where he warns that "[t]he criminal produces an impression, partly moral and partly tragic, as the case may be, and in this way renders a 'service' by arousing the moral and aesthetic feelings of the public." Regardless of the ironic tone of the passage, Marx expresses that there are social processes during which an event is identified as threatening, arousing 'moral and aesthetic sentiments' in the whole population.

There were several original moral entrepreneurs: the authors of the *Malleus* and other religious authorities that condemned witchcraft and heresy;

the exponents of the Protestant Reformation that promoted reform in charity; the promoters of the Poor Laws; businessmen, traders and entrepreneurs that supported the conquest of the colonies. These actors advocated treating social problems as criminal ones, including the resistance to colonialism and occupation of rural lands, behaviors related to leisure, the confrontation of empowered women and the practice of unofficial religions. Moral entrepreneurs presented these conflicts as 'emergencies' that needed to be addressed without delay by crime control. The characterization of these phenomena as 'emergencies' propagated moral panics in the population, particularly the fear of the witch, the heretic, the idle and the wild. Moral panics were used to legitimize the selective criminal practice from a social constructed perception about conflict and control.

Brief Reflections

This chapter allowed us to reflect, on the basis of Marx's *Capital*, about the close link between the foundational process of the capitalist system of production – the primitive accumulation – and the development of the modern punitive system. This parallel helped create a critical concept to understand this process: *original criminal selectivity*. This notion demonstrates two central phenomena: crime control displayed a selective application since the beginning of the capitalist system of production, and it worked as an invaluable tool in forging the new social relations that the system required.

Primitive accumulation required initial capital: precious metals, wool, natural products at low or no cost. Robbery, destruction, torture, and murder were the hegemonic means to obtain them, as was clearly evidenced by Marx in his famous Chapter 24 of *Capital*. Original under-criminalization covered up those acts under the garb of civilizational progress and allowed them to be freely perpetrated. At the same time, absorbing the impoverished populations into the new social order could not have been accomplished without the extreme violence of original over-criminalization. This mechanism was used to destroy communal bonds, traditional values, communal property, and customary rights of the population. It also allowed placing the expropriated population in terrible working conditions to serve the fledgling manufacturing sector. In short, original over-criminalization was needed to subdue this population to the new scenario and to establish the required new social relations.

The clearest breaking point in the use of crime control during primitive accumulation has to do with the fact that it started to operate *permanently*. It stops working occasionally – exclusive to moments of social upheaval – as it did in the feudal structure. To lay the foundations of the capitalist system and to ensure its preservation, it was necessary to maintain crime control as a constant threat to the conflicting sectors. Crime control was imposed as a sword of Damocles that constantly threatened, through the mechanism of original over-criminalization, the rising proletariat. Since then, most of the people would not be punished during their entire life (as was the case with the 'permanent effective punishment' of slavery or the system of 'punishment through traditional links' that dominated during feudalism), but anyone considered controversial could be punished at any time (Ciafardini 2012b). Proof of this change is that the formation of a repressive apparatus had it biggest development between the 15th and 17th centuries (Moore 1987, 13), within the framework of primitive accumulation. Only then, with the birth of this new economic-social system, crime control became structured in a consistent manner and bureaucratically organized by the nascent states.

This constant application of crime control had other relevant features that characterize it as a breaking point between feudalism and capitalism. First, the fact that when the Damocles' sword fell and punishment was effectively applied, it was not just a passing reprimand. Sovereigns did not punish individuals in proportion to the committed offence. They disenfranchised and reduced them to a 'bare life;' they minimized them, converting them to a simple biological phenomenon, a mere body, available to be treated in any way, including the possibility of its annihilation. Agamben states that: "*Not simple natural life, but life exposed to death (bare life or sacred life) is the original political element*" (1995, 55). Second, the over-criminalized behaviors were not those that involved higher social harm but the ones that disrupted the social order that was trying to be imposed. Thus, despite impoverished sectors being accused of acts that caused little or no social harm, sovereigns imposed the most severe punishments. Third, this over-dimensioned and disproportional punishment was legitimized as a legal right of the sovereign to dispose of the bodies of the ruled: a continuity that Agamben detected in modern history. In his words: "the politicization of bare life as such – constitutes the decisive event of modernity and signals a radical transformation of the political-philosophical categories of classical thought" (10). The violent and devastating submission of the impoverished population prevailed through the figure of 'legal punishment' that, thereby, managed to legitimize itself and avoid being tried as a questionable application of terror. Even though the real crime was the excessive punishment – unfairly and selectively imposed over the subjugated population – the fact that it was imposed as a 'legal' action decriminalized (immunized) it from scrutiny. The result was that trivial behaviors perpetrated without legal permission – such as vagrancy or panhandling – were punished with the death penalty or with physical castigation. Meanwhile, those terrible and disproportionate actions perpetrated under legal permission – such as the imposition of death or torture as a response to petty crimes –, became a legitimate punishment.

Here is the axiomatic point: crime control, acting through original criminal selectivity, and notably through the original over-criminalization mechanism, began to serve as a sword of Damocles over the most displaced sectors, transforming them into 'bare life.' In its effective exercise, this approach was embodied in the implementation of cruel punishments, including the death penalty. These sanctions were completely detached from the social harm caused by the acts for which its recipients were accused. These atrocious punishments responded, in turn, to the need of abruptly molding the hitherto proto-proletariat and proto-lumpen-proletariat, and effectively imposing the new social relations. By this logic, although it is this application of terror which should have been read in criminal terms – as the real crime to be persecuted – this character was made invisible, it was excluded from the realm of offense. Punishment de-criminalizes (immunized) itself. This is, perhaps, the most perverse aspect of original under-criminalization.

At this point, we turn our attention to introduce the following pattern of criminal selectivity: disciplining criminal selectivity.

Disciplining Criminal Selectivity

A new socio-economic scheme settled down in the 18th century, following the primitive accumulation. It can be called *disciplining social order* (18th to 20th century) and it started in the transition from a market regulated by tradition and characterized by fatherly relations to a self-regulated market (Pegoraro 2010). It also included the continued development of capitalism to a monopoly configuration under the Imperialist framework, towards the 20th century (Lenin 1916). The disciplining social order found the bourgeoisie struggling with the feudal powers and consolidating in the political and economic arenas. Meanwhile, the working class was already established and its level of organization became increasingly complex.

During the disciplining social order, social conflict encompassed and focused on the opposition between bourgeoisie and proletariat as antagonistic social classes (Marx and Engels 1848). This confrontation was signaled in the late 18th century, developed in the second half of the 19th century (with the paradigmatic manifestation of the Paris Commune of 1871),[1] and preserved a central relevance in the 20th century. It was framed in an even more complex picture as, in the 18th century, the bourgeoisie mobilized the proletariat in its favor, against monarchies and feudal lords. In the 19th century, the intra-class conflict was bordered, in turn, by the international confrontation between the ruling nations that pursued the control of the colonies to capture new markets and raw materials. In the 20th century, the social conflict centered on the two World Wars as well as on the struggles between capitalist and communist blocs in the Cold War. Social control boasted the need to discipline the working class, mainly through the pressure of the labor market and its reserve army. To achieve this aim, the bourgeoisie greatly benefited from the use of crime control but with a different goal than in the primitive accumulation. Crime control no longer served the creation of the working class, but its disciplining. This goal led to the emergence of a new form of criminal selectivity that may be called *disciplining criminal selectivity*.

---

1 This is a historical example that illustrates the use of crime control to resolve a social conflict. After the dissolution of the Commune, the National Assembly held a series of fierce retaliations and imprisoned, and executed those suspected of supporting the Commune. The members of the National Guard who had fought on the side of the Commune were arrested or executed (Marx 1871, 274).

From a materialistic perspective on the particularities of the socio-economic development and the analysis of the disciplining conflict-control, three phases can be identified, each representing different configurations of disciplining criminal selectivity. The *first disciplining phase* is set in the emergence of competitive capitalism and the rise of the bourgeoisie to political power. Criminal selectivity was then configured as *legally-disciplining criminal selectivity* (late 18th century). The *second disciplining phase* is set during the full bloom of capitalism and its transition to a monopolistic configuration of capital. Criminal selectivity was then configured as a *police-medically disciplining criminal selectivity* (19th century). The *third disciplining phase* is set in the framework of monopoly capitalism. Criminal selectivity was then configured as *socio-disciplining criminal selectivity* (early to late 20th century). Far from this being a rigid separation of historical periods, it was a fluid development that encompassed different phases wherein certain forms of criminal selectivity prevailed before evolving to incorporate previous moments into a new predominant form.

This chapter deals with much of Marx and Engels's theoretical contribution, as it directly involves the period in which they lived and developed their work. Their input on the particular topic of criminal selectivity can be found explicitly and implicitly in their complex analyses of the social, enabling tracking of its evolving morphology. In relation to the third disciplining phase, notwithstanding that it chronologically exceeds the life of Marx and Engels, the chapter delves into the contributions of the Marxist tradition.

Table 2 is an explanatory table for the purpose of introducing the variables involved in the framework of the disciplining criminal selectivity:

Where, How and When of the Disciplining Social Order (Late 18th Century to Late 20th Century)

The three phases of disciplining criminal selectivity are framed in the disciplining social order. The term 'social order,' as opposed to 'society,' has been outlined by Pashukanis. He argues that no one can understand the real sense of the criminal practice, unless they depart from the antagonistic character of a class state and that, consequently, "[s]ociety as a whole' exists only in the imagination of these jurists. In fact, we are faced with classes with contradictory, conflicting interests. Every historical system of punitive policy bears tile imprint of the class interest of that class which realized it" (1924, 149).

TABLE 2   *Disciplining criminal selectivity*

Characteristics			Chapter 3 Disciplining criminal selectivity		
			Legally-disciplining criminal selectivity	Police-medically disciplining criminal selectivity	Socio-disciplining criminal selectivity
Section 1 Contextual settings: Where, When and How			First Disciplining Phase (late 18th century)	Second Disciplining Phase (19th century)	Third Disciplining Phase (early to late 20th century)
Section 2 Conflict-Control	Conflict	Social	Unstable alliances and conflicts between the rising bourgeoisie and the working class against feudal lords.	Clashes between pauperism and employed working class with the industrial bourgeoisie; competition between Imperialist nations; conflicts between colonizers and colonized nations.	Clashes between pauperism and employed working class with the monopolistic industrial bourgeoisie; competition between imperialist nations; struggle between capitalist and communist nations.
		Criminal	Urban marginality and peasant resistance.	Urban marginality and members of the emerging labor organizations.	Urban marginality, deviants, individuals with Communist affiliation.

TABLE 2   *Disciplining criminal selectivity* (cont.)

Characteristics				Chapter 3 Disciplining criminal selectivity		
				Legally-disciplining criminal selectivity	Police-medically disciplining criminal selectivity	Socio-disciplining criminal selectivity
Section 2 Conflict-Control	Control	Social		Economic mechanisms and a large egalitarian formal regulatory structure.	Mechanisms of economic coercion and police persecution of the 'dangerous classes.'	Welfare policies.
		Criminal	Under-criminalization	Legal expropriations in European countryside; crimes linked to religion and morality.	Colonial plunder (death, enslavement, torture) and workers' subjugation in European factories.	Gangsterism (organized crime) and white-collar crimes.
			Over-criminalization	Criminalized survival strategies (vagrancy, begging, prostitution), coarse crime (petty crimes against property) and peasant resistance to expropriation.	Criminalized survival strategies (vagrancy, begging, prostitution), coarse crime (petty crimes against property) and union-political activities.	Coarse crimes, deviations, and anti-capitalist activities.

TABLE 2   *Disciplining criminal selectivity* (cont.)

Characteristics		Chapter 3 Disciplining criminal selectivity		
		Legally-disciplining criminal selectivity	Police-medically disciplining criminal selectivity	Socio-disciplining criminal selectivity
Section 3 Who Were Prosecuted?	Under-criminalized social sectors	Mercantile bourgeoisie, monarchies, and feudal remnants.	Emerging industrial bourgeoisie and financial bourgeoisie.	Monopolistic industrial bourgeoisie and emerging international financial bourgeoisie.
	Over-criminalized social sectors	Urban pauperism.	Pauperism and organized dissident.	Pauperism and organized dissident.
Section 4 Punishment	Manifest Functions	Retribution, incapacitation, deterrence, social re-integration.		
	Latent Functions	Disciplining the worker who did not submit to the imposed disciplining guidelines, discipline the modern pauperism, fragmenting the working class.		

'Society' exists only as a pipe dream and "thinking in terms of society, i.e. in a harmony of interests, hides the reality of differences, inequality and hierarchies between dominant and dominated" (Pegoraro 2012, 72). Therefore, there is a theoretical need to refer to the concept of 'social order' because "what exists in the real world is an imposed social order with its relations of domination and subjugation, inequality, and hierarchy" (2011, 59).

As for the adjective 'disciplining,' it shows the transition from 'formal subsumption' (capitalist commands labor process that originates outside of or before the wage relation) to 'real subsumption' (work process is internally reorganized to meet the expectations of capital) in the social division of labor.[2] In parallel, there was a transition from the direct violence of the primitive accumulation to economic disciplining mechanisms – including the establishment of a reserve army that threatens the positions of workers unprepared to submit to the demands of capital. Marx stresses that:

> The advance of capitalist production develops a working class, which by education, tradition, habit, looks upon the conditions of that mode of production is self-evident laws of nature. The organization of the capitalist process of production, once fully developed, breaks down all resistance. The constant generation of a relative surplus-population keeps the law of supply and demand of labor, and therefore keeps wages, in a rut that corresponds with the wants *of* capital (1867, 809).

The essential character of this period, then, is that "in the ordinary run of things, the laborer can be left to the 'natural laws of production,' *i.e.,* to his dependence on capital, a dependence springing from, and *guaranteed* in perpetuity by, the conditions of production themselves" (809). Economic means of coercion become dominant and crime control remains as an adjunct instrument. Together, economic and crime control worked for the imposition of bourgeois power and the protection of private property, as part of a larger disciplining complex. Discipline and punish' mechanisms grow across social divisions (Foucault 1975). It is no longer a moral and religious surveillance with the threat of public punishment (as it happened during the primitive accumulation) but a new

---

2   Real subsumption began with the first industrial revolution. Then, the division of labor was characterized by a polarization process of knowledge, and expressed in the fragmentation and disqualification of the general labor-force and the over-qualification of a minor component of the labor-force aimed at intellectual functions. The attempt to save time, based on the law of value, was accompanied by the transformation of complex work into simple work, and by the improvement of fixed capital (Vercellone 2007).

rigorous discipline within working life and with punishments to correct 'deviations' from it (Pegoraro 2010).

The focus of the disciplining criminal selectivity is Western Europe, where the historical processes were more clearly deployed, and where Marx and Engels made their theoretical contributions. The situation in the United States is analyzed, particularly in the second and third phases of the disciplining social order. It was then that the United States emerged as a key power in the global system, as well as an epicenter of the new forms of organization and crime control, and of the criminological theories that give sustenance to it.

The first disciplining phase – when the disciplining criminal selectivity initially unfolds – took place in the late 18th century, centered in the Industrial and the French revolutions. These events ensured that most European countries buried the remnants of feudal relations and that the bourgeoisie became in charge of political power (Hobsbawm 1962, 157). As Marx shows in *Poverty of Philosophy*:

> In the bourgeoisie, we have two phases to distinguish: that in which it constituted itself as a class under the regime of feudalism and absolute monarchy, and that in which, already formed as a class, it overthrew feudalism and monarchy to make society into a bourgeois society (1847, 13).

Likewise, Foucault (1975, 8) situates the emergence of disciplining societies towards the end of the 18th century. These types of society reached their peak in the early 1900s with the organization of open spaces of confinement. The state, according to the needs of the bourgeoisie, adopted the system of separation of powers and the principles of the Enlightenment. Both elements persist to the present day. Engels emphasizes:

> Only one thing was wanting: an institution which not only secured the newly acquired riches of individuals against the communistic traditions of the gentile order, which not only sanctified the private property formerly so little valued, and declared this sanctification to be the highest purpose of all human society; but an institution which set the seal of general social recognition on each new method of acquiring property and thus amassing wealth at continually increasing speed; an institution which perpetuated, not only this growing cleavage of society into classes, but also the right of the possessing class to exploit the non-possessing, and the rule of the former over the latter. And this institution came. The state was invented (1848b, 59).

The Enlightenment marked the moment when the bourgeoisie openly began its struggle against the nobility, as well as against the clergy and the monarchical absolutism (Anitua 2005, 71). In addition to technological innovations and communications, the bourgeoisie developed new forms of political organization and punitive approaches. Both of them responded to emerging needs within the new social order of larger manufacturing and urban concentrations (75). The new political organization was reflected in a series of legal reforms (particularly relating to criminality) that, centered in England and France, made possible the government of the 18th century. The ideology of the law was crucial in sustaining the hegemony of the ruling class (Hay et al. 1975, 56).

The second disciplining phase (19th century), featuring the deployment of police-medically disciplining criminal selectivity, was marked by the development of competitive capitalism. It was the beginning of the restructuring from a system of free market to the transnational monopolist organization of capital that Lenin called 'Imperialism' (1916). Lenin describes how, in this new phase of capitalism, the ruling nations disputed the domain of the colonies to capture new markets and raw materials to supply the increasing production. In Lenin's words: "It is beyond doubt, therefore, that capitalism's transition to the stage of monopoly capitalism, to finance capital, is connected with the intensification of the struggle for the partitioning of the world" (83). This signaled the breakdown of the equality ideal raised in the first disciplining phase, and the implementation of stark mechanisms to control the working class, in a sharp confrontation with the industrial bourgeoisie. Crime control was deployed in more brutal forms and criminal selectivity was made explicit in the characterization of the working class as 'dangerous,' under the legitimation of a medical discourse.

The third disciplining phase, when social-disciplining criminal selectivity was developed, appeared within the context of a fully developed imperialism. This phase found its center in the Russian revolution of 1917, the economic crises of 1890 and 1929, and the two World Wars. It extended until the oil crisis of 1973. The economic crisis and the development of a communist bloc influenced the establishment of welfare states in the western world. These regimes sought an alternative to the high levels of social conflict, with the aim of preserving it within the margins of capitalist production. Welfare regimes enabled non-punitive mechanisms of social control and more flexible instruments of crime control, both oriented towards social inclusion.

Disciplining Conflict-Control

Given this initial characterization of the disciplining social order, the following analyzes the conflict-control displayed in this historical framework, delving into the three distinct phases and their respective modalities of criminal selectivity.

First Disciplining Phase: Legally-Disciplining Criminal Selectivity (Late 18th Century)

Legally-Disciplining Criminal Selectivity was the modality adopted by crime control in the *first disciplining phase*. The end of the 18th century was the time of the bourgeois revolutions. The new ruling class relied on a legal-philosophical discourse to carry on a drastic legal transformation: the law started to ensure (formal) equal treatment for all citizens. This change consolidated a rupture with the legislation of the primitive accumulation, which had established different regulations according to socio-economic status. However, the emergent formal treatment under the law contrasted with the inequality in the enforcement of the law. The dissimilar operation of criminal law through the new mode of criminal selectivity took shaped in the mechanisms of *legally-disciplining under-criminalization* and *over-criminalization*. *Legally-disciplining under-criminalization* operated on land expropriations, economic crimes and moral-based offenses perpetrated by the mercantile bourgeoisie. *Legally-disciplining over-criminalization* operated on the peasants' reaction against their land confiscation and against the elimination of their communal rights. Over-criminalization also operated on the survival activities perpetrated by the pauperized sectors.

This means that, during this first disciplining phase, the particularities of social conflict rested on the bourgeoisie disputing power with the monarchies and the nobility. At the same time, the new ruling class confronted the popular sectors to ensure their submission to the new rules. The bourgeois goal was to install the respect to private property and to ensure the elimination of the remaining communal rural practices.

Crime conflict found a decrease in murders and physical aggressions, and an increase in property crimes (Foucault 1975, 75). The offenses of the period had its real roots in material poverty (Mathiesen 1987, 50). Urban paupers, facing absolute deprivation, were forced to vagrancy and panhandling. Peasants, suffering the annulment of customary rights, became immersed in illegal activities (Thompson quoted in Pegoraro 2011, 60). Young deserters and stragglers from the military ended up forming bandit groups. The context of incessant wars and bourgeois revolutions, and the chaos and economic turmoil contributed to increase in banditry, theft, and shoplifting at fairs, markets and roads (Emsley 2007, 96–100).

Social control resulted in the construction of a comprehensive regulation of rights and freedoms that went beyond criminal law. It was the end of the explicitly unequal legal treatment of original criminal selectivity: from then on, there would not be different regulations according to social status. It was the beginning of an 'idyllic justice' based on consensual social values (fraternity, equality, freedom) that gave the appearance (at least formally) of non-selectivity. All 'citizens' – a category that continued to exclude entire subsets in terms of race, gender, and age – became formal carriers of uniform rights, regardless of their material conditions. However, these rights were not given for free: they involved the obligation to abide by the norms contained in the new legal system. This means that all citizens became subjected to the law as a hegemonic mechanism of social control. This was true even for those who, in practice, did not have material access to the rights that were assigned to them by the letter of the law. Social control was ensured by merely proclaiming the impoverished as formal right-holders.

The emergence of this broad legislation was also intended to re-affirm the bourgeois social order against the remaining feudal powers. The formal inclusion of all citizens presented the new legal order as 'civilized,' drawing a clear and irreversible separation from the 'barbaric' past. The Enlightenment was key to oppose the ideals of 'reason' and 'light,' against 'despotism' and 'obscurantism,' commonly attributed to the previous period. In this vein, Marx explains in *The Civil War in France* that the bourgeois bureaucratic structure was used to confront the feudal remnants:

> The centralized State power, with its ubiquitous organs of standing: army, police, bureaucracy, clergy, and judicature – organs wrought after the plan of a systematic and hierarchic division of labor- originates from the days of absolute monarchy, serving nascent middle-class society as a mighty weapon in its struggles against feudalism (1871, 66).

Accordingly, Engels says in the *Antiduring* that the bourgeoisie sought to separate the new era from the 'irrational' feudal past:

> Every form of society and government then existing, every old traditional notion was flung into the lumber-room as irrational; the world had hitherto allowed itself to be led solely by prejudices; everything in the past deserved only pity and contempt. Now, for the first time, appeared the light of day, henceforth superstition, injustice, privilege, oppression, were to be superseded by eternal truth, eternal Right, equality based on nature and the inalienable rights of man (1878, 2).

In short, the bourgeoisie used the new legal framework as a mechanism of social control over the impoverished, and as a tool to separate itself from the feudal past. The continuity of the working sectors' dispossession – an inherent element of the development of capitalism – was now hidden behind a legislation that ensured formal equality. Evidence that the bourgeois regulations of the late 18th century were not aimed at ensuring material inclusion is that they were based on a triple inequality: *denial of unequal material conditions through the imposition of an ahistorical and abstract characterization of the law; inequality of the formal law*; and *inequality in the application of the law*. Let us explore them.

First, *abstract and ahistorical characterization of the law*. Contractualism presented the new regulations as abstract and detached from the socio-economic interests of the ruling class. Marx and Engels show that this is particularly indebted to the Hobbesian version of Contractualism. Hobbes espoused that the material life of men and women (and its legal regulation) depended on the mere will of a Leviathan or central power. However, as Marx and Engels highlight, it is not the Leviathan but the mode of production and its reciprocal conditioning of social relations which shape regulatory bodies (1845, 388). They express the same reasoning in *The Communist Manifesto* – as was presented at the meeting for the creation of an international labor movement in London in the autumn of 1847:

> Your very ideas are but the outgrowth of the conditions of your bourgeois production and bourgeois property, just as your jurisprudence is but the will of your class made into a law for all, a will whose essential character and direction are determined by the economic conditions of existence of your class (1848, 24).

This means that legislation is not the result of abstract considerations or the free will of the sovereign (Marx 1847, 45). To illustrate, Marx and Engels criticize Stirner for his claim that the sanction of the law of marriage responds exclusively to the will of the king Frederick William IV, ignoring the socio-economic processes that enabled the emergence of that legislation (1845, 399). As a counterexample, they explain that if the productive forces are not yet sufficiently developed to turn competition unnecessary, the ruling classes would not be able to propose to abolish competition, even if they have the 'will' to do so (387). In short, only an abstract characterization of the law can hide its link with socio-economic processes:

> My inquiry led me to the conclusion that neither legal relations nor political forms could be comprehended whether by themselves or on the basis of a so-called general development of the human mind, but that on

the contrary they originate in the material conditions of life, the totality
of which Hegel, following the example of English and French thinkers
of the eighteenth century, embraces within the term 'civil society;' that
the anatomy of this civil society, however, has to be sought in political
economy.

MARX 1859b, 191

Contractualism was also a key factor that managed to disguise the law from
its historical origin. Referring to a mythic and non-dated foundation when
all citizens accepted to give away part of their freedom to ensure social order,
Contractualism describes the origin of the bourgeois law as peaceful and in-
controvertible. The imposition of the bourgeois legal system remained then
separated from the actual struggles for power and conflicting interests among
different classes. Moreover, this non-historical characterization of the law acted as a mechanism for its perpetuity, avoiding criticism of the legal system's
origins, development, and structure. Presenting the bourgeois legal order as
non-historical imposed it as one incapable of being overcome.

Marx's theory helps denounce these bourgeois legal constructions as half-
rational and half-historical (Cerroni 1965, 95). Indeed, Lenin defines pre-
Marxist Sociology as one that addressed the law as a general one, and not as
an evolving phenomenon that corresponds to particular historical relations
(Kohen 1972, 20). From a materialist perspective, the law – as any other human product – is analyzed as historical, classist and socio-economically conditioned (168). Law needs to be explained in relation to concretely historical
relations (Tadic 1969, 124).

Second, *inequality of the formal law*. The legally-disciplining framework was
doubly unequal even in its formal proclamation: the law treated as equal those
who were in a very different material situation, and the law mainly embodied
the interests of the ruling classes and not the interests of all the existing social
sectors.

On the one hand, *the new legal order was unequal in its forms because it treated the exploited and exploiters on the same basis, even though they were in very
different material conditions*. The law formally treated all citizens as equal, under the model of an 'abstract subject' based on the bourgeois man. This model
neglected the shortcomings of the vast majority of the population who did not
fit in that formal standard. In *On the Jewish Question* (1844), Marx complains
that the bourgeoisie had to give a 'detour' or 'rodeo' – a concept that came from
the Young Hegelians – to defend the existence of a 'society of equals.' Marx
tells us that, under feudalism, men and women could not be recognized as
equal, since the material and physical differences between them were evident.
Because of this explicit inequality, feudal lords resorted to the figure of God to

affiliate men, and place them in a relationship of union and likeness (all men were 'sons' of God). In the bourgeois order, this symbolic 'rodeo' took place through the state: the law became the tool to proclaim that all citizens were equal at some point.

Current differences in the economic position of citizens were explained in relation to a mythic origin when all citizens were equal. The different outcomes were the fair result of dissimilar efforts. While the bourgeoisie had worked hard to achieve its privileged position, the impoverished were lazy. Then, it was not fair to apply affirmative action measures to compensate their disadvantaged situation. As it has been shown in the Second Chapter, this is just a myth: there was neither original equality nor legitimate efforts in the accumulation of resources by the bourgeoisie. There was original under-criminalization of the acts of expropriation and exploitation committed by the dominant sectors, and original over-criminalization of the efforts of the impoverished to achieve minimum material conditions. Therefore, as Marx illustrates in *Critique of the Gotha Program* (1875), treating the impoverished and the well-off equally was unjust. The bourgeois law is class-biased, and even when the law does not give any advantage to the upper classes because it gives the same formal treatment to individuals that are in unequal conditions (Cerroni 1975, 144). The law can be neither class blind nor colorblind if there is class and racial inequality in the material conditions of life. Although, this legal inequality is not surprising. Law is unequal as a result of its correlation to a socio-economic system that requires exploitation of one social class by another. As Marx explains, rights "can never be superior to the economic development and the stage of civilization conditioned thereby" (1875, 31).

On the other hand, *the new legal order was unequal in its forms because it mainly defends the interest of the ruling class and not the interest of all the existing social sectors*. To exemplify, the regulations of the 18th century did not concentrate on the defense of communal property, which was in the interest of impoverished peasants. The new law imposed the protection of private property, which was the main concern of the bourgeoisie.

However, in spite of the clear interests represented in the law, the law was introduced as an embodiment of the interest of society as a whole. Marx and Engels challenge that conception in *The German Ideology* – inspired by the publication of Stirner's *The Ego and Its Own*. They characterize the law as the form through which individuals of the ruling class intend to assert their interests as if they were the shared interest of the community for the purpose of achieving acceptance (1845, 65 and 80)[3] whereas in fact the law embodies the

---

3   Elster (1982) argues that while it is true that the capitalist class can promote their collective interests through the state and its ability to produce norms for their own benefit, this

ideal expression of the existing material relations (64). In *The Class Struggles in France*, Marx notes that this idyllic conception, this intent to sentimentally reconcile class interests with those of society as a whole, constitutes a crime (1850, 64). This statement is based on the fact that the rights of the dispossessed classes are subjugated to the interests of the bourgeoisie. Thus, presenting the law as representative of a 'general interest' becomes a falsehood and a tool to legitimize law's selective application: it is a crime because it is a breach of the rules.[4]

Third, *inequality in the application of the law. Not only the law provided equal treatment to all (despite their material inequality), but inequality was reinforced through the unequal application of the (already formally unequal) law.* The rights that were formally enunciated were not even fully implemented with regard to impoverished sectors, breaching the ideal proclamations. Marx (1844) shows that bourgeois encodings find their foundation in the split between a 'generic' and a 'concrete man.' The 'generic man' is the citizen, who is a rightholder (the ideal face of the law). The 'concrete man and woman' are the ones in the real life, who are conditioned by the socio-economic context which may

conclusion requires a more complex study. He points out that it is necessary to attend the complexities and internal mediations that emerge from the conflicting interests within the ruling class, and even the clashes with other social sectors. Marx and Engels embrace this logic and suggest that, even though laws are presented under the cloak of a 'general interest,' they *tend* to favor the class that promotes and sanctions them. To exemplify, Marx himself offers a complex, non-linear analysis about the bourgeoisie and its control of the political domain. Marx suggests that the bourgeoisie was more interested in leaving the political domain to the aristocracy in Britain and to the emperor and his bureaucracy in France, so that the political struggle between rulers and ruled will blur the outlines of the economic struggle between exploiters and exploited. It is therefore, as Elster argues, not possible to identify the state in a capitalist society as a capitalist state simply by virtue of their favorable consequences to bourgeois economic domination, but it is necessary to delve into its intricacies and internal mediations.

4   The contributions of Marx and Engels have been assumed by much of the subsequent critical tradition. Laws are conceived as rules that tend to protect the interests of the ruling class; the law is the result of inherent conflicts in the class structure (Chambliss 1975, 151; Michalowski 1977; Poulantzas 1969). Thompson, one of the greatest exponents of British Marxism, affirms that the law mediates class relations with a set of rules and appropriate sanctions which ultimately confirm and consolidate the power of existing class (1975, 280). From a utilitarian perspective, the law works as both a mediator and a fortifier of existing class relations. From the ideological perspective, the law legitimizes class relations giving them an appearance of fairness (283–284).

inhibit them from the enforcement of the proclaimed rights (the material face of the law). Using the Hegelian distinction between 'civil society' (the place where the selfishness of men and women rules) and the 'state' (the generic and ideal life of men and women), Marx argues that bourgeois law is valid only for the 'generic man,' but cannot be implemented at the level of everyday life for the 'concrete men.' Going further, Marx draws a parallel between Christianity and the state: both require the man to lead a double life. Christianity promises a full life in the kingdom of heaven that justifies the earthly hardships of the poor. Under the same logic, the state establishes an ideal man with full rights in the political community, while the concrete man, in civil society, is subjugated. Therefore, there is a formal 'freedom to work,' but the market imposes its strictures; there is formally 'free speech' and 'freedom of association' but to exercise them, people need appropriate means. Indeed, the French Revolution of 1789 illuminates the existence of two different spheres: it is the Declaration of the Rights of Man *and* of the Citizen, referring respectively to the material plane of civil society, and the ideal sphere of a political community of citizens.

Moreover, bourgeois rights preserve selfishness and egotism in their conception of rights: the 'right to freedom' is the right to be separated, disassociated, delimited from other men; the 'right to equality' – far from signaling a political community formed on the substantive equality of men and women – only guarantees that all individuals get to be treated in isolation through their individual relation to the law; 'the right to vote' through scrapping wealth requirements, strengthened property rights by presupposing and legitimizing them. The 'right to security' only gets to position man as a wolf of other man, and the police as the privileged arbiter of hunting flocks. Only equal material conditions could cross the narrow limits of bourgeois law (Marx 1875).

We have just analyzed how inequality operated on the law in general. Following the same logic, crime control, as a specific and prominent tool of social control, tended to reproduce the same three aspects of general legal inequality (in its abstract and ahistorical characterization, in its formal regulation, and in its application).

First, *abstract and ahistorical characterization of the criminal law.* The abstract and ahistorical conception of criminal law had to do with the characterization of the offender as a 'legal subject.' Neglecting the historic reasons for the application of punishment and overlooking the socio-economic features of the offender, criminal law formally obliged everybody to abide by the covenant. Disobedience transforms the 'legal subject' into a criminal without analyzing the specific reasons that may have influenced the lack of compliance. Against this backdrop, the materialistic analysis denounces the bourgeois logic that was established in the 18th century and proposes a totalizing view that clarifies the immediate relationship between crime and society (Larrauri 1991, 59–60). Since Marxism, it is possible to provide a necessary historical character to the analysis of crime:

> The superiority of Marx's work lies not in his individual genius, but in his *method*. In part, this method rests on a refusal to separate out thought from society. Thus, for Marx, theoretical reflection is either obfuscation or an exercise in practical reasoning (...) Marx insists upon two features in any proper social analysis. First he says that 'to be radical is to gasp things at the root. For Man the root is Man himself.' And secondly, he observes (necessarily, given some alternative views) that man is inseparable from society. It follows (if these premises are accepted) that to analyze crime, for example, requires that we examine man's position in *society*.
> TAYLOR ET AL. 1974, 462

Indeed, "Marx specifically criticizes those who see law as playing the same general role in all societies, and who thus refuse to analyze the particular effects of a given mode of production" (468). In contrast: "The analysis of particular forms of crime, or particular types of criminals, outside their context in history and society, has been shown in our view to be a meaningless activity" (462). The study of crime should be linked to the historical context in which it occurs, rather than a universal and timeless category. History, contradiction, totality and dialectic are the main methods to find out true elements and, therefore, to dismantle the ideology that presents to the eyes of the investigator a hidden appearance of the essence (Bergalli 1982, 296). Crime deserves to be studied in relation to the "historically determined social structure in which it is inserted" (Baratta 1986, 100).

Inequality of the formal criminal law. As Enlightenment proclaimed the formal equality before the law, punishment – unlike the scenario of primitive accumulation- was consistent with every crime in the abstract. Criminal law stopped making distinctions based on the socio-economic standard of the offender. The key point was that both the citizen and the noble should receive the same sentence when they had committed the same offense. To ensure this equality, the conviction has to be based on the seriousness of the offense, and not on the status of the perpetrator, or the discretion of the judge (Christie quoted in Mathiesen 1987, 180). The French statute of December 1, 1789 proclaimed: "Crimes of the same kind will be punished by the same kind of punishment, whatever the rank and the state of the guilty man may be"

(quoted in Foucault 1975, 12). The epicenter of concern was the crime itself –
understood as a disrespect of the social contract- regardless of the features of
the offender. In the words of Beccaria:

> Some motives, therefore, that strike the senses, were necessary to prevent
> the despotism of each individual from plunging society into its former
> chaos. Such motives are the punishment established against the offend-
> ers. I say that motives of this kind are necessary; because experience
> shews that, the multitude adopt no established rules of conduct; and
> because, society is prevented from approaching to that dissolution (to
> which, as well as all other parts of the physical and moral world, it natu-
> rally tends) only by motives that are the immediate objects of sense, and
> which, being continually presented to the mind, are sufficient to coun-
> terbalance the effects of the passions of the individual which oppose the
> general good. Neither the power of eloquence, nor the sublimes truths,
> are sufficient to restrain, for any length of time, those passions which are
> excited by the lively impression of present objects (1764, 9).

Although this conception seems to be formally equal, it is in fact unequal because it conceived all offenders as alike when they were not. By concentrating
on the offense, criminal law got to ignore the concrete situation of the offenders. The criminal act was always conceived to have occurred according to a free
and unconditioned rational choice to break the social contract.

   Marx and Engels denounce this false equality by referring to the novel of
Cervantes, *Don Quixote*. In Chapter 22, the protagonist and his squire, Sancho
Panza,[5] met the galley slaves of the king and was horrified to find persons so deprived of liberty. Sancho does not understand why the guards want to imprison
in dungeons individuals who have done nothing to them, and he protests that
it seems as if they happen to foreground the category of the stolen. Sancho
provokes them, asking: why do you cry against 'crime'? (1845, 405). With this
literary allusion, Marx and Engels show that the abstract conception of crime
transforms the offense against a man's property, to an attack on the abstract
conception of 'private property.' Thus, the offender in his act desecrates what
the state proclaimed as sacred: the state property (407). This abstraction grants
legitimacy to the state interference in the resolution of conflicts that could

---

5 In *The German Ideology* (1845), Marx and Engels nicknamed 'Stirner' as Sancho Panza because, like Sancho Panza (the character from Don Quixote), he also makes a compliment
   from selfishness and individual output.

have remained in the private sphere. Also, by concentrating on the offense and conceiving the offender as a free and unconditioned man, the bourgeois criminal law gets to ignore that the offense is nothing but the struggle of the isolated individual against prevailing conditions (388). Hegel himself, in 'Who Thinks Abstractly?' (1808), had already written a remarkable essay denouncing the 'criminal' label as an abstraction formulated to override all other characters of human essence, and replacing them with the singular label of 'criminal.' The abstraction that reduces the complexity of a person to a criminal label needs to strip him/her of any associations that constitute him/her as a particular subject (115–118).

Inequality in the application of criminal law. The formal equality under the law did not only hide the different material conditions of offenders, but it also failed to overcome the unequal application of the law. It only meant that, thereafter, criminal selectivity started to operate with greater intensity at the level of secondary criminalization, i.e., at the time of effective enforcement of the law. In light of laws that linked crimes with certain punishments, regardless of the socio-economic status of the offender, criminal selectivity was not so evident in the primary criminalization, but in the everyday application of those laws to distinctive social sectors (secondary criminalization).

The criminal sphere marks the highest point of practical inequality in the bourgeois normative plexus. Foucault (1975) explains that the criminal justice system that emerged in this context, even though it was intended to be egalitarian, "must be conceived as a mechanism intended to administer illegalities differentially, not to eliminate them all" (89). The concept of *legally-disciplining criminal selectivity* shows how the use of criminal law, formally presented as uniform for all individuals (obviating the material differences between each other), and based on an abstract and ahistorical condition of the criminal law, in practice operated as malleable and selective. Crime control, presented under the veil of an idyllic equal standard, worked ambivalently in its application through the mechanisms of *legally-disciplining over-criminalization* (in relation to the acts perpetrated by those who moved away from the social contract at the expense of private property and bourgeois domain) and *legally-disciplining under-criminalization* (in relation to the activities carried out by the bourgeoisie). Let us now delve into the implementation of these mechanisms.

Legally-Disciplining Under-Criminalization
The notion of *legally-disciplining under-criminalization* describes the mechanism that tended to reduce the criminal regulation of the non-coarse impairment of property, the violation of moral and religious standards, and the expropriations of peasants' lands that were mostly committed by the rising

bourgeoisie (primary under-criminalization). It also describes the mechanism that minimizes the effective implementation of that reduced regulation (secondary under-criminalization). Legally-disciplining under-criminalization was legitimized through an idyllic discourse that called for an integrative justice criterion whereby all individuals were included as equals under the law.

Marx and Engels emphasize how the advent of a new class brings a renewed form of law that responds to their material interests (1845, 404). Indeed, authors like Beccaria and Voltaire pushed for changes in favor of primary under-criminalization of those behaviors for which the commercial bourgeoisie was eventually targeted (offenses against religion and morality, suppression of confiscation of property, and laws on libel or defamation) (Rusche and Kirchheimer 1938, 93). Blasphemy and 'illegalities of rights' – fraud, tax evasion, irregular commercial operations- started to be treated in a less severe manner (Foucault 1975, 17).

Primary under-criminalization operated with even more intensity on the expropriations of peasants' lands committed by the bourgeoisie. While the first wave of enclosures that took place in the 16th century was perpetrated by the ruling classes without a legal basis (it was against the law), this second wave rested on strict rules that authorized it. Several laws were passed between 1760 and 1840 in clear relation to the new economic paradigm under construction. In Britain, 159 laws enabling expropriations were enacted between 1750 and 1759; 424 in the 1760s and 642 in the 1770s, reaching a record of 906 acts in the period between 1800 and 1810. The most noteworthy was the Enclosure Consolidation Act (1801) (Campagne 2005, 181). Rather than the law being an obstacle to capitalist expansion (as in the first disciplining phase), it became an instrument to ensure it. The law itself became a vehicle for the depredation of the peoples' property (Marx 1867, 796). In short, expropriations of peasants' land stopped being a crime and became instead an established right.

As a result of this change in their legal consideration, enclosures spread from England and Scotland throughout Europe, and particularly in Denmark, Sweden and Norway (Marx 1867, 800). The discourse that legitimized these expropriations was nourished by the characterization of communal property as the cause of agricultural backwardness. Communal property was supposed to be the responsible factor for the delay in the implementation of new agricultural techniques (Campagne 2005, 182).[6] This brand new legal character of

---

6 Furthermore, in the English and Irish cases, expropriations sought not only to increase productivity, but also to pursue trivial aims such as ensuring the recreation of the ruling class by turning fields into hunting lands. Marx illustrates that: "Everyone knows that there are no real forests in England. The deer in the parks of the great are demurely domestic cattle, fat as London aldermen. Scotland is therefore the last refuge of the 'noble passion'" (1867, 803).

enclosures and its legitimating discourse tried to hide that these were expropriations carried through out violence[7] and without fair compensation, leaving the peasants in a situation of severe impoverishment. As Marx explains: "the agricultural population received a farthing of compensation for the 3,511,770 acres of common land which between 1801 and 1831 were *stolen* from them and by parliamentary devices presented to the landlords by the landlords" (emphasis added) (1867, 800). Besides transforming communal soil in a parcel of capital, enclosures also promoted the migration of the expropriated peasants to the cities (805). The goal was to turn them into factory labor, and also into the consumers that the modern market economy demanded.[8] As a result of these procedures, within half a century, tens of thousands of farms and their workers disappeared from the countryside (Campagne 2005, 186).

Secondary under-criminalization resulted in a *de facto* tolerance of most of the crimes committed by the bourgeoisie in the cities and the countryside. The new ruling class got around its own regulations and laws, ensuring for itself an immense sector of economic circulation by a skillful manipulation of gaps and silences in the law (Foucault 1975, 87). Marat himself said that laws "are decrees of the rulers, who do not respect even his own work and they act with impunity" (1780, 65). Yet it becomes clear that, even if the exercise of justice presented itself as impartial, criminal justice was still "consulted free and everywhere," unlike civil justice which refers to "property disputes of the exclusive interest of the propertied classes" (Marx 1875). The legal advances incorporated by the Enlightenment almost exclusively favored the upper classes. Public processes, free choice of counsel, trial by jury, elimination of torture, defined rules of evidence, and protection against illegal detention were only enforced for the well-off. The lack of knowledge and financial means of the poor forbade them from claiming their exercise (Foucault 1975, 94). The specialization of the judicial circuits assigned transactions, compromises, and offset fines to the jurisdiction

---

Paraphrasing Moro, not only sheep but also deer 'eat' men. As Marx adds: "Deer have received extended range, while men have been hunted [...] as an agricultural necessity, just as trees and brushwood are cleared from the wastes of America or Australia" (804).

7   To exemplify, from 1814 to 1820, 15,000 inhabitants of Sutherland (about 3,000 families) were systematically 'hunted' and rooted out. All their villages were destroyed and burnt, all their fields turned into pasturage. British soldiers enforced this eviction and came to blows with the inhabitants (Marx 1867, 802).

8   Far from being a 'farm cleaning' (as its name indicates), these expropriations swept men. The situation was no different for the few people who managed to maintain their piece of land, since, with the introduction of technical innovations, land productivity grew exponentially and the situation of rural workers became even more painful (Campagne 2005, 201).

of special courts that favored the bourgeoisie (92). Even the formal separation of powers had little impact, in view of the complete corruption of judges who could be bribed by the king, as well as by the parties in dispute. Bribery of judges was a common practice, but it was not criminalized (95). Marx and Engels (1845) illustrate how the division of powers, heralded as a triumph of this historical period, represented only an effect of the division of labor. That is, the division of labor conditioned, within the legal sphere, the emergence of a professional permanent legal apparatus that sought to abide by the principles of Enlightenment, but which mainly responded to the interests of the dominant sectors. In this line, Engels states:

> We know today that this kingdom of reason was nothing more than the idealized kingdom of the bourgeoisie; that this eternal Right found its realization in bourgeois justice; that this equality reduced itself to bourgeois equality before the law; that bourgeois property was proclaimed as one of the essential rights of man; and that the government of reason, the Contract Social of Rousseau, came into being, and only could come into being, as a democratic bourgeois republic (1878, 2).

Judges continued considering the socio-economic status of victims and offenders, even though it had been outlawed. To illustrate, a judge in Auxerre in 1811 explains his sentencing in a case of rape in which he imposed a benevolent punishment because of the low socio-economic status of the victim:

> I vote for the minimum sentence because we must take into account that the victim is a domestic servant. If she were a young lady of high social level, if it were your daughter or mine, I would opt for the maximum. It seems important to make a distinction between the best of society and ordinary people.
>
> Quoted in RUSCHE and KIRCHHEIMER 1938, 124

The persistence of the selective application of the criminal law in favor of the ruling classes is clear in Cervantes' novel. When Sancho crashes into the galley slaves of the king, he urges the slaves to be ashamed of their acts. The thief Gines de Pasamonte refuses to do so and interrupts him, claiming that jailers commit crimes at every step: they steal and embezzle money with no discretion (Marx and Engels 1845, 408). That is, through Sancho's words, Marx and Engels show how criminal law magnifies the crimes of the poor, while the same act committed by a state is not even considered a crime. Using Sancho's words, they conclude that the behavior of the state is violence, but it is mostly called 'right.' Instead, the violence exercised by the impoverished individual is largely called 'crime' (405).

Legally-Disciplining Over-Criminalization

The notion of *legally-disciplining over-criminalization* describes the mechanism that broadened the spectrum of criminalization to include those actions related to the communal tradition, committed by bandits and the rural pauperized sectors that were not included in the production process. It also describes the increasing regulation of petty attacks to private property in the context of growing private, commercial and manufacturing property (primary over-criminalization). At the second level, legally-disciplining over-criminalization describes the over-inclusive enforcement of those regulations (secondary over-criminalization). The legitimization of legally-disciplining over-criminalization rested on an idyllic discourse that called for an integrative justice criterion in which all men were included as equals under the law.

Even intellectuals of the time complained that Contractualism should not justify the prosecution of the most miserable men and women for breaking the social contract, if the social contract has previously failed in respecting their rights. Marat explains that there is a portion of the population that only knows society's disadvantages but is still obliged to respect its laws. If society abandons them, they have the right to return to the natural state and regard any authority that tries to punish them as tyrannical and consider the judge who sentences them to death as no more than a vile murderer (1780, 68). Beccaria himself warned that those accused of theft corresponded to "the crime of that unhappy part of mankind, to whom the right of exclusive property, a terrible, and perhaps unnecessary right, has left but a bare existence" (1764, 32). He reinforces that:

> It is not only the common interest of mankind that crimes should not be committed, but that crimes of every kind should be less frequent, in proportion to the evil they produce to society Therefore, the means made use of by the legislature to prevent crimes, should be more powerful, in proportion as they are destructive of the public safety and happiness, and as the inducements to commit them are stronger. Therefore, there ought to be a fixed proportion between crimes and punishments (1764, 13).

And later, personifying those dispossessed men and women exclaiming against public executions, Beccaria says:

What are, in general, the proper punishments for crimes? Is the punishment of death, really useful, or necessary for the safety or good order of
society? Are tortures and torments consistent with justice, or do they answer the end proposed by the laws? (19).

Foucault also expresses that, in this context, "popular illegality referred not
so much to rights, but goods: pilfering and theft tended to replace smuggling
and the armed struggle against the tax agents. And, in this respect, the peasants, farmers and artisans were often its principal victims" (1975, 84). Unlike
the special courts erected to judge the offenses committed by the bourgeoisie,
ordinary courts were settled for the illegalities of property (87). These local
courts condemned the poor with a total absence of formalism, while the costs
of legal proceedings made it extremely difficult for the poor to appeal those
decisions. The performance of judges was not a problem of personal integrity,
but of the class interests of the landowners, for which the judges were an instrument (Rusche and Kirchheimer 1938, 93). In a primitive form of the broken
windows theory, French guards were authorized to arrest and detain overnight
walkers, criminals, rogues, vagabonds and other idlers who disturbed the public peace (Emsley 2007, 110).

As the broad perspective of less eligibility principle suggests, the growing
incorporation of workers into the production process improved their material
situation in comparison to the earlier primitive accumulation. However, they
were still at a level of extreme pauperization (Rusche and Kirchheimer 1938,
87). Welfare, which was already fully regulated by secular institutions, was
'less eligible' than the slightly better situation of the employed workers. Social
assistance remained tied to the institution of the workhouse, which offered
conditions of severe oppression. Punishment was 'less eligible' than welfare
because the proclaimed rights of the Enlightenment were not materialized in
practice. Instead, legally-disciplining over-criminalization occupied the place
of the promised equality.

While legally-disciplining over-criminalization occurred in both, the rural
and urban European areas, it was more drastic in the former. The bourgeoisie
was already in charge of the cities, but the resistance was more intense in the
countryside. The new ruling class needed to intervene in the rural areas to establish private property (to the detriment of common property freely used by
the peasants), capitalist relations of production (as opposed to communal relations based on the exercise of customary rights) and ordinary justice (in place
of communal justice practices). Moreover, the bourgeoisie required to banish
the remaining rural population, promoting a greater migration to the cities to

increase the supply of wage labor. (a) Legally-disciplining over-criminalization was the mechanism that fell on the rural population that resisted the second wave of enclosure and the banishment of customary rights. (b) Legally-disciplining over-criminalization also fell on those who engaged in demonstrations of social justice (the so-called 'social banditry').[9]

a   *Legally-Disciplining Over-Criminalization on Peasants' Resistance to Expropriations and the Dismantling of Their Customary Rights*
The desperate resistance of rural populations against expropriations was exterminated under criminal law in Prussia, France, the Pyrenees in Southern Italy, and the islands of Sardinia and Sicily (Pavarini 1980, 54). While enclosures were not read as a crime because they were authorized by laws – despite their crudeness and adverse social effects – peasants' resistance was targeted by legally-disciplining over-criminalization. This was part of a larger transformation of their customary rights into crimes, marking the gloomy end of communal property (as the other face of the transformations of crimes into rights favoring the bourgeoisie). From then on, the law made it clear what items could

---

9   In Germany (which Marx studies in particular) these processes occurred later in time than in the more developed nations. Capitalism did not start in Germany before 1830 and, in the late 19th century, the country was still going through a complex relationship between rural and urban populations (Salles 2005, 236). This delay was a general concern among national theorists. Even Weber claimed that Germany opposed to the invasion of the capitalist spirit (1905, 366). Thus, legally-disciplining criminal selectivity took place in Germany in the mid-19th century, while England and France were already in the police-medically disciplining criminal selectivity. Police forces (a key element of the second disciplinary phase) were created in the beginning of the of the 19th century in France and England, but the Berlin police was not born before the second half of the 19th century – after the uprisings of 1848 – and only after that other local policies emerged (Galeano 2007, 113).

   Also the United States experience legally-disciplining order later in time than Western Europe. In the late 19th century, legally-disciplining over-criminalization developed and served to subject the freedman to a new form of forced labor in the fields, ensuring their disciplining on the basis of the law. The U.S. Black Codes (1865 and 1866) were the clear expression of how the expansion of statutes worked as a legal framework to reinforce inequality and foster criminal selectivity. These Codes imposed that every freedman who did not immediately enter into a labor contract could be arrested as a vagrant, and, once a contract was agreed upon, it was a criminal offense for a laborer to fail to carry it out, no matter how unfair the terms might be. In South Carolina, a specific law prohibited Black-Americans from holding any occupation other than farmer or servant, unless they paid an annual tax of $10 to $100 (Novak 1978).

still be taken freely and under what circumstances, which ones could not be taken anymore, and what would be the reproach for each type of offense.

An example of this process can be seen in the *Debates on the Law on the Theft of Wood* (Marx 1842).[10] Rural people were used to freely collect and enjoy firewood and fruits. Because they grew as wild products, they were considered a wholly accidental appendage of property and, if only because of their unimportance, were not an object for the activity of the actual owner.[11] They were considered hybrid goods (neither public nor private) that could be used by the impoverished to satisfy basic needs (9). This changed between the late 18th and the 19th centuries (according to the level of development of the region). What caused the modification of this conception? What pushed the bourgeoisie to plant the flag of private property over these hybrid objects that were previously susceptible to free use? The comments of a deputy of the *Rhenish Diet* sheds light on these questions: "in this area, these berries have already become articles of commerce and are dispatched to Holland in barrels" (10). Economically speaking, wood acquired a high market value: it was required by Holland and England for the scaffolding of railways and the shipbuilding industry, and by Cologne and the Ruhr for industrial and commercial construction, and even for coalmines (Linebaigh 1976, 6). It was also demanded for fuel and heating (Bensaid 2007, 101). This means that peasants' gathering of wild fruits and firewood did not matter until the exchange value of those goods was determined. When wood and fruits became merchandise, the Prussian state was obliged to resolve, for once and for all, the legal problems linked to the contradiction between legal rights and property rights (Lascoumes and Zander

---

10   This series of reflections were published in the *Rheinische Zeitung* between October 25 and November 3, 1842. They show Marx's first analysis about political economy. The dismantling of communal property for the benefit of private property and the consolidation of a fierce parliament that qualified as crimes those usual activities of the rural poor in forests and open fields, encouraged Marx to criticize, for the first time, a particular social problem (Garcia Ramirez 2009, 262). At this moment, Marx had not yet gone through the break with Hegelian philosophy and still retained confidence in the bourgeois state. However, this did not prevent him from pointing out the distance between the selfish character of the Prussian state and the absolute logic of human reason that viewed all men and women through the respect of civil liberties.

11   Marx teaches us that, in opposition to the marketization of fundamental rights, the right of occupation of that grey space that had not been consolidated as private property had yet to prevail. That right belongs to the dispossessed class, but its exercise demands to overcome the hybrid state of this class. Marx then urges the radicalization of the dispossessed as the way to transform this process in an opportunity for the development of class consciousness.

1984, 104). Then, legislation turned unfailingly biased toward private property: "the wooden idols triumph and human beings are sacrificed!" (Marx 1842, 3).

To ensure the respect of what became private property, the bourgeoisie had to send a clear and strong message to that part of the population that, until then, had been enjoying the natural products. After decades of tolerance, the sudden restriction of customary rights had to be firmly promulgated in order to command respect. Over-criminalization became the most suitable tool,[12] and pushed the Diet to break with the rights that the Enlightenment had recently proclaimed. Equal punishment was imposed to the act of cutting the wood and to the act of recollecting the pieces of wood that just fell from the tree – against the principle of proportionality.[13] Private guards were authorized to apprehend the offender and fix the price of the stolen property (18) – against the public monopoly of violence. The burden of proof was on the offender who had to attest the origin of the wood: "everyone could be under suspicion of stealing and concealing wood" (17) – against the principle of presumption of innocence. The third good faith party that obtained the stolen wood from the offender would also be punished – against the principle of individual liability. If the offenders wanted to cite the guard as evidence of his innocence, they must pay the costs for the guard's mobility – against the principle of due process. Full powers were given to the owners of the land and their guards while the judge's role was reduced to the formal implementation of the law (12) – against the principle of impartiality. The victim had the option to make the offender work for free as compensation for the damage – against the

---

12   Marx (1842) explains that the Rhine bill was filed on behalf of Frederick William, King of Prussia, to the Diet, which was composed of deputies of the three social states: the city, the countryside and the nobility, all of them with equal number of votes (25 each), which meant an over-representation of the nobility, principal interested in settling the private nature of the wood and the fruits of the forests. The first deputy that intervened was of the cities and questioned whether to classify the conduct of the peasants as 'theft' or as a mere violation of forest regulations. A deputy of the nobility replied that the reason for the frequency of this act was, indeed, the lack of criminalization. The first deputy insisted that this criminalization would place the honest citizen in the path of crime. The parallel with the present over-criminalization policies that encourage harsh punishment with a deterrent aim is overwhelming.

13   Ironically, Marx (1842) explains that the deputies should criminalize the act of collecting wood as 'wood murder' to punish it as such. Moreover, he insists that, once proportionality between the act committed and the legal framework is lost, law will earn the impunity to accommodate facts to the most convenient normative. He also stresses that, regardless of whether these laws are enforced or not, passing the bill already attached a criminal perception to the act of collecting wood, stripping the activity from its characterization as a right and stigmatizing its authors.

proclaimed end of slavery. The relation between the state and the forest owner became amalgamated (14) – against the ideal of the law as representative of a general interest. Against this backdrop it is clear that the veil of the public nature of the punishment only hid a private interest. The wood, once stolen, had, apparently, the excellent virtue of giving its owner the qualities of the state (24). Thanks to the new legislation, the private guard had the authority to stop the offender and to demand the return of the stolen property, the payment of a fine and the provision of free labor. The state was the spectrum whose shadow legitimized the process of pseudo-private justice:

> The law-giving forest owner confused for a moment his two roles, that of the legislator and that of the forest owner. In one case as a forest owner he made the thief pay him for the wood, and in the other as a legislator he made the thief pay him for the thief's criminal frame of mind, and it quite accidentally happened that, in both cases, it was the forest owner who was paid (23).

Similar laws were passed in the rest of Europe. The impoverished farmers at the Mosel vineyards had to stop using wood to satisfy their basic needs because of the new regulations that favored the Customs Union, controlled by landowners (Marx 1843). In Prussia, from a total of 207,478 prosecutions that took place in 1836, 150,000 were for theft of wood and other forest crimes (Linebaigh 1976). In England, peasants who sought to defend their right to hunt were targeted by the 'Black Law'[14] that criminalized the hunting, harm or theft of deer or fallow deer, hunting hares and rabbits, and fishing without permission on private lands (Thompson 1975, 23). It mattered little, in that regard, that the exercise of customary rights – such as hunting – made a difference between survival and utter destitution (Federici 2004, 103 n 31). The new legislation effectively enforced property rights and strictly distinguished the 'exchange economy' from the 'subsistence economy,' criminalizing the latter (Bensaid 2007, 102). As a result, "many people not of a criminal disposition are cut off from the green tree of morality and cast like fallen wood into the hell of crime, infamy and misery" (Marx 1842, 3).

---

14   The name of the law – also known as the Black Waltham Law – stemmed its name from the 'blackening,' or disguise, worn by hunters contravening the regulations (Thompson 1975, 23–24). Against the proportionality principle settled by the Enlightenment, more than fifty aggravating offenses imposed the death penalty as a punishment. In addition, the diffuse nature of the wording made the law susceptible to be applied to virtually any behavior. This act made it clear that the British state agreed that the essential goal of the law was to protect property, and only eventually the lives and freedoms of the people (23).

This new legal order was not only an intent to discipline the poor and protect private property. It also served the purpose of restricting the arbitrary extralegal power of landowners and fitting them into the legal sphere, as the ruling class believed in those rules and its ideological rhetoric (Thompson 1975, 286). However, they were happy to submit to the rule of law only because this law served and contributed to their hegemonic rhetoric of legitimacy (291).

b   *Legally-Disciplining Over-Criminalization on Social Banditry*
The new legal order also tried to banish informal justice systems for institutionalized and legally-based practices. One of the most common forms of informal justice was 'social banditry,' a universal and uniform practice carried out by some peasants, known as 'bandits,' who attacked and robbed using violence. Banditry arose in remote and inaccessible locales (mountains, plains, marshlands, areas with bad roads and poor communications), where the central authorities did not have access. This practice was accepted and protected by the community of peasants that regarded the bandits as fighters for justice. This practice was also tolerated by the authorities, who described them as a minority form of rebellion that did not require official attention (Hobsbawm 1969, 37). However, with the advent of legally-disciplining criminal selectivity, as a correlate to the advance of capitalist relations of production in these remote areas, these bandits began to be seen as reluctant to take to the expected social passivity. Their regulation was part of the goal of imposing discipline in rural areas, asserting the value of private property and regulating all existing social relations under the capitalist model. Therefore, bandits started to be persecuted and became marginal actors subjected to over-criminalization.

Following this breakdown, they were legally assimilated with criminals, despite the fact that their actions were not considered antisocial in their communities. This offers evidence that over-criminalization did not apply to those acts that harmed the rural community values but to those that were contrary to the order that the bourgeoisie intended to impose.[15] While traditional criminals could harmed the rural population, rural bandits were the embodiment of a popular justice accepted and legitimized by their communities. Despite this, the law did not heed such material differences in community assessments, and pursued bandits and traditional criminals with equal zeal. Any attack on rural

---

15   Social bandits lived in crowded areas where not everyone could find land to work; they belonged to a social group whose status conferred them freedom of action – young men, not integrated into rural society and forced to marginal forms of life –; and – as opposed to the meek and passive social role of the submitted farmer – they were headstrong and stubborn, rebellious individuals (Hobsbawm 1969, 47–49 and 51).

property, any rupture with the new capitalist relations based on ownership, any lack of discipline became forbidden by law and over-criminalized, regardless of the character allocated to such acts by the community.

Another aspect of social-tolerated popular justice were food riots. These actions were direct, disciplined and had clear objectives. They were performed in response to attacks on the moral economy of the poor, such as price hikes, especially of wheat (Thompson 1984). Although traditionally tolerated, the perception of the riots was also modified with the consolidation of capitalist relations of production in the countryside. The bourgeoisie's fear of these revolts, which tested the disciplining of the rural masses, pushed for a change in their conceptualization and treatment (1971, 136). The new legal order imposed new and strict definitions of property that transformed riots into crimes.

In sum, based on *The German Ideology* (1845) among many other texts of Marx and Engels, the above section examined the study of the legally-disciplining criminal selectivity that took place in the first disciplining phase (late 18th century). The construction of a large, formally equal regulatory structure, within and outside the criminal field, was established as an essential tool of social control in the struggle of the mercantile bourgeoisie with the working class and the nobility. The extension of the formal spectrum of rights was intended to cover up the primitive accumulation, leave behind the previous barbarity and hide the perpetuation of crime control over the most disadvantaged sectors.

Crime control operated through legally-disciplining criminal selectivity, under the enlightened discourse that characterized crime as a breach of the social contract, detached from the intentionality and characteristics of the offender. Legally disciplining under-criminalization minimized the legislation and prosecution of those negative social behaviors related to ownership, religion and morality that were committed by the politically-emergent bourgeoisie. Legally-disciplining over-criminalization operated on the peasants' resistance against the plundering of their customary rights, and on the coarse crimes and criminalized survival strategies perpetrated by the urban pauperism.

Under these conditions, the following approaches the next modality adopted by criminal selectivity in the 19th century.

Second Disciplining Phase: Police-Medically Disciplining Criminal Selectivity (19th Century)

In the *second disciplining phase* (19th century) a new mode of criminal selectivity emerged: the *police-medically disciplining criminal selectivity*. This followed from the crisis of the contractual model: legally-disciplining criminal selectivity had invoked and proclaimed 'formal equality' spreading awareness about the possibility of equal rights. However, at the same time, this balance was not put into practice (Pavarini 1995, 35). The contradiction between formal equality and material inequality demanded resolution in order to avoid social unrest. Because the legally-disciplining model had already accomplished its goal (the imposition of the bourgeoisie into the economic and political domain), the referred contradiction was resolved by the use of the new modality of criminal selectivity to overturn the recently proclaimed legal equality.

Police-medically disciplining criminal selectivity was rooted in the activity of the police institutions – in open development – and in the legitimation of a positivist medical explanation of crime. Jointly, police and medical discourse enabled a differential criminal treatment justified by biological reasons. The individuals and subsets of the population that were targeted by crime control started to be categorized as 'dangerous and criminal classes.'[16] Under this pseudo-scientific legitimation, police-medically disciplining criminal selectivity intensively regulated and targeted the political activities of the employed workers, the criminalized survival strategies perpetrated by the pauperism, and the acts of resistance performed by the colonized populations (*police-medically disciplining over-criminalization*). Meanwhile, this new mode of criminal selectivity favored the limited regulation and lenient enforcement of the harmful actions perpetrated by the industrial bourgeoisie – the social sector that embodied 'order and progress' – (*police-medically disciplining under-criminalization*). Police-medically disciplining criminal selectivity shaped crime and conflict not only in Europe, but also in the United States. The latter emerged as a relevant global actor, and an epicenter of criminological theories and new forms of crime control. Indeed, the first criminological work based on a phrenological theoretical approach – in line with positivism – was written in the United States by Caldwell (1846) (Zysman 2013, 194). There, police forces – under the medical discourse – targeted communities of color and other marginalized groups (Mitrani 2013, 6).

In the context of this second disciplining phase, social conflict escalated. The industrial revolution showed that the accumulation of wealth did not bring better conditions for all. Conversely, the economic development of the well-off was accompanied by an accumulation of misery, enforcing the loss of

---

16   This nomenclature was used for the first time in 1840 by Frégier, a Parisian commissioner who described the unintelligent, vicious and ignorant workers. He published two volumes of *Des dangereuses de la population dans les grandes villes et des moyens de les Rendre meilleures*, affirming that, even though there were corrupt and depraved people among the affluent sectors, they were not dangerous. In contrast, the poor and depraved classes had always been and would always be the worst of all kinds of evildoer (quoted in Emsley 2007, 143).

faith in an optimistic future (Pavarini 1980, 40). This growing imbalance, accompanied by the legal proclamation of equality, increased the unrest of the masses that were excluded from the labor market. It also fostered the proliferation of political and union organizations, particularly among industrial workers, struggling with outrageous labor conditions. At the global level, social conflict involved competition among the dominant nations which was intensified by the need to conquest new territories and markets. Asia and Africa became the most valuable resources after the independence of most Latin-American countries.

Crime conflict was confined to the activities of the incipient labor unions and political organizations, coarse crimes, criminalized survival strategies and status-based offenses under the label of 'mala vida' (*Spanish* 'low life').[17] Social statistics and databases, born in the heat of social scientism and nourished by the activity of the police, showed a quantification of crime as had not been done before.[18] Statistics indicated a significant increase of crimes concerning bandits, gangs and the homeless. As for crimes against persons, changes in the understanding of male honor led to a general decline of physical altercations, which were also seen as personal matters and were not reported to the authorities. By contrast, political crimes and offenses against property increased (Emsley 2007, 115–117).[19]

Social control focused on economic coercion through an increasing reserve army. Urban paupers and employed workers were compelled to adapt themselves to the disciplining guidelines if they wanted to enter the labor market

---

17 While the overwhelming majority of people in Europe in the first half of the 19th century did not live in cities or large towns – and certainly not in the new type of dark, dirty industrial cities such as Manchester – authorities expressed an urgent concern about public order and social hygiene (Emsley 2007, 135–136).

18 The French lawyer Guerry and the Belgian academic Quetelet were surprised by the regularity and uniformity of criminal statistics, assimilating the phenomena of crime and criminalization and without noticing the interference of criminal selectivity between them. However, Quetelet realizes that there could be an unknown gap between the number of crimes committed, and those cited by the police authorities: "our observations can only refer to some known and judged crimes, from the totality of crimes" (quoted in Emsley 2007, 118).

19 They were usually committed by young men, and they increased during winter (especially firewood robbery) and when the price of cereal grew. These variations seem to respond to the fact that over-criminalization grew in winter times and when grains were expensive in order to promote deterrence. Variations could also respond to a greater social sensitivity that increased the amount of reports to the police during those critical moments (Emsley 2007, 115–117).

or preserve their employment. Crime control retained an important place to contain those who disobeyed the ideal of 'order and progress,' and were not subjected to economic constraints.

Crime control divorced from the jurists and philosophers who produced the legitimating legally-disciplining discourse, and engaged with doctors and police-forces that explicitly proclaimed its selective functioning. Unequal criminal treatment became justified by invoking biological deficiencies 'detected' in over-criminalized individuals, who were identified by the newly-formed police forces. Doctors came to resolve the paradox that assumed a social contract between free and equal individuals and the selective application of crime control only against certain classes of people. The reasoning behind this apparent inconsistency was that the over-criminalized were inferior beings and did not deserve to be considered peers but targets of crime control.

The new police forces were based on the French (1800) and English (1829) models.[20] They emerged with the purpose of occupying colonized territories but their functions soon extended to the control of the major urban concentrations in the metropolitan cities. Police began to intervene in urban spaces to treat the internally displaced masses with the same (biased) instruments and ideology used in the colonies (Zaffaroni 2011, 88). For example, the police practices and attitudes toward Black people in the United Kingdom are rooted in the imperialist logic (Lea and Young 1984, 143). To justify the selective profiling, doctors brought a medical-based discourse that gave birth to criminological positivism (Zaffaroni 2011, 95). Medical studies were conducted in prisons (i.e. on those already criminalized as a result of biased police actions) and, from them, the doctors individualized the traits that characterized 'criminals.' The medical knowledge affirmed that certain morphological characters (Mongoloid and African physical features) were evidence of atavism. The holders of these features – which also corresponded to the colonized – were considered as biologically inclined to commit crimes; they were 'born criminals' (Lombroso 1897). The methodology (studying those who have been already criminalized)

---

20   Police forces were developed in Europe to systematically perform the activities that, until then, where circumstantially carried out by the Gendarmerie during conflictive situations (Merriman 2006, 4). The French police (known as the first modern police force) was created in 1800, and the English metropolitan force was established in 1829. Both became the early models for the creation of modern policing systems in the rest of Europe (O' Brien 1978, 510). France developed a centralized and militarized system, while England supported a system of unarmed civilians (Emsley 2007, 96). In the United States, the first police forces were created in Boston (1838) and New York City (1845) and, by the end of the 19th century, all the major u.s. cities had their police forces (Walker and Katz 1996, 29).

assumed (and legitimated) the identification between the 'criminalized individuals' and the 'real criminals.' Those who were in prison were presumed as accurate representatives of the population that commits crimes, ignoring the incidence of the mechanisms of under-criminalization and over-criminalization. This self-legitimizing mechanism that assimilates 'criminals' with the 'criminalized' has been preserved until the present.

The following develops how crime control was embodied in the mechanisms of police-medically disciplining under-criminalization and police-medically disciplining over-criminalization.

Police-Medically Disciplining Under-Criminalization

The notion of *police-medically disciplining under-criminalization* refers to the scarce and narrow legislation of the harmful actions against the life as well as the physical and economic integrity of the industrial workers and the colonial populations, committed by the liberal industrial bourgeoisie (primary under-criminalization). It also refers to the rare enforcement of that already narrow legislation (secondary under-criminalization). The explanation that legitimizes this mode of under-criminalization rested on the need of ensuring progress and civilization, while repressing those who delayed them. Police-medically disciplining under-criminalization operated differentially (a) in the colonies, to the detriment of local populations; and (b) in Europe, at the expense of the working class.

a   *Police-Medically Disciplining Under-Criminalization on the Colonial Populations' Oppression*

In line with the primitive accumulation, the 19th century hosted a new wave of land occupations and economic subjugation in pursuit of new markets and sources of raw materials. As Marx and Engels point out in *The Communist Manifesto*, "the need of a constantly expanding market for its products chases the bourgeoisie over the entire surface of the globe. It must nestle everywhere, settle everywhere, establish connections everywhere" (1848, 16). And then:

> The conditions of bourgeois society are too narrow to comprise the wealth created by them. And how does the bourgeoisie get over these crises? On the one hand by enforced destruction of a mass of productive forces; on the other, by the conquest of new markets, and by the most thorough exploitation of the old ones (17).

Engels (1888) emphasizes that English dominion, as the epicenter of industrial development, was built not only in the heat of high modern industry, machinery and steam power but also through the imposition of terrible working conditions in the colonies and the massive extraction of natural resources. Indeed, in the framework of the police-medically disciplining criminal selectivity, the European great powers divided the African continent in the Berlin Conference (1884–1885). Millions of African died as an effect of the extraction of rubber and ivory between 1890 and 1910. Prohibition of slavery was already established in England in 1833, and there was a widespread recognition of the character of 'person' of all the inhabitants of the colonies. However, extremely violent acts (death, enslavement, torture, extortion, smuggling and trade and tax prey) were still neither legally regulated nor effectively prosecuted. Paradoxically, the extended application of the death penalty by the colonizers in Africa, took place when Europe had already banned it from its territory (Ternon 2007 quoted in Codino 2010, 15). England was the colonial power par excellence and the privileged actor of the police-medically disciplining under-criminalization.

The 'police-medical' characterization describes the positivist medical discourse that conceived non-Europeans as 'savage' and 'primitive,' and therefore susceptible to repression and domination by military forces operating in a policing manner (Zaffaroni 2011, 95). This violence was legitimized by an ideology that showed that there were 'good intentions' behind the necessary evil: the inferior species should give way to superior ones, and that goal justified the killings (Bensoussan 2008, 11 quoted in Codino 2010, 16).

The 'disciplining' objective of the police-medically disciplining under-criminalization was two-fold: reducing the colonial population to slave labor and nullifying their resistance while utilizing this work to press down wages of the European workers. On this point, Marx illustrated that to be 'free' at home, John Bull must enslave people who are outside the borders of this state.[21] By this logic, the accumulation of wealth on one side of the globe means the accumulation of misery, labor, torture, ignorance, brutalization and moral degradation on the other (1859c). Paradoxically, attempts at resistance against these under-criminalized behaviors were stymied and resulted in the over-criminalization of the oppressed.

In India, Britain systematically practiced slavery, torture and economic crimes. Even though Britain had approved the abolition of slavery and flaunted

---

21   John Bull was the national personification of England. The immediate political conclusion that Marx drew was that if the colonial subjugation was not overcome, European workers could not be able to triumph. Even Engels had formulated the principle that a nation cannot win freedom if it keeps oppressing others (Levrero 1979, 24). This position is reinforced in a letter to Marx in which he explains that British upper classes' freedoms are based on the oppression of the colonies (Engels 1856 quoted in Levrero 1979, 28).

its zeal in suppressing this crime by other countries, it systematically applied it in India. The distance between the abolitionist discourse and the under-criminalized slavery practice allowed England to get rid of competition and take advantage of slave labor in its colonies in order to dominate the global trade market. Ironically, England used the anti-abolitionist discourse even to perpetrate the conquest of East Africa and displace its 'slave-holder' competitors, diluting the ideals of equality between men for the sake of conquest (Marx 1858b).

Torture was also routinely used by the English in Indian territory. Marx (1857) describes how local workers were mistreated and tortured for complaining about their pay: stones were put on their backs while stooping in the burning sand. In spite of the extension of torture, its under-criminalization prevailed because victims had to exhaust several bureaucratic requirements in order to have access to courts. Marx illustrates that even the English commission in charge of investigating torture was impressed by the difficulties that victims have to overcome to obtain reparations. When despite all these difficulties the reports acknowledged the systematic application of torture, under-criminalization still persisted: British authorities sought to offload responsibility on local officials, releasing any link between them and the Crown. Britain got to stand removed from the accusation and even used them to characterize torture as a barbaric behavior, more typical of backward nations:

> The universal existence of torture as a financial institution of British India is thus officially admitted, but the admission is made in such a manner as to shield the British Government itself. In fact, the conclusion arrived at by the Madras commission is that the practice of torture is entirely the fault of the lower Hindoo officials, while the European servants of the Government had always, however unsuccessfully, done their best to prevent it (1857).

Even in the cases where it was not possible to hide the responsibility of British agents, under-criminalization assumed a particular form: crimes were attributed to individual actors, ignoring the systematic nature of torture as a required tool for colonial domination. Then, criminal prosecution characterized the acts of torture as an 'excesses' of individual agents, but without links among each other. Torture was the responsibility of a few 'rotten apples.'

Besides these crimes against persons, the conquest of India involved economic crimes. As happened with the double-speech that surrounded the crime of slavery, England imposed its commercial monopoly in the colonies by fire and sword, while it demanded a free trade from foreign economies. "Thanks to this happy mixture of both systems, at the end of the wars, in 1815, she [England] found herself, concerning all important branches of industry, in possession of the virtual monopoly of the trade of the world" (Engels 1888). In India, the monopoly took place through the East India Company and was founded on bribery:

> The power the East India Company had obtained by bribing the Government, as also did the Bank of England, it was forced to maintain by bribing again, as did the Bank of England. At every epoch when its monopoly was expiring, it could only effect a renewal of its Charter by offering fresh loans and by fresh presents made to the Government.
>
> MARX 1853b

Economic oppression also operated through the application of excessive taxation on the Indian population. Marx noted that the vast mass of the people of India were in a state of absolute impoverishment and gloom, with even slight taxation seeming to reduce them to dire poverty (1858c). If the local people did not pay, torture was used to compel them or the British would expropriate their land.[22]

This sequence of crimes – though never perceived as such – encouraged armed uprisings against the English in 1857. These rebellions were reduced the following year with the defeat of Muslim guerrillas in Kashmir and, paradoxically, persecuted as crimes. The twisted logic of colonialism regarded Indian resistance as the real crime deserving of prosecution. Marx states: "if the English could do these things in cold blood, is it surprising that the insurgent Hindoos should be guilty, in the fury of revolt and conflict, of the crimes and cruelties alleged against them?" (1857b). Marx denounces the lax treatment of the actions committed by the Crown, and the excessive treatment of the same actions when perpetrated by locals. He explains that the cruelties of the English were reported simply and quickly, without dwelling on unpleasant details, while the outrages of the native populations are deliberately exaggerated. Engels (1858) reinforces that, far from being less violent, the acts committed by the English included looting and outrageous expropriations. He compares

---

22   In 1783, the English Governor in India enacted a law that implemented the system of 'zemindari' in Bengal and other provinces. According to this law, lands that belonged to village communities were delivered to the 'zemindars' (landowners collectors). British authorities also implemented the 'ryotwari' system in the presidencies of Madras and Bombay in 1818, which transformed the 'ryot' (Indian peasant) into a tenant of government land. The new tenants were obliged to pay high income-taxes to the Company and, if they could not pay, they were condemned to lose their property rights. This system gradually passed the lands into the hands of loan sharks.

English colonialism with the hordes of Mongols, and defines it as a "new accumulation of wealth through repression:"

> The calmucas hordes of Genghis Khan and Timur, fly over a city like a
> swarm of locusts and devour everything in their path, should have been
> a blessing for the country, compared with the arrival of these British sol-
> diers, Christians, civilized, chivalrous and courteous.

English domination also spread to China and Ireland. In China, Britain imposed its power through economic subjugation, achieved by implementing
compulsory monopolistic practices – particularly the forced importation of
opium.[23] While England "openly preaching free trade in poison [in relation
to the unrestricted sale of opium in China], it secretly defends the monopoly
of its manufacture" in India (1858d). To that end, Marx describes how England
resorted to criminally forbidden acts such as extortion and smuggling, in addition to the massive deaths caused by opium. These lethal consequences were
charted by Marx, who recalls the words of an English slaver who claimed that
the damage caused by the drug was markedly more harmful than the slave
trade:

> Why the 'slave trade' was merciful compared with the 'opium trade'? We
> do not destroy the bodies of Africans as it was our immediate interest to
> retain life [...] But the seller opium kills the body after it has been cor-
> rupted, degraded and annihilated.
>
>   MARX quoted in LEVRERO 1979, 97

The criminal acts of smuggling and piracy also produced extraordinary
losses for the Chinese trade balance, harmed by the opium contraband that
brought misery to the population. Marx (1858d) illustrates that: "The importation was estimated, in 1856, at about $35,000,000, while in the same year,

---

23   The beginnings of the conflict date back to 1798 when the East India Company ceased to
      be the direct opium exporter and became its direct producer: the monopoly of opium was
      established in India, while the vessels of the company were not permitted to take part in
      drug trafficking and licenses were issued to private ships trading to China. Because of the
      massive consumption of opium, the Chinese Emperor banned its importation and its use.
      But then the East India Company introduced its sale through smuggling, which led to the
      First Opium War (1839–1842), in which the British empire succeeded and imposed free
      importation of opium and other British goods to China, while opening five major ports
      and imposing its domain in Hong Kong.

the Anglo-Indian Government drew a revenue of $25,000,000, just a sixth of its total State income, from the opium monopoly." Again, however, they were under-criminalized, while the press collaborated in this process by avoiding the characterization of those behaviors through a criminal prism:

> How silent the press of England about the blatant violations of the treaty, committed daily by foreigners living in China under British protection! Nobody heard of this illicit trade of opium annually thickens the British treasury at the expense of human life and morality. Nobody heard the incessant conclusions of subordinate officials, thanks to which the Chinese government is defrauded their legitimate income from import and export of goods.
>
> MARX 1857C

In Ireland, the English carried out enclosures to provide meat and wool at the lowest possible price, while forcing the Irish peasants to migrate to the cities and compete with British workers. This process helped reduce wages and worsened the material and moral situation of the English working class (Marx quoted in Levrero 1979, 213). Cleaning fields resulted in the fact that, from 1855 to 1866, 1,032,694 Irish peasants were replaced by 996,877 head of cattle, while the remaining population was physically and psychologically deteriorated (35–38). Periodic famines killed more than a million people, and forced another million to migrate, while the remaining peasants were heavily exploited by the English landowners (Marx 1855). A seizure of this magnitude in an independent country demanded a high dose of terror and repression, but these was not sufficient to give rise criminal liability. Conversely, crime control was used to subjugate the local population through their over-criminalization: Irish peasant uprisings were cruelly quelled and rebels were criminally persecuted (Marx quoted in Levrero 1979, 150). Even the institute of *habeas corpus* was canceled making evident that the legal values of the first disciplining phase could be flouted for the purpose of securing English dominion. Over-criminalization also fell upon those who did not rebel in political terms and just committed prohibited acts as a result of their state of misery.

Regarding Latin-American territories, slavery persisted in Cuba until the mid-19th century in favor of the British government. Spain signed a treaty with Cuba in 1835, which imposed severe punishments to prevent the trafficking of slaves. However, the law was enforced only ten years later, without any criminalization of the acts of trafficking committed in the interim. On the contrary, the press covered the subjugation as a sign of civilizational progress for Cuba, correlating with the prevailing police-medically paradigm. Marx (1857c) acknowledges that wrongs are inflicted 'even unto death' upon misguided and bonded emigrants sold in the costs of Peru and into Cuban bondage. In contrast to the complacency of the acts committed by England in Jamaica, the local peasantry was subjugated: the troops mutilated, beat, and hanged the local people, burning more than a thousand huts, under the banner of civilizational progress. Meanwhile, "one of the most monstrous enterprises ever chronicled in the annals of international history" took place in Mexico (Marx 1861), when England, France and Spain started a military action to demand the payment of Mexican foreign debt. In Panama, during the construction of the Suez Canal, France committed huge embezzlement, to the detriment of thousands of small shareholders, without criminal consequences.[24] Marx claims that 1,500 billion francs disappeared into the pockets of fraudulent politicians and journalists. 22,000 Latin-American, Chinese and Indian workers were forced to work in appalling conditions. Most of these succumbed to malaria and yellow fever (1867c, 527). Colonial escalations included the British occupation of the Falklands Islands in 1833, Belize in 1834, and Roatan and other Honduran islands in 1838. The French aggression against Mexico between 1838 and 1839; the French (1838–1840) and Anglo-French (1845–1850) blocks of Buenos Aires; the British occupation of the Nicaraguan port of San Juan del Norte (1841 and 1848), and Honduran islands in the Gulf of Fonseca (1848), and the French intervention against Ecuador (1853) (Scaron 1972) can be added to this list.

b   *Police-Medically Disciplining Under-Criminalization*
        on the Workers' Oppression

Marx and Engels also offer a detailed descriptions of the new manufacturing ventures in Western Europe. Widespread and systematic unsanitary conditions imperiled the life and health of workers there. The developing labor and administrative regulations operated as a reinforcement of these conditions, as they legitimated the illicit character of the productive activities and the disciplining of workers. Indeed, legislation tended to minimize the reception of

---

24   Around 1879 the Universal Panama Canal Company was created to build the Canal, but the funds were not allocated. The directors of the Company bribed hundreds of parliamentarians and, in violation of various laws, obtained an authorization to sell lottery tickets intended to fund the construction. Huge sums of money were paid to ministers, judges and journalists to pass over or disregard the catastrophic situation of the Company. But despite these 'investments,' and partly because of them, on February 4, 1889, the Universal Panama Canal Company went bankrupt. They almost obtained the ideal that Marx attributed to Louis Bonaparte: stealing all the money from France to buy France with the same money (Marx 1867c, 527).

the harmful actions committed by the bourgeoisie in the factories (primary under-criminalization). That scarce legislation was accompanied by a limited persecution of those acts, notably through the complicity of factory inspectors and judges (secondary under-criminalization).

The 'disciplining' character has to do with the fact that cultivating workers' tolerance to the terrible conditions of the factories was part of the process of framing and regimenting them. The goal was forcing the proletariat to accept whatever working conditions if they wanted to preserve their jobs. The 'police-medically' character has to do with the legitimation of under-criminalization through the characterization of the workers as 'atavistic' and 'dangerous.' The prevailing positivist discourse justified the implementation of a hard regime of work by the factory-owner acting in a police function. The common goal of disciplining workers, shared by the private factory owner and the bourgeoisie in the political domain, facilitated the development of cooperation and impunity networks among them. As a corollary, harmful behaviors against the life and physical integrity of workers were committed with the collaboration of public agencies, and primary and secondary under-criminalized, under the veil of a positivist discourse that characterized workers as vicious, needing to be subdued and disciplined to increase capitalist profit.

Primary under-criminalization ranged from non-criminal perception of behaviors involving social harm to the life or integrity of the workers to its inclusion in the prevailing civil law. When criminalized, these actions were linked with lenient punishments in disproportion with the caused social harm. Secondary under-criminalization rested on the fact that law enforcement agents had almost no control over what happened inside the factory. It also rested on the difficulties of evidence' gathering, and the ridiculous punishments imposed in the courts that did not manage to offset the gains arising from breaking the law. Let us analyze each of the forms adopted by primary under-criminalization.

The first form of primary under-criminalization describes how behaviors that caused serious social harm against the workers were not considered offenses by the existing legislation, and they were even regarded as a legitimate part of the labor discipline. These behaviors included the subjection of children to harsh working conditions, a situation of such gravity that it was likened to covert slavery.[25] Their working hours exceeded those of the adults without

---

25   Marx notes: "While the cotton industry introduced child-slavery in England, it gave in
      the United States a stimulus to the transformation of the earlier, more or less patriarchal
      slavery, into a system of commercial exploitation. In fact, the veiled slavery of the wage-
      earners in Europe needed, for its pedestal, slavery pure and simple in the new world"
      (1867, 833).

any law criminalizing this overwork (Marx 1867, 432).[26] Harsh working conditions included torture and injurious abuses, which were not referred to as criminal acts either (831).[27] Most of the children were employed without requiring the consent of their parents or obtaining the consent through threats that were not identified under a criminal prism (529, n 2). The silence of the law in relation to over-work, torture and threats was necessary to ensure the sustained development of the production: "the necessity of child-stealing and child-slavery [served] the transformation of manufacturing exploitation into factory exploitation" (830). Social harms perpetrated at the expense of the most vulnerable representatives of the working class (the children) were accepted as legitimate labor practices. Abuses against children were not even regulated by the existing legislation, in what is an eloquent example of primary under-criminalization in the manufacturing space.

Primary under-criminalization also involved the civil and administrative regulation of harmful acts that could have been considered crimes. To illustrate, adulteration of bread was a systematic practice regulated by administrative law, despite the serious injuries for the health of the workers who consumed it as their most important food (194, n 4). And even these administrative regulations were only formal, as there were no specific procedures to enforce them (274). Bread adulteration was an effect of the replacement of traditional bakeries for mass bread production encouraged by commercial competition (277). This process shows that the expansion of capitalist relations of production within the framework of this second disciplining phase was, again, the factor that conditioned the systematic violation of workers' rights that, despite its harmful character, escaped prosecution.[28]

---

26   Marx states: "Men, women and children lie at night huddled together; and as regards the men, the night-shift succeed the day-shift and the day-shift the night-shift in un- broken series for some time together, the beds having scarcely time to cool; the whole house badly supplied with water, and worse with privies; dirty, unventilated, and pestiferous" (1867, 726).

27   Marx recounts that "in many manufacturing districts, especially Lancashire, cruelties of the most heart-rending sort were practiced upon the unoffending and friendless creatures who were consigned to the charge of master manufacturers. They were harassed to the brink of death by excess of labor [...] were flogged, fettered and tortured in the most exquisite refinement of cruelty; [...] they were in many cases starved to the bone while flogged to their work and.... even in some instances [...] were driven to commit suicide" (1867, 726).

28   Marx states: "The adulteration of bread and the formation of a class of bakers that sells the bread below the full price, date from the beginning of the 18th century, from the time when the corporate character of the trade was lost, and the capitalist in the form of the miller or flour-factor, rises behind the nominal master baker. Thus was laid the foundation

The few recognized workers' rights were circumvented by factory owners who evaded the provisions without criminal consequences. For example, the Factory Act (1844) incorporated some improvements – such as the granting of a minimum 30-minute break every five hours before noon –, but this rule did not clarify that it was mandatory during the afternoon. Based on this loophole in the law, the employer insisted on the 'crime,' not only of making 8-year children work without interruption from 2 pm to 8.30 and half of the night but also making them starve during that time (315). It should be noted that Marx named these behaviors 'crimes,' regardless their regulation in the civil law since they implied a reinforcement of the extreme exploitation and a threat to the physical integrity of adult workers and children.

The third form of primary under-criminalization describes how the few criminal regulations of the acts perpetrated by the industrial bourgeoisie provided such light punishments that they were considered a benefit for the factory-owner. As Engels clarifies:

> [...] the law is sacred to the bourgeois, for it is his composition, enacted with his consent, and for his benefit and protection. He knows that, even if an individual law should injure him, the whole fabric protects his interests; and more than all, the sanctity of the law, the sacredness of order as established by the active will of one part of society, and the passive acceptance of the other, is the strongest support of his social position (1845, 227).

To exemplify, although as an effect of the workers' organization, working hours started to be regulated, punishments in case of infringement were so mild (contraventions and fines) that capitalists found it more convenient to violate the law than to respect it. Engels points out that they "disregard the law, shorten the meal times, work children longer than is permitted, and risk prosecution, knowing that the possible fines are trifling in comparison with the certain profits derivable from the offense" (174).

Regarding secondary under-criminalization, in the few cases regulated by criminal law, law enforcement agencies, specifically factory inspectors, significantly reduced the number of cases in which punishment was applied. Marx reports that even when the ruling classes acceded to pass criminal laws

---

of capitalistic production in this trade, of the unlimited extension of the working day and night labor, although the latter only since 1824 gained a serious footing, even in London" (1867, 277).

to punish abuses, they showed "the hesitation, the repugnance, and the bad faith, with which it lent itself to the task of carrying those measures into practice" (1867, 541).[29]

Secondary under-criminalization was expressed, first, in the fact that acts of serious injury to the rights of workers were absorbed into the silence and immunity of the factories' jurisdiction, beyond the reach of administrative, police or judicial control. They remained under-criminalized, filed under an accident, a consequence of the unforeseen. Engels described the owner of the factory as a 'legislator' who regulates what can be done in the plant, even when it came to sexual abuse. Collusion or submission to the owners' desires was part of what workers had to endure to preserve their jobs (148). Repeatedly, the harsh working conditions led to the deaths of workers. Far from understanding this as mere accidents, Engels claims that the risk of death was covered by the employer for the purpose of achieving greater productivity and was therefore not only known, but encouraged. Therefore, Engels qualifies these acts as 'murder.' It is a murder that "does not seem what it is, because no man sees the murderer, because the death of the victim seems a natural one since the offense is more one of omission than of commission. But murder it remains" (96).[30]

Secondly, secondary under-criminalization persisted due to the difficulties of evidence collection arising from the same control exercised by the employer on stage work. Marx shows that to increase profit, they could not resist the temptation of breaking the law.[31] The extraordinary gains that could be

---

29   Marx illustrates that, in 1867, the Royal Assent, the Factory Extension Act (applicable to large factories) and the Workshop Regulation Act established criminal punishment for employing children. They also imposed fines to the owner of the workshop and to those who benefit directly from the children's work. However, the Factory Extension Act was not enforced because of a series of emergency regulations and the Workshops Regulation Act, wretched in all its details, remained a dead letter in the hands of the municipal and local authorities who were in charge of its implementation (1867, 540–541).

30   Marx explains that, in 1863, the London press ran a story of an employee at a luxury dressmaker who had been subjected to a 26 hours working-days along with sixty other women, all accommodated in two minuscule rooms. In the evenings, they slept two by two in a bed installed in a hole, with a few partitions improvising an alcove. This workshop was one of the best fashion shops in London (1867, 280). The doctor reported that "Mary Anne Walkley had died from long hours of work in an over-crowded workroom, and a too small and badly-ventilated bedroom" (281). Marx then refers to the work of the blacksmiths who died at a rate above the national average. So this occupation, which is almost an instinctive art of humanity, is made intolerable by a mere excess of work (282).

31   Here, as elsewhere, Marx makes the parallel between the acts committed within the factory and the primitive accumulation. He notes that smuggling and slave-trade were part of business ventures during primitive accumulation, despite being forbidden by law.

obtained by lengthening the working hours above the legal standards pushed them to see how many illicit practices they could get away with (266). These speculations raised the fact that the manufacturer had complete control over the workplace, and it was tough for the workers to prove infringements. Indeed, even the inspectors encountered insuperable difficulties to gather evidence and make a case. Despite the invisibility of these behaviors, Marx warned about their criminal character, calling them 'small thefts' of capital from the laborer's meal and recreation time (267).[32]

Another example of secondary under-criminalization in relation to the lack of denounce or enforcement of the law was the practice of paying salaries with products, although it was prohibited by law. In many cases, the factory owner also owned the products used to pay wages, redoubling his gain. Engels explains that "payment in truck orders was declared void and illegal, and was made punishable by fine; but, like most other English laws, this has been enforced only here and there" (1845, 182). Even if the facts made their way to the state authority, the difficulty encountered by the workers in demonstrating the criminal nature of the conduct perpetrated at their expense was overwhelming, leading to under-criminalization.

Third, secondary under-criminalization was imposed when, even if there was enough evidence to bring the case to justice, the courts ruled against the worker or applied derisory penalties. Convictions consisted of small fines that failed to compensate the money earned through the perpetrated crime (1867, 464). Marx shows that when the factory owners see the small amount of penalty, and the costs for making the laborers illegally over-work, "they find that if they should be detected there will still be a considerable balance of gain"

Following the same logic, torments in the manufacturing sphere were practiced besides being criminalized by the law. This shows that "[t]he cupidity of the well-off whose cruelty in the pursuit of gain have hardly been exceeded by those perpetrated by the Spaniards in the conquest of America in the pursuit of gold" (1867, 268, n 2).

32   Marx adds that the same factory inspectors who had to enforce the law were the ones that commit irregularities and minimized these 'thefts' of the workers' time. Marx describes these acts as 'thefts' – 'petty pilfering of minutes' or 'snatching a few minutes'- clarifying how they were considered by the inspectors as an unimportant matter. But, says Marx, this technical language was not enough to hide the severity of those behaviors, as the minutes detracted were the only available moments that the workers had to eat and rest. Because of this, the workers called this action 'nibbling and cribbling at meal times' (1867, 267). Another resonant case charted by Marx appears in Chapter 19 of *Capital* when he analyzes the situation of the workers that got paid only for the perfect pieces that they produced. Marx affirms then that "[p]iece-wages become, from this point of view, the most fruitful source of reductions of wages and capitalistic cheating" (605).

(1867, 267). This can be illustrated with a case in which the owners of eight large factories were denounced for breaking the Factory Law[33] and, though the defendants admitted liability, the court sentenced them to the insignificant amount of a 20 pound fine (187, n 22).[34] All judicial complaints proved unsuccessful, as the courts and county magistrates almost always absolved because, in these tribunals, employer-lords administered justice themselves (317). The class judged was the same class that occupied the offices of the magistracy. The interests pursued by factory-owners, inspectors and judges tended to coincide (463–464). The influence of personal relations in court decisions promoted the dissimilarity of the sentencing in different regions. Even the factory inspectors claimed the government to sort this anomalous and anarchic situation. A litigant report expresses that after "having endeavored to enforce the Act [...] in seven magisterial divisions, and having been supported by the magistrates in one case only [...], I considered it useless to prosecute more for this evasion of the law" (317–318). Finally, not only did the judiciary ensure undercriminalization of the behaviors of the factory owner through lenient and inconsistent sentencing, but, paradoxically, the courts compelled workers to meet the imposed working conditions under the threat of criminalizing them.[35]

---

33 Marx states the facts were that "[s]ome of these gentlemen were accused of having kept at work 5 boys between 12 and 15 years of age from 6 a.m. on Friday to 12 p.m. on the following Saturday, not allowing them any respite except for meals and one hour for sleep at midnight. And these children had to do this ceaseless labor of 30 hours in the 'shoddy-hole,' as the hole is called, in which the woolen rags are pulled in pieces, and where a dense atmosphere of dust and shreds forces even the adult workman to cover his mouth continually with handkerchiefs for the protection of his lungs" (1867, 267 n 1).

34 Marx points out that they admitted guilt because their Quaker origins prevented them from lying (1867, 267, n 1).

35 Marx brings up an example that demonstrates that the principles laid down by the Enlightenment (in this case the *ne bis in idem*) were only alive in the letter of the law: "One occurs at Sheffield at the end of 1866. In that town, a workman had engaged himself for two years in steel works. In consequence of a quarrel with his employer he left the works and declared that under no circumstances would he work for that master anymore. He was prosecuted for breach of contract and condemned to two months' imprisonment (if the instructor breaks the contract, he can be proceeded against only in a civil action, and risks nothing but financial damage). After the workman has served his two months, the master invites him to return to the works, under the contract. Workman says; no: he has already been punished for the breach. The master prosecutes again; the court condemns again, although one of the judges, Mr. Shee, publicly denounces this as a legal monstrosity, by which a man can periodically, as long as he lives, be punished over and over again for the same offense or crime. This judgment was given not by the 'Great Unpaid,' the provincial Dogberries, but by one of the highest courts of justice in London" (1867, 229).

The effects of these mechanisms of primary and secondary under-criminalization were reflected in the fate of the workers who suffered atrocious working conditions and abuse without legal consequences. Engels character-izes the employment contract as an 'as if' because the law did not exceed the level of a mere formality. In practice, the worker's conditions were comparable with slavery:

> The proletarian is, therefore, in law and, in fact, the slave of the bour-geoisie, which can decree his life or death. It offers him the means of living, but only for an "equivalent" for his work. It even lets him have the appearance of acting from a free choice, of making a contract with free, unconstrained consent, as a responsible agent who has attained his ma-jority (1845, 76).

Life and health of workers were threatened by individual capitalists that side-stepped regulatory compliance to increase the exploitation of employees. Harmful and unlawful activities were used to discipline workers and as a rein-forcement of the lawful productive activity of the factories. The possibility of raising a venture respectful of existing labor rights and the bureaucratic and legal requirements was very complex because violations were widespread. If the owner did respect workers' rights, he would lead the business to ruin, pressed by the existing competition. In this regard, as Bonger highlights, these crimes were intimately connected with the system of production, to the point where they are inseparable (1905, 600). Private capitalist and public sectors were united by ties of economic and cultural homogeneity. Thus, there was not symbiosis, as Sutherland would characterize it years later (1940 and 1949), but a link that could be called 'collaboration.' Factory inspectors and judges were not actively involved in the harmful actions but they provided a cover-up.

Police-Medically Disciplining Over-Criminalization

The notion of *police-medically disciplining over-criminalization* describes the mechanism that broadens the criminal regulation of the political activities performed by the organized working class, and the criminalized survival strat-egies committed by the pauperized sectors (primary over-criminalization). It also describes the over-dimensioned enforcement of these new legislations (secondary over-criminalization). These mechanisms of primary and sec-ondary over-criminalization rested on the characterization of their targets as 'dangerous classes' that contaminated the social organism. This justification rested on a supposedly scientific basis, which promoted racist and xenophobic statements.

Following the expropriations in rural areas during the first disciplining phase, the rural poor were forced to migrate to the cities. Under these conditions, in the 1840s and 1850s several counties were already on the verge of an absolute loss of population and, since 1850, the exodus from the countryside became general (Hobsbawm 1962, 148). Thus, in this second disciplining phase, police-medically disciplining over-criminalization arose mainly in the urban European territory, affecting both the urban pauperism and the organized dissident. 'Urban pauperism' refers to the impoverished masses that could not enter the labor market and who were persecuted under the moniker of 'low life,' on the basis of the prevailing positivist paradigm. The notion of *organized dissident* refers to both, the employed workers that were unionized and politically organized, and the partisan activists that supported the demands of the working class. The latter category includes Marx and Engels, who developed theoretical production and advocacy activities in support of the working class. Indeed, the fathers of historical materialism themselves were subjected to such over-criminalization, particularly when they promoted the International Workingmen's Association. Let us then analyze separately the police-medically disciplining over-criminalization of (a) the criminalized survival strategies committed by the urban pauperism and (b) the acts of resistance perpetrated by the organized dissident.

a   *Police-Medically Disciplining Over-Criminalization of the*
        Criminalized Survival Strategies Committed by the Urban Pauperism
The 19th century found Europe suffering from a severe increase of industrial unemployment. The reasons were an overabundance of labor and the replacement of adult-labor with women and child-labor. Upon the introduction of machinery – mainly in the textile industry but also gradually in other areas – male adult labor was not as necessary as before. In the opening pages of *The Condition of the Working Class in England* (1845),[36] Engels illustrates that in England, as in the rest of Europe, workers were not guaranteed the satisfaction of their basic needs. Misery configured a state of permanent social insecurity, affecting the most populous sectors, as it acted as a principle of demoralization

---

36   While Marx was describing the situation of the rural people who were criminalized for stealing firewood (1842), Engels was studying the effects of British capitalism in the local proletariat. He began his work in 1843 and he published it in 1845 after twenty-one months of research. It is noteworthy that, though the title of Engels' work refers to the situation of the 'working class' in general terms, it shows its further development on the part of this class who was unemployed and living in extreme poverty (which is described here as 'pauperism').

and social dissociation (Castel 2003, 40). They lived in terrible conditions of life: "no cleanliness, no convenience, and consequently no comfortable family life is possible" (63).[37]

Which mechanism of control could be used over this population excluded from the labor market? Searching for an answer, Engels published an article in a newspaper of Leipzig in 1868 explaining that this subset became an industrial reserve army. This reserve army provides workers that, when necessary, perform work for wages that are lower than the market value, and that most often are unemployed and let to the mercy of public charity. This 'army' is indispensable for the capitalist class to provide hands in times of great prosperity and to always press wages down (Engels quoted in Gomez Crespo 2012). Most of the time, the labor market did not exercise control over this mass of unemployed workers ('it did not put eyes on it'). The medical, legal and charitable agencies did instead:

> Political Economy, therefore, does not recognize the unoccupied worker, the workman, in so far as he happens to be outside this labor-relationship. The cheat-thief, swindler, beggar, and unemployed man; the starving, wretched and criminal working- man – these are *figures* who do not exist for *political economy* but only for other eyes, those of the doctor, the judge, the grave-digger, and bum-bailiff, etc.; such figures are specters outside the domain of political economy.
>
> MARX 1844c

In other words, when the economic mechanisms did not exercise social control over the paupers to accomplish a disciplining function, crime control mostly occupied those spaces, under the legitimation of a medical discourse and the support of welfare. This means that all institutions of social control (medical, legal, charitable), beyond their explicit purposes, worked under the police-medically disciplining paradigm to support crime control. As Engels warns: "The only provision made for them is the law, which fastens upon them when

---

37   Engels drag some elements of the prevailing hygienist theory, linking physical unhealthiness with moral poverty. He uses the variable 'demoralization' to show how, as a result of material conditions and the inability to invest in a long-term project, workers acquire an impulsive and irrational character. He claims that "all who are more intimately acquainted with the condition of the inhabitants will testify to the high degree which disease, wretchedness, and demoralization have here reached" (1845, 36). The minimum loss of moral conditions was also incumbent upon the bourgeoisie itself. So, Engels says, they "will not confess, even to itself, that the workers are in distress, because it, the property-holding, manufacturing class, must bear the moral responsibility for this distress" (18).

they become obnoxious to the bourgeoisie. Like the dullest of the brutes, they are treated to but one form of education, the whip, in the shape of force, not convincing but intimidating" (1845, 114). Thus, the worker "is not only without bread but without a shelter, a vagabond at the mercy of the law which sends him, without fail, to the treadmill" (184).

As was clarified in the introduction of the second disciplining phase, the peculiarity of the medical discourse serving crime control was that it operated as a self-fulfilling prophecy. Law enforcement agencies worked through a selective orientation targeting the poor. To illustrate, the English Vagrancy Act (1824) ordered the arrest of any individual under suspicion of idle behavior, by discretion of the police agents (Emsley 2007, 106–109), in an early configuration of stop-and-frisk. Then, these over-criminalized individuals were studied under a medical discourse that identified their physical appearance as the one of the criminals. The resulting stereotype of the 'criminal' was one with outrageously morbid characteristics, typical of the wild man: steep fronts, deep eye sockets, eyes far apart, facial asymmetry, and a disproportionate jaw (Lombroso 1887). The persistence of these inferior classes was explained through the atavism theory: remaining populations in the path of social progress were condemned to disappear. In addition, hygiene principles, which were part of this medical approach to crime, affirmed – on a pseudo-scientific base – that poor neighborhoods also helped to spread crime, besides the individual biological determination. Positivism's representatives asserted that the inferior and depraved social environment of the large cities contributed to expanding crime and that "it was in the popular classes, in the underworld, natural and fatal place, where the crime appeared and multiplied" (Prins 1886, 17 quoted in Codino 2010, 17).

Based on this police-medically orientation, it was not necessary to 'wait' for the criminal to commit the crime. As it was possible to detect the 'born criminal' and the social neighborhoods where crime spread, crime control could now rely on pre-criminal dangerousness procedures. The mere identification of criminal features by doctors allowed the intervention of the police forces to 'find' them in the urban space. Welfare – through schools, families and other institutions that affected the lives of people considered likely to become criminals – would be essential to pursue this 'preventive' criminal program (Cooper quoted in Platt 1969, 28). The greatest criminal persecution of this second disciplining phase targeted life-style behaviors: criminalized survival strategies, coarse crimes and the low life. All of these were read as symptoms of a 'dangerous state without crime' that should be controlled as a measure social defense.

Criminalized survival strategies included panhandling, vagrancy and prostitution. For women, prostitution was persecuted as a moral threat, channel of transmission of sexually transmitted diseases, and even as a potential threat to state security (Emsley 2007, 158). From the criminological positivist perspective, Lombroso and Ferraro (1915) dedicated a book to the topic – *The Donna Delinquente, the Prostitute, and the Normale Donna* – claiming that prostitution was the way in which women show their criminal character, given their weakness for other conducts. From a different perspective, Engels acknowledges that these criminalized survival strategies were not volunteer actions that emerged from an unconditioned free will. Panhandling or vagrancy were imposed as daily necessities: "When people are placed under conditions which appeal to the brute only, what remains to them but to rebel or to succumb to utter brutality?" (1845, 128). In the United States, criminalized survival strategies were traversed by a clear racial bias: Latinos, Native-Americans and Black-Americans were criminalized and even lynched for status-based offenses, including 'being too Mexican' (Delgado 2009, 299).

Coarse crimes began to increase significantly by the end of the 17th century and even worsened during the first decades of the 19th century (Rusche and Kirchheimer 1938, 115). Bonger explains that European statistics that portray crime show that 55% of criminalized people responded to crimes of vagrancy and panhandling, and secondly to crimes against property (1905, 546).[38] Needless to say, these statistics reflected a false association between crime and poverty, and fail to show that in a general context of absolute deprivation, subsets of the impoverished sectors committed attacks against property. The dramatic increase of crime statistics was the result of the growing number of coarse crimes but also of their over-criminalization. Not all the pauperized people engaged in crime, because even in desperate situations alternative outlets may arise, without being meritorious to claim a direct association between deprivation and crime. Moreover, it does not mean that the crimes showed by the statistics were unique, or even the most grievous – as we demonstrate through the mechanism of under-criminalization – but only that they were the most over-criminalized. The increase of coarse crimes unfolded in the context of the growing need to discipline the working class as a whole, and protect the increasing number of goods in circulation. As an effect of the industrial expansion, the cities developed numerous ports, large warehouses, and workshops with a considerable mass of raw materials, tools and manufactured objects that belonged to the employer. The difficulties in monitoring all this turn crime

---

38   Regardless of the quality of much of his thought, it is noteworthy that Bonger fails to break away from the prevailing etiological paradigm and fails to distinguish the over-representation of disadvantaged sectors in criminal statistics, which leads him to defend the positivist criminological perspective that sustains the existence of a 'natural crime' (Pegoraro 2010).

against property into an intolerable behavior that required constant policing and a rigorous repression (Foucault 1975, 87). Crime control expanded for the purpose of settling the essential need of respecting private property, regardless of poverty constraints.

Police-medically disciplining over-criminalization was also a key instrument for the discovery of new categories of 'bad' behaviors: what until then was considered as private and tolerable by the community, now called for the intervention of crime control, in line with the conversion of customary rights to offenses during the first disciplining phase. This means that crime control was not limited at this stage to legislating existing offenses, but was aimed at 'creating' crimes out of mere social transgressions:

> Violations of the law are a result of economic causes beyond the control of the legislature but, as evidenced by the implementation of the law on juvenile offenders, to some extent it depends on the official society that certain violations of its rules are a qualified crime or mere transgressions. This difference in nomenclature far from being indifferent decides the fate of thousands of men and determines the moral climate of society. The law can not only punish crimes, but it also can invent them.
>
> MARX 1859

These created crimes focused on the low life – different status-based offenses such as alcoholism, prostitution, gambling, practice of unofficial religions, drug use, "and everything that did not fit the model of bourgeois life, or its imitation model for disciplined proletarians" (Anitua 2005, 190) –. Even the size of a family could attract crime control: criminological positivism argued that there was an inverse relationship between prolificacy and crime, legitimating the bourgeois family model. It was also affirmed that there was a relation between intelligence and crime, asserting the inferiority of the 'dangerous classes' (Lombroso 1887)[39] – a precedent of the contemporary book *The Bell Curve*.[40] Also here, Marx acknowledges that it was in the context of

---

39 Marx himself experienced police-medically disciplinary criminal selectivity because of his physical appearance. Hyndman recounts that when Marx and his family were in deep misery, he set out pawning the silver of his wife's family. The father of historical materialism did not dress too well and did not master English at that time. As he entered the store on a Saturday night, the manager called the police, who detained him until Monday, based on his description as 'a foreign Jew.' Only on Monday was the founder of scientific socialism able to demonstrate, thanks to the statements of 'respectable' friends, that he was not a thief, and that the Campbell silver crown was his legal property (Enzensberg 1974, 390).

40 From the 15th century to today, the coverage of the selective matrix of crime control has led to risky association between criminal behavior and the over-representation of vulnerable

misery and industrial vacancy that "the earnings of the worker are lower, and the young people, deprived of their playground, go to the beer-shops" (1854, 283). Alcoholism spread because "the temptation is great, he cannot resist it, and so when he has money he gets rid of it down his throat. What else should he do? How can society blame him when it places him in a position in which he almost of necessity becomes a drunkard; when it leaves him to himself, to his savagery?" (Engels 1845, 93). Drinking worked even as a food substitute because it was cheaper (Emsley 2007, 140). And it were also these conditions of extreme poverty that promoted prostitution as a possible source of income for female workers.

Marx and Engels are well positioned at the forefront of prevailing criminological schools. At the height of positivism, which conceived the law as a mere regulation of 'natural crime' (Garófalo 1891), the fathers of historical materialism laid the foundation for what a hundred years later would become the labeling approach theory.[41] Marx and Engels identify the mechanisms of primary over-criminalization through which the law selects, from all behaviors that could receive the protection of criminal law, only those that threat the social order, regardless of their social harm. They also perceived another relevant aspect of the police-medically disciplining over-criminalization that was detected by the labeling approach theory in the 1960s as a privileged effect of penal reaction: how it leads to a process of stigmatization. This effect of crime control was clearly foreseen by Marx when he illustrates that "this difference of nomenclature [between crime and transgression], so far from being indifferent, decides on the fate of thousands of men, and the moral tone of society." Criminal intervention encourages segregation. But Marx goes beyond labeling approach – which would be criticized for assessing crime only as a process of definition, neglecting the analysis of the socio-economic structure. In contrast, Marx notes that "it depends to some degree on official society to stamp certain violations of its rules as crimes or as transgressions only." He argues that these processes of 'crime' creation should not be analyzed in isolation, as they respond to the interests of the prevailing social order. In line with the thesis of

---

groups in the crime statistics. To exemplify, *The Bell Curve* (Murray and Herrnstein 1994) suggests a correlation between IQ, the desire to work, and propensity toward crime. Ignoring the selectivity of the criminal justice system can lead to dangerous atavism and biological explanations as enough foundations for crime and disruption.

41   The labeling approach was a breaking point in the study of crime. As mentioned in Chapter 1, in the 1960s, this theory introduced crime control as part of criminological research. Becker (1962), one of its greatest exponents, explains that the social challenged actions of the 'outsiders' were classified as crimes under criminal law, even though they did not involve actual social damage, or it was mild enough not to require the intervention of the criminal justice system.

this book, Marx even suggests that the origin of this process of creating crimes is not new, as it dates back to the Inquisition.[42] The capitalist evolution reinforced conflicts between classes to become more frequent and violent, and further defines more and more behaviors as criminal (Chambliss 1975, 151).

As part of this process of over-criminalization of social transgressions that were previously tolerated, crime control also started to focus on a previously unattended subset of the population: the impoverished youth. Those who until now were considered 'children' began to be approached as 'minor pre-delinquents or criminals,' under the medical discourse of 'moral distress.' Both in Europe and the United States, movements calling for the prosecution of these sectors emerged.[43] The charges consisted of criminalized survival strategies (vagrancy, panhandling) and low life' accusations (immoral conduct). The targeted children were usually detected in fragmented families but only impoverished families were evaluated, while the decency of middle-class families was presumed. The promoters of these reforms professed the union of criminal and medical remedies to avoid contagion, as well as immunization and treatment for the recovery of the 'minors.' They were treated as pathological cases, patients, for whom the medical science had miraculous cures (Anitua 2005, 218).

The increasing concern about criminalized survival strategies, coarse crimes, and the emergence of low life offenses, along with the introduction of new sectors of the population – the poor youth- to crime control, broadened the spectrum of criminalization beyond the traditional limits. Primary

---

42   Marx (1859) identifies the clergy as a social sector with influence on the production of legal standards. Clergy, Marx says, has been exerting influence on the criminal law, broadening the scope of what is considered illegal. Wryly, he remarks that, with its dark views about human nature, the clergy has created more crimes than the sins it has forgiven.

43   The movement of The Child Savers had great resonance in the United States. It was a moral crusade held by a group of reformers that took place in the mid-19th century and operated under the positivist discourse. They were self-proclaimed humanitarians and philanthropists concerned about the economically disadvantaged youth that was not reached by the public education system and that was in a situation of moral vulnerability. Its most active and visible supporters came from the professional middle class. Clergy and doctors were hoping to reform youth, while lawyers provided the technical expertise for drafting and enforcing the new laws. In Europe, England was at the forefront of these processes through the Juvenile Offenders Act of 1874 that initiated a series of reforms in the legislation to take the youth away from the ordinary procedure and subject them to local courts. The Juvenile Courts were established by law in 1908. In most of them, the figure of a medical specialist assessed the defective physical or mental conditions of the children for the purpose of determining their inclination toward crime and suggesting a treatment (Platt 1969, 26).

police-medically over-criminalization transformed 'paupers' into 'criminals:' mere violations committed by urban pauperism to mitigate its absolute impoverishment were converted into crimes, turning poverty into a criminal condition. The moral arguments insisted on the fact that even mere habits of low life – drinking alcohol, non-formal sexual behavior, or loitering in public – needed to be regarded as criminal offenses to defend the social organization. This expansion of crime control molded and stigmatized the lives of ever-larger subsets of the impoverished populations, and it was not the end. *After primary over-criminalization created 'new' crimes and transformed the poor in 'new criminals,' secondary over-criminalization meant that law enforcement agencies, particularly institutions of confinement, turned these 'new criminals' into 'workers,' closing the disciplining circle.*

The leading institutions that became the basis of the logic of confinement were the workhouses (intended for the poor in need of assistance), reformatories (aimed at young people with moral or material distress) and the nascent prisons (aimed at those who had committed a criminal offense). Welfare and crime control became amalgamated under the vein of the medical diagnosis. All three were aimed at including marginal populations in the productive logic. It was not that these sectors (the poor, the youth, the offender) were currently needed in the oversupplied labor market; however, they were needed as a disciplined reserve army. The aim was educating (or retraining) the 'criminal' (the non-proprietary) so that he becomes a benign proletarian; that is, to make him a non-owner that does not threaten property (Pavarini 1980, 194–195). By this logic and although punitive institutions have never been 'useful' in their commercial function, they were successful in their tacit purpose, namely the transformation of the criminal into a proletarian (190).

Workhouses. As an effect of the extensive pauperization, the cost of public assistance significantly increased, and the propertied classes began to rebel against these expenses.[44] At the same time, forced labor in the workhouses was not useful anymore, given surplus masses in the cities (104). Marx and Engels observed the paradoxical consequences of the structural inability of the system to give the proletariat minimum conditions of survival through work: this bourgeoisie was forced to support it, instead of being supported *by* it (1848, 47). The mechanisms of social control – deployed for the purpose of

---

44   Theorists of this new system insisted on the re-educational value of hard work and the superiority of collective versus individual work tasks in cells (Pavarini 1980, 158). The internal organization of prisons, through silence and work, imposed the organization that should shape proletarians in the free world. This 'inside' emerged as an ideal of what should be the 'outside' model (195).

disciplining the unemployed – puzzlingly configured a significant economic burden for the state and a loss of revenue for private capital. Indeed, Marx (1849b) defines workhouses as "those public institutions where the redundant labor population is allowed to vegetate at the expense of bourgeois society." With great irony, he says that "charity is cunningly combined with the revenge which the bourgeoisie wreaks on the wretches who are compelled to appeal to its charity," and states:

> These unfortunate people have committed the crime of having ceased to be an object of exploitation yielding a profit to the bourgeoisie – as is the case in ordinary life – and having become instead an object of expenditure for those born to derive benefit from them; like so many barrels of alcohol which, left unsold in the warehouse, become an object of expenditure to the dealer.

In this context of increasing population in need, and no demand of production in the workhouses, the British New Poor Laws (1834)[45] became a model for all Europe: pauperism stopped being alleviated by charity and started to be systematically redirected to workhouses as the unequivocal solution. In correlation to the principle of less eligibility and in considering the extreme impoverishment of the urban masses, workhouses acquired the character of a last refuge: the last option for the pauperized, only sought as an alternative to dying from poverty-related causes. Welfare was not a 'right' and instead was a degradation of citizenship: workhouses were places where the individual exchanged his freedom for minimum support, acquiring the status of classless or pariah (Ciafardini 2012b). Thus, despite the cruel conditions offered by the factory environment, workhouses were sufficiently terrible to be even 'less eligible' than factories.

Marx warns in *Capital*; workhouses were expected to be 'haunted houses' where people work fourteen hours a day. The idea was transforming them into 'dream job houses' to extirpate "idleness, debauchery and excess, promoting a spirit of industry, lowering the price of labor in our manufactories, and easing the lands of the heavy burden of poor's rates" (1867, 303). People in workhouses lacked enough clothes, food and minimum recreational spaces, while they were obliged to perform unproductive and monotonous activities, as well

---

45   The theoretical foundations of these laws was the Malthusianism – which affirmed that poverty was the result of the fact that the poor increased faster than the production of goods – and the Disciplinarian approach – which asserted the central role of discipline to define policies – (Lopez Castellano 2004).

as being deprived of contact with their family. The conditions were so painful that many died of starvation in this slavery havens-workshops, these 'prisons of misery' (1850, 57). This 'cruel charity' responded to the practical fact that if all the poor in Britain had been suddenly thrown into the street, without any contention, the bourgeois order and the commercial activity would have suffered to an alarming degree.[46] On the other hand, the industry alternated between periods of feverish overproduction that demanded extra labor force and periods of low demand. Therefore, it was necessary to keep this population in reserve during times of unemployment, to have them available when the market required it.

As noted, although England was the paradigmatic model, the situation was similar in the rest of Europe.[47] Meanwhile, in the United States the conditions were even more pronounced: until the 20th century, the poverty line was similar to the one of the pre-industrial and proto-industrial Europe, with the fear of hunger and chronic malnutrition as an everyday reality (Emsley 2007, 253–254). In the beginning, welfare was religiously-oriented and consisted of productive work[48] but this change with the massive industrial deployment of the country. By the 1860s, the United States was already the second most industrialized nation in the world and the primitive ideal of a territorially stable community life was lost. As a result, the private welfare system was abolished and replaced by public aid, forced labor and terrorist-profile workhouses (Pavarini 1980, 135–160).

Prisons. Continuing with the less eligibility analysis, conditions in prisons were even 'less eligible' than those of the workhouses. Through a productive

---

46   Assistance was anchored as a public function at the expense of private charity. It was conceived as an instrument of social protection against the risk of poverty. Charity lost its philanthropic role and began to purely work as a form of containment of the masses with nothing to lose. For this last reason, as Lopez Castellano (2004) points out, the state criminally pursued workers' associations, and mutual aid societies, as a means to prevent rebellion.

47   For example, in Spain, the Law of Vagrants (1845) established a typology of vagrancy, different workshops where they should be detained, and the punishment of imprisonment for two to four years in correctional penitentiaries for bums with aggravating factors. Only paupers with written permission from the Board of Charities were allowed to beg. The Criminal Codes of 1850 and 1870 increased the penalties. Finally, with the General Law of the Charity (1849), the liberal welfare system was configured, providing that public establishments could admit those capable of working (Lopez Castellano 2004).

48   It was a religious approach attached to rigid positions on the static social order and a great sense of community, typical of the first agricultural-colonial settlements. It distinguished between 'guilty' and 'not guilty' poverty, relegating charity to the former and criminalizing the non-resident poor through severe laws against vagrancy, while also trying to absorb the pauperism in the agricultural colonies.

profile in the United States or a place of mere confinement in Europe, prisons offered cramped conditions and operated under oppressive policies that configured them as 'houses of terror' (Marx 1849, 232–245 and 1867, 304). The conditions were atrocious, and a fifth of the detainees died each year (Melossi 1980, 57).

In the United States, the model of absolute solitary confinement was introduced through the Philadelphia system, advocated by Quakers, who encouraged containment and religion as the sole and sufficient basis for re-education. The Philadelphia Society for Alleviating the Misery of Prisons, directed by Benjamin Franklin, was the first organization to "rediscover their good nature solitary confinement as an opportunity to regret." By this logic, the prison of Philadelphia, which became a worldwide model, imposed 23 work-hours a day and three meals a day in the cells. During the hour that prisoners could spend outside, they had to have their head covered to avoid being recognized by the other offenders. There were punishments established for chatting and the only object that the prisoners could have in the cell was a Bible (although freedom of religion was already recognized in the First Amendment to the Constitution). Racial inequality ensured that some jobs were predominantly performed by Black-Americans – such as the work in the kitchens – and others mainly carried out by whites – such as pressing clothes. Because of the number of people who went mad and committed suicide, after 1821, the Pennsylvanian system was replaced by the Auburn model, which consisted of joint work during the day and solitary confinement during the night, always without chatting. This change also responded to the need to alleviate the acute shortage of labor; a product of the rapid industrial development experienced by the country. Europe copied the U.S. model, but the isolated cell system prevailed.[49] When the imprisoned men and women were allowed to work, it was only for punitive purposes, assigning them useless tasks to increase their suffering and the effectiveness of punishment (Pavarini 1980, 161–188).[50]

---

49   In some parts of Europe, prison as a form of punishment was imposed lately or incompletely. In the Netherlands and certain Italian cities, the usurious and commercial capital failed to become industrial capital, and, after a deep recession, the accumulation process resumed its original form: the consequent deterioration of living standards of the exploited classes, and the proletariazation of peasants took place. The principles of differentiated charity prevailed over the large segments of the poor, distinguishing 'useless' poor and 'working' poor, and providing assistance only for the former, while for the latter corporal punishment was applied, essentially through gallows and emigration (Pavarini 1980, 102–105).

50   Pavarini systematizes, following the logic proposed by Rusche and Kirchheimer, that when the labor supply exceeds the demand, prison plays a role in destroying the workforce

Reformatories. As part of the tutelary movements that advocated for the protection of poor young people – the new over-criminalized sector – reformatories and juvenile courts were created. As workhouses and prisons, these new institutions intended to transform the poor youth into a skilled and disciplined labor force (Platt 1969, 23). The courts operated as an instrument of class oppression to restrain urban working class children and assimilate them into the realities and discipline of industrial life (200).

b   *Police-Medically Disciplining Over-Criminalization of the Organized Dissident' Resistance*

Having settled how the mechanisms of police-medically disciplining over-criminalization applied to the urban pauperism, the situation of the organized dissident demands a separate analysis. Organized dissidents were those individuals of the occupied working class that, through their different levels of organization (individual rebellion, trade union, political organization), questioned the existing social order, and the political activists who promoted their interests (such as Marx and Engels). For the organized dissident, the overabundance of the labor force – especially between 1760 and 1815 – conditioned that the silent compulsion of economic relations' regulation replaced violence as the privilege disciplining strategy (Melossi 1975, 58). Marx explains that the pressure of the economy over the occupied workers was such that the laws regulating maximum wages and restrictions on labor mobility became useless: the pressure of the reserve army was enough to push wages downward, thanks to the wide competition for the available jobs (1867, 106).[51] Even though the wages were not even sufficient to cover basic needs (471, n 1)[52] and factories

---

(terrorist profile) and prison labor is applied only as a punishment. In the reverse situation, with steady jobs and increases in wages, prison usefully employed the workforce for reclassifying it and re-inserting it into the labor market (1980, 161–180).

51   The bourgeoisie had no more need for coercive measures as it used to have during the mercantilist period. English laws restricting labor mobility of workers and traders began to fall into disuse in the 18th century and they finally disappeared. Judges abstained from setting rates of wages and all the mechanisms for its regulation also began to disappear; its objective, minimum wage fixing, was no longer necessary (Marx 1867, 106). Specifically, laws stipulating maximum salaries were repealed in England in 1813: "They were an absurd anomaly since the capitalist regulated his factory by his private legislation" (812). That is, they began to be unnecessary because the economic mechanism of capitalist production itself began to regulate the conditions for the sale of the workforce.

52   During the 19th century, European workers experienced conditions of such severe economic oppression, particularly in areas dominated by the manual technique, that they had to combine their salaries with the help of parish charity to survive (Marx 1867, 471, n 1).

were unhealthy places, the pressure of the reserve army was enough to subjugate the industrial workers (Geremek 1986, 252).[53]

The extreme economic oppression and the risk of relapse into pauperism seem to have been powerful enough to render the tool of crime control dispensable. However, Marx shows how the methods of coercion, although typical and dominant in the early establishment of capitalism (primitive accumulation), were preserved in the era of developed capitalism (Mansilla 1965, 44). Crime control was employed to undermine workers' attempts to unionize and as a disciplining assurance against any dissent. Police-medically disciplining over-criminalization took shape under the aegis of the positivist discourse, which characterized the organized dissident as 'dangerous.' This perception helped legitimize the permanent control of the police, even inside the factory (secondary over-criminalization). Police acted with the support of broadly prohibited conducts that incorporated under the criminal prism behaviors that were previously regulated through civil and labor law (primary over-criminalization).

The positivist discourse characterized the organization of the workers as an attack against the social organism and assimilated the characteristics of political activists (particularly those of socialists or anarchists) with those of the 'dangerous' offenders. This discourse found a supposedly scientific foundation in criminal statistics that confirmed that common criminals, troublemakers, radical workers and activists were one and the same thing: a dangerous and criminal class that constituted a serious and growing threat to the existing way of life (Emsley 2007, 134). Newly created offenses, such as conspiracy, corresponded to those fears, and Lombroso's list of 'born criminals' included the anarchists (Ciafardini 2012b). In his work *L'uomo Delinquente* (1887), Lombroso – the greatest exponent of Italian criminological positivism – refers to the 'anarchist' as a criminal stereotype. Along with Laschi (1890), he warns that this type of political offense occurs when progress is too 'sudden and violent,'

Marx notes that there were areas that remained under the manual technique, where the wages of handloom weavers were so inadequate to meet the most basic material needs that the workers had to supplement their pay with parish relief. To illustrate, Marx says that in the textile field, while the power looms shifted to the manual, the latter survived thanks to the handloom weavers, who were employed in a position that allowed them to undergo a reduction in wages that were insufficient to meet basic needs (456, n 1).

53   The fragility of the working class was not reduced to their place in the labor market but absorbed the complexity of their existence: the industrial revolution destroyed their traditional way of life without offering anything in return. Traditional support such as family and community disappeared, while an increasing insecurity challenged the alleged 'economic rationality' of capitalist order (Hobsbawm 1977, 88).

and can lead to 'rebellion.' As opposed to 'revolution'- which is a historical expression of social evolution – 'rebellion' is "a hasty, artificial incubation, with exaggerated temperature, of embryos that are condemned to death." In *Gli Anarchici* (1894), specifically dedicated to the anarchist offender, Lombroso describes this criminal as associated with political offenses. The anarchist – Lombroso argues – was not a true propeller of revolutions but of undesirable premature rebellions. This characterization justified the repression of those who held such ideas and, above all, their admission in mental hospitals to undermine the respect that popular sectors professed for them (Anitua 2005, 186). Meanwhile, Garofalo (1895), the most conservative exponent of criminological positivism, rallied against anarchists and socialists, and Le Bon (1895) denounced 'the multitudes' warning that they emerged when the paleopsíquis and higher brain functions are neutralized (quoted in Zaffaroni 2011, 117).

Positivist discourse helped to legitimate secondary over-criminalization, embodied in the exercise of police power. As an example, the Prefect of the Paris police, named after the revolutionary events of 1848, assimilated activists and offenders in the same category: "It is likely that most of the people involved in these disturbances are swindlers and vagabonds who are only motivated by the desire to plunder and theft. Perhaps some of them are paid by the government's enemies to excite people to disturb the public peace" (quoted in Emsley 2007, 134). In the same vein, the president of the Dutch Society of Prisons expressed its concern that "the prisoners released [by the events in Paris] could play a pernicious role and could threaten and endanger the peace, the possessions, the health and the life of many in the city" (134). Meanwhile, Bonneville Marsagny, theoretical leader of the Second Empire, claimed that the 'moral anarchy' of 1848 was the direct result of the improved treatment of prisoners. Secondary over-criminalization was mainly exerted by continuous policing. Police and factory guards treated workers according to the hegemonic criminal stereotype: they represented the atavistic nature of some on the social fringe that put at risk the society as a whole, their activity contesting the idea of progress:

> No other class is subjected to a surveillance of this kind; it is exercised almost in the same way as that of released prisoners; it seems to place the workers in the category that we now call the dangerous class of society.
>
> *L YATELIER* 1845 quoted in FOUCAULT 1975, 323, n. 22

Also in the United States, and particularly in Chicago, the elites called for the creation of police forces to control the industrial working class that claimed for better-working conditions trough strikes and riots (Mitrani 2013, 6).

This police surveillance rested on an expansive primary over-criminalization that made waywardness committed by the worker subjected to criminal liability. In a promiscuous confusion between labor law and criminal law, the most trivial behaviors were absorbed by crime control. The extensive catalog of prohibited conducts ranged from small faults to political organization. Indeed, all practices of resistance became a crime: mere disobedience, professional misconduct or rebellion perpetrated through the destruction of machinery and goods. All these offenses received the harshest penalties and strict persecution, including torture and the death penalty (recently challenged by the Enlightenment ideal) against political activists and trade unionists. Over-criminalization included the dismantling of liberal rights proclaimed only a few decades earlier. The 'dangerous' character of the working class and its political representatives legitimized the transformation of the liberal rights proclaimed by the Enlightenment (mainly, right to freedom of expression and association) into crimes. Let us analyze them in greater detail.

'Indiscretions' or 'small faults' in the workplace were subjected to primary over-criminalization through a triple overlapping: police functions were confused with those of the factory inspectors, the Civil Code was amalgamated with Criminal Code, and labor rebellion was assimilated with criminal offenses (Marx 1849b). The English Labor Code of 1823 "punished the workers by prison for breaches of contract and the employers merely by modest fines" (Hobsbawm 1962, 192):

> Materially the new factory proletariat was likely to be somewhat better off. On the other hand, it was unfree; under the strict control and the even stricter discipline imposed by the master or his super- visors, against whom they had virtually no legal recourse and only the very beginnings of public protection. They had to work his hours or shifts; to accept his punishments and the fines with which he imposed his rules or increased his profits (208).

A clear example of this mechanism was the Worker's Card, a document issued by the police or municipal authorities, with information about the physical description and trade of its holder. When a worker was hired, he had to accept the terms of the Card's provisions and deliver it to their new employer and, at least in theory, could not get the job otherwise (Emsley 2007, 101–113).[54]

---

54   This card reinforced the workers' subordination and allowed the police to stop them in the street. If they were apprehended on the roads without it, they were charged as vagrants and sentenced to imprisonment. Moreover, hotels and guest house owners had to

The provisions included that, in case of drunkenness, disturbance of the peace, or involvement in brawls, the consequences were the immediate dismissal of the worker. The card also contained indications such as: 'Disobedience and insubordination will mean immediate dismissal;' 'If you arrive ten minutes late to your workplace, you will not be given work on that particular day;' 'If this happens three times, you can be fired;' 'Working hours are from six thirty to noon and from one until darkness' (unspecified fixed schedule); or 'The dismissal is recorded in the worker's Card and, if that the reason has been a punishment, the worker may not file a request for re-employment or in the same workplace or other municipal works.' The Card established that the police must be given notice whenever workers were dismissed as a form of punishment. Marx (1849b) asks then about the relevance of the police intervention in the cancellation of a civil agreement, such as a contract of employment: "Is the municipal worker a convict? [...] Would you not deride the citizen who denounced you to the police for having broken some delivery contract, or failed to pay a bill when it was due, or drunk too much on New-Year's eve? Of course, you would!"

The first attempts of rebellion were also absorbed by crime control. The most emblematic form was the destruction of industrial machines by groups dubbed as 'Luddites' (named after a fictional character, Ned Ludd, created to unify the claims of the workers), which was a primitive form of rebellion against the steam power loom (the emblem of the Industrial Revolution). The workers thought that they could abolish capitalism by destroying the machines, which were the apparently responsible for layoffs and lower wages:

> They direct their attacks not against the bourgeois conditions of production, but against the instruments of production themselves; they destroy imported wares that compete with their labor, they smash machinery into pieces, they set factories ablaze, they seek to restore by force the vanished status of the workman of the Middle Ages.[55]
>
> MARX and ENGELS 1848, 18

---

inform local commissioners about their visitors. Thus, everywhere in Europe in the early 19th century, men began to measure and take note of what was considered the problems of crime and criminal classes (Emsley 2007, 101–113).

55   Marx and Engels add that "[t]he rebels workers, destroy the goods of others that make them competitive, destroy the machines, set fire to factories, struggling to return to the situation and buried the medieval worker." Destroying the machines was intended to return society to a previous, idyllic situation, roll back production, and that, therefore, was a form of rebellion that could not succeed. Marx affirms that workers did not know how to distinguish the machinery from its capitalist employment (1867, 355). This form of rebellion was restricted in time and space: the biggest wave of Luddite attacks occurred

These acts were severely over-criminalized and gave "the anti-Jacobin governments of a Sidmouth, a Castlereagh, and the like, a pretext for the most reactionary and forcible measures" (Marx 1867, 468): new laws condemned the
destruction of machinery with the death penalty and banishment to Australia
(Rude 1964, 88–92). This means that a rebellion that damaged only material
goods was assigned the most severe punishments for the purpose of disciplining the 'dangerous classes.'

The first attempts of union and political organization received an even
more stern response from crime control. The worker stood as an irreducible
adversary of the bourgeois, the bearer of an inadmissible hope: the revolution
for a classless society (Pavarini 1980b, 42). Workers' associations were defined
as associations of criminals and criminal proletarian as potential criminals.
Primary over-criminalization even applied to the use of the press by workers'
organizations.[56] In this context, Engels claimed that persecution was redoubled towards immigrant activists, in a striking parallel with the 21st-century
over-criminalization towards foreigners:

> Half of the editorial staff were prosecuted; the other half were liable to
> deportation as non-Prussians. Nothing could be done about it, as long
> as a whole army corps stood behind the government. We had to surren-
> der our fortress, but we withdrew with our arms and baggage, with band
> playing and flag flying, the flag of the last, red issue (1884, 174).

The right to freedom of expression proclaimed in the very first disciplining
phase found its limit in its use as a form of organization and protest. Disrespect for the disciplining guidelines was the turning point for the conversion
of rights into crimes. The most dramatic example was the 'crime of anonymity:'
a common resistance mechanism that consisted of writing anonymous documents, especially letters, that were broadcast as social protest, through riots, revolts, rebellions or insurrections (Thompson 1984). This harmless offense was

---

between 1811 and 1812, beginning with lace and weavers' stockings Nottingham, Leicester,
and Derby. There were then minor waves in 1814 and 1816 (Rude 1964, 88–92).

56   The Prussian edict of 1819 prohibited the freedom of the press as a mechanism for mobilization of the working class (Marx 1843). French laws of 1835 allocated imprisonment and
large fines in cash to acts of the press that attempted to undermine the current political
regime (1871). Marx and Engels themselves suffered the close of the Communist Party
newspaper. In Germany, "[t]he repressive laws by which the declaration of a state of siege
was left to the discretion of the government, the press still more firmly muzzled, and the
right of association annihilated, absorbed the whole of the legislative activity of the National Assembly during the months of June, July, and August" (1850, 115).

assigned the punishment of the death penalty, as it was considered an extraordinary crime. Likewise, attempts to unionize were also subjected to primary over-criminalization to such an extent that, even in England, the strike and the abandonment of the workplace were punished with galleys and confinement in houses of correction.[57] In France, the right of association, proclaimed by the Revolution of 1789, was taken away from the workers just two years later.[58] An Executive Order declared all labor coalitions as an 'attack on freedom and the Declaration of the Rights of Man.' The punishment was a fine of 500 pounds, and deprivation of active citizenship for one year.[59] By parliamentary legerdemain, resources that could defend workers during strikes were subtracted from the common law and incorporated into criminal emergency legislation (Marx 1867, 813). Regarding political organization itself, the most terrible prosecution was carried against the Fenians, who attempted to act for Irish independence in 1870. Marx wryly says:

> Above all, the British government is rich and the press, as you know, incorruptible. Moreover, the British régime is a model government [...] Of course, it would also be a crime against freedom of speech if I told these countrymen that in the country of the bourgeois freedom is punishable by twenty years of forced labor what in the country of the headquarters [in Ireland] is punishable by six months in jail.
>
> 1870 quoted in LEVRERO 1979, 203

A hundred years after the birth of the prison as a replacement for torture, the latter still governed crimes related to labor organization: Fenians were

---

57   The formation of coalitions of workers was considered a great crime and, between 1799 and 1800 different laws prohibited them. These laws were only partially repealed in 1825. In practice, persecution of coalitions and even simple propaganda for the accession of the workers to unions and participation in strikes were considered 'coercion' and 'violence' and treated as a common law offense (Marx 1867, 811).

58   Although this legislation chronologically corresponds to the beginning of the social-disciplinary order, its characteristics respond to the police-medically disciplining prism that tended to undermine the formal proclamations of the first disciplining phase.

59   Article I of the act stated that: "As one of the foundations of the French Constitution is the abolition of all kinds of associations of citizens of the same state and profession, it is prohibited under any pretext or restore them in any form." Article IV stated: "[...] if citizens of the same profession, industry or trade conspire and agree to refuse jointly exercise their industry or job or not paid to exercise rather than a certain price, these agreements and confabulations [...] shall be regarded as contrary to the Constitution and as prejudicial to liberty and the Rights of Man" (Marx 1867, 47 n 4).

subjected to corporal punishment, 35 days in a dark cell, an iron neck chain
that linked them with a cart loaded with stones, a bread and water diet, permanent transfers, etcetera, all worse than the treatment of ordinary prisoners
(204). Since 1793 the British government:

> [...] suspended all laws except that of the brutal violence. Thus, thou-
> sands of men were imprisoned in Ireland, just because they were sus-
> pected of Fenianism, without even being convicted or taking to court,
> even without being charged. But the government was not content with
> stealing freedom, and still tortured them in the cruelest way (205).

In Germany, the government unleashed a wave of repression against the
uprisings of 1848, particularly in 1851 and 1852, including communists' prosecutions and the incorporation of the criminal offense of international conspiracy. Marx's wife expressed in a letter to A. Claus: "You can imagine how the
'Marx Party' is active day and night [...] All the allegations of the police are lies.
They steal, forge, break open desks, swear false oaths [...] claiming they are
privileged to do so against Communists, who are beyond the pale of society!"
(J. Marx 1852 quoted in Hirst 1975, 275). Engels (1852) and Marx (1852b) described how the Communist Party, along with others, was barred from being
legally organized by the suppression of association and assembly rights. Their
leaders were deported or imprisoned. In 1852, eleven members of the Communist League in Cologne were accused of high treason, and seven were
sentenced to imprisonment in a fortress for periods of 3 to 6 years (Marx and
Engels 1848, 7). Over-criminalization was a permanent obstacle to attempts of
political organization by the founders of the First Communist International.[60]
   In Spain, primary over-criminalization banned the right of assembly and
association.[61] Although, in practice, a clear distinction was made between the

---

60   They even moved from one place to another, chasing the kindest legislation. When they
     had to decide where to install the party newspaper, Engels pointed out that, in Berlin, the
     political processes were judged by professional judges, while on the Rhine, the Napole-
     onic Code was unaware of press crimes because it assumed the censorship regime and a
     jury jurisdiction that qualified only for political offenses. Likewise, after the revolution,
     Schlöffel was sentenced to one year in prison for a small offense in Berlin; however, in the
     Rhine, they enjoyed an unconditional freedom of the press, and they took full advantage
     of it (1884, 174). Of course, they did not only assess the level of permeability of the rules:
     Marx and Engels assumed the importance of the law as a thermometer of the material
     conditions for the organization of the workers.
61   The Criminal Code of 1822 expressly provided the elimination of societies that did not
     have a license from the government. While acknowledging the right of assembly, it held it

rights of those groups considered harmless (mutual aid, recreation, charity, culture-instruction), and those suspected of attempting to violate the current order. The Criminal Code of 1848 devotes several articles to "riots, [...] illegal associations [and] machinations to alter the price of labor," describing them as "crimes against internal security." In 1855, disturbance of the order was met with capital punishment. In 1874, the government established the dissolution of all political organizations and societies, such as the International Working-men's Association. The argument was that they violated property, family and other social bases (Lopez Castellano 2004).

Thus, throughout Europe, police-medically disciplining over-criminalization meant that, at the level of primary over-criminalization, any waywardness committed by the worker was liable to fit a criminal offense, in a promiscuous confusion between labor law and the criminal law. That is, the more trivial behaviors, regardless of the administrative or labor nature of the conflict, were absorbed by crime control, the indispensable ally of economic discipline. The medical aspect responded to the characterization of the workers as 'dangerous classes,' legitimizing their exceptional treatment by the criminal law. In turn, secondary over-criminalization, perpetrated by police and factory guards, applied the rules on the workers, treated through the hegemonic criminal stereotype: they represented the atavistic nature of some on the social fringe that put at risk the society as a whole, their activity contesting the ideal of progress:

> No other class is subjected to a surveillance of this kind; it is exercised almost in the same way as that of released prisoners; it seems to place the workers in the category that we now call the dangerous class of society.
>
> L YATELIER 1845 QUOTED IN FOUCAULT 1975, 323, n. 22

Ultimately, the capitalist mode of production demanded a docile labor force and the protection of the means of production: these goals are secured through repression or ideology, depending on the degree of social consciousness and the level of organization of the dispossessed sectors (Pierce 1976, 84–85). With the escalation of such social conflict during the 19th century, repression was the answer and all practices of resistance became a crime: mere disobedience, professional misconduct, or rebellion perpetrated through the destruction of

---

to authorization by the local authority, and it criminalized as 'public uproar' or 'scandal' any meeting with more than forty people. The decree on political associations of 1834 underlined the evils that secret societies produced in social and political life and stipulated for them punishments ranging from a simple fine to imprisonment and exile (Lopez Castellano 2004).

machinery and goods, all received the harshest penalties and strict persecution. This included torture and the death penalty (recently challenged by the Enlightenment ideal) against political activists and trade unionists. Finally, over-criminalization included those liberal rights proclaimed only a few decades earlier to fall within the criminal orbit: the 'dangerous' character of the working class and its political representatives legitimized the transformation of the rights of expression and into crimes, with the crudest penalties and the most relentless persecution.

In sum, based on the various works of Marx and Engels, this second disciplining phase showed disengagement with the disciplining legal ideal of the late 18th century, as a result of the collision between formal proclamations and the prevailing social inequality. This was justified through alleged biological deficiencies of the criminalized individuals, who were identified by the nascent police forces following the positivist paradigm. The social and crime conflict was intensified in light of the increasing impoverishment of the excluded masses, and the proliferation of unions of industrial workers, in parallel to the expansion of imperialist competition for the conquest of new territories and markets. Crime control was deployed through the mechanism of police-medically disciplining under-criminalization and police-medically disciplining over-criminalization. The former applied to the acts perpetrated by the great powers in the colonial territory, oriented towards the plunder of natural resources and local labor forces, and to the acts perpetrated by the manufacturing bourgeoisie to orient the working class to the industrial discipline, both acting under the legitimation of the prevailing positivist discourse. Over-criminalization particularly focused on the conflicting sectors, that were classified as 'dangerous and criminal classes,' including the urban pauperism and the organized dissident.

Under these conditions, the next modality adopted by the criminal selectivity in the 20th century will be analyzed.

Third Disciplining Phase: Socio-Disciplining Criminal Selectivity (*Early to Late 20th Century*)

At the birth of the 20th century, imperialism was in plain development (Lenin 1916). It was characterized by the formation of monopolies and oligopolies in various branches of the economy, the concentration of capital that displaced those smaller capitalists that were unable to compete successfully, and the intensification of international competition for markets and raw materials. In this framework, a new form of criminal selectivity, that will be called *socio-disciplining criminal selectivity*, took place. This modality of criminal selectivity adopted by crime control in the *third disciplining phase* was built on more flexible criminal policies and based on a sociological discourse that encouraged the social inclusion of 'problematic' sectors in the context of welfare states. This modality was utilized through the mechanisms of *socio-disciplining under-criminalization* and *socio-disciplining over-criminalization*.

While it took place after the theoretical production of Marx and Engels, the analysis of this modality is constructed from a materialistic approach, using various inputs from the Marxist contemporary thought as well as some passages in which Marx and Engels have tangentially addressed elements of the social processes of this period.

The transition from police-medically disciplining criminal selectivity towards this new modality came earlier and was more pronounced in the United States. The country became the most dynamic nation after World War I, the center of an exponential economic growth and a magnet for migrant masses from Europe. In Europe, welfare policies were equally developed but the positivist paradigm remained relevant until the 1970s.

Regarding conflict-control, the social conflict found its axial points in the first major economic crisis of modern capitalism (1890 and 1929) and the two World Wars. These episodes ended the illusion of the linear and indefinite progress of capitalism. Moreover, the revolutionary processes in the eastern hemisphere, with its axis in the Russian revolution of 1917, sowed fear among elites in regards to the possible destabilization of the western workers. Finally, this social conflict became deeper in the context of the confrontation between the capitalist and the communist blocs during the Cold War.

Social control took place through the emergence of welfare states, which introduced interventionist policies to prevent the social disintegration caused by the self-regulating market system (Polanyi, 1944) and to discourage revolutionary outputs. Welfare states assumed the emerging problems but characterized them as non-structural (as opposed to the vision of communism) and, therefore, susceptible to reform through social policies and monitoring practices within the framework of capitalism. This deployed the 'wage society,' a society of full employment, increasingly homogeneous, where wage labor afforded status and dignity through labor rights and social protection in exchange of discipline (Castel 2003, 45). The state worked to reduce risks and provide social protection through the registration of individuals in collective organizations such as collective labor, unions, collective regulations of labor law, and social protection, which ensured their control (50–51). This led, both in Europe and in the United States, to a marked reduction in the gap between the most favored and the worse-off sectors (Piketty 2013).[62]

---

62   In Europe, the top 10% of the population with more resources lost part of them due to the war of 1914–1918, and the concessions that the bourgeoisie gave throughout the struggles

Crime conflict found the United States in a process of great economic development and heavy industrialization with an abundance of capital and lack of manpower. The growing cities received a huge migratory movement from internal rural areas and from the poorer countries of Europe. This resulted in what was termed 'social disorganization:' socio-cultural difficulties in the integration of large heterogeneous populations concentrated in anonymized cities.[63]

These masses were not in a situation of 'absolute deprivation' (the inability to meet basic material needs), characteristic of the primary and second disciplining phases, because the current great economic growth incorporated them into the labor market (at least until the crisis of 1929). However, the problem of 'relative deprivation' (Merton 1949) emerged. This refers to the impossibility of individuals to meet imposed cultural standards (the so-called 'American Dream') through the available legitimate means. These masses had basic means of subsistence but were 'relatively' deprived in relation to the goods that the consumer society disseminated as necessary to achieve success and happiness (certain cars, new technological devices, clothing of specific brands, etcetera). Relative deprivation represented the desire of a great mass of people to consume and their inability to earn enough money to meet those desires (Chambliss 1975, 150). This process had been previously warned of by Marx, who mentioned how the modern factory, even in his time, produced huge quantities of goods that fed the public's desire, which increased the greed of people (1867, 674). Similarly, Bonger showed that property crimes were not strictly linked to poverty (1905, 572).[64]

---

that took place after the World War I. The decline continued after World War II for the same reasons, and the share of the richest 10% reached its minimum in 1975 (a little less than 60%). The wealth held by the richest 1% described the same curve going from a little over 50% in 1810, to just over 60% in 1910. The decline began in 1910 and reached the lowest values between 1970 and 1975 (20%) and then began to increase again. The development of the United States followed the same timeline, leading to a historically low level of private capital in the years 1950–1960 (Piketty 2013).

63   The Chicago School and its most representative work, *The City* (1925) written by Park, Burgess and Mckenzie, sustain that the problem of crime no longer resided in the biological conditions of the individuals (as positivism affirmed), but in the characteristics of the urban area in which they live that can cause 'social disorganization.'

64   Bonger illustrates that the division between rich and poor people goes back centuries and does not belong exclusively to capitalism, but the particularity of this system is the distance between those extremes. Cities where the contrasts between poverty and wealth were higher, also show very high levels of property crime. Bonger defended the improvement of the socio-economic conditions to prevent 'crimes of misery' (what is referred to here as absolute deprivation), but noted that such improvement increases 'crimes of greed' (1905, 572). Outside Marxism, Quetelet also raises the concept of 'relative poverty,'

The concept of relative deprivation was of great importance in explaining criminality in all social classes, unlike the classic concept of 'absolute deprivation' that linked crime to poverty. Relative deprivation also served to unravel why crime did not decrease despite the inclusive policies, as it clarifies that, although there was a distributive improvement, society remained strongly unequal; "between the bottom and the top of the scale of wages hierarchy, incomes' differences [were] substantial" (Castel 2003). Those differences in income, in combination with strong consumption patterns that were unattainable for those at the bottom of the ladder, conditioned the tendency to commit coarse crimes.

However, the focus of attention for crime conflict was not on the coarse crimes because they were partially absorbed through inclusive policies of non-punitive social control. Crime control focused on the organized dissident who challenged the existing cultural goals and proposed the construction of a different political organization (the 'rebellion' mode of adaptation in Merton's categorization). Particularly, crime control focused on those with communist affiliations and supporters of the Russian revolution of 1917, on African-American activists who challenged racial inequality, and on anti-war activists. Crime control was also deployed on the one sector that ignores the existing cultural goals: the 'retreatism' mode of adaptation in Merton's analysis – or 'deviant' as identified by Becker (1962) – who did not fit the disciplining guidelines that encouraged submission to wage labor.

Crime control was deployed through the mechanism of over-criminalization which focused on the mentioned sectors with more lenient approaches than in the previous disciplining phases. It was not possible to stand the ideal of equality that arose from the social contract of the legally-disciplining criminal selectivity. It was not possible either to expose selectivity in the explicit and grotesque way in which the police-medically disciplining criminal selectivity did. Biological atavism as an explanation for why certain populations and social sectors were determined to be criminals was discredited by scientific progress. Moreover, the positivist paradigm was also disgraced by the great economic crisis of 1890 and 1929 that belied its proclamations of unlimited 'order and progress.' The experience of Nazism, operating as an application of positivists postulates, also shattered confidence in the positivist discourse

---

even prior to Merton, and says that the great inequality between poverty and welfare in the same area incite the commission of violent crimes inspired by envy. He affirms that this is especially true when changes in economic conditions cause the impoverishment of some people, while others retain their status (quoted in Taylor et al. 1974, 37–38).

(Zaffaroni et al. 2000, 161).[65] In consequence, crime control chose to ignore the general equality of all before the law, and mediated conflicts between unequal sectors. Any idea of contract was definitively lost and discipline triumphed (Melossi 1999, 87); i.e. this modality of criminal selectivity finally buried the contractual remnants that still lingered in the legally-disciplining criminal selectivity and it applied control in indulgent ways that pursued the disciplining of conflicting sectors, based on a sociological explanation of crime.

Durkheim (1895, 1917), who would be recognized as the father of sociology – conceiving society through a paradigm of order and control –, was the one who developed the theoretical guidelines that explained conflict-control throughout the first half of the 20th century. His theoretical perspective avoided the ambitious goal of eliminating crime and conceived it as a 'social fact' that was positive because its reprimand strengthened 'social cohesion.' For Durkheim, the only limit was the amount of crime: to be considered a normal social fact, crime did not have to exceed certain level. In contrast to this theoretical position, Marx, ironically praised the advent of crime for its encouragement of a multiplicity of productive areas:

> The criminal produces not only crimes but also criminal law, and with this also the professor who gives lectures on criminal law and in addition to this the inevitable compendium in which this same professor throws his lectures onto the general market as "commodities" [...]The criminal moreover produces the whole of the police and of criminal justice, constables, judges, hangmen, juries, etc.; and all these different lines of business, which form just as many categories of the social division of labor, [...] Torture alone has given rise to the most ingenious mechanical inventions, and employed many honorable craftsmen in the production of its instruments [...]In this way he keeps it from stagnation, and gives rise to that uneasy tension and agility without which even the spur of competition would get blunted. Thus he gives a stimulus to the productive forces (1861–1863).[66]

---

65   However, the positivist paradigm was not completely eradicated: it has been shaping the exercise of criminal selectivity up to the present, but no longer as the hegemonic modality of crime control.

66   Marx's palpable irony in this passage, read in the context of his overall theoretical contributions, illustrates that he did not believe crime to be inevitable: "What Marx had seen more clearly than later functionalists, such as Durkheim, was that viewing activities in functional terms drives one into the absurd position of seeing crime as a necessary feature of society. For Marx and us it is not. This passage must be read as a polemic against functional analysis [Indeed,] Marx is asserting the possibility of a crime- free society by

Marx mocks the possibility of considering crime as a productive activity that could encourage the 'social division of labor' and 'social cohesion.' On the contrary, he acknowledges that the current economic and social system must have something 'rotten' to be continually producing crime (1859). In his later work, Engels also argues that crime, far from being something positive, was a reprehensible act inherent to the functioning of capitalism, where the supreme value of private property governs: "From the moment when private ownership of movable property developed, all societies in which this private ownership existed had to have this moral injunction in common: Thou shalt not steal." Engels continues:

> Does this injunction thereby become an eternal moral injunction? By no means. In a society in which all motives for stealing have been done away with, in which therefore at the very most only lunatics would ever steal, how the preacher of morals would be laughed at who tried solemnly to proclaim the eternal truth: Thou shalt not steal! (1878, 52).

Indeed, the positive value that Durkheim gives to crime was grounded in a legitimization of the capitalist system of production, which was (and remains) unable to eradicate crime because it cannot solve the social conflicts that condition its emergence.[67]

Socially-Disciplining Under-Criminalization

The concept of *socially-disciplining under-criminalization* refers to the scarce and narrow legislation of those negative social behaviors mostly committed by the ruling classes (primary under-criminalization) and its rare prosecution (secondary under-criminalization). The two World Wars and economic

---

demonstrating, albeit ironically, the normal interdependence, not of an industrial society or a certain division of labor and crime, but quite specifically, of capitalist productive social relationships and crime" (Taylor et al. 1973, 226).

67   In other words, according to Marx and Engels, crime is a 'normal social fact,' as Durkheim says. However, it is not 'normal' because it has positive effects but because of its inherence to the capitalist mode of production. As demonstrated during the previous sections, the current system of production, since its foundation, has been associated with the perpetration of crimes. Moreover, unlike Durkheim, for Marx it is not possible to say that crime is functional to the social order, as it is a complex phenomenon that involves both functional and dysfunctional elements. As was evident even in the context of the primitive accumulation, crime justified the application of a functional crime control, but was also a dysfunctional element that damaged the interest of the ruling class in protecting private property.

crimes were the focus of socially-disciplining under-criminalization. It will be suggested that the purpose of these behaviors was to recover and fortify capital following economic crisis, while they were justified as normal (and even desirable) social facts.

Economic crimes were developed in the form of white-collar crimes – which referred to the great variety of wrongful acts committed by individual practitioners in the course of their business (Sutherland 1940 and 1949) – and organized crime – namely, a type of corporate crime whose maximum expression was the U.S. mafias (Virgolini 2005).

'White-collar crimes' were defined as "crime[s] committed by a person of respectability and high social status in the course of their occupation" (Sutherland 1949, 65). Following the great wave of immigration in the United States and the industrial development of the 'golden years,' a huge amount of liberal professions developed (bankers, pharmaceutics, small shops owners). Their particularity was that they combined their lawful occupation with systematic violations of the activity's regulations. Regardless of its extension, white-collar crimes preserved most of the features of the crime perpetrated by the manufacturing bourgeoisie in the framework of police-medically disciplining criminal selectivity: they had an individual character (they were committed by private individuals under a decentralized mode) and were perpetrated in the course of lawful activities (and, thus, their authors did not respond to the marginal stereotype, but to the average professional one).

Meanwhile, 'organized crime' referred to a set of culturally disapproved activities: gambling, prostitution, distribution of alcohol during Prohibition, and an extortive protection system. These activities increased with the exponential population growth and increasing buying power (particularly until the crisis of 1929 and after World War II). They were perpetrated by people linked to the criminal stereotype: members of a hierarchical organization linked through bonds of fidelity founded on racial identity, secret societies, family ties and the use of violence (Virgolini 2005, 335). Organized crime was a type of offense no longer committed by an individual (as it was the case of the white-collar crimes), but collectively. It was not the result of a combination of legal and illegal activities, but it rested almost exclusively in illegal activities. Its most widespread expression was the U.S. mafias that emerged during Prohibition, through the development of a large black market of alcohol, mainly in Chicago and New York.

Despite the expansion of white-collar crimes and the rawness of the organized crime, they were mostly under-criminalized. With regard to primary under-criminalization, the mechanisms designed to favor these behaviors multiplied (Veblen 1989). Under the welfare state, bureaucracy steadily increased and its agents played a crucial role in minimizing the sanction of criminal laws that regulate economic crimes. Bills aimed at strengthening the criminalization of this kind of behaviors were systematically frustrated: for example, between 1879 and 1907, 140 laws on food and drugs were introduced in Congress and all failed because of the influence of the people who might be affected by the regulation (Sutherland 1949, 175). In the few cases regulated by criminal law, the prescribed penalties were relatively light compared to crimes such as theft, especially in relation to the differential damage that they caused (Bonger 1905, 606).

In regard to secondary under-criminalization, the number of people imprisoned for economic crimes was very limited (607), and the treatment that the criminal agencies provided to them was markedly more benevolent than in the case of ordinary crimes: while the thief or fraudster who had won great wealth with his crimes was more likely to avoid the severe punishment meted out to the coarse criminal (Veblen 1989). While the crimes of the lower classes were handled by police, prosecutors and judges who imposed imprisonment and death, the crimes of the highest class resulted in total official inaction or they were manipulated by inspectors or administrative commissions. These public servants only gave warnings, occasionally the loss of a license, to the economic criminals. Only in extreme cases, fines or prison sentences were imposed (Sutherland 1949, 179).

Particularly interesting was this type of under-criminalization that treated these economic crimes through civil proceedings, in a continuation with the logic of the police-medically disciplining criminal selectivity. Many acts that had a criminal content, such as the intentional breach of the law with serious social harm effects, violence and injury, were not judged under criminal law, but by civil proceedings (179). While statistics exposed that less than 2% of persons subjected to prison belonged to the highest class, those numbers did not respond to the criminal reality, but to 'biased samples' and therefore produced misleading conclusions. Sutherland contributes to shape the concept of 'black holes' – materialization of the mechanism of secondary under-criminalization – that refers to a hidden criminality, officially unknown, and concealed through distorted criminal statistics.

The central element of secondary under-criminalization of white-collar crimes had to do with the link between the private and the public sector. From a relationship of mere cooperation between state agencies and perpetrators during the second disciplining phase, white-collar crimes initiated a path towards a symbiotic confluence between public and private interests (Pegoraro 2011). Indeed, the socio-economic configuration of imperialism, with the growth of the monopolistic concentration that absorbed the smaller merchants in a fierce competition for markets, favored all kinds of illegal behaviors in the struggle for business survival, including this initial symbiosis in pursuit of permanent impunity.[68] This was noted by Marx in Volume III of *Capital*, where he describes the tendency of the rate of profit to decline, and the process of capital concentration and centralization by expropriation of small capitalists. He adds that this process finally results in the centralization of existing capital in a few hands, and the undercapitalization of many capitalists (1867, 355).

Concerning organized crime, the symbiosis raised on the widespread corruption of the police and the public servants engaged in control, as well as on the extension of violent crimes linked to business (Trasher 1927; Wayne 2010, 1168). This means that the initiatory symbiosis with the public sector not only empowered secondary under-criminalization, but also facilitated the perpetration of the crimes. In Chicago, the homicide rate increased 21% in response to the emergence of organized crime linked to alcohol smuggling, while 250,000 people died nationwide by drinking alcohol produced in poor condition (Escohotado 1983). However, this did not lead to the investigation of this kind of illegal behavior: the figures show that in 1920 Chicago had 35,000 gang members and 10,000 young adults working in organized crime groups, and that from 975 murders, only two derived in a sentencing (Hagedorn 2009). Just as an anecdotal example, the famous Al Capone was sentenced to eleven years in prison when he was found guilty of 5 of the 23 charges for the crime of fraud on October 11, 1931, but not for the acts of smuggling or for the multiple homicides that he perpetrated to consolidate his business (Brown 1915, 729).

The other side of the secondary under-criminalization was the over-criminalization of the most vulnerable individuals who violated the Prohibition by consuming alcoholic beverages (consumers). Consequently, federal prisons had 4,000 prisoners before the ban, but, in the early 1930s, they had more than 25,000 (Asbridge and Weerasinghe 2008. 361–362). This was seen by public opinion as a 'crime wave' when, in fact, crime rates as they pertained to events outside the Prohibition had stabilized and the arrests linked with alcohol consume were the ones that filled the prisons (Wayne 2010, 1168).

In the military field, socio-disciplining under-criminalization was reflected in the imperialist escalation, which enabled the perpetration of large exterminations: eight million people were killed in 1884 in the colonized Belgian

---

68   While trusts and cartels were banned by federal law in 1890, in the 20th century a large
      number of mergers in holding companies were authorized by other regulatory laws, in
      what was known as the 'societies revolution.' Specifically, the annulment of competition
      was associated with the crisis of 1929. Interestingly, opposition to monopolies was en-
      couraged by farmers and workers, while the less advanced capitalist sector of the econo-
      my developed a popular movement to defend their own interests (Duménil 2006, 181).

Congo, a million Armenians were massacred between 1915 and 1922, and between two and three million individuals were eliminated in Bangladesh by the Pakistani government in 1971 (Morrison 2006). The two World Wars were also unfolded under a form of conquest, banditry and theft, in which the predatory centers of global power dragged everyone to war (Lenin 1916). Polanyi proposes a reading of these great wars as a massive reorganization of capital, the state, and social relations, what he characterized as a 'great transformation.' He argues that the propelled destruction of society was neither the result of the devastation of war, nor the revolt of the proletariat in Russia or the fascist lower middle class in Italy, Germany or Spain. It was the conflict between the market and the basic requirements of social life, compared with which the great wars were simple accelerators of the process (1944, 110).

Regardless of the severity and extent of these crimes, their prosecution was minimal, both nationally and globally. With regard to its legal reception at the international level, primary under-criminalization tended to adopt a minimum amount of criminal provisions related to the socially harmful actions of the great powers. In this sense, the most relevant international standard was the Convention on the Prevention and Punishment of the Crime of Genocide of the United Nations (1948), but it limited the legal definition of 'genocide' to render it inapplicable for most of the committed acts because it "was developed to measure the great powers at the beginning of the Cold War" (Zaffaroni 2011, 423). The annihilation of political groups was excluded from the definition of 'genocide,' with the object of under-criminalizing the acts committed in the Union of Soviet Socialist Republics (U.S.S.R.) against dissenters. The requirement of 'annihilation' in categorizing genocide tended to exclude the European neocolonialist massacres in Asia and Africa, as well as the bombing of Hiroshima and Nagasaki at the end of the World War II (424–425). Meanwhile, the Nuremberg Trials introduced the concept of 'crime against humanity,' consolidating a breakthrough for the prosecution of these acts. Notwithstanding this, primary under-criminalization appears in the conspicuous absence of the crime of 'torture,' as well as in the absence of the concept of 'human rights' (Sueiro 2008, 1339).

Concerning secondary under-criminalization, the Nuremberg statute empowered the creation of an International Tribunal constituted of representatives of the four main countries that won the World War II. It authorized them to exercise universal jurisdiction on behalf of the international community for crimes against humanity and war crimes committed outside their national territories and against non-citizens. By this logic, and despite the significant progress of these statutes, the only specific processes for acts committed during the great wars had been the Nuremberg and Tokyo Tribunals.

Socially-Disciplining Over-Criminalization

The concept of *socio-disciplining over-criminalization* refers to the broad and abundant legislation (primary over-criminalization) and emphatically prosecution (secondary over-criminalization) of coarse crimes – in continuity with primitive accumulation. The focus was also on those activities considered politically controversial or deviant. Deviance referred not only to the committing criminalized survival strategies but also to alcoholism, gambling, playing jazz, consuming marijuana and incurring in homosexual practices (Becker 1962), in a logic that perpetuated the over-criminalization of the 'low life,' as it happened during the second disciplining phase.

Welfare policies generated better conditions for all strata of the working class, whose wages and employment benefits improved. Only in the United States, more than a hundred of welfare programs were created (Piven and Cloward 1969). These social policies operated as privileged mechanisms of social control, in relation to the prevailing economic and social needs, demanding the reduction of social unrest and the appeasement of possible revolutionary outputs, under an inclusive and reform-driven discourse (577–582). Against all conspiratorial reading, many theorists and welfare agents actually trusted in the humanistic character of the change. In *The Affluent Society* (1958), Galbraith optimistically predicted that it was possible for the United States to overcome poverty and that an affluent society could be achieved. Galbraith, however, kept characterizing the causes of poverty as individual-based and claimed that those causes could be transformed through social policies oriented to create citizens in the full sense. As Marx express, aid to the poor was just one of several necessary 'capitalist production expenses' in critical moments of the class struggle (quoted in Mishra 1975, 298).

In accordance with a broad reading of the principle of less eligibility, this expansion of welfare conditioned the benevolence and laxity of crime control. The latter preserved its selective and disciplining matrix but under more lenient forms that promoted the rehabilitation of offenders in order to ensure their disciplining and to placate the possible revolutionary outcomes of social turbulence. This lenient crime control found a double orientation. On the one hand, it was deployed in more flexible interventions as an alternative to traditional sentences (probation, mediation, parole) that were shaped by the rehabilitative paradigm. Described as 'penal welfarism,' this new form of crime control encouraged specialization and professionalization (Garland 2001, 74–81). Technical teams consisting of psychologists and social workers were in charge of evaluations, reports and treatments, as the new experts of the criminal justice system; all to the detriment of the medical profession which was hegemonic during the second disciplining phase. As Garland clarifies, "[i]nstead of the illustrate principle of 'no punishment without a crime' here it was 'no treatment without a diagnosis' and 'no penal sanction without expert advice.'" (2001, 23–26). Prison, which retained a hegemonic place throughout the disciplining social order, was now re-oriented particularly towards those offenders identified as dangerous, recidivistic or incorrigible, who could still be detained for lengthy periods. Although, even in relation to prison sentences, their length was not fixed but attached to the behavior of the offender, with the possibility of early release and parole supervision (indeterminate sentences)[69] that stressed the re-educative purposes of imprisonment (34). Wacquant (2009) explains that when Foucault published *Discipline and Punish* (1975), the international consensus among professionals in the criminal field was that the prison was an outdated and discredited institution. Moreover, there were just 380,000 people behind bars around 1973, and the United States seemed ready to raise the flag of freedom and bring other nations on the road to 'a world without prisons.'

On the other hand, crime control mechanisms were not only deployed through strict punitive measures but also through activities in the community, upon an etiologic-social perspective. State intervention tried to strengthen community control through the actions of primary groups (community groups, parishes, associations, mutual aid, cooperatives) and interdisciplinarian approaches. These interventions helped modeled a 'master change' from the era of 'great imprisonments' to the 'era of decentralization' and 'deinstitutionalization' (Melossi 1990, 19). While in the 19th century capitalist despotism tried to transform society into a factory-based model, in the 20th century the democratic capitalism of mass societies encouraged a diffuse but constant control (75).

The discourse that legitimized this modality of crime control was endorsed by sociological schools that, based on the thought of Durkheim, continued to focus on individual and etiological analyses about the causes of crime. They no longer supported biological degeneration justifications, but sustained that individual bad socialization was the cause of crime and that it could be overcome through inclusive social policies. Thus: "Social problems become individual problems in an ahistorical criminology; and the task of criminology is reduced to the examination of 'the causes of crime' largely in terms of individualistic

---

69   Until the 1970s, sentences were imposed by the courts, but the judicial sentence was often modified by other sentencing authorities (mainly, parole board) that exercised discretional decisions, pursuing the rehabilitation of the offender through individuation techniques. The sentence had to take into account whatever punishment was needed to rehabilitate the offender, regardless of the requirements of proportionality.

explanations, with the occasional dash of social factors or determinants" (Taylor et al. 1975, 44). The current thinking proclaimed that "social reform, along with economic affluence, eventually reduce the frequency of crime," and that the state was responsible for assisting offenders, both as a punishment and as a control mechanism (Garland 2001, 88).

With regard to the prosecution of the organized dissident, and in continuity with the second disciplining phase, the tighter criticism of political activists, unionists and intellectuals evolved in an effort to discipline those that could operate as mobilizers of the working class. Its period of greatest intensity occurred in the context of McCarthyism in the United States and during the Cold War, particularly between 1950 and 1956. In February 1950, McCarthy, a U.S. senator representing Wisconsin, denounced a communist conspiracy in the bosom of the State Department, and started a so-called 'witch-hunt.' It consisted of widespread persecution, based on mere presumptions, of anyone who might be minimally linked to communist activities. Against prevailing basic constitutional standards, the Senate Committee, chaired by McCarthy, was entitled to summon defendants to secret interrogations or public hearings, under presumption of guilt, to prove their loyalty to U.S. liberal values. As part of this prosecution, the official program, COINTELPRO (1956) pursued "increase factionalism, [to] cause disruption and win defections" inside the Communist Party, as a governmental strategy to destroy movements for self-determination and liberation, and other progressive organizations (Poynter 2016). Later on, COINTELPRO intensively focused on organized communities of color and, particularly, on the Black Panthers. On June 15, 1969, J. Edgar Hoover, director of the F.B.I., declared: "the Black Panther Party, without question, represents the greatest threat to internal security of the country," and he pledged that 1969 would be the last year of the Party's existence (quoted in P.B.S. 2016). A final aspect of the socio-disciplining over-criminalization of the organized dissident included those who opposed to the Vietnam war, who were associated with the use of drugs in order to ensure their subjection to crime control, as a Nixon's advisor publicly admitted (LoBianco 2016).

Over-criminalization of the organized dissident was not deployed particularly through imprisonment but through further policing, social pressure, persecution and harassment in working life, summons, subpoenas for the purpose of accounting statements or policies affiliations, blacklisting aimed at preventing the use of their members, passport removal, censorship of artistic works (amounting to 30,000), espionage to dismantle possible infiltrations in public administration, the use of the media and academic powerhouses to harass suspects, and even censures and persecution in Hollywood (Rovere 1959). The goal of crime control was to settle a non-confrontational integration among the population. Indeed, half of u.s. social scientists had been interviewed by the f.b.i. in the first twelve months of the witch-hunt, with a third of them interviewed on three occasions; Marxist books were censured; school curricula were rewritten; and Merton himself had to change the Jewish character of his name, which eventually limited his critical position towards criminal issues (Lazarsfeld 1958 quoted in Young 2012, 142). The traditional form of crime control still worked and was applied in to the most problematic cases, finding its apotheosis in the execution of Ethel and Rosenberg in June 1953, accused of transmitting the secrets of the atomic bomb to the Soviet Union (Rovere 1959). Also in relation to the Black Panthers, prison has been used as the primary tool of control and some of this group members are still imprisoned in solitary confinement (Allen-Bell 2014).

In sum, as we have seen, during this third disciplining phase, and based on the contributions of the Marxist tradition and some applicable contributions from the works of Marx and Engels, socio-disciplining criminal selectivity (20th century) was conceptualized. Given the lost of scientific legitimization of positivism and its failure to achieve 'order and progress,' social control persisted in addressing the most vulnerable sectors but it was deployed through social and inclusive policies within the framework of welfare states. These efforts were aimed at appeasing the prevailing social conflict, which was the great confrontation of the Western capitalist world with the Eastern bloc, centered on the Russian revolution of 1917. Crime control continued targeting individuals through a selective matrix, but was implemented under a discourse with a sociological basis, that was compatible with the implemented social policies. It operated through the mechanism of socio-disciplining under-criminalization that was applied to white-collar crimes and organized crime in the context of the exponential expansion of cities and commerce, and, in a more drastic level, to the war crimes in the context of imperialism. The mechanism of socio-disciplining over-criminalization focused on coarse crimes associated with urban pauperism and deviations that challenged the disciplined social order, as well as on those behaviors that disputed the existing political order.

Let us now analyze the social sectors of the disciplining criminal selectivity across its three phases.

Who Were the Social Sectors Targeted by Disciplining Criminal Selectivity?

Delving into individuals targeted by the under-criminalization, it is possible to understand that they are likely to be characterized differently in the three disciplining phases. Briefly, in the first disciplining phase (late 18th century) the privileged focus of under-criminalization was the mercantile bourgeoisie, which had assumed political power and was struggling with the remaining feudal and monarchists powers. Then, in the second disciplining phase (19th century), it was the free-trade industrial bourgeoisie that prevailed politically and economically in the European and colonial territory. Finally, in the third disciplining phase (early to late 20th century), it was the monopolistic industrial bourgeoisie and the emerging international financial bourgeoisie (Boron 2001, 41), as well as middle-class professional sectors and the mafias of organized crime.

In regard to the social sectors over who the mechanisms of over-criminalization were particularly applied, the focus was on the organized dissident and the pauperism (both rural and urban). The organized dissident was targeted during critical moments of social conflict between dominant sectors and workers, while over-criminalization of the pauperism took place throughout the development of the disciplining social order.

Recalling, the organized dissident refers to those members of the working class that were unionized and politically structured to challenge the existing labor order. The notion includes those political activists that were also targeted because of their theoretical production or advocacy activities in support of the working class. Marx and Engels themselves were subjected to such over-criminalization, particularly when they promoted the International Working-men's Association. Although persecution of this sector was already present in the first disciplining phase, the organized dissident became a privileged focus of crime control in the framework of police-medically disciplining criminal selectivity (essentially, socialists, anarchists and unionized workers), when the confrontation between bourgeoisie and proletariat was in the spotlight. Over-criminalization of the organized dissident concentrated in very different behaviors, ranging from trivial forms of resistance against the harsh conditions of employment (such as absenteeism) through embryonic attempts of resistance (such as destroying machines) towards political organization. Crime control over this sector ranged from private reprimands within the factory to criminal prosecution of riots and protests along with censorship of unions. During the second disciplining phase, crime control absorbed civil and labor law, while the freedoms proclaimed by the Enlightenment (freedom of association, expression and organization) became criminal offenses, under the prevailing medical discourse that categorized the workers as a 'dangerous class.' Similarly, in the context of the socio-disciplining criminal selectivity, over-criminalization of the organized dissident was reinforced, particularly against those with communist affiliation, protestors against the Vietnam war, and Black activists.

The sector identified as pauperism was the most affected by crime control. But, who were these paupers? In Chapter 23 of *Capital* and using the Law of Pauperization, Marx defines 'pauperism' as an analytical category. Marx exposes that this sector emerges from the same functioning of the capitalist economic system:

> This change in the technical composition of capital, this growth in the mass of means of production, as compared with the mass of the labor-power that vivifies them, is reflected again in its value-composition, by the increase of the constant constituent of capital at the expense of its variable constituent (1867, 681).

This means that, as the composition of capital changes with the increase of fixed capital over variable and the supply of labor tends to increase, those who are not successful in the sale of their labor force must survive on their own resources (Bonger 1905, 261–262). So, the working population is excessively increasing in relation to the operating capital needs, forming masses of remaining people that Marx called 'relative surplus.' This surplus constitutes a reserve army available for capital (1867, 533).[70] This 'army' acts as a 'thermometer' of the wages of the occupied working class, preventing their growth from putting the accumulation of capital at risk. This 'army' is not cyclical and it is inevitably destined to grow (regardless of intermittent regressions) (694–695).[71] Based on this, Engels says that the situation of the workers is even

---

70   Engels likewise defines this sector as a 'permanent surplus' (1845, 82). Bonger, against the Malthusian thesis, proclaims that this evidence that the surplus cannot be attributed to the biological reproduction of workers, but to the character of the capitalist system of production that causes overpopulation (1905, 217). On the other hand, Marx makes a distinction between three forms of relative surplus inside the 'army.' The 'fluctuating' has to do with the fact that the production repels and attracts workers alternately; the 'latent' that has to do with the fluctuations of certain branches of industry or seasonal agricultural economy; and the 'intermittent,' that has to do with those individuals with a very irregular insertion, that work long hours for low wages (1867, 706–707). All these forms of relative surplus act as a reserve army.

71   Marx states: "The whole form of the movement of modern industry depends, therefore, upon the constant transformation of a part of the laboring population into unemployed or half-employed hands [...] When this periodicity is once consolidated, even Political Economy then sees that the production of a relative surplus population – i.e., surplus with regard to the average needs of the self-expansion of capital- is a necessary condition of modern industry" (1867, 694–695).

worse than that of a slave; the latter had his daily survival assured, while the former is always at risk of falling into the category of relative surplus.[72]

As the industrial reserve army increases, it also tends to lower the revenues of the occupied working class, producing growing pauperization (Law of Pauperization). This process is accompanied by a concentration of wealth in the economically advantaged sector, who appropriates the greater surplus value extracted from the employed worker, polarizing classes. Piketty (2013) shows that, in the case of Europe, the share of total wealth monopolized by the top 10% amounted to more than 80% of assets in 1810 and increased during the 19th and early 20th until it reached 90% in 1910. The Law of Pauperization does not indicate that wages never increase or improvement is impossible (indeed, wages' improvement was the highlight of the third disciplining phase). What this Law tries to stress is the condition of relative impoverishment of the proletariat; the fact that even when their wages increase, they do so in lesser proportion than the wealth accumulated by capital (Mandel 1967, 154).

Following the analysis of Chapter 23 of *Capital*, Marx identifies another dispossessed sector: the pauperism, made up from those able to work who managed to escape from this category in times of economic upswing; orphans and pauper children who were also likely to be incorporated in the labor market in times of great prosperity; and "the demoralized and ragged, and those unable to work, chiefly people who succumb to their incapacity for adaptation due the division of labor" (1867, 706–707). He states that

> Pauperism is the hospital of the active labor-army and the dead weight of the industrial reserve-army. Its production is included in that of the relative surplus-population, its necessity in theirs; along with the surplus-population, pauperism forms a condition of capitalist production, and of the capitalist development of wealth. It enters into the *faux frais* of capitalist production; but capital knows how to throw these, for the most part, from its own shoulders on to those of the working-class and the lower middle class (707).

---

72   In point VII of the *Principles of Communism* (1847), Engels wonders what the difference is between the proletarian and the slave, to answer that the slave is sold only once and for all his life, however, the proletarian has to sell himself, every day and every hour. Moreover, slaves, owned by a certain lord, have already assured its existence, however miserable it may be; but the proletarian is purchased only when he is needed, and his existence is not secured. Because of that, Engels affirms that the slave can have a better existence than the proletarian.

Pauperism is constituted, then, from those extremely poor sectors, chronically unemployed or employed in sporadic and precarious jobs, whose integration into the labor market takes place only in special occasions of economic strength, but that fail to keep jobs throughout time. Returning to Marx's words, it is "that part of the working-class which has forfeited its condition of existence (the sale of labor-power), and vegetates upon public alms" (554). It is in the context of the disciplining social order that pauperism exponentially grew and that an increased number of workers, employed and unemployed,[73] were at constant risk of relapse into this category (Geremek 1986, 250–252). So extended was this phenomenon that, in the 1840s, the Real-Enzyclopädia Brockhaus incorporated the German word 'pauperismus' to designate those extremely impoverished masses who thronged the increasingly mighty cities (Emsley 2007).

Recalling, only in the first and second disciplining phases did pauperism find itself in a situation of absolute deprivation. In the first disciplining phase,

---

73   It is relevant to highlight that, even though the paupers were generally excluded from the labor market, Marx and Engels still considered them as part of the working class. This is visible in *The Communist Manifesto* where they define the proletariat as "a class of laborers, who live only so long as they find work, and who find work only so long as their labor increases capital" (1848, 18). The workforce is a commodity like any other, subjected therefore to market fluctuations. This means that the actual occupation of these masses does not define their character as working class, as they may be temporarily unoccupied. In a note to the English edition of *Capital*, Engels confirms that by bourgeoisie they meant the class of modern capitalists who are the owners of the social means of production and who exploit wage labor. Meanwhile, by proletariat, they meant the class of modern employees that do not own means of production and that depend on selling their labor to live (Engels 1888 quoted in Gomez Crespo 2012). In Marx and Engels' terms, 'working class' represents the entire population that needs to sell their labor in the market to meet their basic needs of existence and to reproduce their workforce, regardless of the fact that they may not actually be able to rent their labor. Then, 'working class' includes the unemployed workers that have both the need and the willingness to sell their labor, even though the system cannot absorb them; they are slaves seeking a master who does not respond to their call. This becomes clear in the work *The Condition of the Working Class in England* (1945), where Engels analyzes not only the occupied working class, but also those who begged along the banks of the English cities to try and fulfill their basic needs. Of course the need to sell their labor force is enough to be considered as a 'class in itself,' but what worried Marx and Engels was the ability to become class for itself, i.e., to develop awareness of their class. This concept describes the sense of collective identity that a class has as opposed to another, which results in clashes that develop class-consciousness; the process through which individuals perceive themselves within the socio-economic structure.

pauperism had a greater presence in the rural areas, as an effect of the second wave of enclosures and the prohibition of use of the common lands, which started to be considered private property. Those masses could not get the minimum goods that were necessary for subsistence. Paradoxically, those who challenged the new rules to avoid a situation of absolute deprivation met with legally-disciplining over-criminalization. In the second disciplining phase, a fully urban pauperism, mostly coming from the expropriated lands, could not enter into the labor market. Plunged into a situation of absolute deprivation, they were stigmatized under the moniker of low life and were recipients of police-medically disciplining over-criminalization, under the actions of police officers guided by a positivist and hygienist discourse that conflated urban sanitation, poverty, morality and crime. In the third disciplining phase, most of the pauperism was not suffering from extreme poverty. Unlike previous times, especially in the United States, the economic situation and the social policies implemented tended to increase the standard of living of workers in general and, with them, even the conditions of the pauperism. However, they were in a situation of relative deprivation by which, although their basic needs were satisfied, they had insufficient means to meet the social goals identified with success.

Based on Marx and Engels's conceptualization of the pauperism, it is possible to propose a categorization within the purpose of clarifying *how* they could follow different solutions to overcome their situation of marginalization (far from ensuring a false link between pauperism and crime), and *how* disciplining criminal selectivity shaped them in different manners during the disciplining social order. Engels distinguishes that the workers in a disgraceful situation could (a) brutalize themselves until devoid of personal will, (b) accept the imposed social habits and dive into the war of all against all, (c) embark on the struggle for socialism, or (d) steal and resort to crime.

a.   In the first case (absolute brutalization), Engels seems to pursue a deterministic logic; poverty brings loss of will and turn men and women into mere objects. However, in opposition to the biological determinism of the positivist academics, Engels develops a determinism that is no longer the product of the organic composition of the individuals, but of the socio-economic situation that surrounds them. It is the socio-economic determination what could eventually deteriorate and demoralize men and women to such extent that they could abdicate their ability to exercise free will. Over this category of pauperism, crime control was exercised through institutions of confinement. Prisons, workhouses and asylums made up the 'disciplining continuum' plotted by Foucault (1975). During the third disciplining phase, more flexible mechanisms of crime control became the privilege disciplining tool.

b.   In relation to the pauperized individuals that dissolved themselves in the stark struggle against their peers, Engels calls attention to the inefficacy of this method. Conversely, he points out that "if *all* the proletarians announced their determination to starve rather than work for the bourgeoisie, the latter would have to surrender its monopoly. But this is not the case" (1845, 76). Selfishness and competition were the most common outlets for desperate masses that became immersed in the most repulsive behaviors. Engels is referring here to the lumpen-proletariats that were characterized not only by being excluded from the labor market and holding a low social status (like their counterparts in the other categories of pauperism), but also because they lack class consciousness and play an active and reactionary role in the class struggle, fostering an attitude of 'all against all.' Crime control was not applied to the lumpen-proletariat in an overbearing manner: when the lumpen-proletariat fulfilled a useful need of the ruling class, crime control was waived.[74]

c.   Third, Engels contemplated the possibility for the pauperized subsets to change their situation by changing their socio-economic circumstances (213). This analysis makes clear that, for Engels, demoralization did not put the paupers in a deterministic path to crime, as the prevailing positivist paradigm affirmed. Engels claimed that it was possible for the impoverished workers to transcend demoralization through collective action. Even the unemployed could become part of the organized dissident and fight for political transformation.

d.   Engels also addresses the case of the paupers who perpetrate crimes. He notes that the condition of the workers appeared as a steeplechase in which if they did not succeed in getting a job, they had to commit illegal acts as the only alternative to starvation. That is, Engels placed coarse crimes in the context of the absolute deprivation experienced by pauperism (particularly in the first and second disciplining phases). The

---

74   Understanding the lumpen-proletariat as part of pauperism clarifies that Marx and Engels' rejection of this category should not be confused with a repudiation of all the extremely impoverished and unemployed masses. In addition, and away from determinism, Marx and Engels had considered that the lumpen-proletariat could transform their role in the historical process. In the *Communist Manifesto*, Marx and Engels affirm that the context of the proletarian revolution can drag the lumpen-proletariat to the worker's movement (1848, 39). In other words, far from being a tight category, the lumpen-proletariat can move from place to place within the framework of class conflict.

alternative to crime was perishing by starvation because of the impossibility of meeting the most basic needs. The situation was so extreme that if the worker intended to avoid crime and did not want to succumb to starvation, the remaining option was suicide (115).[75] However, far from a romantic vision, the offense was considered by Marx and Engels as an inappropriate way to transform poverty because it was oriented towards the immediate acquisition of goods (Hirst 1975, 274). In this regard, Engels affirms that, at the dawn of industrial development, "the first, the crudest, the most horrible form of such rebellion, was crime" (1845, 191), but the working class quickly realized that such a method was not the path for change. Change would come from the collective organization of the working class, while crime was just an individual input. This analysis of Marx and Engels might be interpreted as a preview of the left realism's critique of critical criminology in the 1980s: the challenge of not idealizing the offenders because their activities usually harm their class peers.

The suggested categorization contributes to understand that, far from a linear and univocal relationship between pauperism and crime, there were several alternatives for the impoverished. However, all of them were subjected to some form of crime control: asylums for people with mental health problems, political subjugation for the lumpen-proletariat as an alternative to avoid criminal prosecutions, and the fiercest criminal punishment for the organized dissident and those who relapsed into crime and marginal activities.

Mixed Insertion in the Disciplining Social Order
As it happened during the primitive accumulation, the most pauperized masses of the disciplining social order also combined coarse crime and criminalized

---

75   Even before the great work of Durkheim (1897), Marx and Engels had already warned how suicide, far from being an individual act, responded to social conditioning. In various newspaper articles, Marx questions those who analyze suicide as a moral problem, and, in contrast, he encourages its analysis as a social problem. Based on the records of police archives, he asks: "What kind of society is this, which is in the midst of millions of souls, the deepest solitude; in which one can have the inexorable desire to kill, and no one can feel it? This society is not a society; as Rousseau says, it is a wilderness inhabited by wild beasts. In the bourgeois world, a man and a woman persist, subjected to the tragic events of evil ordinariness, which seem to offer a unique way to overcome: lacking anything better, suicide is the most extreme resource against the evils of private life" (Marx 1846 quoted in Abduca 2012, 98).

survival strategies with temporary and precarious jobs. Then, mixed insertion persisted in the framework of disciplining criminal selectivity.

As evidenced by Engels in his study of the urban working class in England, crime was a concrete possibility for those left at the mercy of material deprivation. Coarse crimes were a regular livelihood for the paupers in combination with work, when it was available (1845, 56, 73 and 82). Engels states: "The 'surplus population' of England, which keeps body and soul together by panhandling, stealing, street-sweeping, collecting manure, pushing handcarts, driving donkeys, peddling, or performing occasional small jobs" (85). Marx (1867) points out that paupers' chances of getting stable or occasional jobs were almost zero. The economic degradation of the employed and unemployed working class was shameful, particularly in the first two phases of the disciplining social order. For the purpose of supplementing the wages or any revenue they could get, illegal activities were a necessary source to compensate for the lack of legal gain. In the third disciplining phase, the phenomenon of mixed insertion acquired new characters: as noted, the offenses were linked to situations of relative deprivation. This means that stable employment was sufficient for minimum needs, but not for the purpose of achieving the consumption levels that were culturally promoted. Paupers combined social assistance and sporadic jobs with illegal activities for the purpose of achieving the culturally imposed goals.

Having settled the characterization of the social sectors targeted by criminal disciplining selectivity, the following section analyzes how punishment was legitimized through manifest discourses that clashed with underlying latent functions.

Punishment during Disciplining Criminal Selectivity

What follows replicates the analytical structure of the second chapter, distinguishing between those ideological discourses that tried to justify the exercise of punishment along the disciplining social order (manifest functions) and the implicit purposes that undermined those discussions (latent functions).

Manifest Functions
In the long historical period covered by the disciplining social order, many ideological discourses that tried to legitimize the application of punishment were developed in the form of theories of punishment: retribution or just deserts; specific deterrence/incapacitation; general deterrence; and rehabilitation.

Retribution or Just Deserts

Retribution (or just desert) theories focus on the crime itself as the only and sufficient reason for imposing punishment. This theory holds an ecclesiastical origin,[76] although it spread in the heat of the 18th century during the first disciplinary phase through the voices of the leading representatives of German Idealism: Kant (1785) and Hegel (1821).[77] Retribution theory was particularly welcomed by Contractualism and Disciplinarism. For the former, the reason for punishing was related to the conception of men and women as individuals with free-will that had signed a social contract by which they agreed to comply with certain rules. As a consequence, if they break those rules, it is fair to apply punishment without considering mitigating or aggravating incidents. For Disciplinarism, the criminals should be punished with a penalty proportional to the pain they caused. In both versions it is not required to consider other justifications or useful purposes for society or the offender; it is sufficient to look at the breach of the social contract or the proved damage (that is why they are called 'absolute theories'). It follows that the punishment should be imposed in proportion to the committed harm as an outrageous/expressive condemnation of the crime. In Mathiesen's words: "A coherent theory of compensation provides an answer to the question of what acts should be punishable, and to the question of how severe should be the punishment to satisfy justice" (1987, 56).

---

76   Divine retribution conceived a correspondence between the universal order as a divine creation and the organization of earthly justice. Pope Pius XII proposed this concept at the 6th International Congress of Penal Law of 1953, when he said: "But the supreme court in its final judgment, applies only the principle of retribution. It must therefore have a value that cannot be ignored" (quoted in Mir Puig 2008, 46).

77   Kant argues that only compensation avoids the use of men and women as a means to convey a message to society, and ensures that the individual suffering will not be subjected to reasons of social utility. The law is conceived as a 'categorical imperative' that stipulates conditions devoid of utilitarian justice requirements. Thus, Kant questions the possibility of imposing punishment only because of further effects, even if they are positive. This is the central element of his theory that utilitarianism has not been able to solve. Kant brings his theory to the extreme of arguing that in a community where only a murderer survives, he should be punished anyway. On the other hand, Hegel (1821) sustains that the punishment has to restore the legitimacy of the law, that has been challenged through the action of the wrongdoing. Hegel insists on the need for respect for the free status of the accused individual. So, he commented that "[t]he criminal is honored as a rational being, from the moment it is understood as something that contains its own right. This honor would not correspond to him if the concept and measure of punishment were not considered upon the committed act; if he were seen as a harmful animal, which must be transform in a harmless one, or as someone who has to be intimidated and reformed."

The theory followed the logic of the 'fair return:' the disciplining working class was assigned a 'fair' wage that was 'equivalent' to the work that they had to do; the law was assigned a 'fair' punishment that was 'equivalent' to the harm that had been caused by the offender. Both, wage labor and workers' free will, had to comply with the ordering patterns to receive their compensation. If they met the work requirements, they received a pay that was proportional to their tasks. If they failed to comply with their social obligations, they received a sentence in proportion to the committed offense. The postulates of this theory, however, were not effectively exercised. As has been shown throughout this chapter, workers must accomplish the assigned task but they did not receive the promised 'fair' compensation; 'citizens' must respect social rules and avoid breaking the law, but they did not see the promised rights materialize in their everyday lives. Moreover, people were criminalized not just because of the committed offenses, but in relation to their level of conflictivity.

To justify an abstract application of punishment, retribution theory affirms that – regardless of the conditions of the environment – criminals must always be judges of their own crimes (Marx and Engels 1845, 220). Kantian and Hegelian views[78] prioritize the value of personal autonomy and self-realization as arguments for the legitimacy of retributive punishment. The state decision to punish was interpreted as an exercise of rights by the offenders that misused

---

78   Kant argues that, to be morally justified, coercion must be established in such a form that the individual can rationally desire punishment. However, he falls on an abstract and ideal vision of a 'rational and calculating man' that does not exist in reality, or at least does not correspond to all men. The contributions of cultural criminology, developed in recent years, teaches that individuals are often motivated by impulses and irrational passions, and not necessarily responding to rational criteria (Ferrell et al. 2008). On the other hand, Hegel argues that punishment restores the breakdown of the normative order caused by the offender: "Violence is eliminated with violence. As the second violence, that consists in the removal of the first one, it is therefore just, not only under certain conditions, but necessarily" (1821, 93). But the salient feature of punishment is that, concomitantly to the recovery of legal balance, it also plays a beneficial role for the offender, as it works as a right that allows him to compensate the caused harm. In *Philosophy of Right*, Hegel explains that "[t]o adhere obstinately to the equalization of punishment and crime in every case would reduce retribution to an absurdity. It would be necessary to institute a theft in return for theft, robbery for robbery, and to demand an eye for an eye and a tooth for a tooth, although the criminal, as we can easily fancy, might have only one eye or be toothless. For these absurdities, however, the conception is not responsible. They are due to the attempt to equate crime and punishment throughout their minute details. Value, as the inner identity of things specifically different, has already been made use of in connection with contract, and occurs again in the civil prosecution of crime (95). By it the imagination is transferred from the direct attributes of the object to its universal nature" (93).

their freedom. Against this backdrop, Marx tells us that the postulates of Con-tractualism brought legitimacy to state coercion, conceiving it as an (impos-sible) tacit agreement between the state and the sanctioned individuals who accepted the rules then applied to them (220):

> Hegel says: 'Punishment is the *right* of the criminal. It is an act of his own will. The violation of right has been proclaimed by the criminal as his own right. His crime is the negation of right. Punishment is the negation of this negation, and consequently an affirmation of right, solicited and forced upon the criminal by himself.'
>
>   HEGEL quoted in MARX 1853

Hegel's conception of men as free and self-determined is nothing but a fallacy that responds to an abstract conception of men, detached from their material conditions. Only from an idealist perspective is possible to consider punish-ment as the result of the criminal's own will. So Marx asks: "Is it not a delusion to substitute for the individual with his real motives, with multifarious social circumstances pressing upon him, the abstraction of 'free-will' – one among the many qualities of men..." (1853). This is why Hegel's theory of punishment cannot survive outside abstraction.[79] Kant does not realize either that the the-oretical thoughts of the bourgeoisie do not pursue a fair and abstract applica-tion of punishment. Theories of punishment are constrained by the material conditions of production (Marx and Engels 1845, 220).[80] Indeed, retribution might be the only theory of morally defensible punishment because it only takes into consideration the offense and not further social utilities. However, this is true only in the abstract; in the real world, within the unjust conditions of our social orders, the theory becomes inapplicable. Neither are all men and women equally positioned to respect the law, nor does the law treat all men and women equally. Thus, a combination of Kantian postulates on punish-ment and social analysis of Marxism conducts to challenge the very institution

---

79   Hegel pretends to use punishment to make men control their impulses. However, Marx and Engels point out that when the impulses do not appear and the crime is committed, uselessly is to reprimand the absence of repression that should have worked. Punishment cannot require the self-repression of the offender precisely because punishment, as well as violence, contradicts human restraint (1845, 220).

80   Rusche and Kirchheimer also confirm that retributive theories fail from the start because they perceive the relationship between guilt and atonement as a mere problem of legal allegation, that analyze the individual acts as a direct product of free will (1938, 3). That is, retribution pays no attention to the material conditions in which free will is manifested.

of punishment, which can only be valid in abstract and ideals terms. In Murphy's words:

> If we think that the institutions of punishment are necessary and desirable, and if we are morally sensitive enough to want to be sure we have the moral right to punish before we inflict it, then we had better first make sure that we restructured society in such a way that criminals genuinely do correspond to the only model that will render punishment permissible [...] Of course if we did this then – if Marx and Bonger are right- crime itself and the need to punish would radically decrease if not disappear entirely (1973, 243).

Murphy concludes that the legitimacy of an absolute theory is conceivable only in materially equal conditions. Until then, retributive theory is formally correct but materially inadequate. Only egalitarian material conditions might have the right to give the same fair treatment to all the individuals that commit an offense. This keeps strict relation to Marx's expressions in his *Critique of the Gotha Program* (1875), where he affirms that it is only possible to apply a fair law under materially equal conditions.[81]

---

81   Following Murphy's reflections, it is possible to inquire whether those who live in extreme poverty have a duty to obey the law. For them, the law has not been a means of gaining freedom or achieving self-governance, but rather an instrument that has oppressed them. Therefore, it is problematic if it is not justified that they challenge and even resist such legal order (Gargarella 2007c, 3). Indeed, the legal order has not ensured the protection they need, but – on the contrary – has been partly responsible for their oppression. To the extent that the law is causal and morally implicated in their suffering, certain forms of resistance should be seen, in principle, morally permissible (20). In other words, in unfair and structural situations of systematic deprivation of certain basic goods, the state lacks legitimacy to punish conducts that have been promoted by that structural depravation (31). Tadros (2009) invokes the possibility of exempting or reducing the criminal responsibility of those who are in a situation in which the state has not assured their minimum material conditions. Distributive injustice implies a disregard for the conditions that make crime possible: The state has wronged the offenders, and this enables them somehow to shirk responsibility guidelines imposed by the state. Also, Green (2011) wonders if a retributive justice system depends on previous standards of socio-economic justice. Likewise, Duff (2000) has argued that social exclusion does not meet the preconditions for the application of punishment. While this does not prevent the state from calling individuals to answer for the acts that they committed, it is a condition of legitimacy that the state recognizes, simultaneously, the hardships that the person has experienced in the course of life, in a doubly communicative activity toward the offender and to the community. Gargarella (2011b) brings up the case *United States v. Alexander* (1973) in which the

In addition to its abstract and unequal character, retributive theory can be criticized because it does not respond to the Enlightenment ideal, as it proclaims. Conversely, this theory perpetuates the confusion between 'civil justice' and 'religious righteousness' (particularly in the version called 'divine retribution') as well as between 'law' and 'ethics.' Marx and Engels observe that, even though the retributive punishment is presented as a sign of the Enlightenment and against the previous barbarity of the primitive accumulation, it preserves a religious content that requires remorse and suffering, and not just proportional punishment (1845, 234). Analyzing a book, *The Mysteries of Paris*, which defends the retributive theory through the story of a schoolmaster who imposes the law of retaliation to an offender (taking him the eyes to lock him inside himself), Marx and Engels point out that this form of punishment is strictly linked to Christian tradition, confusing punishment with a religious morality that requires atonement and repentance from the offender. Punishment is conceived as embodying the revenge of society that falls upon the criminals and requires their penitence and remorse. This theory asks for an alliance among corporal punishment, moral and physical pain, and repentance; it demands punishment as a Christian and moral mean of education. Ironically, Marx and Engels claim: "Compared with this Christian cruelty, how humane is the ordinary penal theory that conforms to behead the man he wants to annihilate!" (231), without requiring remorse. They mocked the Paris novel, stating that the schoolmaster rejects capital punishment on the grounds that the passage from the court to the scaffold is too fast, and does not encourage repentance and remorse (1845, 218).[82]

On the other hand, Kant's theory also fails to meet the proclamations set forth by the legally-disciplining ideal, by mixing up 'law' and 'ethics.' Arguing that the offender seeks to break the existing legal system and that the punishment repairs the violated norms implicates a confusion between law and ethics, which collides with the proclaimed separation between these two spheres (Marx and Engels 1845, 403). The result is that Kant's theory does not succeed in breaking the confusion of the primitive accumulation and fails to acknowledge the complex relations between the law and the offender, reducing it to an ethical conflict. If it seeks to justify punishment, it must value the

---

judge Bazelon considered a link between a violent crime and the social background of the offender as a justification for adopting redistributive measures.

82   This persistence of 'religious justice' in the retribution theory was recognized by contemporary thinkers, including Ferrajoli, who stresses that religious ideas have always had an irresistible fascination for reactionary political thought, and have never been entirely abandoned by criminal culture (2001, 254).

interests protected by the rule as universals and, therefore, insert them in an
ethical analysis (Pavarini 1995, 64–65).[83]

Specific Deterrence/Incapacitation

By the 19th century, with the acknowledgment of the fictional character of
Contractualism and the bourgeois proclamations of legal equality, the retributive argument failed to answer why punishment was imposed. If the contract
was a legal form capable of representing the abstract social relations but it
was not a fair representation of material relations, the ratio of value-crime and
value-punishment also ceases to be credible (Pavarini 1995, 20). From then on,
theories would be called 'relative,' because they maintain that the purpose
of punishment could not be just a mere application of proportional harm; it
must pursue further goals. Relative theories would include specific and general
deterrence.

Specific deterrence seeks "to discourage the defendant from committing
further crimes by instilling fear of receiving the same or a more severe penalty
in the future" (Frase 2005, 70). In close relation to this discourse, incapacitation
theory looks at those offenders that were considered especially dangerous or
violent to take them out of circulation, i.e. to isolate, neutralize or eliminate
them in order to avoid recidivism. This theory supports that punishment must
impact the body of the offender: "[i]ts effects result from the physical restraint
placed upon the offender and not from his subjective state" (Wilson 1998, 149).
It was one of the hegemonic ideological discourses of the police-medically disciplining criminal selectivity and was particularly sustained by Italian positivism. This school relied on penalties of deportation, prolonged imprisonment
or capital punishment (Lombroso 1887; Garofalo 1891),[84] pursuing the physical

---

83   There is another relevant critic to the Kantian version of retributive punishment, apart
      from those highlighted by Marx and Engels. Kant argues that it is important to ensure
      that those who disobey the law not gain an advantage over those who voluntarily obey it.
      Thus, the Kantian postulate slips into its own critique of the utilitarian theories, through
      a 'counter-utilitarianism' that also positions utility in its center: the imposition of punish-
      ment is encouraged to prevent an extra profit, an additional utility, for the offender, to the
      detriment of the respectful members of society.

84   Prins proposes deportation for the poor, indeterminate prison for criminals, and intern-
      ment for alcoholics and vagrants. He understands that migration to Africa will transform
      the poor into useful producers (quoted in Codino 2010, 15). Because recidivist offenders,
      Prins explains, have no morality and they do not have the habit of work, their remain-
      ing physical strength is not enough to 'regenerate' them. As a result, it made no sense to
      send them to the colonies (14). Garofalo (1895) proposes deportation for those who com-
      mitted crimes against property (crime associated with the loss of probity) and capital

elimination or neutralization of those criminals that were considered unrecoverable because of their biological degeneration. Positivism often combined incapacitation (for those who suffer atavism) and rehabilitation (for those who, through an appropriate treatment, could become socially functional) (Zysman 2013, 151; Alagia 2013, 249).

Incapacitation theory was proven to be false. The evidence presented in this chapter makes it clear that police-medically disciplining over-criminalization did not address the most serious or harmful offenses of the period, i.e. it was not oriented to neutralize dangerous perpetrators. That is, the proclaimed purpose of isolating those who caused serious harm to society seems inconsistent with the application of punishment to criminalized survival strategies and coarse crimes. Marx and Engels point out that the roots of crime are to be found not in the antisocial individual will, but in the antisocial and inhuman character of capitalist society (1845, 242). Then they mock of those who hold that penalties serve to protect the good people, ignoring that crime control itself is a tool for the consecration of social differences: law does not create anything itself but sanctions those behaviors socio-economically perceived as deservers of punishment (242). Likewise, Engels remarks that the law is necessary only because there are people who own nothing, and that if a rich man is brought up, or rather summoned to appear before the court, the judge regrets that he is obliged to impose upon him so much trouble (1845, 282). This means that the parameter of punishment, far from being rooted in the seriousness of the committed acts, is applied in relation to the socio-economic background of the offender.

Moreover, incapacitation theory was mostly applied through the punishment of imprisonment, which extracted religious content from the retribution discourse. Detention and solitary confinement were mere forms of intersection between legal punishment and theological torture. Imprisonment had its greatest development and encouragement in the United States in the 18th and 19th centuries at the hands of the Quakers, with isolation, meditation and religious practice as guidelines. The classics of Marxism bring to light that this method was recognized for its bloody and tortuous content: the absolute isolation conducted criminals to madness or suicide (Marx and Engels 1845, 220).[85]

---

punishment for crimes against life or health (crime associated with lack of pity). Social defense is common to all legitimating discourses of shame, but in the deterrence theory, this aspect is radicalized: the punitive selectivity eliminates the most vulnerable individuals (Alagia 2013, 266).

85   Later on, in *The Communist Manifesto* (1848), Marx and Engels refer to the Brussels Congress of Charitable and Philanthropic Lawyers' resolution about criminal detention.

The victims died no longer because of being tied to a wheel for long days and nights, but they perished spiritually in the high prison buildings, distinguished from asylums in name only (Horkheimer and Adorno 1944, 244).

The most extreme version of incapacitation was the application of capital punishment, which physically eliminates the offender. Marx notes that, while Quetelet wonders if crime responds to psychological or social causes, it was better to question if we should transform the system that gives rise to those crimes instead of extolling capital punishment as a magic solution. In his words:

> That it is not so much the particular political institutions of a country as the fundamental conditions of modern *bourgeois* society in general, which produce an average amount of crime in a given national fraction of society [...] is there not a necessity for deeply reflecting upon an alteration of the system that breeds these crimes, instead of glorifying the hangman who executes a lot of criminals to make room only for the supply of new ones?
>
> MARX 1853

Here, Marx also questions the effectiveness of capital punishment as he notes that, although many criminals are killed by the executioner, it is only to physically eliminate new ones. This means that, in spite of capital punishment' effectiveness in terms of incapacitation (after all, it kills the dangerous offender), its effects in terms of general deterrence are void because, although it is extensively applied, the number of condemned criminals also increases, diluting its intended effect. Marx explains that: "It would be very difficult, if not altogether impossible, to establish any principle upon which the justice or expediency of capital punishment could be founded, in a society glorying in its civilization" (1853). In opposition to the supposedly civilized discourse that confronted the bourgeoisie with the feudal past, Marx reminds us that, even in times of expansion of the prisons, capital punishment was still in force. To overcome that old *jus talionis*, Marx adds, we should not combat the crimes for which the death penalty was applied, but wonder about a society that allowed those crimes to emerge.

The resolution concluded that, to improve the 'moral level' of prisoners, the best tool was to impose solitary confinement. Marx and Engels, again ironically, repudiate that solution. In the *Critique of the Gotha Program* (1875), Marx insists that, in place of isolation as punishment, offenders should perform productive prison labor to avoid losing their class condition.

Finally, Marx directly challenges the central argument for the legitimation of punishment in the second disciplining phase: social defense. He asks: "what a state of society is that, which knows of no better instrument for its defense than the hangman, and which proclaims through the 'leading journal of the world' its brutality as eternal law?" (1853). Marx questions the cornerstone of the prevailing criminological thought and its functionality in a socio-economic system that uses the criminal justice system as the main tool against behaviors that undermine it.

General Deterrence

General deterrence was also developed in the 19th century. It maintains that the goal of punishment is to send a message to deter people other than the offender from committing crimes. The offender serves as an example to the rest of the population. The punishment applied to the offender reinforces the 'general interest,' the values of the entire social group. The positive version of general deterrence[86] affirms that "criminal penalties serve to define and reinforce important social norms of law-abiding behavior and relative crime seriousness" (Frase 2005, 72). Such rules guide and restrain behavior even when the chances of detection and punishment are slight (79). In its negative formulation,[87] the message is oriented to intimidate would-be offenders through an adverse incentive – the fear of being punished –. Its goal is to increase the fear of being caught to condition the cost-benefit analysis of committing a crime.

Marx and Engels criticize the proclaimed end of sending a message that represents a 'general interest:' "but what does this mean? [...] This public interest that you personify is nothing but an abstract term and does not represent more than the mass of individual interests" (1845, 168). As has been shown in the context of legally-disciplining criminal selectivity, the construction of the bourgeois juridical order was viable by sustaining the existence of a 'general interest' that helped reduce existing social conflicts. General deterrence defends

---

86 This version is known as positive general deterrence or denunciation. It is also known as communicative, educative, or expressive function of punishment, or just positive general prevention.

87 The negative version is called just 'general deterrence,' though 'negative general deterrence' could be more accurate to clarify its use of fear as a discouragement. Its first variant was formulated in the 19th century by Bentham – as well as by Feuerbach and Romagnosi – who made special reference to the 'psychological coercion' of punishment that should serve to confirm to the citizens the seriousness of defying criminal law. Bentham reinforced utilitarianism, incorporating calculations of the amount of pain expected to be enough to override the attractiveness of the offense (Mari 1983, 95).

the use of the offender as a medium to send a message that is the abstraction of the interest of the ruling class presented as the interest of all. In *Capital*, Marx challenges Bentham – an exponent of general deterrence – noting that the parameter of 'normality' that regulates 'deviation' is the one of the bourgeois man (1867, 668 n 2).[88]

The aim of sending an intimidating/reinforcing message to the general population is not reflected in the concrete application of punishment either. This is because, on the one hand, the type of individuals that are punished are not representative of the existing social diversity (they are just the over-criminalized). On the other hand, the message does not target the population in general; it focuses on specific social sectors considered conflictive (the yet non-criminalized peers of the over-criminalized). Punishment is applied to (certain) type of individuals to transmit a message to (certain) type of in-dividuals. Overturning the Kantian legacy, human dignity of the former is dissolved to settle social control over the latter. Under this logic, Marx (1853) asks: "what right have you to punish me for the amelioration or intimidation of others?" Moreover, as punishment does not respond to the severity of the committed offense but to the goal of deterring potential offenders, propor-tionality is lost.

Finally, if the punishment that is applied intends to send an intimidating message, it has proved to be ineffective as "since Cain the world has neither been intimidated nor ameliorated by punishment" (Marx 1853). This means that the Kantian postulate is broken as a result of an alleged social utility that cannot be borne out in practice; i.e., despite the severe messages transmitted by punishment, people keep on perpetrating crimes all over the globe. The problem is that, as retributivism did, this theory also relies on an abstract con-ception of man as purely rational, ignoring that most of the over-criminalized crimes are emotional and impulsive-driven. Paradoxically, under-criminalized offences, such as white-collar crimes, are the ones with a more calculated or thoughtful structure that could fit with the theory of general deterrence. But those ones are not the focus of deterrence.

---

88   Marx makes fun of Bentham and his principle of utility, and explains that though nature is modified in each historical epoch, "Bentham makes short work of it. With the driest na-iveté he takes the modern shopkeeper, especially the English shopkeeper, as the normal man. Whatever is useful to this queer normal man, and to his world, is absolutely useful." Marx reinforces that Bentham uses this logic to analyze past, present, and future, and nicknames him as "a genius in the way of bourgeois stupidity" (1867, 668, n 2). The alleged utilitarian aims, far from being a representation of useful means for the 'general interest,' embody the utilitarian means of bourgeois men.

Rehabilitation

In the 20th century, rehabilitation theory appeared. It is aimed at reforming and rehabilitating offenders through a treatment model based on making them re-think their morality or physiology (Alagia 2013, 265).[89] Rehabilitation theory considers that prison is the most efficient tool to fulfill the re-educational purpose (Ferrajoli 2001, 271). While this theory had some historical background (mainly in the police-medically disciplining criminal selectivity in relation to offenders that were considered capable of reform), it became hegemonic in the third disciplining phase. Under the Fordist production model, the assumption was that the factory, Keynesianism and the 'normalization' function of prisons shared a functional link. Unemployment and social exclusion were seen as results of the individual inability to enter into the labor market and became addressed through welfare. Meanwhile, prison worked as a subsidiary recourse; as a disciplining mechanism to include those individuals with higher deficits (De Giorgi 2002; Bergalli 1997).

Criticisms of this theory rely on the concrete experience and criminological research that has tirelessly demonstrated that prisons do not fulfill its proclaimed function of social rehabilitation. The quintessential contributions of Foucault (1975) and the work of Baratta (1995), among many others, help confirm this analysis. Rehabilitation is just a correctional fiction that is functional to the good governance of prisons (Daroqui 2002). Defenders of rehabilitation argue that the impediments to social re-integration have to do with technical and not historical problems (Rusche and Kirchheimer 1938, 3). This argument has been promoting the re-legitimization of the rehabilitation theory, despite centuries of failure.

Latent Functions

Disciplining criminal selectivity developed together with imprisonment[90] as the hegemonic form of punishment. As Foucault (1975) explains, the establishment of subtraction of time as a disciplining punishment in lieu of corporal punishment[91] and bloody legislations (typical of the primitive accumulation)

---

89   Its most prominent exponent was Kaufmann, who states that punishment has a threefold function: inform about the content of the law, foster trust for the law, and spread respect for the enforcement of the rule of law. Similarly, Welzel claims that the aim of punishment is to strengthen social, ethical values (Mir Puig 2008, 30).

90   This date certainly coincides with the end of torture. Prison as a hegemonic penal institution ends up settling at the end of the 19th century, in a gradual process of conversion of workhouses into prisons (Pavarini and Melossi 1980).

91   Frederick The Great condemned torture as cruel and useless, a penalty that hardened the hard offenders and weakened the innocents, and thus restricted it shortly after

took place between 1750 and 1820, i.e. the beginning of the disciplining social order.[92] How did it happen? Was it an effect of Enlightenment values acting against the previous barbarism? Punishment rested on a triple implicit purpose: disciplining the worker that resisted the new social order and its guidelines (while ensuring the invisibility of under-criminalized behaviors); disciplining the entire working class; and fragmenting the working class.

Disciplining the Worker That Resisted the New Social Order and Its Guidelines

The first latent function of punishment had to do with its orientation to discipline the rebel worker. In the 'Preface' to the first edition of *Capital*, Marx illustrates that commodities are the economic cell of bourgeois society (1867, 12). How is this value measured? For the amount of labor that it contains. In turn, the amount of labor is measured by its duration (labor time) which is finally calculated into different fractions of time: hours, days, and so on. This calculation of the commodities' value is not determined by the individual workers' performance, but by the 'abstract labor.'[93] Thus, the entire Chapter I

---

succeeding his father in 1740, finally abolishing it in 1754. A generation later, Gustav III of Sweden abolished torture and adopted a series of policies aimed at a more rapid and equitable criminal justice system. Austria, Baden, Bavaria, Saxony, Württemberg and other minor German states, restricted or just ceased to use torture, though its formal abolition had to wait until the French domination of the early 19th century. In Hanover, it was used as late as 1818, but it was abolished four years later. In France, the 1670 Ordinance limited its use (Emsley 2007, 30).

92   This transition was far from harmonious, because the prison did not appear as a desirable replacement against torture. At first, prison was accepted for specific crimes (particularly freedom violations such as abduction, or those resulting from the abuse of liberty, as disorder and violence) and as a condition to enforce certain punishments (for example, forced labor). Many other critics rejected prison for diverse reasons: it was not able to respond to the specific nature of crimes; it did not exert effects on the public; it was useless and costly to keep convicts in idleness, multiplying their vices; it is hard to control and there was a danger of exposing detainees to the arbitrariness of their guardians; it could constitute an exercise of tyranny, etcetera (Foucault 1975, 119). Also, even though prison's legitimacy responded to an alleged overcoming of the barbarity of corporal punishment, i.e. in seeking a transfer from a corporal to a carceral punishment, the body remained there: prison or forced labor maintained a punitive supplement either through food rationing, sexual deprivation or beatings. In what looks like a rephrasing of the principle of less eligibility of Rusche and Kirchheimer, Foucault says that it is considered fair that a convict physically suffers more than other men (16).

93   Thus, "abstract human labor is the expression of equivalence between different sorts of commodities that alone brings into relief the particular character of value-creating labor,

of *Capital* enlightens us about the vital importance of 'time' as the measurement of the value of the assets, which are the heart of the current economic
system. If capitalism reduces everything to an abstract, divisible, equivalent,
homogeneous and constant unit of time; that is, to time dissociated from the
concrete human purposes, then time is everything. If time is everything, then
man is nothing, or, in the best case, is the housing of time (Marx quoted in
Bonefeld 2010). Since all goods are reducible to 'abstract labor' and time becomes even more relevant than the worker's own value, it is not surprising
that, when capitalism was settling down, subtraction of time became the hegemonic punishment. As Pashukanis shows through his Theory of Equivalent
Compensation, the link between time, contract and imprisonment is inherent
to this historic moment:

> Deprivation of freedom – for a definite term previously indicated in the
> judgment of a court – is the precise form in which modern law, that is,
> bourgeois capitalist criminal law, realizes the basis of equivalent retri-
> bution. This method is profoundly, but unconsciously connected with
> the concept of the abstract man and of abstract human labor time. It is
> not accidental that this form of punishment grew intense and eventually
> seemed natural and expected in the nineteenth century, i.e. when bour-
> geois society was fully developed and had consolidated all its particular
> features. Prisons and dungeons, of course, existed even in ancient times
> and in the Middle Ages, alongside other means of physical coercion. But
> at that time prisoners were usually confined until their death or until the
> payment of a ransom (1924, 188).

It is a historic moment in which time can be measured, economically quanti-
fied and, because of this, prison became a must; the element that allows the
principle of equivalence to become historically manifest (Pavarini 1995, 18). Of
course, the punitive response of the state as a 'legal compensation' was valid
only in formal terms. In practice, that equivalence does not occur. Marx evi-
dences it by stating:

---

and this it does by actually reducing the various varieties of labor embodied in the different kinds of commodities to their universal quality of human labor in the abstract"
(Marx 1867, 59). The work of each individual producer is subsumed into the general form
of 'abstract labor' and the individual worker becomes the collective worker. Through this
process, capital stunts the individual subjectivity of the worker and prevents the work
from depending on personal characteristics. Then, it turns out that the time of abstract
human labor is the unit of measure par excellence that gives value to the goods.

[t]his sphere that we are deserting, within whose boundaries the sale and purchase of labor-power goes, is in fact a very Eden of the innate rights of man. There alone rule Freedom, Equality, Property and Bentham (1867, 195).

This means that the 'sphere of circulation' is the realm of abstract rights and governs the exchange of equivalents, as opposed to the 'sphere of production' where exploitation and accumulation reign. Analyzing the prison system, in the 'sphere of circulation' all human being possess time. Time is a good that – on the abstract level – all people dispose of in a homogenous manner (or its quantitative distribution does not respond – at least directly – to the economic and social organization, or to human beings' will) and, therefore, it configures imprisonment as a formally equal punishment. Thus, Foucault asks: "How could prison not be the penalty *par excellence* in a society in which liberty is a good that belongs to all in the same way and to which each individual is attached, as Duport put it, by a 'universal and constant' feeling?" (1975, 232). In contrast to the 'sphere of circulation,' the disciplining objective predominates at the 'production level,' and within it, over-criminalization of the working class, and more particularly of the pauperism, takes place to the detriment of the proclaimed egalitarianism.[94]

Prison as a privilege tool for workers' disciplining makes evident why the first form of freedom deprivation was the workhouse – where punishment and work were combined –, and why its continuation was the prison-factory – where the transgressor repaired the 'damage' by paying with his employee time, and must be disciplined in order to be reintegrated into society as a docile proletarian – (Melossi 1980, 86).[95] The link between prison and disciplining also explains why prison has been preserved over time despite its inability

---

94   Pavarini notes that retribution and the disciplining aim coexisted. The role of the legal and penal retribution is a translation of the social relations that are based on the 'exchange of equivalents' that is 'in the exchange value' (1995, 228) and thus, prison as deprivation of freedom becomes the privileged punishment (229). In this coexistence between retributive and disciplining aims, the central contradiction of the capitalist production system is evident: the general legal form that guarantees equal rights system (compensation) is neutralized with socio-economic and political inequalities (231).

95   Meanwhile, the introduction of the clock in the daily lives and the imposition of a new sense of time, were strictly linked to work-discipline. With the clock, the rhythms of industrial life were imposed and the naturally synchronized time was abandoned. Puritanism was a key factor that introduced a new value of time and the notion that 'time is money' (Thompson 1984). Closing the circle, the link between Puritanism and the invention of the prison, particularly in the United States, was explicit: the philosopher and

to meet its proclaimed goals – which were not the same over time, as was described in the first part of this section. The key to understand this apparent contradiction, Foucault (1975) explains, is that imprisonment, far from being aimed at eliminating infringements, was established to distinguish them, to distribute them and to use them. That is why no one can believe that imprisonment was 'invented' by philosophers and jurists: its origin lies elsewhere, in the necessity to discipline the working class (Pavarini 1995, 72). Prison is not the result of a humanization of punishment and it is not an invention of the Enlightment. Imprisonment was a punishment consistent with a production system in booming development, which determined the value of goods based on the measurement of abstract time. For the purpose of compelling the labor force that did not submit to the expected discipline, over-criminalization was embodied in the removal of the same amount of time that the offender refused to meekly surrender. Meanwhile, over-criminalization of the most vulnerable groups also helped cover-up the tendency to under-criminalize those acts linked to the processes of capital expansion, both in Europe and the colonies.

Disciplining the Entire Working Class

Notwithstanding that prison was prescribed to the worker who did not submit to the new disciplining guidelines (the effectively over-criminalized), it was not limited to that social sector. Punishment was also aimed at controlling the entire working class. Prison was not imposed as an isolated device but as part of an elaborate scheme of disciplining devices, including school, military, hospital and factory. That is, the punishment of confinement has been reproduced by institutional segmentation, and by the new categories of knowledge (psychiatric care, therapeutic, legal, etc.) (Pavarini 1995, 11). Punishment within these other disciplining devices was aimed at taming individuals (13). All this operated under the strict model of surveillance and punishment, as Foucault describes. The pattern of the Panopticon materialized the metaphor of the bourgeoisie's panoptical power in the late 18th century (42). In Foucault's words:

> By means of a carceral continuum, the authority that sentences infiltrate all those other authorities that supervise, transform, correct, improve. It might even be said that nothing really distinguishes them any more except the singularly 'dangerous' character of the delinquents, the gravity

---

reformer Quaker Rush described prisons as Republican machines in which the uncivilized should be converted into a good citizen and good worker (Melossi 1997, 73).

of their departures from normal behavior and the necessary solemnity of the ritual (1975, 303).

Clearly, there are institutions that serve the capitalist organization of work – the family, school, hospital and prison – (Melossi 1980, 71). That is why, during the first disciplining phase, the factory was amalgamated into a prison through the model of the workhouse. Marx describes the continuity between the factory and the prison as a disciplining mechanism, held with the purpose of molding the working class:

> The factory code in which capital formulates, like a private legislator, and at his own good will, his autocracy over his workpeople, unaccompanied by that division of responsibility, in other matters so much approved of by the bourgeoisie, and unaccompanied by the still more approved representative system, this code is but the capitalistic caricature of that social regulation of the labor-process which becomes requisite in co-operation on a great scale, and in the employment in common, of instruments of labor and especially of machinery. The place of the slave driver's lash is taken by the over-looker's book of penalties (1867, 463–464).

It is then that:

> Economy of the social means of production, matured and forced as in a hothouse by the factory system, is turned, in the hands of capital, into systematic robbery of what is necessary for the life of the workman while he is at work, theft of space, light, air, and of protection to his person against the dangerous and unwholesome accompaniments of the productive process, not to mention the robbery of appliances for the comfort of the workman. Is Fourier wrong when he calls factories 'tempered prisons?' (465–466).

In plain words: prisons acquired the symbolic representation of factories; the former was conceived as a machine that creates machines to work with other devices (Anitua 2005, 125). This does not seem strange because the goal of the prison was to subject the offender to a general discipline and specifically to the factory discipline, to the capitalist logic. So disciplining punishment was imposed as a modulating mechanism, in and out of the prison. The prison sentence was not reduced to this cycle of 'punishment-reproduction' (the prison's triumph understood as the failure of the goals that it explicitly proclaims);

it also organizes the transgression of laws in a general tactic of submission (Foucault 1975, 277). In the words of the French philosopher:

> [...] if one can speak of justice, it is not only because the law itself or the way of applying it serves the interests of a class, it is also because the differential administration of illegalities through the mediation of penalty forms part of those mechanisms of domination (288).

Marxist tradition explains that prisons do not control the future of prisoners' activities; the presence of those prisoners is what monitors the rest of the population (Young 1976, 18–19). In short, crime control of a few was aimed at crushing the entire working class.

Fragmenting the Working Class

The third implicit aim pursued by punishment was the fragmentation between the over-criminalized subsets of the working class (listed as 'dangerous' and 'savage') and the disciplined ones (listed as 'civilized'). Even the punitive enforcement of welfare introduced conflicts between the 'true' poor (those who have a disability and deserve mercy) and the 'false' poor (those who refuse to endure harsh working conditions, and so, were criminalized). To illustrate, in 1782 the English Gilbert's Law ordered that the parish should assist the capable poor until they could get a job. However, the employed workers – as well as the upper classes – refused to pay taxes to support relief for the 'false' poor. Later on, in the 19th century, the use of imprisoned workers sparked protests in labor organizations that saw them as an 'unfair' competition (Pavarini 1980, 161–188). Instead of joining together to demand better working conditions for all, the conflict evolved into a strong fragmentation in which imprisoned people were seen as enemies of the free working class.[96] In the *Critique of the*

---

96   In Chapter 8 of *Capital*, Marx says: "In the year 1863, an official inquiry took place into the conditions of nourishment and labor of the criminals condemned to transportation and penal servitude. The results are recorded in two voluminous blue books. Among other things it is said: 'From an elaborate comparison between the diet of convicts in the convict prisons in England, and that of paupers in workhouses' and of free laborers in the same country it certainly appears that the former are much better fed than either of the two other classes,' whilst 'the amount of labor required from an ordinary convict under penal servitude is about one half of what would be done by an ordinary day laborer.' A few characteristic depositions of witnesses: John Smith, governor of the Edinburgh prison, deposes: No. 5056. 'The diet of the English prisons [is] superior to the one of ordinary laborers in England;' No. 50. 'It is the fact...that the ordinary agricultural laborers in Scotland

Gotha Program (1875), in contrast to these positions, Marx himself advocated for prison labor to strengthen the working class, and to push prisoners and free workers to organize themselves together for better working conditions (Melossi 2012, 134). Marx acknowledges that the use of prison labor conditioned the downward trend of wages in the market. However, he insists that the goal of a workers' movement should not be to fight against prison labor but to fight against the way in which it is practiced (134, n 19), i.e., against the alienation and workers' exploitation. Finally, in the 20th century, McCarthyism intended to confront the 'orderly and disciplined' working class with those linked to the 'red terror,' and the 'undisciplined' Black-American workers with the 'hardworking' whites, reinforcing class and racial divisions.

This fragmentation of the working class through punishment also had its expression outside the national borders. Colonized workers (listed as 'savages') were opposed to the 'civilized' working class of the central countries, obstructing their joint organization. Even within Europe, Irish workers were linked to crime, vagrancy and vices, and as competitors for employment. This characterization pushed the confrontation between English and Irish workers, hampering their joint organization for better working conditions. This is charted by Marx when he says that all industrial and commercial centers in England now have a working class that is divided into two hostile camps: English vs. Irish proletarians. The ordinary English worker hates the Irish proletarian because he is a competitor who lowers his standard of life; the English understand themselves as members of the dominant nation, refusing to acknowledge the Irish as peers. Racism, propagated by the criminogenic characterization of the Irish people, was based, in contrast, on extremely solid material reasons: the impotence of the English working class, despite the strength of their organization (Levrero 1979). British workers have religious, social and national

---

get very seldom or any meat at all;' Answer: No. 3047. 'Is there anything that you make you aware of the necessity of feeding them better than ordinary laborers? Certainly not.' No. 3048. 'Do you think that further experiments ought to be made to ascertain whether a dietary might not be hit upon for prisoners employed on public works nearly approaching to the dietary of free laborers?' He [the agricultural laborer] might say: 'I work hard, and I have not enough to eat, and when in prison I did not work hard and I had plenty to eat, and therefore it is better for me to be in prison again than here'" (1867, 746–747). In fact, factory conditions were so harsh that they appeared to be even bloodier that the conditions of prison life. While this may have occurred during a particular moment, it was not preserved over time, and less eligibility of prison, relative to the factory, generally prevailed. In addition, the documents cited by Marx may not have been accurate as to the true conditions of the prison.

prejudices against the Irish. They behaved more or less as the poor whites did toward blacks in the u.s. slavery states (Marx quoted in Levrero 1979).

Moral Entrepreneurs and Moral Panics

Sensationalism, evident in sections of the English press during the 18th century, spread throughout Europe during the 19th century. Newspapers permanently published stories of nighttime robberies, encouraging 'panics' in the population. Articles and books related to crime referred to the 'dangerous classes.' Growing literature helped develop the image of the criminal as an individual against the respected society, bringing together all fears for the safety of life, property and family. The memoirs of Vidocq (1828), a former offender who had organized the Criminal Investigation Department of Prefecture of Paris for nearly twenty years, were in the spotlight (Emsley 2007, 20). In 'Whose atrocities?' (1857c), Marx warned that the press hid the heinous acts committed against India under colonialism, while reinforcing the fear of residents.

The moral entrepreneurs of the period were the owners of the press and businessmen associated with it. Misrepresentation or amplification of existing coarse crimes spread, and newspapers invented stories of roadside robberies to increase their sales. Even Paris' General Attorney declared his suspicion that some of the published stories were made up (Emsley 2007, 26). In contrast, the press concealed the crimes of people with advantaged social position: in a case of notorious forgery involving the twin brothers Daniel and Robert Perreau, and Margaret Rudd, the press did not comment on it, fearing social pressure. Only exceptional novelists such as Balzac, Dickens and Trollope reported the crime of the bourgeoisie, illustrating some of its most odious characters and describing events ranging from embezzlement to financial corruption and fraud (152). Dickens criticized the system of solitary confinement and, until today, the prison of Philadelphia remembers his description of that model as a punishment on the souls that could drive people crazy (Eastern State Penitentiary 2016).

The effect of these moral panics on over-criminalization was palpable. Although the vast majority of individuals brought before the criminal courts were charged with relatively minor offenses, they were assimilated into the dangerous crimes and criminals promoted by the press and literature. This affected the outcomes of the jury trials: until the early 20th century, juries were composed of members of the liberal professions, owners and men engaged in business and commerce. Influenced by their own social position and by the spread of these moral panics, they were not likely to show mercy to beggars, prostitutes or vagrants. The result was increasing sentences to the detriment to those subsets of the population (Emsley 2007, 150). In the United States, the movement of The Child Savers was a cornerstone for the over-criminalization of the poor youth in the 19th century, and for the creation of specialized criminal courts and reformatories.

Moral entrepreneurs also incentivized working class fragmentation. In a letter to Meyer and Vogt (1870), Marx states: "the press, the public, the humoristic newspaper – all the means at the disposal of the ruling classes – stoked and artificially increased class-antagonism." Marx expresses that this antagonism explains the scarce results of the English working class' struggle, and empowers the capitalist class. He points out that the burden of the workers' hostility was particularly sensitive between the British and the Irish, whose confrontation was detrimental to overall output (Marx 1870 quoted in Enzensberger 1970, 35). This eloquent insight warns about the link between the press and the ruling class, and how that association harms the potential of the working class' organization.

In the 20th century, the multiplicity of media expanded the influence of moral entrepreneurs in the spread of over-criminalization, disciplining the working class and fostering fragmentation. The most emblematic case was the media propitiation about the evils of drinking and its effects on social degeneration in the United States. Those messages facilitated the sanction of the Dry Law or Prohibition (1920), which made a crime of the manufacture, sale, exchange, transport, import, export or supply of any intoxicating liquor. The Anti-Taverns League, in the vanguard of the criminalization battle, was one of the most efficient groups in the history of U.S. political action. Wheeler, one of its members, negotiated punishments among legislators on the eve of the law's enactment (Auerhahn 1999, 442). Other relevant moral entrepreneur that influenced the sanction of the Dry Law was The Woman's Christian Temperance Union, one of the most influential women's groups of the 19th century that focused primarily on Prohibition.

Meanwhile, the extensive foreign participation in the commercialization of alcohol promoted the characterization of those activities as part of an international conspiracy. The League helped disseminate the fear of "an invasion of our homeland by foreign hordes, many of which have brought and preserved inferior moral and political ideas," leading to a restrictive legislation on immigration in 1920. The act placed limits on immigration from southern and eastern Europe, as those regions were linked with the vice of alcohol (430). This act also served to encourage the fragmentation between the U.S. working class and the waves of migrants who arrived earlier in the century.

The over-criminalization of Black-Americans was also fueled by moral panics, and even by an epic movie, The Birth of a Nation (1915), which cultivated the image of the Black-American male as a dangerous criminal, the image of the White-American woman as the innocent victim, and the Ku Klux Klan as the heroic group that brings justice back (13th 2016).

Brief Reflections

The 18th century, with its axis in the Industrial Revolution and the bourgeois domination of political power, became the turning point for the emergence of what has been termed *disciplining social order*. Poised in the framework of the transition from the competitive to the monopolistic organization of capital, this social order was set on a new form of exercise of crime control. In lieu of the direct violence of the primitive accumulation, the overabundance of labor made possible the use of economic mechanisms to subjugate the working class. Crime control, under a selective matrix, worked to complement the financial mechanisms in satisfying a disciplining purpose. This established the core concept of this section, namely *disciplining criminal selectivity* and its three interior phases: legally-disciplining criminal selectivity (late 18th century), police-medically disciplining criminal selectivity (19th century) and socio-disciplining criminal selectivity (early to late 20th century).

Legally-disciplining criminal selectivity (late 18th century) was settled on formal proclamations of rights and guarantees as an inescapable requirement of the modern legal system. Since it was no longer possible to maintain a differentiated regulatory treatment based on the social status of the offenders, secondary criminalization was reinforced as the privileged space of selective exercise of crime control. An expansive legislation operated as a mechanism of social control aimed at holding the impoverished sectors to the 'social contract' settled by the bourgeois political revolutions. In other words, the sectors that were excluded in the feudal regime were now considered part of the social whole. In return, they must respect the emerging legislation and submit to the demands of capitalist development: (employed and unemployed) workers must become disciplined. However, the inclusive formal proclamations were not materialized for the impoverished sectors. This period shows the material impossibility of the full exercise of the bourgeoisie's illustrated announcements; material inequality prevented real individuals from invoking the rights assigned to them as abstract persons.

This contradiction between formal proclaims and enforcement of the law was reinforced in the criminal field. Offenses became codified in the civil law countries, and rights and guarantees specifying procedural requirements as a prerequisite for implementing punishment were incorporated. However, as the law was allegedly equally treating individuals who were in fact unequal, the result was a continuation of unfairness. Moreover, at the level of secondary criminalization, unfairness was expressed through the mechanisms of legally-disciplining over-criminalization of the acts perpetrated by the pauperism, and legally-disciplining under-criminalization of the acts committed by the mercantile bourgeoisie, feudal lords and monarchic powers.

When it was no longer possible to sustain the incompatibility between formal proclamations of equality with the material inequality of the real world, police-medically disciplining criminal selectivity (19th century) emerged. This mode of criminal selectivity affirmed that there were biological differences between human beings that supported their unequal terms under the law. The medical discourse was in charge of explaining the biological inferiority of both, the impoverished classes and the organized workers and activists (the organized dissident), who were detected and detained by the nascent police forces. The goal was the disciplining of those who, taken as an atavistic holdover on the evolutionary scale, should be legitimately persecuted. The populations of the colonies were subjected to the same treatment, thus allowing the looting of their territories and the subjugation of their workforce, along with the conditioning of the lowest wages of the European working population through competition. The figure of the 'born criminal' was the appeal to arrogate to police-medically disciplining over-criminalization of the colonized masses, the pauperism and the disobedient workers, who were denied rights recognition. The flipside was police-medically disciplining under-criminalization that covered with impunity the subjugation of industrial workers and the colonization conducted by the industrial bourgeoisie.

Towards the end of the disciplining social order, socio-disciplining criminal selectivity (early to late 20th century) was confronted with the harmful effects – the violation of rights and the extermination of human lives – of the prior mode of criminal selectivity. Economic crises and scientific advances also disparaged positivist proclamations, while an alternative communist movement was spreading worldwide. This framework conditioned the emergence of the new mode of criminal selectivity, under a sociological discourse that encouraged the inclusion of the pauperism via welfare states. Disciplining of paupers and organized dissident continued under the guise of socio-disciplining over-criminalization. Socio-disciplining under-criminalization operated on gangsters, white-collar crimes and even massacres perpetrated directly or with the connivance of the monopolistic industrial bourgeoisie.

At this point, we can move on to the next (and last) mode of criminal selectivity: bulimic criminal selectivity.

Bulimic Criminal Selectivity

During the last quarter of the 20th century, and particularly after the economic crisis of the 1970s, a new form of capital accumulation characterized as 'globalization' became the new worldwide-economic standard. It has been marked by a raw hegemony of financial markets (Levy 2006), a concept already outlined by Marx (1857–8) through the notion of 'general intellect.' In this context, a break occurred in the very inclusive process of socio-disciplining criminal selectivity, conditioning drastic changes in the composition of the labor market (increasing precariousness, relative impoverishment and mass expulsion of workers), in correlation to the Law of Absolute Pauperization (1867). This economically expulsive matrix has been taking place concomitantly with a culturally inclusive process (consumption and 'success' patterns have been infused indiscriminately) that permeates even deeper into the impoverished sectors.

In this socio-economic setting, a renewed form of criminal selectivity that continues to the present took shape: *bulimic criminal selectivity* (late 20th century to today). This concept aims to emphasize the patterns adopted by crime control in the *bulimic social order*: growing layers of paupers are incorporated (ingested) into cultural patterns that enforce consumption as integral to success and happiness. However, these layers of paupers do not have access to the economic means to achieve those levels of mass consumption. Moreover, they cannot even be incorporated (digested) into the work discipline. The result is a process of cultural inclusion and economic exclusion, in which the criminal justice system operates on behalf of the work discipline over those who have been expulsed from the economic matrix. This is the basis of the mechanism of *bulimic over-criminalization.*

Bulimic criminal selectivity has another side to be explored: it encourages processes of capital expansion that produce (ingest) larger amounts of capital. This financial-based process is performed in such short periods of time that it cannot afford a productive inversion of these sums of money (they cannot be properly digested). Conversely, these wealth is ejected as speculative capital. This is the basis for the mechanism of *bulimic under-criminalization.*

This study uses analytical contributions from the works of Marx and Engels to address the effects of criminal selectivity in the 20th century. Although there are clear differences between the analyzed socio-economic context and the enunciation framework of the authors, it is proposed that their theoretical

contributions offer a basis upon which to understand the functioning of criminal selectivity in the present. The analysis of Marx and Engels's works will be
supplemented by the contributions of contemporary Marxist thinkers, particularly on issues that were not identified by the former.

To introduce the variables of the bulimic criminal selectivity, the following
explanatory table is presented:

TABLE 3   *Bulimic criminal selectivity*

Characteristics			Chapter 4 Bulimic criminal selectivity
Section 1 Contextual settings: Where, When and How.			Bulimic Social Order (late 20th to 21th century).
Conflict	Social		Clashes between modern pauperism and monopolistic industrial, and financial bourgeoisie, between workers and employers, employed and unemployed, local and immigrants, ethnic-racial minorities and majorities. Conflicts over the appropriation of markets and natural resources among nations.
	Criminal		Urban marginality that responds to the process of bulimia.
Control	Social		Global subjugation of the working class and deepening of criminal control.
	Criminal	Under-criminalization	Illegal occupations, extermination, robbery and complex business-crime.
		Over-criminalization	Criminalized survival strategies (vagrancy, begging), coarse crime (petty crimes against property).
Under- criminalized social sectors			Monopolistic industrial bourgeoisie and international financial bourgeoisie.
Over- criminalized social sectors			Pauperism (social junk and social dynamite).
Manifest Discourse			Delegitimizing theory of punishment, and new versions of the theories of social order disciplinary.
Latent Functions			Incapacitating problematic sectors, controlling the modern pauperism, fragmenting the working class, encouraging a 'crime control industry' and an omnipresent control of the social whole.

Where, How and When of the Bulimic Social Order (Late 20th to 21th Century)

Bulimic criminal selectivity is framed in a new social scheme that can be called *bulimic social order*. The concept of 'social order' is preferable to 'society' to account for its antagonistic nature (Pashukanis 1924, 149) and not hide the differences, inequalities, and hierarchies between those who are rulers and those who are ruled (Pegoraro 2012, 72). The concept of 'bulimia' (or process of inclusion – exclusion) is based on the notion of relative deprivation (Merton 1949) within the specific characteristics of late modernity (Young 2007). In this context, deprivation lies not only in the conditioned exclusion of social sectors and their lack of access to culturally deployed goals, but in the fact that those social sectors are *firmly included* in the cultural paradigm of consumption while they are *systematically excluded* from its materialization, deepening their relegation (49). As opposed to a binary analysis in terms of 'included social sectors' and 'excluded social sectors' – each one with their own territorial and cultural categories[1] – the notion of 'bulimia' (Young 2007) shows a continuous flow in which the most impoverished sectors are (economically) excluded, but (culturally) included. Indeed, these economically excluded subsets are more culturally included than the well-off sectors as a result of mass consumption, television as the daily information-source and violence as the expression of manhood. At the same time, it is not possible to perceive geographic 'outsides' and 'insides;' on the contrary, both sectors coexist in spaces delimited by porous borders that are easily passable: the gated-communities of the rich depend on the work of the poor to maintain them (55). 'Cultural inclusion,' then, shows how these impoverished sectors are strongly adapted to the First World Dream that becomes the basic narrative for their lives, even though they have to confront it with their economical exclusion (Young 2012, 148–149). In short, during the bulimic social order, the most impoverished sectors are culturally included and economically excluded, or, more briefly, they are subjected to a process of inclusion – exclusion.

---

1 Young points out that this binary reading is based on the reduction of complex social phenomena to simple opposites: high class v. lower class; unproblematic v. problematic population; community v. disorganization; employment v. unemployment; independence v. unemployment insurance; stable families v. single parents; natives v. immigrants; legal drugs v. illicit drugs; victims v. criminals. These are false dichotomies, as neither such extreme has a strictly delimited form. In Young's words: the construction of the problem in a binary mode hides the problem of disparities in a late modern society, while the concept of social exclusion ironically exaggerates the degree of exclusion and underestimates its seriousness (2007, 46).

Going further, 'primitive' societies were 'cannibalistic' (they swallowed strangers, gaining strength from them), as was evident during primitive accumulation when the undesired members of society were physically exterminated. This mode of functioning was taken up by socio-disciplining selectivity, when welfare policies started to absorb 'strangers' (the impoverished sectors) who were 're-habilitated' and incorporated to the labor and welfare system in a non-conflictive manner. In contrast, modern societies swallow these impoverished sectors through the education system, the media and the market, imposing global images of success, expectations and desires, but then they economically expel them (Young 1999b, 35). Crime control operates as the ultimate expulsion, after an excessive culture intake, through increasing over-criminalization. In the context of crisis and removal of the paupers from the productive matrix, crime control, selectively applied, has broadly expanded to fill the space left by the economic restraint mechanisms (those developed during the disciplining social order in general and that were particularly extended during the third phase of the disciplining period, the socio-disciplining order). Bulimic criminal selectivity operates, then, to avoid conflict and to neutralize the included-excluded population.

Where does bulimic criminal selectivity take place? Although the bulimic social order involves a new socio-economic configuration on a global scale, the book maintains the focus on the United States and Western Europe. There are two reasons behind this decision: first, historical trends occur first and in more definitive form in those regions; secondly, focusing on those areas maintains the analytical continuity with the geographical scenario discussed in the previous modalities of criminal selectivity. A peculiarity of this period is that the United States becomes even more important as a center of global power: The White House at the heart of political power; the Federal Reserve, Treasury and Wall Street as icons of international financial markets; and its various cities as multilateral financial institutional bases (Boron 2004). Especially in the criminal field, the United States became the dominant producer of theories on crime and punishment. However, the most relevant aspect of its centrality is its configuration as an outlier state, where the size of the repressive agencies and the harshness of punishment – with pronounced classist and racist features – acquired magnitudes not comparable with any other Western nation.

When did bulimic criminal selectivity take place? It mainly arose in the 1970s, in the context of the oil crisis and the end of the Fordist production system (Foucault 1977–8; Deleuze 1995; Wacquant 1999; Taylor 2001; De Giorgi 2002; Garland 2001; Castel 2003; Young 1999, 2000 and 2007; Harvey 2005; Piketty 2013).

How does bulimic criminal selectivity take place? Through the development of a financial-based and hyper-globalized capitalism, settled over a processes of economic exclusion and cultural inclusion of impoverished social sectors.

Economic Exclusion

At the end of the 20th century, the financial conformation of capitalism was built upon the processes of displacing productive investment into its speculative form (with its effects on the expulsion of labor). Financial capitalism was also built upon an increasing automation in the remaining productive investments (with its effects on expulsion of labor because only a small number of people is required for the control of machinery). Speculation and automation favored insecurity for employees and increasing pauperism for unemployed sectors. In short, it favors the economic exclusion of impoverished sectors.[2]

Concerning the first process (changes in the reproduction of capital from a productive to a speculative from), it materializes in the hegemony of new means of production, which are nothing but parasitic speculation mechanisms (exchange transactions, fictitious acquisitions, swaps, financial loans).[3]

---

2   Marx illustrates that the decline in variable capital in the process of capital accumulation is a direct result of the Law of Absolute Pauperization and reinforces the Tendency of the Rate of Profit to Fall (1867, 3). Capitalists are paradoxically harmed by the expulsion of labor from the labor market, because the rate of profit declines as a result of increased technical capabilities (proportion of machinery in comparison with labor) and the growth in the organic composition (ratio of constant capital in relation to variable capital) generated by the automation and financial character of capital accumulation. This trend has been questioned by two arguments: first, the compensatory function of the increase in the rate of surplus value and, secondly, the stability of the organic composition. However, this does not discredit Marx's analysis that, far from seeing it as an irrefutable law, characterized it as a 'trend.' In other words, a 'functional' principle which includes two opposing movements: one towards the fall and the other to the attenuation of the declining percentage of profit. 'Marx well established that the law referred to an intrinsically downward movement of the rate of profit, which he called a tendency to consider that the decline unfolds in a "countered, hampered, attenuated" manner [...] Its main objective was not to clarify the unstable and irregular nature of the reproduction of capital, but the effects of the structural imbalances in crisis recovery (Katz 2000).'

3   From the 1970s, the fall of the general rate of industrial profit, especially in the United States, led to the accumulation of an enormous amount of money without the ability to find out a way to invest it in the production of goods and services. The acceleration of monetary circulation, the unbridled expansion of credit to unproductive functions, the proliferation of shares, bonds and all kinds of false values, the transnational interconnection of Stock Exchanges as a means of concentration of capital and the relentless growth of state debt produce conditions for a final transformation of the historical relationship between the process

Marx warns about the importance of the financial component of capitalist competition within credit itself, which at first appears as favoring the small capitalist but was a new weapon that eventually became a giant social mechanism of centralization of capital (1867, 436).[4] In other words, bulimic social order occurs in the transition of productive capital to financial capital: more than 400 billion dollars are exchanged every day on currency markets, while the flow of commercial transactions is only about $12 million (Calavita et al. 1997, 29). Or, to give another startling figure, 95% of the capital that circulates daily in the international financial system is equivalent to a number greater than the combined gross national product of Mexico, Brazil and Argentina (Boron 2014).[5] These sums of money are unthinkable when it comes to productive capital: they are deposited for less than seven days, a period incompatible with the time-frame required in a production process to be able to generate economic growth and social well-being.[6] Then, instead of being productively invested (digested), capital is discharged (ejected) in a speculative manner.

The second aspect of this new economic configuration, as proposed, is linked to new forms of division of labor. As an effect of automation, the

---

of production and financial speculation. The latter becomes the dominant form of reproduction of transnational capital with its permanent threat of collapse and depression, its concomitant destabilizing fluctuations in prices of raw materials, agricultural and industrial products, of coins, of the life quality of the population and of the political stability of States (Cervantes Martinez et al. 2000, 185–186 quoted in Ciafardini 2014).

4   Marx analyzes financial institutions based on the study of bank capital, which was the leading financial institution when he was writing. He describes it in terms of a new class of capitalists who contribute to the advancement of capital without being involved in the management (financial capitalist). On the other hand, Marx describes another category of capitalists who provide capital and exercise management functions (active capitalist). The new phase comes with the creation of the director position, who acts as a manager while the capitalist is removed from the production process. Under the banking system, the distribution of capital is subtracted from the hands of private capitalists (1867, 782).

5   This effect occurs through a movement of gradual privatization and transfer of public wealth into private property from the 1970s to 1980s, and a long-term readjustment of real estate asset prices and the stock market in the 1980s and 1990s, in a global political context that was favorable to private equity in comparison with the period after World War II (Piketty 2013, 273–274).

6   Strange (1986) characterizes the current status of capitalism as a 'casino capitalism:' in a few minutes, it is possible to lose a fortune; "the big difference between a normal casino, where you can enter or not, with the global casino of high finance, is that its daily bets concern all of us [...] From recent graduates to pensioners, what occurs in the casinos of major financial centers may have a sudden, unpredictable and unavoidable consequence for individual lives. The financial casino takes us on a roller coaster."

workforce is no longer the primary input in the production process, but a mere
inspector of the machines. This change can be traced in the work of Marx
(1857–8) and his concept of 'general intellect.' Marx notes that the maximization of the form of work of the industrial period would bring a new social
order governed by knowledge as the prime productive force. He explains that
the development of fixed capital reveals how general social knowledge has
become an immediate productive force (230). Thus, the development of the
productive forces of society, measured in fixed capital, is merely objectified
social knowledge that the capital appropriates. This evolution of productive
force has resulted in an increased automation that disregards human labor
as the primary input, so that the creation of real wealth comes to depend less
on material human work, and more on the general state of science and the
progress of technology. That is, "the man behaves as a supervisor and a regu-
lator with respect to the production process itself" (228), instead of being its
chief actor. Marx explains that this process would push capital to its own dissolution and that humanity will achieve free time for artistic and scientific
purposes. While this did not happen, it is possible to use Marx's anticipatory
analysis to highlight how abstract knowledge (automation) has tended to become the primary productive force of society, relegating physical human work
to a marginal position. Castillo (1996) characterizes this process as 'organizational lyophilization:' the process by which living substances are eliminated,
since living labor is increasingly replaced by dead labor (quoted in Antunes
2003).[7] The off shoring and internationalization of productive capital in the
globalized context also tend to affect the mobility of investments into regions
that ask for lower investment in terms of wages, which increases the levels of
impoverishment at a global level.

---

7   Authors such as Moulier Boutang, Lazzarato, Negri and Vercellone argue that we are in a dif-
    ferential phase of capitalism that they call 'cognitive capitalism.' It proposes that intellectual
    and immaterial labor becomes dominant. The surplus value has to do with making workers
    voluntarily put their knowledge at the service of the company and the capital. Moreover,
    exploitation is not limited only to the extraction of surplus value, but also to the absence of
    democracy in the organization of production, and the loss of purpose in the activities that
    the workers perform. In short, the term cognitive intends to highlight the changing nature of
    work and sources of value and surplus value, forms of ownership and relations of exploita-
    tion which, today, supports capital accumulation (Vercellone 2011). Although it is possible to
    agree with this analysis in relation to the increase of immaterial labor and the importance
    of scientific knowledge as elements of this new stage of capitalism, these thoughts should
    not make us overlook the fact that the production of goods remains the genuine 'pillar' on
    which the everydayness of life is based (even though it is based on an in-depth automation
    of production).

These structural changes (automation and globalization) had a political translation in the dismantling of the welfare state and the declining social satisfaction of the economically excluded sectors. This process has been described as a return to the primitive accumulation to "re-establish the conditions for capital accumulation and to restore the power of economic elites" (Harvey 2005, 19). These political changes wrought the supremacy of individual freedom over social responsibility, competition over cooperation, free market over state intervention, mobile capital over financial regulation, and business interests over the rights of the organized labor (20).[8]

The increase of financial capital, the automation-dislocation of the production process, and the disarmament of welfare led to a deepening of what Marx conceptualized through the Law of Absolute Impoverishment (1867, 540). It refers to capital's encouragement of the creation of a reserve army, steadying the wages of employed workers, and protecting the needs of capital against the oscillating demand for labor, which tends toward a relative impoverishment of the working class.[9] Under the bulimic social order, this process becomes even deeper, relapsing to the de-structuring of the third phase of the disciplining social order, which had fostered workers' rights and welfare policies. The main expressions of this overturn are (a) the precariousness of the labor market; (b) the expansion of the distributive gap; and (c) the exponential increase of pauperism.

a. When discussing the precariousness of the labor market, industrial manufacturing became more capital-intense and technologically sophisticated, resulting in fewer jobs for more skilled workforces (Garland 2001, 81–83). This collapse of the industrial production took place with a decline in the strength and size of trade union membership – which was a central tool for activism and rights-empowerment during the disciplining social order. In addition to this expulsion-sophistication of the industrial sphere, a transition from physical labor (characteristic of the primitive accumulation and the disciplining social order) to immaterial labor inherent to the service sector occurred.

---

8 Consider the United States, social spending is the scarcest among the major industrialized countries (after Australia and South Africa). The population officially classified as 'very poor' (those living on less than 50% the amount of the poverty line) doubled between 1975 and 1995, reaching the figure of 14 million people (Nun 1999, 996). After that, the 1996 reduction of the Aid to Families with Dependent Children, the broadest social program of the country, conditioned that the amount of families living on less than $2.00 per person per day went from 636,000 in 1996 to about 1.5 million (with three million children overall) in 2011.

9 Marx states then that law entails "an accumulation equivalent to capital accumulation misery," conditioning increases in wealth at one end of the class spectrum to have proportional effects upon the other (1867, 536).

This transition conditioned the emergence of a new sector of workers, the so-called 'precariat' (Wacquant 2011), characterized by insecure short-period contracts (Young 2007, 41).[10] In other words, on the one hand, classic industrial and rural workers (dominant sectors in the disciplining social order) are in severe retraction and configure a privileged category in relation to the whole working class with precarious and temporary jobs.[11] On the other hand, the number of workers in the service-sector is steadily increasing. These workers lack strong unions and full labor rights, they are intermittently employed and they receive asymmetric salaries in comparison with the formally employed worker. Their unfair and unstable economic situation undermines the coherence of their personal narratives, under the 'vertigo of late modernity,' which is to say that they suffer from a "sense of insecurity, insubstantiality, uncertainty, and fear of falling" (Young 2007, 35). They experience that the nature of their jobs, the number of hours that they work and their compensation are unfair; as if they were outside the norms of "a fair wage for a fair work day." They are part of the labor market but are not full citizens (115). As an example, the largest employer in the United States, Walmart, keeps their employees on such low salaries that they have to combine them with food stamps and Medicare (Walmart1Percent 2015).

Thus, far from the prophecies about the end of work, what is taking place is a "new polysemy of work" (Antunes 2003), i.e. the end of work with stable wages and well-paid jobs as a real and achievable perspective (Nun 1999) and its

---

10   This secondary market relies on tasks that neither have a rigid center of supply nor require the coexistence of workers in the same space and at the same moment. Conversely, they are the subject of a multifunctional and versatile de-specialization that makes them expendable. Since the 1970s, this process has deepened as a result of labor deregulation laws, with its drop in regulatory coverage for stable employment, expansion of de-collectivization dynamics, re-individualization and de-standardization, and increasing insecurity within the erosion of wage society (Castel 2003, 58). The incorporation of women into the labor market, which reaches 50% in advanced countries, accentuated this process, as they hold precarious and deregulated jobs, with lower wage income and higher destabilization (Antunes 2003). In 2006, the 'informal sector' came to almost a billion people, what makes it the fastest growing sector, unprecedented in history (Davis 2006). Even this impressive number may be higher, as the statistics of most countries collaborate to hide their real numbers: one hour of work per week is enough to be removed from the index of unemployment (Wacquant 1999, 86).

11   This process is valid for the analyzed geographical areas (Western Europe and the United States), while the situation of countries like China or India deserves a separate analysis because of the constant incorporation of former peasants into industrial production. Because of the global character of capitalism, this process may influence the composition of the universal labor market.

fracturing into: structural unemployment, underemployment, part-time and precarious work, full incorporation of women and flexible modes of employment, all of which accounts for one-third of the available global labor force.[12] Within the 'precariat,' there is an even lower substrate that can be called *under-precariat*: the immigrants who are often coerced to remain illegal. They occupy the flimsiest jobs within this already weak category, and are continually exposed to relapses into the lower stratum of pauperism. The under-precariat consists of the gastarbeiters in Germany, lavoro nero in Italy, chicanos in the United States, immigrants from Eastern Europe (Poles, Hungarians, Romanians, Albanians, etc.) in Western Europe, dekaseguis in Japan, Bolivians in Brazil, brasiguayos in Paraguay (Antunes 2003).

b. The second effect of the process of economic exclusion is the massive increase in the distributive gap. In Europe and the United States, the most advantaged sector reached 65% of assets in 2010, a level of prosperity unknown since 1913. Currently, 10% of the most economically advantaged globally own between 80% and 90% of the world's wealth, while the 50% poorest population have less than 5%. On this basis, it is predicted that the 21st century will hold even greater levels of inequality and, therefore, more social discord (Piketty 2013).[13] In the United States, the Walton family (owners of Walmart) hold the same amount of money as 40% of the U.S. population at the bottom of the distribution range (Walmart1Percent 2015). Indeed, it is the first time in U.S. history in which the American Dream has entirely fallen apart: it is not

---

12   Boron clarifies that "[t]oday, capitalism not only subjects the industrial proletariat but, as recalled by Houtart, there is a real and formal subsumption of the vast majority of the world's population to the logic of capital, that has expanded remarkably the number and diversity of social actors who today are in contradiction with the bourgeoisie. A rough calculation shows that under these conditions about three billion people are directly involved" (2008, 124–125). Boron explains that, though, "the centrality of the working class [...] has to do with its unique insertion in the productive process and its irreplaceable role in the valorization of capital, which means that only that class can eventually meet the necessary conditions for subverting the bourgeois order" (128) and, citing Miliband, he adds that "the principal (but not the only) gravedigger of capitalism still is the organized working class" (129). Likewise, Iñigo Carrera (2003).

13   Piketty (2013) explains that the average return on capital exceeds the growth rate of the economy and that inherited wealth always has more value than what an individual can accumulate in a life time. He concludes that capitalism is incompatible with democracy and social justice, as it tends to a constant increase of inequality: the 1% and 10% of the most economically advantaged individuals enhance their wealth, while the amount received by the poor drops. While this book focuses its analysis on Europe and the United States, it is noteworthy that Piketty's analysis is not concentrated only in Western developed countries, but also in Russia, China, and developing countries.

enough for parents to work hard in order to provide their children with a better life (Chetty 2016). The American Dream's destruction particularly affects Black-Americans and Latinos as well as families headed by single mothers; all of them are far more likely to earn lower wages than average and live below the poverty line (McKernan et al. 2009).

   c. As a corollary to the described processes, pauperism increased. The restructure of the labor market works "systematically expulsing low-skilled, poorly educated, young, urban and minority population for whom long-term unemployment was the prospect" (Garland 2001, 83). As it was predicted by Marx, the enlargement of the pauperism is linked to the growth of the reserve army which, in turn, increases the rhythm of social wealth:

> The greater the social wealth, the mentioning capital, the extent and energy of its growth, and, therefore, also the absolute mass of the proletariat and the productiveness of its labor, the greater is the industrial reserve-army. The same causes which develop the expansive power of capital develops also the labor-power at its disposal. The relative mass of the industrial reserve-army increases therefore with the potential energy of wealth. But the greater this reserve-army in proportion to the active labor-army, the greater is the mass of a consolidated surplus-population, whose misery is in inverse ratio to its torment of labor. The more extensive, finally, the lazurus-layers of the working-class, and the industrial reserve-army, the greater is official pauperism. *This is the absolute general law of capitalist accumulation.* Like all other laws, it is modified in its working by many circumstances, the analysis of which does not concern us here (1867, 707).

In short, economic exclusion expresses in the enlargement of the distributive gap and the ensuing conditions: the deepening of the relative pauperization of employed workers and the exuberant increase in pauperism. The latter became the primary target of bulimic over-criminalization.

Cultural Inclusion

Economic exclusion intersects with several superstructural variables. Within these, as has been argued, the most relevant is the conjunction of material exclusion and cultural inclusion. The culture defined by those who are economically included also absorbs those who are not. Everybody is pushed to incorporate the high social values of the American Dream, a cult of success and a celebration of consumption (Young 2007, 73). Malls are an obvious example: although they offer exclusive brands with unaffordable prices for the paupers, crowds from the suburbs come in pilgrimage to these temples of consumption. Most devotees covet things that their pockets cannot afford. Entire suburban families undertake the journey to these malls, to these capsules of consumption, where an aesthetic-focused market has designed an amazing landscape of models, brands and labels (Galeano 2005).

This excessive cultural inclusion generates iatrogenic effects in the pauperized sectors, configuring a phenomenon that could be called *supra-culturization*. It describes disproportionate consumption standards – in relation to the use of the goods that are acquired – and a culture of violence oriented to (re) construct incoherent personal narratives. Material barriers do not only represent a mere economic deprivation, but also the impossibility of belonging, of being somebody, in a social order that assimilates having (something) with being (someone). As a response, supra-culturization operates in the form of a 'reaction formation'[14] to this economic and biographical exclusion. It takes place in the form of an over-acquisition of goods which cost in excess of their use-value because their functionality consists in providing identity, or membership, as the saying goes 'tell me what you have and I will tell you what you lack.' If the included population is encouraged to acquire technology, paupers seek to buy the latest innovations; if the use of clothing brands is promoted, the poor value the brand above the usefulness of the garment; if consuming television programs is a widespread option for leisure, paupers remain watching television for hours and hours, super-idealizing and imitating those famous individuals identified with the ideal of 'success;' if buying a car or a motorcycle is conceived as synonymous with status, the poor assume it as a way to build identity. In short, paupers get involved in a maximization of cravings, and a hunger for immediacy (they want it all, and they want it now). The narratives are clear about this: people in some slums of the United States do not even know how to sign or write their names, but they know the names of very exclusive brands as Prada or Gucci because they are bombarded with promotions or advertising all day long (Hayward 2004). These impoverished sectors are seduced by the idealization of brands such as Gucci, BMW or Nike. They watch television 11 hours a day. They share the obsession of a violent culture. They supported the U.S. incursions of the Gulf War. They worship success, money, wealth and status and even the racism of society (Young 2007, 49).

---

14   'Reactive formation' refers to the influence of the unconscious on the formation of symptoms (what Freud calls 'defense mechanism') that consist of behaviors, habits or attitudes that are opposed to repressed desires. It emerges as a defense against the disturbing pulsion, i.e., the individual constructs a reaction against the expression of his desire to protect himself from it (Laplanche and Pontalis 1996).

Supra-culturization also encourages the radicalization of those features that enable the included-excluded masses to sustain a certain superiority over others. This process takes place through an intimidating physical presence, the use of violence to solve problems, and racist attitudes against their class peers that are part of a racial, ethnic, gender or sexual minority. A violent, racist and misogynistic culture helps them to reinforce their identities against 'weaker' subsets.

Through excessive consumption and re-enforced violence, supra-culturization is markedly more pronounced in young people with dissonant expectations about their future. They are pressured by cultural inclusion but they have little opportunities to achieve material integration. They are even denied access to full citizenship status due to daily harassment by police, or being unfit to occupy the patriarchal role within the family. Frightened by stereotypes and prejudice, the youth underclass has the most extraordinary crisis of identity and self-esteem. It is not only about the relative deprivation, but also about ontological crises (Young 1999, 79). Then, goods and violence acquire an extra – value and they become the core of their identities. Being young is understood as incorporating symbols, practices and consumer spaces (Bermudez 2001).

To further this process of inclusion – exclusion within the bulimic social order, the following pages explore the pair bulimic conflict-control.

Bulimic Conflict-Control

Social conflict of this radical stage relied on the need to control the impoverished masses embedded in the process of inclusion – exclusion. In the case of immigrants or ethnically relegated populations, this process is exacerbated by the burden of xenophobia. This has resulted in clashes between employed and unemployed workers, local and immigrants,[15] ethnic-racial minorities and majorities, and the fundamental struggle between industrial and financial bourgeoisie with the employed workers. Finally, there are conflicts among nations, in a continuation with the third disciplining phase. The crucial domain of the United States which is responsible for half of global spending on armaments and possess bases and missions of military training in 121 countries across the

---

15   The undermining fear is that the migrant worker harms the local worker, through employment hoarding. Focusing on Britain, Cohen (1995) suggests that this fear may not be real because immigrant population demands jobs that involve, in principle, lot of hours of work and commitment that national citizens tend to find acceptable. Cohen notes that if those jobs were not fulfilled by immigrants, they would probably not be occupied at all.

planet, constitutes an unprecedented phenomenon. Globalization is a new phase of the imperialist stage of capitalism (Boron 2014).

Concerning crime conflict, the process of inclusion – exclusion and its effects on supra-culturization as a 'reaction formation' may condition the commission of coarse crimes or those linked to the use of violence by paupers. In the bulimic social order, coarse crimes do not only involve illegal ways to satisfy material needs (absolute deprivation) – as it was more evident during the primitive accumulation and the first and second disciplining phases.[16] They do not consist either in illegal ways of obtaining essential goods, as a result of cultural pressure (relative deprivation), as it happened during the third disciplining phase. Coarse crimes during the bulimic social order are an apotheosis of that relative deprivation: they involve offenses against property that are configured as the most suitable way (apart from random situations, or very exceptional cases of sporting prowess) to obtain the financial inputs needed to acquire what is required for exacerbated cultural inclusion, as well as reinforcing identity and belonging. This means that, in the context of the bulimic social order, coarse crimes do not respond to a lack of culture but to an extreme embrace of a culture of success and individualism (Young 2007, 31).[17] By this logic, cultural inclusion is what broadens the scope of exclusion, and what encourages the treatment of the excluded as deviants (Giorgi 1997, 93–95). The commission of coarse crimes is even physically facilitated in late modernity by the mass presence of portable high-value goods (particularly cell phones), less situational controls (self-service shops, empty houses during the days while people are working, downtown areas such as entertainment facilities without residents, cars unattended in the streets), and reduced social and self-control mechanisms (less informal social controls in families, neighborhoods, schools and streets; more anonymous life; relaxation of norms; questioning of authorities; less normalized repression) (Garland 2001, 90–92). It is important to stress, though, that this reasoning does not imply a linear association between

---

16   Geremek explains that since the mid-20th century the social evolution of developed countries gradually leads to the disappearance of physiological poverty as a mass phenomenon (1986, 22). Of course, this is not a global phenomenon, as evidenced by statistics of South Asia and Africa, which show that between 25% and 30% of the population is in a state of chronic malnutrition (261).

17   Contrary to the views of liberal thinkers who assume a direct causal relation between unemployment and criminal behavior, this relationship is mediated by the characteristics of capitalist social ties (Bohm 1984, 214). Taylor (1982) expresses that crime is not an effect of unemployment, but of the way in which the capitalist mode of production sets man against man and 'systematically' prioritizes individual interest as a rational social practice.

inclusion – exclusion and crime. More accurate would be to understand the latter as a determining factor to justify the application of crime control over the paupers. Crime control exceeds crime conflict, as it has been imposed as an instrument of social control, revisiting a pattern of primitive accumulation.

Crime control under bulimic social order, indeed, functions as a mechanism of social control replacing the undermined economic constraints. The stage of primitive accumulation, which had been displaced by the disciplining social order through the massive incorporation of workers into the market, has been recovered. After being culturally swallowed and economically expelled, crime control operates as last hurdle of the paupers. As an effect, they become stigmatized and their chances of re-entering the labor market become more constrained. Modern paupers end up being a multitude of criminal records-holders, with even more fractured lives than before the interaction with crime control. Retreating further into the criminal space becomes a plausible alternative, reinforcing even more crime control.

In the transition from the disciplining social order to the bulimic social order, crime control was transformed. During the former, crime control was a stable institutional structure with a consolidated intellectual framework of penal-welfare, characterized by a liberal political conception and acting as a guarantor of order and safety. However, challenges to the legitimacy and effectiveness of welfare institutions spread-out. Complaints point out the permanent inadequacy of budgets, the tendency of rising expectations and the inefficacy of the bureaucratic machinery. These critiques along with the fading of the collective memories of depression make the state appear to many as the problem rather than the solution (Garland 2001, 92–94). Crime control acquired, then, a retributive, vindictive and deterrent approach to punishment (74–81). It did so through the mechanisms of *bulimic over-criminalization* and *bulimic under-criminalization*, which are developed below.

Bulimic Under-Criminalization

The notion of *bulimic under-criminalization* refers, on the one hand, to the narrow and scarce legislation of behaviors that produce social harm, particularly the territorial occupations in the context of the so-called 'war on terror,' and financial maneuvers in the context of increasing financial capitalism (primary under-criminalization). On the other hand, bulimic under-criminalization describes the rare implementation of the already scarce legislation that regulates those behaviors (secondary under-criminalization). Primary and secondary bulimic under-criminalization serve the purpose of promoting accumulation and globalization of capital. The following analyzes bulimic under-criminalization of (a) the war on terror and (b) financial maneuvers.

Bulimic Under-Criminalization of the War on Terror

Under the war on terror, bulimic under-criminalization finds a double manifestation: at the individual and the supra-individual level. Concerning the latter, bulimic under-criminalization describes the process by which certain state actors (those characterized by the u.s. State Department as 'state sponsors of terrorism'[18]) and certain non-state actors (those considered neither 'civilians' nor 'state parties' which are accused of conducting or supporting acts of terrorism – e.g. ISIS, Al-Qaeda and Hamas-) are expelled from the international legal framework in the context of the war on terror, allowing the consideration of counter-terrorist actions against them as legitimate (and, thereafter, under-criminalized).[19] Meanwhile, at the individual level, those accused of committing or supporting acts of terrorism are expelled from the traditional criminal law framework, based on the application of the 'law of the enemy', allowing, also here, the consideration of counter-terrorist actions against them as legitimate (and, thereafter, under-criminalized).

The turning point for the expansion of the counter-terrorist actions does not seem to be exclusively anchored in terrorist attacks; it was also marked, on the political level, by the fall of the Soviet bloc, which enabled an unrestricted expansion of Western powers in the new unipolar context dominated by the United States. The 'war on terror' has also been influenced, at the economic level, by the oil crisis. The latter showed the need for this dominant country to exercise control over the territories that hold non-renewable energy resources, to ensure the strength of the monopolistic mode of production. This process was described by Marx as a component of the Tendency of the Rate of Profit to Fall (1867), which refers to the geographical expansion and global spatial reorganization for the reproduction of capital and the reduction of the impact of the overproduction crisis. Territorial occupations, key element of the 'war on terror,' are characterized as a 'new wave of enclosures' – in parallel with the ones of the primitive accumulation. These new enclosures serve the appropriation of natural resources, territories and knowledge through the same mechanism of 'accumulation by dispossession' that took place in the foundation of capitalism (Harvey 2003, 111).

War on Terror at the Supra-Individual Level. When discussing the global war on terror, the process of bulimia describes a double process: since the two World Wars and in a process that is still going on, a massive incorporation

---

18   The u.s. State Department included Iran (1984), Sudan (1993) and Syria (1979) as 'State Sponsors of Terrorism.' *See* http://www.state.gov/j/ct/list/c14151.htm.

19   Reluctance to incorporate Non-State Actors to the international legal framework responds to the fear that giving them human rights obligations could 'legitimize' them (Clapham 2010, 53).

(*ingest*) of all the international actors into a global legal framework that settled rights and obligations has been taking place. The core of the obligations has to do with respecting universal values, while the central aspect of the recognized rights involves protection against abusive actions committed by other international actors. After this 'ingestion,' a process of expulsion (*ejection*) of those actors accused of supporting or committing acts of terror from the legal protections that had been universally granted took place. This means that the international legal framework could not digest those actors labeled as 'terrorists,' and expelled them from their scope of influence and protection. This expulsion opened the path for the under-criminalization of counter-terrorist actions committed against those 'terrorist' actors.

Even though the counter-terrorist actions perpetrated by the leading powers can be as harmful as the terrorist ones, they are regarded as legitimate (and under-criminalized) because they are allegedly aimed at confronting those acts that they themselves had previously labeled as 'terrorist.' Concerning primary under-criminalization, the Convention on the Prevention and Punishment of the Crime of Genocide of the United Nations of 1948 is the universal legal framework for defining and outlawing genocide, crimes against humanity, war crimes and crime of aggression. Those crimes are judged by the International Criminal Court (I.C.C). However, in a clear expression of the primary under-criminalization of counter-terrorist nations, the United States avoided being subjected to the Convention and the I.C.C through the non-ratification of the Rome Statute that created the court. Moreover, in 2002, the U.S. Congress passed the American Service-Members Protection Act to protect the military personnel and other elected and appointed officials against criminal prosecution by an international court to which the United States is not a party. This means that the law undermines the prosecution of U.S. citizens in the I.C.C. The effects of this federal law include prohibition of both, extradition of citizens to the court and provision of assistance to it.[20] The lack of ratification of the I.C.C. jurisdiction is part of the general U.S. foreign policy in international law, including its abandonment of the Anti-Ballistic Missile Treaty and its rejection of the Kyoto Treaty – the protocol to strengthen biological weapons treaties (Iadicola 2009/10, 105). This phenomenon has been described as the

---

20 It is accurate to refer to illegal occupations because Afghanistan (2002) and Iraq (2003) have not been authorized by the United Nations (in accordance with the provisions of the statute). On the other hand, occupations are regulated as an invasion of one state by another without authorization from the United Nations (crime of aggression), which was only incorporated to the Rome Statute in 2010. Accordingly, the occupations in the Middle East could not be retroactively judged by the I.C.C., even if the United States were part of it.

'Law of the Empire,' namely, a process through which a global power seeks to arrogate the role of sovereign over the rest of the nations while pleading itself as the exception (Bartholomew 2006, 163).

Concerning the mechanism of secondary under-criminalization, the crimes committed in the domestic and foreign jurisdictions have remained generally unpunished. As the most significant example, the United States committed worldwide massacres throughout its history, although only once did an international tribunal indict it. In *Nicaragua v United States* (1986), the International Court of Justice (I.C.J.) determined that the United States supported acts of international terrorism that produced tens of thousands of victims in the effort to overthrow the Nicaraguan President Daniel Ortega. The United States refused to participate in the trial, invoking lack of jurisdiction and legitimacy of the court. It intensified the attacks on Nicaragua and vetoed a Security Council resolution calling on all states to observe international law. In 1990 the Nicaraguan presidential candidate supported by the United States won the elections and withdrew the charges before the I.C.J. The case was closed.[21] Chomsky says: "the United States is, after all, the only country condemned by the International Court of Justice for international terrorism – for the illegal use of force for political purposes, as the Court points out" (quoted in Iadicola 2009/10, 102).[22]

The apotheosis of this process is that the laws that regulate 'terrorist' actions are extremely similar to the ones that serve to under-criminalize the 'counter-terrorist' ones. Young affirms that, when comparing terrorist and anti-terrorist

---

21   The U.S. magazine *Time* pointed out that the methods implemented by the country were ruining the Nicaraguan economy and maintaining a long and deadly proxy war until the exhausted local powers shot down themselves the unwanted government. With a minimal cost to the United States, these methods left Nicaragua with destroyed bridges, sabotaged power plants and ruined fields, providing the U.S. candidate with a winning platform: the end of the impoverishment of Nicaragua's people (Chomsky 2001).

22   Closer in time, and in response to the absence of instances of formal criminalization of the Iraq invasion, an unofficial tribunal (International Tribunal on Iraq) met in the city of Istanbul in 2005. The court stated that the invasion and occupation were illegal and that the reasons invoked by the governments of the United States and the United Kingdom were false, while the most relevant cause of the attack was to control and dominate the Middle East and its vast oil reserves. The court also recognized the impotence of the formal international legal mechanisms. In this regard and that the 'impunity that the U.S. government and its allies enjoy has created a severe global crisis that questions the importance and significance of international law' (Iadicola 2009/10, 105). Later on, in October 2009, the War Crimes Tribunal in Kuala Lumpur agreed unanimously and stated that a head of government cannot unilaterally refuse to comply with the provisions of international law, such as the Geneva Conventions (104).

regulations, only the word 'unlawful' can distinguish the actions of terrorism committed by the targeted actors, as opposed to the self-defense actions undertaken by the United States and its allies (2007, 184).[23] Indeed, even though there is no internationally-agreed upon definition of the word 'terrorism,' the Federal Bureau of Investigation (1998) defines it as "the *unlawful* use of force or violence against persons or property to intimidate or coerce a government, the civilian population, or any segment of it, in support of political or social objectives – emphasis added -" (quoted in Young 2007, 184). As a result of this type of regulations, a vast number of actors became subjected to external control under terrorism accusations (allowing their territorial occupations) while the attacks performed by the United States and its allies are described as mere 'self-defense mechanisms' performed against previous unlawful attacks, allowing their under-criminalization. Thus, "modern conventional warfare has become a 'terror terrorism'" (192).

The legitimating discourse that protect counter-terrorist acts qualifies the 'East' as chaotic, violent, disorderly and irrational, in contrast to the 'order' represented by the 'West.' Following this logic, u.s. attacks are read as a necessary action against an 'other' that is threatening the western civilization (Said quoted in Young 2007, 184). Thus, far from being detected as criminal actions, the illegal occupations are endorsed (or at least uncontested) by the international political community, reinforcing the historical characterization that, since the primitive accumulation, affirms that they represent an advance in the civilization.[24]

---

23   Under international law it is unlawful to use force "against the territorial integrity or political independence of any state, or in any other manner inconsistent with the Purposes of the u.n." (Art. 2(4) of u.n. Charter). The only two exceptions are self-defense against armed attacks (Art. 51) and Security-Council's Authorization (Chapter 7). A main issue regarding self-defense is whether the conduct of terrorists can be attributed to that of the state. Additionally, whether states can use force against terrorists based in another country is much discussed and the u.n. Charter does not provide a conclusive answer.

24   Not only those countries that have been accused of terrorism have been the target of over-criminalization. Also, countries for which the risk of terrorist attacks is not a fundamental or current concern have been dragged to this war on terror by the pressure of international organisms and the leading nations. The underlying message is that if they do not support international conventions against terrorism if they do not help the nations that are leading the war on terror, and if they do not incorporate the crime of terrorism in their national legislations, they are also suspects. It is the imposition of a Manichean world where the options as terrorism or counter-terrorism, and nothing else. As an example, Argentina and Chile have been compelled by the United Nations Counter-Terrorism Committee and of the Financial Action Task Force (F.A.T.F.) to pass certain laws related to terrorism. Both countries finally sanctioned the laws, and the experience shows that

War on Terror at the Individual Level. When analyzing the war on terror's effects on individuals, bulimic criminal selectivity describes a double process in which bulimic over-criminalization and under-criminalization become engaged. Following the legacy of the legally-disciplining order, all individuals have been massively incorporated (*ingested*) to the national and international legal framework that protects them against abusive state actions. However, there is a later process of expulsion (*ejection*) of certain citizens from the legal protections that were nationally granted, under the allegation of terrorism charges.[25] This exceptional treatment invokes the Enemy Criminal Law theory (Jakobs and Cancio Melia 2003),[26] which promotes the existence of one type of law for 'citizens' (who are treated under the traditional liberal criminal law) and another one for 'enemies' (who can be dealt with under exceptional rules). Under this warlike discourse[27] and during the Bush Administration, terrorist

---

they have been applied distortedly. The result has been higher punishments in cases that were not related with terrorism, such as native peoples' protests against mining projects.

25   This process of bulimia is also manifested in the fact that, although all U.S. citizens are formally included on an equal footing in the national and global fight against terrorism, wealthy citizens are excluded from its materialization. Only the U.S. low-income people are the ones that offer their bodies for the purpose of concretizing the armed occupations. Thus, when Galbraith consulted the Dean of Harvard University at the time that the Gulf War was unfolded, how many students had joined the war, he said 'very few.' Galbraith lobbied to know the exact amount. The Dean replied: 'Zero' (Young 2007, 84).

26   Jakobs and Cancio Meliá states that: "The penalty is coercion [...] response to the fact [...] of a rational person, [...] disavowal of the standard, an attack on their validity and it also means anything, it means that the complainant's allegation is irrelevant and that the rule continues to apply unchanged, maintaining therefore the configuration of society [...] the author is taken seriously as a person [...] it does not just mean something, but it also produces something physically [...] individual prevention [...] effect of insurance. To this extent, coercion intended to mean nothing, but want to be effective, which means that is not directed against the person in law, but against the dangerous individual" (2003, 23–24). Their theory rest on three essential aspects: criminal law tends to punish prospectively in a bid to prevent future harms; it imposes disproportionate sanctions in the name of security, and it departs from conventional procedural protections.

27   More than a decade later of 9/11 and Bush's announcement of the war on terror, Attorney General Eric Holder (2012) re-affirmed the spirit of the authorization, expressing: "We are a nation at war. And, in this war, we face a nimble and determined enemy that cannot be underestimated [...] there are people currently plotting to murder Americans, who reside in distant countries as well as within our borders." Recently, President Obama (2013) reasserted this aggressive approach: "We are at war with an organization that right now would kill as many Americans as they could if we did not stop them first. So this is a just war – a war waged proportionally, in last resort, and in self-defense."

actions had been considered neither crimes (protected by due process[28]) nor war acts (protected by Geneva Conventions[29]). This uncertain legal status has facilitated the under-criminalization of counter-terrorist actions, even when they included killing and torturing.

Outside u.s. borders. When discussing the use of lethal force, 2001 was the date when President Bush signed a secret Memorandum of Notification giving the Central Intelligence Agency (C.I.A.) the right to use it anywhere in the world. The legitimating discourse referred to a 'global war' against Al Qaeda and other armed groups and individuals. U.S. Congress endorsed this Memorandum (Authorization for Use of Military Force, Pub. L 107–40), using the legitimating concept of 'anticipatory' self-defense. Recently, in 2015, the Authorization for Use of Military Force was broadened to be applied to I.S.I.S. and other Islamic groups. Lately, drones[30] have become the center of the lethal force discussion.

---

28   Since November 2001, President Bush ordered that individuals suspected of terrorism could be held indefinitely in third countries without being charged, and could be judged by military commission, rather than under civil courts. Prisoners have been detained in secret facilities abroad for years, and even the International Committee of the Red Cross has been denied access to them. Notably, the Patriot Act includes authorization to impose indefinite detention time to immigrants, permission to search homes or business without the need of consent of the owner; and increased surveillance by the Federal Bureau of Investigation (F.B.I.) through the expansion of the National Security Letters (N.S.L.). The Patriot Act punishes a threatened action (conspiring) with no need for real action, and it also reverses the burden of the proof by imposing penalties "for anyone who cannot reasonably prove that they are using a biological agent, toxin or delivery system..."

29   In February 2002, President Bush ruled that the Geneva Conventions, underwritten by the United States in 1949 and applicable to all combatants and civilians captured in an international armed conflict, do not apply to Al Qaeda suspects detained in Afghanistan. The reasoning was that the detainees must be considered under a third category, named as 'unlawful combatant.' Lawful combatants receive prisoner of war status and the protections of the Third Geneva Convention. Unlawful combatants do not. Al-Qaida members are considered unlawful combatants because they are members of a non-state actor terrorist group (Council on Foreign Relations 2002). By now, these considerations have changed and, at least in a theoretical framework, it is well accepted that, in contemporary international human law, there is growing customary international law that applies to all conflicts, whether international or non-international. This means that event those accused of terrorism are protected by the principles of humanity, proportionality, distinction, and military necessity. However, there is still no determination of the legal framework applicable to all persons held in the fight against terrorism by the U.S. authorities (ICRC 2016). Moreover, international humanitarian law has been sporadically and selectively applied and in many respects has been ignored or violated with respect to the detainees accused of terrorism (Gill and van Sliedregt 2005).

30   Drones are remotely controlled aerial vehicles that were used by the U.S. military and the C.I.A. initially for surveillance, but that are currently used to launch missiles against

The most problematic action is the secret c.i.a. drone program,[31] which works without any level of accountability or transparency[32] even in countries where the United States is not at war, including Pakistan, Somalia, and Yemen. There are no official numbers of people killed, but it is estimated that 3,000 people have been targeted, including hundreds of noncombatants and even u.s. citizens (Drones Watch 2013).

Bulimic under-criminalization followed all the cases in which the Memorandum or the specific killings have been challenged. u.s. judiciary has insisted on the 'political question' doctrine, which describes judicial deference to executive decision-making, especially in foreign affairs, in matters of national security and the command of military action (Savage 2014).[33]

Concerning torture, it also became lawful when the Office of Legal Counsel of the u.s. Department of Justice signed the 'torture memos' directed to the c.i.a., the u.s. Department of Defense, and the President. These memos were intended to restrict the definition of torture as it is internationally recognized and to establish that it was a foundation of necessity and self-defense against 'extreme acts,' and therefore, it could be justified (Zysman 2011). Following this suggested framework, the Bush administration prepared a torture program under the direction of the c.i.a.[34] Although most of the 119 tortured people who were subjected to the program have never been charged with a

---

      human targets. Drones are the expression of a new form of warfare in which the killer and the killed do not share physical space. Drones erase the acknowledgment of the act of killing: there are no people, but 'targets'; there is no killing, but 'neutralization'; there is no civilian death, but 'collateral damages.'

31   There is a military drone program that is publicly acknowledged: it operates in the recognized war zones of Afghanistan and Iraq, targeting enemies of u.s. troops stationed there and it follows the patterns of a conventional warfare by new means (Mayer 2009). Conversely, the c.i.a. drone program, which is aimed at finding terror suspects around the world, is hidden.

32   Drones are also being deployed domestically, particularly by Customs and Border Patrol to search illegal immigrants and drugs, and by metropolitan police and county sheriffs to assist s.w.a.t. operations (Drones Watch 2013).

33   E.g. federal district Judge John Bates dismissed the suit to enjoin the targeted killing case of Anwar Al Awlaqi, who was killed in a drone attack, only one week before his 16-years old boy was also murdered by a u.s. missile in Yemen (Savage 2014).

34   The program was created by the military psychologists James Mitchel and Bruce Jessen with the aim of exploiting and abusing captives to achieve complete psychological destruction to extract information easily, in a remake of the most outrageous interrelations between medicine and torture. The techniques include prolonged isolation, sleep deprivation, sensory deprivation and overload, forced nudity and sexual humiliation (Brown 2015). The most sophisticated one was 'water dousing,' a technique that elicits a drowning sensation and lowers body temperature, which has been used in at least thirteen cases.

crime, the United States has largely failed to prosecute those responsible of the acts of torture that the prisoners had suffered, and all the claims for reparations had been rejected (Ackerman 2015).[35] Under-criminalization of torture is part of the unpleasant choice that the war on terror compelled 'us' to take against 'them,' under the 'lesser evil' principle. The most outrageous example occurred when in 2004 the 60 Minutes II of CBS released a large number of photographs of tortured prisoners, which had been taken as a 'trophy' by some of the U.S. guards with their cameras or personal mobile phones at the Abu Ghraib prison in Iraq. Despite the abusive use of violence against the prisoners, only low-ranked guards had been convicted by U.S. courts for those actions,[36] and those few convictions involved no prison time,[37] very short periods of incarceration,[38] or larger convictions with early release.[39]

---

35 In an unprecedented decision, one of the cases involving three men that were held for years undergoing 'enhanced interrogation' without being charged with any crime, including one that died of hypothermia, found a different resolution. Federal Judge Quackenbush ruled that the victims' lawsuit can move forward, and discovery may begin. Far from being an expression that neglects the under-criminalization of the torture program, it seems to be an exception; the director of the A.C.L.U.'s national security project, Hina Shamsi, expressed: "This has never happened before ... There have been so many cases brought by torture victims, Iraq, Afghanistan, elsewhere, and not one of them has been able to go forward for shameful reasons" (La Ganga 2016).

36 In one of the most widespread photographs, it is possible to see "[a] prisoner hooded, precariously situated over a cardboard box with arms outstretched, electrical wires attached to his fingers. He had been led to believe (by the Sergeant Davis) that if his legs failed, he would be electrocuted" (Zysman 2011).

37 Santos Cardona, accused of using his animal to threaten detainees at Abu Ghraib prison, was sentenced to 90-days hard labor, a reduction of rank, and must forfeit $600 of pay per month for a year. Ambuhi pleaded guilty, and he was discharged from the Army without prison time. Jordan was the only one charged with prisoner abuse, besides disobeying an order, dereliction of duty, cruelty, false statements, fraud and interfering with an investigation, and he was sentenced in 2007 with a reprimand. In 2008, the conviction and reprimand were removed from his record. Karpinski was in charge of all 12 Iraqi detention facilities, including Abu Ghraib, and she received a demotion from brigadier general to colonel. Pappas was reprimanded, fined, and relieved of command after using muzzled dogs inside interrogation rooms. Phillabaum was reprimanded and relieved of command (CNN 2016).

38 Harman was sentenced to six months in prison. Sivits was sentenced to a year of confinement, discharge for bad conduct, and demoted. Davis pleaded guilty and was sentenced to six months in a military prison, and he was early released after three months (CNN 2016).

39 Frederick II pleaded guilty and was sentenced to eight years for conspiracy, dereliction of duty, maltreatment of detainees, assault, and committing an indecent act under a plea agreement and he received parole after serving three years in prison. Graner was

After Abu Ghraib, the Obama's administration adopted a dual approach (Alston and Goodman 2013, 274–275). On the one hand, it tried to overturn primary under-criminalization: Obama's Administration recognized that the U.S. applied torture (Gerstein 2014) and, prospectively, banned any ongoing or future use of torture, including C.I.A. investigation, revoked all legal opinions analyzing the law on interrogations (i.e. revoked the Torture Memos), and ordered the closure of C.I.A.'s secret overseas detention centers (the so-called black sites) where high value detainees had been held incommunicado. Obama and his Attorney General also unequivocally affirmed that waterboarding constitutes torture and made publicly available C.I.A.'s interrogation practices, related communications and legal opinions adopted by the Bush Administration. On the other hand, retrospectively, the Obama's Administration preserved secondary under-criminalization: the government generally avoided prosecutions or pursuit of individuals responsible for authorizing or engaging in torture in the past, even though both President Bush and V.P. Dick Cheney admitted that they authorized waterboarding and had no regrets (Alston and Goodman 2013, 275). Moreover, detainees are still outside the U.S. territory in facilities where they suffer torture, they are not subjected to U.S. law,[40] and, in the past, they have been deprived of the elementary right to *habeas corpus*.[41]

---

sentenced to ten years but he was released after serving six years. England was found guilty of maltreating detainees, conspiracy, and an indecent act and convicted to three years of imprisonment (CNN 2016).

40   Since January 2002, Bush disclosed that the expulsion of terrorist suspects from the established legal framework could be even more intensified: they would not be incarcerated in traditional facilities. The government opened Camp C-Ray at the U.S. Guantanamo Bay Naval Base in Cuba. Because of the mixed jurisdiction between Cuba and the United States, it has been intensively debate if U.S. law applied to the detainees.

41   This decision to transfer the detainees to Cuba was followed by a back and forth between Congress and the Supreme Court about military commissions. The Congress supported those procedures, while the Supreme Court pushed for the respect of constitutional rights for the detainees. In 2004, in *Rasul v. Bush*, 542 U.S. 466 (2004) ruled that the detainees must be given an opportunity to be heard in civilian courts and refute the evidence that classified them as 'unlawful combatants.' Also in 2004 in *Hamdi v. Rumsfeld*, 542 U.S. 507 (2004), the Supreme Court established that U.S. detainees retain due process rights and the writ of habeas corpus within it. The U.S. Department of Defense responded creating the Combatant Status Review Tribunals (a set of tribunals that are in charge of deciding if the detainees of Guantanamo are correctly designated as unlawful combatants). The U.S. Department also proposed the Detainee Treatment Act (it protects captives against torture, but it also restricted the submissions of additional habeas corpus). The Supreme Court answered back in *Hamdan v. Rumsfeld* 548 U.S. 557 (2006) that the President does not have the authority to settle military commissions. The Congress passed then the

After receiving more than 20 amicus curiae from organizations, such as the American Civil Liberties Union (A.C.L.U.) and the Center for Constitutional Rights (C.C.R.), the Supreme Court finally guaranteed the right to *habeas corpus* to Guantanamo's detainees and held that the Military Commissions Act of 2006 was an unconstitutional suspension of that right (*Boumediene v. Bush*, 553 U.S. 723). However, in line with the dual approach, the U.S.S.C. did not imposed on the Executive a clear framework governing the detention of alleged terrorists and it did not give sufficient protection to those challenging their status as enemy combatants (Gill and van Sliedregt 2005). Also, as Alston and Goodman (2013, 275) explain, none of those who created, regulated, administrated and executed these unconstitutional conditions of incarceration have been targeted by crime control (secondary under-criminalization).

Inside U.S. borders. Under-criminalization of right-depriving and potentially unconstitutional measures conducted under the protective label of war on terror rests on expansive surveillance and law enforcement profiling.

In terms of surveillance, the United States can detect any communication traffic that passes through the country or the United Kingdom (Macaskill and Dance 2013).[42] After 9/11, the Patriot Act amended and broadened the existent regulations to allow the collection of certain wire or electronic communication that might be relevant to terrorism or espionage investigation. Section 215 of the 2001 Patriot Act[43] allows national collection of U.S. citizens' phone metadata.[44] 2008 F.I.S.A. Amendments Act, renewed in 2012, allows the collection of communications without a warrant when at least one end of the communication is a non-U.S. person. Executive Order 12333 – signed in 1981 by

---

Military Commissions Act (2006) which states that there are no habeas actions for Guantanamo detainees and establishes a narrow review of the military commissions' decisions and only in the DC Circuit Court of Appeals. It also allows the submission of evidence extracted using 'enhanced interrogation techniques' that took place before the Detainee Treatment Act.

42 F.I.S.A. was intended to curtail the National Security Agency (N.S.A.)'s ability to use its capabilities against U.S. citizens. The Act was a response to the unlawful surveillance by the intelligence agencies of U.S. political activists, trade union leaders, and civil rights leaders in the mid 20th century. However, at the level of its application, F.I.S.A. was not as effective, and surveillance stayed broader that just oriented to spy foreign actors (Macaskill and Dance 2013).

43 Its formal name is Uniting and Strengthening America by Providing Appropriate Tools Required to Intercept and Obstruct Terrorism Act of 2001 (Pub.L. 107–56).

44 The particular letter of the section refers to the allowance of the government to obtain information of "any tangible things for an investigation to protect against international terrorism."

President Reagan, and amended by Bush in 2004 – authorizes the collection of all information for the purpose of 'national defense' if it is not prohibited by other applicable laws. Groups such as the Electronic Frontier Foundation and the American Civil Liberties Union (A.C.L.U.) warn that the scope of the surveillance exceeds Congressional authorization, violates the U.S. Constitution, undermines civil liberties that have been the moral foundation of the country, and it is not even useful.[45] However, there has been almost no accountability for those who design and enforce this, allegedly unconstitutional, surveillance.[46]

When discussing law enforcement profiling in the war on terror in U.S. soil, being Muslim or a national from certain countries has been assumed as a 'proxy' to being a terrorist. Hijabs and Muslim attires are enough to arouse police suspicion.[47] Around 3,000 immigrants have been annually detained in

---

45   In regards to its usefulness, the N.S.A. argues that surveillance is necessary to prevent terrorist attacks. However, its director, Inglis, conceded that, at most, one plot – which he has not specified – might have been disrupted by the bulk phone records program alone (Macaskill and Dance 2013). Even disregarding ethical considerations and accepting surveillance just because of it ability to prevent terrorist attacks, this last point has not been proved. By the same logic, U.S. government is developing the biggest biometric collection program of the world. This program does not only encompass encroaching civil liberties in the name of security and public safety – as the Patriot Act did-, but it also has been operating with a high percentage of error rate (20% in the NGI's facial recognition program contained errors) (Markowitz 2016). Surveillance has not only been undermining civil rights, but that did so with inaccurate results that lead to the over-criminalization of citizens with no proved relation to terrorist activities. Even when effective criminalization does not take place, the expansive surveillance implicates a potential threat of over-criminalization over all the individuals that are a target of this spying net.

46   The only exception was *A.C.L.U. v. Clapper* (2015), in which the Second Circuit Court of Appeals decision held that the collection of phone records by the NSA, as applied, violates the Patriot Act. However, the court withheld any injunction 'pending Congressional review.' In legislative terms, pressure on the government conditioned that, in 2015, the Freedom Act incorporated modest reforms to reduce the scope of surveillance. The changes affected the dissolution of bulk data collection of U.S. citizens' phone records and Internet metadata. However, the bill authorizes the government to obtain records 'two hops' removed from its target, by proving that there is 'reasonable' suspicion about the connection among them (Washington Post 2015). The weakness of this limitation can be seen in numbers: 10,000 is the golden number of people suspected of terrorism that is needed to allow the control of all the population of the United States, through the 'two hops' rules. Meanwhile, no limits are imposed for surveillance of non-U.S. citizens outside the country.

47   A policy paper issued by the Air Force Research Laboratory under the title 'Countering Violent Extremism: Scientific Methods & Strategies,' contained a characterization of women that use hijabs as 'passive terrorists' (Buncombe 2016).

immigration raids since 2001 (Wonders 2007, 45).[48] At the local level, the New York City Police Department (N.Y.P.D.) established a secret surveillance program that mapped, monitored and analyzed American-Muslim daily life throughout the city,[49] and even in its surrounding states, breaking jurisdictional limits[50] (Shamas and Arastu 2014). Six years of undermining civil rights of the N.Y.C. Muslim community on a biased and discriminatory basis (affecting religious practice, censoring speech and stunting political organizing) without results[51] did not result in accountability. Bulimic under-criminalization covered the actions of the authorities that violate constitutional rights to enforce bulimic over-criminalization by using religion as sufficient ground for suspicion.

Entrapment is the core of law enforcement actions: through this technique, the Federal Bureau of Investigation may have created terrorists out of law-abiding individuals by conducting sting operations that facilitated or invented the target's willingness to act. People who would have never participated in a terrorist act on their own initiative and might not even have the capacity to do so were prosecuted for serious, yet government-created, terrorism plots. In numbers, nearly 50% of the more than 500 federal counterterrorism convictions resulted from informant-based cases, and, among those, almost 30% were sting operations in which the informant played an active role in the underlying plot (Human Right Watch 2014). Even though a successful strategy should focus on persecuting the 'radicalizer,' and not the (vulnerable) 'radicalized,' anti-terrorist enforcement replicates the same mode that is used for ordinary crimes: entrapment technique focuses on the desperate and impoverished individuals, and even on those suffering from mental health issues. In spite of the impractical and unconstitutional character of this law enforcement activity, it has been subjected to under-criminalization, under the scope of the war on

---

48   In the United States, the annual budgetary allocations for the activity of the Border Patrol increased almost three times during the 1990s, while the government estimates the cost of national security in $100 billion per year. The militarization of the borders is also underway in Europe, especially in Italy, Germany and Spain (Wonders 2007, 45).

49   This program includes monitoring and planting informants to detect terrorist activity in mosques, Muslim neighborhoods and Islamic university clubs (Kaleem 2012).

50   N.Y.P.D. implemented surveillance in mosques situated in Newark (Star-Ledger 2012).

51   In 2012, the Chief of the N.Y.P.D. Intelligence Division, Lt. Paul Galati, admitted that in the six years of his tenure the program had not yielded a single criminal lead (Shamas and Arastu 2014).

terror. Also, the judiciary has restricted essential constitutional rights, such as freedom of expression, in the name of this 'war.'[52]

Bulimic Under-Criminalization of Financial Maneuvers

Considering economic crimes, bulimic under-criminalization describes the reduced regulation and scarce enforcement of those financial transactions that – through illegal procedures – use significant amounts of capital, to later eject (expel) them into a new financial venture, without investing (digesting) them productively. This process does not only deprive states of tax returns but also undermines productive assets, constraining the labor market. The u.s. misappropriation of government bonds in 1980[53] was the breaking point of this new form of economic crime that takes place outside the realm of production or manufacturing, and focuses on the manipulation of hedge funds (Calavita et al. 1997, 23).[54]

---

52   The Supreme Court decision in *Holder v. Humanitarian Law Project* (2010) constrained freedom of speech, by characterizing teaching and discussion literature as 'material support for terrorism.' This decision broadened the traditional consideration that understood 'material support' as providing funds or personnel. Chief Justice Roberts legitimated his position by expressing that the involved organization was part of those that are "so tainted by their criminal conduct that *any contribution* to such an organization facilitates that conduct." This argument seems to be replicating the broken windows theory but now for international terrorist crimes: only by criminalizing every level of terrorism with the tougher punishments is it possible to stop the 'big fishes.' Justice Breyer, in his dissent, acknowledged the risks of those analogies that unreasonably expand crime control: "In my view, the majority's arguments stretch the concept of 'fungibility' beyond constitutional limits."

53   The events analyzed led to the S&L crisis (savings and loan crisis) of 1980, with the bankruptcy of 747 of the 3,234 savings and loan associations in the United States. It involved the fraudulent actions of savings and loan financial institutions (also called 'secondhand') that accepted savings deposits and mortgages, or granted personal loans with them, and that, in order to conceal the insolvency in which they relapsed, fraudulently produced the emptying of the entities themselves. Keating, Milken, and Boesky were charged with insurance fraud, manipulation of junk bonds, insider trading, and securities fraud, among other crimes (Calavita et al. 1997, 26). After this case, u.s. and European banks went bankrupt in the financial crisis of July 2007, involving the collapse of Bear & Sterns and the investment bank Lehman Brothers in September 2008. Also, AIG, Merrill Lynch, Wachovia, Citibank, Goldman Sachs, Bank of America and Deutsche Insurance, among others, went bankrupt, and countless frauds committed by business leaders became known worldwide.

54   Moreover, in some cases, the real purpose of the organization is to enact its hollowing, and the corporation is considered both the criminal and the 'victim' (Calavita et al. 1997, 28).

Economic crime has been a permanent element for capital accumulation throughout the entire capitalist system. The link between capital accumulation and economic crime was intuited by Marx, who warned that "[b]anking and credit, however, thereby also become the most powerful means for driving capitalist production beyond its barriers and one of the most effective vehicles for crises and swindling" (1867 v3, 742). In the purpose of preserving the rate of profit, regardless of productive investments, illicit activity increased. This logic is preserved and accentuated in the bulimic social order, when economic crimes adopted peculiar characteristics that further favored their under-criminalization: they are developed through a symbiosis between crime and business; they also involve a symbiosis between the public and the private sector; they are perpetrated in a collective and corporative manner; they meant a 'mediate' type of violence that is not easily perceived; and their perpetrators are part of the non-criminal stereotype of the business world.

Symbiosis between crime and business. Evolution of economic crimes shows that, during the primitive accumulation, they were perpetrated by adventurous individuals under state control that could be easily identified. Later on, the industrial capitalists who owned factories during the second disciplining phase were also easily identifiable because they acted at an individual level and using crime to support their primary legal activity. Organized crime during the third disciplining phase was perpetrated at a supra-individual level but its criminal profile was evident because their main activity (e.g. production of illegal alcohol) took place outside the legal market. Even in the case of white-collar crimes, where legal and illegal activities were mixed, the author was susceptible of being identified because the illegal actions were committed by specific individuals. Conversely, in the bulimic social order, economic crimes are perpetrated by large corporations through activities in which the line between legal and illegal business, and between the public and the private sectors, become blurred.

Thus, business is not classifiable as entirely illegal, but it inevitably turns to forbidden behaviors to ensure its development and success (Bales 1984). This crime-business is facilitated by the free enterprise model (abstract and impersonal entities, internationalization of companies, the complexity of the dependency relationships between corporations that make it difficult to individualize responsibility, etc.) (Tiedemann 1975). Indeed, crime has become an essential part of 'doing business' in the context of a 'Darwinian competition' for status and resources (Currie, quoted in Bergalli 2008, 5). The resulting symbiosis between crime and business is one of the major obstacles posed by prosecutors and law enforcement to investigate these crimes. It facilitates their under-criminalization, particularly in cases such as money laundering (Virgolini 2005).

Symbiosis between the public and the private sector. Symbiosis also occurs between the public and private sectors, facilitating primary under-criminalization.[55] Public senior officials whose political careers depend on a steady flow of campaign funds are especially susceptible to the demands of those with the resources to make large contributions (Calavita et al. 1997, 28), helping to limit the scope and severity of punishment attached to the economic crime. In addition, despite the limited circumstances wherein economic crimes are criminalized, complex and ambiguous wording facilitates secondary under-criminalization: the law generally requires the fulfillment of complex administrative requirements to avoid incurring in a crime, so that no one can actually abide them all. As a consequence, enforcing those laws is part of the discretion of state agencies that benefit from the same legal system (Chambliss 1978, 35–37). In other words, the regulations of these offenses involve an oversubscription of requirements that cannot be fully satisfied and are left to the discretion of officials who are linked to the offenders in complex networks.

Moreover, the same individuals and organisms that must prosecute economic crimes are often part of the illicit operations. The scenario is complex, and it is not possible to make a linear division: while the state is not completely co-opted by corporate interests, there is not an absolute confrontation between them but various competing interests cross the public and private hierarchical levels (Calavita et al. 1997, 28). What is possible to affirm is that the states are forging a stronger link with the private sectors: it is no longer a cooperative relationship (as described by Sutherland in relation to the disciplining social order) but a complete symbiosis between public and private actors, where it is no longer possible to clearly distinguish between each other as they take part of the same networks, favoring secondary under-criminalization in a process of 'selective abolitionism.'[56]

---

55   To recall, Pegoraro calls this 'economic organized crime,' which describes the criminal organization dedicated to legal-illegal businesses of a certain political complexity with the necessary participation of institutions and state officials, that produce a significant financial reward, and enjoy criminal impunity and social immunity (2002, 52–53). This definition clarifies the assimilation between crimes and businesses: a particular type of criminal conduct constitutes a certain way of doing business. So, while white-collar crimes (Sutherland 1940 and 1949) have to do with individuals that act in the field of their profession under the omission of control of state agents, 'economic organized crime' encompasses situations in which state actors are an active part of the criminal network.

56   Van Sweninberg uses the concept of 'selective abolitionism' to refer to the non-prosecution of coarse crimes by the actuarial criminology because of the superabundant prison population, favoring the prosecution of only the most severe cases (1997, 392). However,

Collective and corporative features. Under-criminalization is also facilitated by the increasingly collective and corporate character of economic crimes, under the bulimic social order. Their authors are named as 'collective scammers' who do not act alone and are not lower-level employees but owners and managers of corporations that operate in networks within and outside them (28–29).[57]

A 'mediate' type of violence. The increasing social harm caused by economic crimes does not undermine their under-criminalization because they affect non-hegemonic social interests. They harm the interests of the losers, the taxpayers the processes of accumulation and, particularly, the working class. Therefore, they are not easily perceived (Pavarini 1975). As an example, in the case of the embezzlement of U.S. government bonds in 1980, the high cost of the operation, which amounted to 87.9 billion dollars, was paid by taxpayers, forming the basis of budget deficits in 1990 (Calavita et al. 1997).

Besides the extension of the produced harm, it seems to be less evident than in petty offenses, discouraging social demands for their prosecution. These might respond to a differential violence in comparison with the rough, physical and immediate violence of over-criminalized behaviors. In this sense, it is feasible to identify economic crime with what might be called *mediate violence*: its effects involve greater social damage but are uncollected as 'immediate' for the affected population. As another example, environmental crimes include the destruction of natural resources to increase profits and achieve productivity rates in the context of necessary modernization and technological upgrading. However, the relation between the environmental damage produced by factories and the weakened health of the population is not easily perceived. Even worse, some productive activities are paradoxically seen as economically beneficial for local development, making its criminogenic character hardly identifiable.

The non-criminal stereotype of the business world. Finally, the perception of these crimes is mediated through the mythologized image of the business world as a space of 'good people,' an area of neatness, oblivious to the vices

---

this concept could be used to demonstrate that many of the prosecution of economic crime are abolished in practice, through secondary under-criminalization.

57 At the lowest level of responsibility in regulatory agencies there are sporadic cases of co-operation (by offering better salaries to work with them), favoring secondary under-criminalization. The strategy that better ensures illegal investment is to include as partners those whose work consists in controlling which acts are illegal (Chambliss 1978, 55). On the other hand, hierarchical officials of regulatory agencies are less susceptible to accept political and financial pressures, because of structural reasons (Calavita et al. 1997, 31–34).

of the underworld (particularly evident in the label of white-collar crimes). They do not constitute a symbolic threat to the capitalist mode of production but, on the contrary, they are the example of individual creative freedom, a political logarithm of economic liberalism (Neuman 1997, 7). Far from regulating their excesses, the liberal law property is the instrument that ensures individual freedom [and property]; therefore, the liberal rule of law is a rule of law for owners (Aniyar de Castro 1988, 45).

The resulting primary and secondary under-criminalization of economic crimes during the bulimic social order could be characterized as a process of 'immunity,' namely a further configuration of impunity that has structural characteristics: not only catering to the quality and position of the people, or the value and appreciation of their own activities, but allowing those prohibited practices to continue to unfold (Virgolini 2005). This protection becomes a permanent barrier against crime control. Even in the specific cases where particular individuals are criminalized, those actions are classified as 'withdrawal of coverage' (Zaffaroni et al. 2000, 11).[58] Efforts are aimed at preserving the allocation of responsibility at the individual level, leaving intact the 'infrastructure' of that crime (Lascoumes and Weinberger 1978). The goal is to reduce all the complex organization of the crime to the individual responsibility of the defendant, to not extend attention to the interweaving of the practices throughout the economic sector in which that person worked.

Another point to note is the role of legal academia. Notwithstanding the link between business and crime, and its permanent under-criminalization since the dawn of capitalism, the first criminological analysis of this topic only occurred in the last century (Sutherland 1940 and 1949). Even though critical criminology claimed that it was necessary to show how the legal infractions by the most economically advantaged sectors are institutionalized (Taylor et al. 1974, 450–451), the few contributions on economic crimes did not come from Marxist criminological schools.[59] Although today there are proliferating

---

58   This expression makes reference to the very exceptionally criminalization of some individuals who, being in a position that makes them virtually invulnerable to crime control, takes the brunt of a conflict as a scapegoat of hegemonic power and suffers for it, falling to a vulnerable position (criminalization for retirement of coverage) (Zaffaroni et al. 2000, 11).

59   The failure of critical criminology to approach economic crimes could have to do with the fact that they dedicated more to analyze criminal matter within the social complex in general rather than to specific researchers. In this sense, it did not detract the need to address this type of crime in particular, but it assumed it from a more abstract theoretical perspective. Left realism relegated economic crimes as a second-level concern because it mistakenly understood that general population was not worried about these type of

studies, what is still missing a reading of economic crime as an inseparable part of the function of the production system, especially in its bulimic
configuration.[60]

In sum, the explanation for economic crimes' under-criminalization and
the insufficient investigation about these behaviors can be summarized as follows: no society can criminalize activities that are foundational to its dominant economic and political relations (Virgolini 2005).

Bulimic Over-Criminalization

The notion of *bulimic over-criminalization* describes how the spectrum of criminalized survival strategies and coarse crimes committed by (economically) excluded and (culturally) included sectors are broadly regulated in statutes that
incorporate more severe procedural requirements and harsher punishments
(primary over-criminalization). It also describes the increasing persecution of
those offenses through law enforcement profiling, courts' discretion and differential penalization (secondary over-criminalization). The targeted social
sectors are those collected by crime control – after being culturally swallowed
and economically expelled – to reduce their unrest. Over-criminalization is
reinforced to the detriment of the most vulnerable racial, ethnic, religious,
gender and age subsets of the impoverished population.

Social control over the economically included workers remains linked to
economic mechanisms (they are subjected to the order of work). The question
is what happens to the economically excluded sectors, in a framework of lack
of access to social mechanisms for containing poverty (welfare policies): What
kind of control operates over them? Or, as Christie states, we have a surplus
population (those who are out of production) and we have the classic problem
of how to control the dangerous classes (1993, 67). The answer that arises is that,
at the end of the 20th century, states 'managed' the situation with criminal repression devices (De Giorgi 2002, 127). Crime control expanded and occupied

---

crimes. Left realism was so 'realistic' that it did not realize that other criminal realities
exist despite not being visible, or rooted in popular fear, or on the tops of the daily news
(Cohen 1998, 5). This delay in the analysis of economic crimes condition the recurrence
to Sutherland's work, despite it has been so long since he wrote his work.

60   It is striking that social theory does not analyze economic organized crime as a social
fact, as it is a constituent part of capitalism. This form of social order could not have been
possible or developed without the participation of organized crimes, such as those that
have historically produced and continue to produce the massive accumulation of capital
in private hands (Pegoraro 2011, 79).

those spaces formerly filled by social policies[61] in what has been called the passage from the 'welfare state' to the 'badfare state' (Rodriguez 2008); from the 'social state' or 'providence state' to the 'criminal state' or 'penance state' (Wacquant 1999); from a 'social state' to a 'security state' (Castel 2003, 73). Social integration policies have been replaced by governance strategies to contain and segregate the 'left over' (Castel 1995) and the penal system survived as an instrument of class terror (Pavarini 1980, 87). In numbers, "the United States spends over $80 billion on incarceration each year, while local state and federal governments spend anywhere from $20,000 to $50,000 annually to keep an individual behind bars" (A.C.L.U. 2016). Meanwhile, social and health expenditures play a race to the bottom.

This punitive transformation exceeds the control of the course of crime rates. Far from being an exclusive response to crime conflict, it was a response to a social insecurity generated by the increasing precariousness of wage labor

---

61   Studies show that the seven countries with the highest imprisonment rates spend below-average proportions of their G.D.P. on welfare, while the eight countries with the lowest incarceration rates all spend above average percentage of their G.D.P. on welfare, with the exception of Japan. Denmark, Sweden, and Finland spend the highest proportion of their GDP on welfare and have the lowest imprisonment rates. Meanwhile, the United States spends the smallest percentage of its GDP on welfare and has the highest imprisonment rate (Downes and Hansen 2006, 144–145). The finding indicates that a country that increases the amount of its GDP spent on welfare sees a greater decline in its imprisonment rate and that the links are becoming more rather than less significant over the past ten or fifteen years (152). Although the relation is highly mediated rather than simple or direct (particularly by the relevance of altruism and social harmony), welfare is the principal and even the primary protection against mass imprisonment (154).

      Analyzing the United States, Beckett and Western claim that state governments that provide more generous welfare benefits also have lower incarceration rates, while those with less generous welfare programs have higher incarceration rates (2001, 47). Lerman and Weaver (2015) affirm that United States has developed an exceptionally small (or private) welfare state, which is correlated with the trajectory of punishment and policing. The numbers confirm that the reduction of the U.S. budget allocated to social assistance was inversely proportional to the increase in the budget for security purposes. Bratton in New York increased its police budget by 40% over five years, bringing the number of local police to 12,000. In the same period social services suffered an amputation of one-third of their loans and 8,000 jobs were lost (Wacquant 2009, 31). In California, each prisoner demands $22,000 per year, or 3.3 times the amount of the highest social assistance (1999, 95). Kohler-Hausmann (2015) disputes the relation between penal and welfare policies. However, and taking into account her contributions, it would be more accurate to affirm that the correlation is verified for the lower classes, and not for the middle and upper classes. As Kohler-Hausman shows how programs destined to the impoverished, such as the Aid to Families with Dependent Children, were reduce and even eliminated.

(Wacquant 2009). The retraction of the labor market along with the processes of job insecurity and the reduction of social assistance within political, geographic, gender, cultural and racial constraints, have strongly influenced the increase of bulimic over-criminalization. A clear evidence of this is that, although an increase in crime rates initially fueled crime control, most of the tough-on-crime policies were implemented when crime rates were already stable and decreased.[62]

Thanks to this punitive transformation, the modern pauperism is culturally swallowed, economically expelled, and finally absorbed by bulimic over-criminalization. This instance operates as the last post of expulsion, conditioning personal narratives wherein their economic exclusion seems irreversible. Thus, criminal justice works as a support for social control to contain poverty,

---

62   In New York City, crime began to fall in the city before the Bratton Commissioner took
      office as head of the Police Department (Young 2012, 150). Crime levels dropped not as
      a consequence of zero tolerance policies, but were declining even before. Indeed, while
      crime in New York has been declining since 1992, the number of people arrested and
      convicted is increasing (Wacquant 1999, 39). For example, in 1998, the 77 judges of the
      criminal courts of New York that exercise jurisdiction over offenses and minor infractions
      attended 275,379 cases, or more than 3,500 each, twice the amount of cases than in 1993.
      The average delay is 284 days per case (against 208 in 1991), even for trivial cases such as
      a simple shoplifting. It is common that a judge examines up to a thousand cases per day.
      Although the incidence of crime victimization (outside homicidal violence) in Canada is
      similar to the United States, the imprisonment rate in Canada has stagnated at around 110
      prisoners per 100,000 inhabitants, in comparison with 740 per 100,000 in the United States
      (Wacquant 2013). Also "John Eck and Edward Maguire reviewed the empirical evidence
      and studies on broken-windows policing in their contribution to Alfred Blumstein's *The
      Crime Drop in America,* and found that there was little evidence to support the claim that
      broken-windows policing contributed to the sharp decrease in crime during the 1990s"
      (Harcourt 2013, 260–261). In 2001, George Kelling and William Sousa published *Do Police
      Matter?* where they proved that places with most intensive broken-windows policing dur-
      ing the 1990s were the ones that experienced the largest increases in crime during the
      city's crack epidemic of the mid-to- late 1980s (263). Also, Steve Levitt's 2004 study shows
      that "policing practices probably do not explain much of the crime drop in the 1990s be-
      cause crime went down everywhere, even in places where police departments did not
      implement new policing strategies" (263). In relation to the axiom of 'broken windows
      policies' – the relation between petty disorder and crime – Robert Sampson and Stephen
      Raudenbush, in their 1999 study Systematic Social Observation of Public Spaces, found
      that disorder and predatory crime could not be proved (261). Garland (2016) explains
      that since 1996 crime rates have decreased in all Western Societies, and not just particu-
      larly in the United States. Indeed, in Britain, crime rates also fell, imposing a high level
      of concern and prosecution for less severe violations (Young 2012, 152), which increased
      criminalization.

as it had happened in the context of the primitive accumulation. However, the difference is that, in the original context, crime control was aimed at creating a working class that the industrial development would eventually absorb. The current situation shows a more hopeless exclusion: the expansion of crime control is not aimed at creating future workers but at disqualifying those left over.

So, is there a direct relation between economic surplus and crime control? As noted by Rusche and Kirchheimer and other authors that complemented and verified their work,[63] there is a close relation between unemployment rates and the exercise of crime control, although this relation is not direct or unequivocal. States could have addressed the surplus population by developing more comprehensive social programs oriented to their support and control (as happened during the third disciplining phase). States could even have resorted to medical devices, pathologising poverty, by expanding the scope of asylums to include the poor (as it happened during the second disciplining phase). Simon suggests that social control could have been conducted even through empowerment of labor unions, environmentalism and through the civil rights movement (2007, 26–29). The fact that the surplus population has been addressed by crime control responded mainly to the end of welfare policies and the precariousness of the labor market, but also to cultural, political, ethnic, gender and even geographical transformations:

Ethnic, racial and geographic variables. The spread of the private automobile and mass transportation relaxed the need for proximity between home and work, making possible the migration to the suburbs and the concentration

---

63   Just to name some of them, Chiricos and Delone examined 44 empirical studies that confirm the importance of surplus labor in punishment increases. They also found that this process was often independent of crime rates, giving evidence that state criminal practices had a direct role in controlling surplus labor (1992, 432). Box and Hale (1982) confirm the same trend in England. On the contrary, Jankovic (1980) could not prove Rusche and Kirchheimer's hypothesis of an immediate effect of increased incarceration on unemployment rates, as prison population is numerically depreciable in connection with the numbers of the unemployed population. The only exception against it could be the United States, where incarceration rates are so high, particularly since the 1970s, that they have influenced statistics, by hiding part of the unemployed population: it is estimated that incarceration decreased by two points U.S. unemployment rates (Wacquant 1999, 103). Regarding Black-Americans, if prisoners were included in the unemployment statistics, unemployment would reach 7% (De Giorgi 2002, 77–78). Of course, prison hypertrophy is a double-edged mechanism: while in the short-term, it beautifies the employment situation by cutting labor supply, in the long term it aggravates it, making millions of people less than unemployable (Wacquant 1999, 103).

of poor and minorities families in areas quite far from the city. In the United States, as Black-Americans migrated to the northern and mid-western cities from the 1940s onwards, many white city residents moved away, promoting the formation of racial segregation (Garland 2001, 84–85). The old and new Black-American neighborhoods experienced a transformation from spaces dominated by networks of informal control and solidarity to 'hyper-ghettos' dominated by social unrest and insecurity.[64] Prisons replaced ghettos as the primary instrument of population control, particularly for those considered deviant, dangerous and unnecessary (Wacquant 1999, 104). The main vehicle for this process of racial over-criminalization was the so-called 'war on drugs,' which operated as "a stunningly comprehensive and well-disguised system of racialized social control" (Alexander 2010, 4).[65] Evidence of this use of crime control as a tool to sort out social and racial problems is that the war on drugs was announced even before crack cocaine became an issue in the media or a crisis in poor black neighborhoods (12). Indeed, the use of this 'war' as a tool

---

64   Wacquant's notion of 'hyper-ghetto' defines a situation of absolute space exclusion, even
      when it is more accurate to describe a situation of inclusion – exclusion. Far from being a
      place of exclusion, ghettos constitute an apotheosis of the United States and a complete
      immersion of the population in the American Dream (Young 2007, 49).

65   Using data on white, black, and hispanic male drug offenders sentenced in three U.S.
      district courts, Spohn and Sample (2008) find that fitting the stereotype of a dangerous
      federal drug offender (i.e., a male drug trafficker with a prior trafficking conviction who
      used a weapon to commit the current offense) affected the length of the prison sentence
      for Black-American offenders but not for white or hispanic offenders. Further analysis re-
      vealed that this effect was confined to Black-American offenders convicted of drug offens-
      es involving crack cocaine. On the other hand, Forman (2012) highlights that the war on
      drugs is not the only explanation of mass incarceration (it only explains 10% of the prison
      population). He suggests that Alexander uses this type of crime in particular because it
      is rhetorically convenient as an explanation as it refers to victimless, mainly nonviolent
      crimes. Drug offenses can also expose more clearly the unfairness and racial bias of the
      system, and the underlying behaviors are similar between races (whites use as much or
      more drugs than Black-Americans, but are not equally criminalized). Moreover, though
      the racial aspect of the criminal justice system in the United States cannot be ignored, it
      does not explain mass incarceration on its own: what's more, if all Black-Americans were
      freed from prison, the United States would still have the great imprisonment rate of the
      world. Finally, the 'New Jim Crow' misses the interrelation between race and class, and
      the fact that – while Jim Crow targeted all Black-Americans – in times of mass incarcera-
      tion there are Black-Americans that are not targeted, and lot of poor whites who are actu-
      ally criminalized: indeed, for graduate Black-Americans students, the chances of being
      incarcerated are dramatically less.

of social control was recognized by Nixon's domestic policy chief, John Ehrlichman, who said:

> You understand what I'm saying? We knew we couldn't make it illegal to be either against the war or black, but by getting the public to associate the hippies with marijuana and blacks with heroin, and then criminalizing both heavily, we could disrupt those communities, we could arrest their leaders. raid their homes, break up their meetings, and vilify them night after night on the evening news. Did we know we were lying about the drugs? Of course we did.
>
> quoted in LOBIANCO 2016

In Western Europe, processes of social insecurity led to the demonization of the 'other' through the projection of negative attributes to those who are different: illegal immigrants and ethnic-racial minorities are perceived as dangerous and criminal. A stigmatizing spatial distribution has concentrated those subsets in 'sink estates' and decaying inner cities (Young 2007, 35 and 84–85).

Cultural factors. Overwhelming, crime control is also related to the emergence of a 'new culture of control.' Garland (2001) explains that underlying the debate of crime and punishment was a fundamental shift in the interests and sensibilities of the public, highly charged by emotions of fear, resentment and hostility. Televised images of urban race riots, violent civil rights struggle, anti-war demonstrations, political assassinations and worsening street crime reshaped the attitudes of the U.S. public in the late 1960s. Meanwhile, stories of 'mugging' and increased street crime, militant trade unionism, chronic industrial disputes, and long lines of unemployed workers convinced British voters that social democracy was finished. The experience of the public was that experts (judges, parole boards) were not doing a good job because the crime was increasing and they were failing the public. While 80–90% of the people were not re-offending, public tolerance for any new risk had waned significantly (Stuntz 2011). Welfare policies for the poor were represented as an expensive luxury, while penal-welfare measures for offenders were depicted as absurdly indulgent and self-defeating (Garland 2001). Thus, a new morality, typical of periods of economic recession, emerged and rejected deviation, becoming a fertile input for law and order campaigns (De Giorgi 2002, 84).[66] Public policies

---

66   While it is relevant to analyze social panics in relation to the proliferation of law and order policies during the economic crisis, they cannot be analyzed as an independent variable, as they have a critical dependence of the conjuncture of class struggle. For example, in the United States in 1929, the existence of the latent danger of communism in

BULIMIC CRIMINAL SELECTIVITY

abandoned the goal of rehabilitation, encouraging a generalized defensive cultural attitude (Castel 1995, 6). Analyzing surveys to measure public opinion, Enns explains that there have been rising levels of punitive feelings from the mid-1960s into the 1990s (204, 862). Support for being 'tough on crime' explains over 30% of the changes in the incarceration rate (865). The public's rising punitive feelings appears to be a fundamental determinant of the incarceration rate, mediating the relationship between the latter and the crime rate (869).[67]

---

the working classes, among other factors of class struggle, prompted welfare policies in lieu of law and order policies, as well as the expansion of the sociological approach to crime and punishment rather than a more conservative one.

67   A relevant question is how the public digests the outcomes of a racial, punitive and selective criminal justice system. Alexander uses the framework of 'states of denial' of S. Cohen, who shows how individual and institutions know about, yet deny, the occurrence of oppressive acts during slavery, genocide, torture, and every form of systemic oppression, through the 'myth of choice' (telling themselves that the oppressed 'deserve' their fate) (2010, 177–178). Denial is facilitated by persistent racial segregation in housing and schools, by political demagoguery, racialized media imagery, and by the ease of changing one's perception of reality simply by changing television channels. About mass incarceration, denial is even easier than with slavery or Jim Crow, because Black-Americans are confined in prisons and ghettos and officially targeted as criminals. Moreover, because mass incarceration is officially colorblind, it seems inconceivable that the system could function much like a racial caste system. Finally, it is more convenient to imagine that a majority of young Black-American men in urban areas freely choose a life of crime than to accept the real possibility that their lives were structured in a way that virtually guaranteed their early admission into a system from which they can never escape (Alexander 2010, 177–179). Neuroscience studies show that dehumanization of the oppressed automatically reduces the pain and empathy that emotionally underpins rights based attitudes and behavior (Murrow and Murrow 2015).

This 'myth of choice' operates even in the Black-American communities, who supported punitive policies. Fortner criticizes the invisibility of black victims with no sympathy or empathy with perpetrators of crime in their neighborhoods (2015, x-xii). Fortner recalls that, in 1973, when New York Governor Nelson Rockefeller announced new punitive antidrug measures (mandatory life sentences for individuals convicted of selling any amount of 'hard' drugs, including heroin, cocaine, and hashish), leaders of Black-American neighborhoods endorsed the plan. While white liberals denounced these laws as inconsistent and useless in resolving drug addiction and trafficking, the silent black majority supported the regulation and removal of the poor, whom they blamed for urban blight and violence in the streets, laying the groundwork for mass incarceration (9–10). In the same line, Forman points out that the NAACP Citizens' Mobilization Against Crime demanded "lengthening minimum prison terms for muggers, pushers, [and first] degree murderers," and that, essentially, Black-Americans were "actors in determining the policies that sustain mass incarceration." However, this conditions a 'double frustration:' while communities want better crime policies and law enforcement presence in their

Social and institutional components. U.S. states with lower levels of trust in people's honesty and in the criminal justice system have higher incarceration rates. These levels have decreased in the country since the 1980s (Lappi-Seppälä 2016). The fact that a part of the population has not protested against the reduction of welfare, even though this left the lower-classes unprotected, constitutes an expression of low levels of solidarity and social commitment. Accepting the lack of social assistance to their fellow citizens inculcates a culture of individualism in which people do not think that they have an obligation to the other. An expression of this sentiment can be found in the formulation of the American Dream: everything is possible in the United States; you just need to 'work hard and play fair.' As getting what you want only requires effort, it is understandable that housing, education or healthcare are not universally available but only granted to those people who work hard to 'succeed' in the market. The equation fostered the characterization of the recipients of social assistance as 'lazy people.'

Following the same logic, if it is tolerable that 'good citizens' lack basic rights because they did not put in enough effort to obtain them, the burden is double for those who break the social contract: they must be punished. This reasoning reduces failure to a wholly individual-based explanation, without considering structural barriers. Indeed, both development and reduction of welfare and punitive-welfare rest on the same individual-based explanatory basis: social and criminal outbreaks are explained as individual-based and voluntarily chosen (as integration difficulties that could be addressed by social policies in the welfare state; and as laziness that has to be discouraged by withholding help in the post-welfare state).

Political variables. Social discontent encouraged right-wing realignments and tougher approaches to social problems in response to the perceived crisis of the welfare state. These policies were conducted by the governments of Reagan, Bush and Clinton (1981–2000) in the United States, and by Thatcher, Major and Blair (1979–2007) in the United Kingdom. Simon (2007) characterizes this process as a 'governance' technique that consists of 'governing *through* crime' (as opposite to governing crime) raising the fear of crime to the level of a hegemonic concern. He explains that "crime offered the least political or legal resistance to government action" to control the poor (31). Moreover, Simon clarifies that this form of governance does not only apply to the criminal sphere but also to schools, gated communities and workplaces. Crime control operates as

---

neighborhoods, they understand that this may well lead to their children's conviction (2012, 204).

the Damocles sword behind all legal regulations: "[a]ll governance is 'through' the implied threat of making resistance at some stage a 'crime'" (14).[68]

Gender relations. A number of gender-related changes (namely the mass entry of married women and mothers into the paid workforce, women marrying later, having fewer children, re-entering the paid workforce soon after giving birth, the rise of divorces and more children born to single mothers) helped diminish social control in the family sphere, affecting poor populations. And welfare was seen as responsible for encouraging these changes that de-structured families (Garland 2001, 82–83).

Having analyzed the factors that conditioned the irruption of bulimic over-criminalization, it is relevant to note that this mode of over-criminalization operates in a different manner according to the level of conflict of its targets and the availability of non-punitive means of social control. Analytically, without pretending to fall into fixed and static divisions but looking for general guidelines for analyzing the current situation of crime control,[69] it is possible to separate the over-criminalized population into two categories: 'social junk' and 'social dynamite' (Spitzer 1975). These nomenclatures are interesting because of their colloquial and even provocative character that omits the label-frauds and explicitly states the genuine perception and treatment given to these sectors, i.e., how they are effectively addressed by crime control. The response seems to be that social junk is perceived and treated as a tax burden, an expense, while the social dynamite is perceived and treated as a source of undesirable crime. It is necessary to analyze these categories separately.

---

68   Simon describes the deployment of criminal law and the technologies, mentalities, metaphors and narratives associated with it figure in efforts to govern non-criminal issues like land use in the central business district, the flow of transnational migrants and political refugees, in efforts to guide the post-patriarchal family (2002, 8–9). In the case of schools, Simon expresses that punishment and policing have come to compete with teaching as the dominant mode of socialization, not only in those that suffer from a crime but also in those that suffer from 'fear to crime' (2007, 210). In the United States, governing through crime is centered in the figure of the American prosecutor. In the political sphere, the prosecutor became the new model of leadership, in which mayors, governors, and presidents define their objectives in prosecutorial terms. On the other hand, the prosecutors themselves expanded their power at the expense of juries, judges and defense attorneys. Their sphere of influence extends beyond the judiciary to the governance (33–36).

69   The suggested categories are just 'ideal types' (Weber 1922) that are not intended to reflect a static description of the dynamics of classes and social strata, since individuals may eventually fluctuate between these subcategories, and even join the formal labor market, or modify its position regarding expectations produced by the exacerbated cultural inclusion.

Bulimic Over-Criminalization of the Social Junk

Social junk represents those individuals who have a disability, or who fail or refuse to participate in the expected productive roles of capitalist society, which makes them costly to the state by demands of assistance, but relatively harmless. Social junk identifies the group of people who have fallen or jumped through the cracks of our social system, and now rely on others to supply their basic needs (Spitzer 1975, 405).

While Spitzer uses the term to refer to retirees, the physically handicapped and people with mental health problems, the category is expanded here. It is defined to include all those who, facing a highly competitive labor market and imbued by class, racial, cultural, political, gender and geographical conditionings, can only survive on charity, the scarce remnants of social assistance, sporadic jobs and subsistence self-employment (very precarious autonomous economic ventures that provide insufficient and irregular incomes). The essential feature of the social junk is that, even though it is an expensive burden on the state, it is hardly troublesome. Its members tend to passively accept their status as economically-excluded, while they evade supra-culturization (the exacerbated incorporation of cultural patterns conditioned by a distorted and iatrogenic cultural inclusion). Taking us back to the very division of the primitive accumulation, social junk represents the 'true' and 'good' poor; the 'non-working' sectors that accepted governmental aid and the permission to beg. As mentioned above, the most drastic difference from the original framework is that, far from a draft economic expansion that tends to a future inclusion of those sectors, the current orientation is towards a greater breakdown of inclusive mechanisms.

Essentially, the social junk has been the target of bulimic over-criminalization as a result of the perpetration of minimum-harmful behaviors: mostly, criminalized survival strategies and the absorption of social assistance into a criminal logic that turns it into what may be called *punitive welfare*. Once targeted, social junk is addressed through flexible crime control, namely the application of restorative justice mechanisms that operate as a latent control: if restorative mechanisms fail, the traditional procedural mechanisms are applied as a back-up. This approach reflects the lower level of conflict of the social junk, as well as the structural inability of the criminal justice system to absorb them as a whole through traditional repressive mechanisms (prison).

Bulimic Over-Criminalization on the Criminalized Survival Strategies. Criminalized survival strategies became extensively regulated by criminal legislation (primary over-criminalization), while also their effective prosecution expanded (secondary over-criminalization). These strategies include criminal treatment of behaviors such as hawking, misuse of public space, occupation

of public roads, encroachments, car care without legal authorization, prostitution, vagrancy, drinking alcohol in public, loitering, panhandling, playing loud
music, marijuana possession and sleeping on the subway, among others.

Over-criminalization of such kind of activities may suggest that the state's
failure to provide health and social rights, far from being challenged (or criminalized) is translated in the over-criminalization of those whose rights have
been neglected. The transformation of fundamental and unsatisfied rights of
the population into crimes is a logic that has been sustained since primitive
accumulation. The effect of this change has been the over-criminalization of
those individuals that precariously seek meeting those needs through informal
means. Belonging to the targeted class and racial subset of the population constitutes their members in a privileged flank of criminal legislation that awards
'criminal' character to behaviors that were once addressed through healthcare,
therapeutic or administrative services.

Bulimic Over-Criminalization of the Punitive Welfare. The other main transformation has to do with the absorption of social assistance from a criminal
perspective, forming what may be called *punitive welfare.* This phenomenon
has been more prevalent in the United States. Although it has also occurred
in Britain, Sweden, Holland, Belgium, Spain, Italy and France, European countries still retain a high welfare framework (Wacquant 1999, 44). Increasing
populations need social assistance while public resources for these provisions
continue to shrink. In the few cases where welfare is provided, it links its recipients to crime control through two mechanisms: the imposition of criminal
consequences for non-compliance with the obligations and administrative requirements imposed within social assistance, and crime control as a latent and
constant threat in the everyday life of the assisted.

The first mechanism – criminal consequences for non-compliance with obligations or administrative requirements imposed within social assistance –
has its origin in the break with, and mistrust of, social support. It was
emphasized that welfare states had failed because their aid programs were
too 'permissive' and imposed no strict obligations on the conduct of its recipients.[70] Murray, as an exponent of the demands for welfare transformation, notes that it was necessary to prevent the poor to live at 'our' expense.
He argues that there was a need to bury the welfare state, to save society from

---

70   In the United States, President Reagan categorized the assisted population as 'welfare
     queens:' that is, the image of the widespread and criminal depravity among low-income
     women of color. The stigmatizing effects reverberated such that, by 1984, two-thirds of
     adults living below the poverty line were single mothers, who were five times more likely
     to live in poverty than two-parent families (Gustafson 2009, 653–658).

the underclass who sow social ruin and moral desolation (quoted in Wacquant 1999, 42). The challenge was to overcome the passivity of the poor, and
particularly, of Black-Americans, through labor discipline and authoritarian
remodeling of their 'dysfunctional lifestyle.'[71] As a reverse of the innocence
principle, the demanding population had the burden to prove that they were
not just lazy and that they sincerely needed and deserved assistance. The
parallel is striking if we recall the over-criminalization of vagrants during the
primitive accumulation (when they had to prove that they were not able to
work) and the over-criminalization of peasants during the legally-disciplining
order (when they had to prove the legal origin of collected wood). Punitive
welfare even led to a discursive shift: recipients of aid were no longer characterized as active citizens claiming a right that the state guaranteed, but mere
'beneficiaries;' i.e. passive individuals that were given a 'benefit,' a 'favor,' a
'grace,' a 'plus,' an excess from the regular considerations that – unlike rights –
can be discretionally removed. Even though the welfare state had operated as
an instance of crime and social control, it did so with a soft glove, which now
was no longer available because it was no longer useful.

As for the second mechanism – the link between crime control as a potential and constant presence behind welfare-, it was cemented in the discourses
of the 1990s that characterize social assistance bearers as criminals. To better
administrate the use of state resources, there was a greater crime control over
the 'lazy' and 'criminal' people. Investigations of possible fraud increased and
urged the analysis of the criminal background of petitioners as a requirement
for granting aid.[72] Those convicted of crimes related to drugs could not receive

---

71   Wacquant notes that the new social paradigm is 'compensatory' as it is no longer free,
      but requires return duties (1999, 45). In a later work (2009), he delineates the concept
      of 'workfare' which designates the public assistance programs that condition the accep-
      tance of low-wage jobs by the potential assisted population, or their engagement in un-
      paid activities under the promise of future employment, such as training or internships.

72   In the United States in 1993, 23 had established fraud investigation units as a pre-con-
      dition of eligibility, including interviews with family, friends, neighbors, employees and
      owners of the housing of applicants. In 1996 the Personal Responsibility and Work Oppor-
      tunity Reconciliation Act imposed severe measures to control fraud at the federal level.
      In California, the assisted population has to inform about their criminal records, report
      on their partner status, immunize their children, and refrain from consuming drugs. The
      financial information provided is contrasted with multiple databases and personal in-
      formation (along with photograph and fingerprints) that is of free access for any public
      official. In 1997, the county of San Diego, California, established a program that subjects
      assisted people to home visits without notice, directed by a fraud investigator that can
      present criminal evidence against the petitioner (Gustafson 2009, 659–660).

aid ever again in their lifetime.[73] The Fugitive Felon Prohibitions (1996) prohibited those who have an arrest warrant or those who had violated the terms
of probation or parole from receiving any aid. Based on this legislation, the
General Accounting Office reported that, in 2002, 110,000 recipients were identified as fugitives (Gustafson 2009, 665). Punitive welfare became a privilege
extension of the criminal justice system.

These features of punitive welfare also ban all kinds of potential petitioners
from even asking for social assistance, strengthening their economic exclusion
in a self-enforcing cycle. For those who passed the background check and received support, the result was becoming exposed to a permanent control by
the social assistance agencies. Extreme situations include calling fugitives and
inviting them to pick up food stamps for the purpose of capturing them, transforming the welfare system into a trap for hungry violators of the law (668).[74]
Between early 1997 and September 2006, this mechanism led to the arrest of
10,980 people across the United States: 31% were for misdemeanors such as
turning dead checks (668–670).

In light of the fact that welfare and penal institutions can compromise a
single policy regime aimed at addressing problems associated with deviance
and marginality (Beckett and Western 2001), a broad analysis of less eligibility
should be preserved. In the bulimic social order, the inclusive social assistance
fostered during the third disciplining phase becomes punitive welfare. It provides worse conditions than those in precarious and poorly paid jobs, mostly
destined to the precariat. In this respect, the requirement of fulfilling obligations in exchange for social assistance rises to the rank of civic duty (in particular, reducing the chance of survival outside the unskilled labor market), without
which they will not find anyone to employ them (Wacquant 1999, 44).[75] Thus,

---

73 In 15 U.S. states, any charges related to drug offenses – including possession of small
quantities – is sufficient for lifetime disqualification from public assistance. As a result,
approximately 92,000 adults were excluded from the welfare rolls between 1997 and 2002
(Gustafson 2009, 671–672).

74 Talon Operation was created to expedite the implementation of outstanding warrants
and to enable the offices that provide food stamps to conduct covert operations to arrest
fugitives, citing them under the guise of providing a benefit (Gustafson 2009, 667–669).

75 In the 1970s, bureaucracy increased, access to social benefits was more difficult, and the
number of advantages were reduced. In the United States, since 1967 and especially since
1988, Aid to Families with Dependent Children lost its character of federal law and introduced an income qualification through another federal program known as Temporary Assistance for Needy Families. There is an obligation to follow rules of behavior and report
all details of income and household composition. Failing to comply with these requirements after receiving the benefit includes penalties and exclusion from the program,

punitive welfare helps reduce public spending: not only is the quality of the provisions reduced but many individuals prefer to refrain from requesting it so as not to be exposed to the consequences of that submission. Punitive welfare also exerts social control by introducing a latent crime control over petitioners and recipients. Finally, punitive welfare also pressures the informal labor market by compelling under-skilled workers to accept bad-paid jobs as a better alternative to being the target of these instances of harsh control (46). In addition, the drastic conditions of social aid have the effect that over-criminalization follows those employed workers to ensure their submission to the workplace order under the threat of becoming criminalized. For example, the u.s. federal government has encouraged drug testing in the workforce through the 1986 Drug-Free Federal Workplace Executive Order issued by President Reagan. Other mechanisms include pre-employment screening, drug testing, fraud prevention and investigation, and violence threat assessment and response. Preventing violence, drug use and fraud are used as justifications for control (Simon 2007, 236–241).

As for the hegemonic form of punishment that applies to the social junk when they commit criminalized survival strategies or they fail to fulfill the requirements of punitive welfare, it rests mainly on restorative justice mechanisms. This approach is a result of the lower level of conflict reported in the acts committed by this social group and, at the structural level, because they represent "the extreme poverty of three-quarters of humanity, too poor for debt, too numerous for confinement" (Deleuze 1995). Hence, the implementation of prison sentences becomes materially unfeasible to contain the growing over-criminalized population. The use of restorative justice mechanisms (probation, parole, mediation, summary trial, and file) and alternative procedures (community courts, specialized courts) facilitates covering a much larger population at a markedly lower economic cost than prisons. In numbers, the United States had 7.3 million people on probation and 4.3 million on parole in 2008 (Garland 2016).

What is remarkable is that these restorative justice mechanisms, created with the aim of rehabilitation in the context of socio-disciplining criminal selectivity, are still formally presented under this logic, but this is a euphemism. Far from replacing the traditional criminal justice system, these institutions expand it horizontally in a net of crime control that acts in concert with imprisonment. These new requirements of order are graded regarding capillarity and extension, under ambiguous control, so that the prison population represents

often permanently. Meanwhile, the amount of average benefit went from $854 in 1969 (in 2001 dollars) to $456 in 2001 (Gustafson 2009, 644–660).

a minority of the total number of people who are criminally-controlled (Pava-rini 1995, 52–53). The traditional criminal process works as a latent threat for those who do not surrender to the first line of crime control. To exemplify, the guidelines established for the imposition of alternative mechanisms (estab-lishment of domicile, abstaining from drug use or alcohol, performing com-munity work, among others) operate as a 'notice' that their breach involves a referral to traditional criminal proceedings. The purpose is not to rehabilitate offenders but to collect the waste of the inclusion – exclusion process, ensur-ing their non-confrontational control.

Bulimic Over-Criminalization on the Social Dynamite

Social dynamite refers to individuals (especially young people) with a high level of conflict that present them as a threat to the existing social order. So-cial dynamite is configured by those who have the potential to question estab-lished relations, especially the relations of production and domination. They are those who have fallen or jumped through the cracks of our social system; those who respond rebelliously and potentially violently to failure (Spitzer 1975, 405).

Expanding the characterization of Spitzer, this book proposes that, with re-gard to social dynamite, unlike social junk, supra-culturization is accentuated because of their age and their relation to the culturally imposed consumption patterns. Taking us back to the analysis of the primitive accumulation, mem-bers of the social dynamite are perceived as 'bad' or 'false' poor. They are those who resist being incorporated into the shameful conditions of available em-ployment, and that question the existing order with their disruptive behavior. The difference from primitive accumulation consists in the low expectations of being fully included in the near future but also in the burden that the situ-ation of inclusion – exclusion involves. By this logic, most of the members of the social dynamite do not even apply to social assistance because they do not meet the requirements that it demands. Some individuals may not even have the basic social strategies needed to manage the bureaucratic constraints and expulsive efforts of administrative agencies to enable access to aid (what is known as 'functional illiteracy'). The rebel attitude of the social dynamite – conditioned by supra-culturization – also distances them from the institutions and agents that mediate among potential recipients and the state.

Resorting to the re-analysis of the less eligibility principle, it is proposed that the sort of crime control that operates over the social dynamite is 'less eligible' than the one used to monitor the social junk (the lowest members of the free working class, linked to criminalized survival strategies and puni-tive welfare). Supporting this analysis of the less eligibility principle, former

Massachusetts governor William F. Weld expressed that prisons should be a "tour though the circles of hell," where detainees should learn only "the joys of bustling rocks" (quoted in Worth 1995). Or, as Shaw says. "[i] f the prison does not underbid the slum in human misery, the slum will empty, and the prison will fill" (Petersilia 2003, 5).

Thus, the level of conflict of social dynamite fosters bulimic over-criminalization, which operates over this social sector through a warlike approach: the 'war on crime.'[76] This 'war' expresses in a quantitative (larger number of criminal types) and qualitative (stiffer penalties and more stringent procedural mechanisms) expansion of the regulations applicable to the acts committed by this sector (mainly coarse crimes). It also conditioned a reinforced persecution by law enforcement (particularly higher levels of arrest and prosecution), court's discretion, degraded prison conditions and harsher collateral consequences of convictions. To exemplify how punishment got harsher to ensure its less eligibility in comparison with the situation of the 'good' citizens, in 1994, the U.S. Congress eliminated the Pell, which covered the tuition for college during incarceration. Today, 1,600 people are released each day, having served an average of 2,5 years. Three in four have a history of substance abuse, and one in six suffers mental illness, while infectious diseases, illiteracy or lack of skills, unemployment and learning disabilities are common patterns. At the moment of their release, they receive a bus ticket and are told to report to the parole office in their community the next business day. Some states provide a set of clothing but this practice has been declining (Petersilia 2003, 5–7). This humiliating treatment transforms 'citizens in prisons' into 'inmates;' 'citizens with criminal records' into 'outcasts,' and their 'rights' into 'underserved privileges.' Let us analyze this in detail through the study of how primary and secondary bulimic over-criminalization operate on the social dynamite.

Primary Bulimic Over-Criminalization of the Social Dynamite. The core of primary over-criminalization was the expansion of drug offenses at the federal and local level. N.Y.C. Rockefeller Drug Laws (1973) incorporated extremely harsh punishments for possession or sale of illicit drugs, even for small amounts, and worked as a model for the federal level (Kohler-Hausman 2010). The Federal Crime Bill of 1984 and the Anti-Drug Abuse Act of 1986 triggered the national 'war on drugs.' The latter imposed twenty-nine new mandatory

---

76   Wacquant calls this process 'prison-fare' (2009) by analogy with 'workfare,' referring to the policies that send the unemployed, marginal employees, and petty criminals to prison, and to the active deployment of police, criminal courts, and prisons (and its extensions: parole, the criminal databases and various surveillance systems) in (and around) marginalized neighborhoods, where the postindustrial proletariat live.

minimum sentences,[77] which have been characterized as the cause of the growth of incarceration at the federal level. The expansion of statutes under this 'war' ended up configuring an overwhelming number of 21,323 drug-related offenses from the total 75,836 federal offenses (Federal Sentencing Statistics 2014). These laws are not only punitive but also biased, as mandatory minimum sentencing laws target crimes for which Black-Americans are more likely to be arrested. A clear example is the 100-to-1 law (1986) that punished sales of crack cocaine as severely as sales of a hundred times larger cocaine powder when crack cocaine sales mostly involve Black-Americans and powder cocaine mostly involves whites. Although this law was replaced by an 18-to-1 model in 2010, the new law only slightly reduces the disproportionate effects (Tonry 2012).

Breaches of immigration regulations followed a similar path in terms of primary over-criminalization. By 2014, 22,238 federal crimes were related with this type of behavior (Federal Sentencing Statistics 2014). This process started in the 1980s when new federal laws intensified the priority of identifying and removing criminal aliens, lowered the seriousness of crime required for mandatory deportation, and eliminated state court waivers. These federal laws include dispositions of internment in expulsion centers or detention centers for migrants. These facilities have a high degree of privatization and provide lower wages to their employees, resulting in worse conditions than those of the average state prisons for felons (Simon 1998, 580).

Following the primary over-criminalization trend, severe behaviors such as domestic and gender violence went beyond the private sphere and became public policy issues. More than a dozen states and many municipalities in the United States adopted policies mandating police to make an arrest when they find probable cause that an act of domestic violence occurred. Some states passed mandatory jail terms and others created specialized domestic violence courts (2007, 183–187).[78] Also, sixteen states adopted new commitment laws

---

77   Mandatory minimums require offenders to be sentenced to a minimum specified amount of prison time, as part of a withdrawal of trust in decision-making by judicial actors or parole boards, and a stronger confidence in the political sphere to decide a 'fair' punishment. These minimums implicate an abandonment of individualization as a basis of punishment because they establish fixed sentences for each offense. They also lead to disparate charging decisions by prosecutors: while no offender was charged with mandatory minimums in some districts, in others as much as 75% received it.

78   Without ignoring that the latter is a delicate and seriously problematic, these laws tend to over-criminalize the impoverished sectors involved in those critical situations. While the upper-classes might have similar problems, they can resolve them through mental health assistance or counseling in the private sphere. A punitive approach to domestic and

aimed at sexual offenses, which substantially broaden the reach of preventive confinement, potentially for life (2006–2006, 2139).

Primary over-criminalization also involves the introduction of more rigorous procedural mechanisms, including determinate sentences, truth in sentencing schemes, life-without-parole, elimination of parole boards' discretion about when to release, three-strikes and-you-are-out laws, the treatment of juveniles as adults and the expansion of preventive detention. These punitive instruments, as well as capital punishment, strengthen the characterization of the United States as an outlier. In Europe, these institutions are unconstitutional and life-time sentences only take place after the rejection of parole.[79] These institutions can be legally established in the United States as a result of the country's abandonment of rehabilitation as the goal of punishment, which is still the paradigm in the European law (Subramanian and Shames 2013). International human right treaties signed by the European countries provide a human rights-framework for the criminal justice system that, although it may not be respected in all its terms, brings a legal support to claim for the ideal conditions provided in the letter of the law.

Determinate sentences. The passage from indeterminate to determinate sentences introduced fixed prison terms established by sentencing guidelines. State and federal sentencing commissions created ranges of sentences for given offenses and offender characteristics.[80] Racial injustice became relevant here as a result of the discretional application of the guidelines that allows

---

gender violence is not likely to improve the situation of victims, but mostly constitutes a new form of criminal selectivity. Willis uses the concept of 'pyrrhic victory' to describe how young members of the working class create a myogenic and tough culture to protect themselves from the humiliation of being economically excluded and how this culture harms their interest (quoted in Young 2007, 84). Also here, the violent culture of these subsets facilitates their over-criminalization instead of their emancipation.

79   Some European countries have shown tendencies to harshen criminal procedures: for example, the British Labor government weakened defendants' procedural protections by abolishing the double jeopardy rule, changing evidentiary rules and narrowing jury trial rights (Tonry 2007). However, as Subramanian and Shames (2013) show, overall, European countries give great possibilities for prosecutors to implement alternatives to imprisonment. In the Netherlands, a widely used transaction is a form of diversion in which an offender voluntarily pays a sum of money or fulfills one or more financial conditions to avoid prosecution. Transactions are available for offenses for which the maximum penalty is less than six years, which covers the majority of crimes. Prosecutors in the Netherland and Germany can also divert through a penal order, which can comprise a fine, community service, compensation, driving restrictions, mediation, forfeiture, or confiscation of assets obtained by or used in the conduct in question.

80   Some states incorporated 'presumptive guidelines' (the judge could decide something different from the guidelines, and they can be appealed) and some others gave 'strict

biased departures.[81] Even though determinate sentences pursued sentencing uniformity in order to respond to demands that came from both conservative and liberal positions,[82] they did not accomplish that goal.

Truth in sentencing schemes. Sentencing schemes (1984) made it mandatory to serve a substantial portion of the sentence – generally, 85% of the time that the judge imposed -. Parole eligibility and good-time credits became restricted or eliminated. The emergence of these schemes had to do with claims from the public and the representatives that understood that it was a scandal that offenders were charged with long sentences but only served a short period of them. To promote and extend the truth in sentencing schemes, the U.S. Congress passed the Violent Offender Incarceration and Truth-in-Sentencing Incentive Grants Program in 1994. This program gave grants to build or expand correctional facilities only to those states that could demonstrate that the

---

guidelines' (the judge must follow the guidelines). At the federal level, since *United States v. Booker*, 543 U.S. 220 (2005), the guidelines are applied as advisory.

81   Assuming Arendt's framework on the 'banality of evil' (1963), it is possible to question when it is morally permissible to punish. Arendt formulated the concept of the 'banality of evil' in *Eichmann in Jerusalem* (1963) to portray the perpetrators of the Holocaust. She describes how Eichmann, far from being an extremely cruel character (a monster), was just a bureaucrat operating within a system based on extermination, and who executed orders without ethically questioning them. Regardless the differences between the Holocaust and everyday criminal practice, Arendt's concept helps reflect on the functioning of bureaucracies as shortchanging justice criteria. Moreover, it is possible to think about how the judiciary operates through similar 'techniques of neutralization' (Sykes and Matza 1957) than those that concern the stereotype criminal. They first work through 'denial of responsibility' with expressions such as 'we do not know what is the current status of prisons because it is not possible for us to monitor the excessive number of cases that we are assigned,' or 'we are not unjust, the offenders are the ones who committed a harmful act.' Second, 'denial of injury,' including claims such as 'the law says that prisons are healthy and clean.' Third, 'appealing to a higher loyalty,' used by superior courts to say that they are just implementing the law, by district judges to express that the responsibility is of the superior courts, and by employees to mean that they just do what the judge orders. Fourth, 'blaming the victim,' where officials express that the offender deserves punishment or that the offense has been proved, without questioning the conditions of the offender and the offense. Finally, 'condemn the condemners' led officials to sustain that critics are ideological, or that it is easy to criticize from the 'outside.'

82   Liberal critics argued that indeterminate sentencing was discriminatory and biased because most of the people released sooner by the parole board were white middle class. Conservatives also alleged that indeterminate sentences were inappropriate because they were soft on crime and unfair because people did not serve the time that their sentence had established.

average time served in prison was not less than 85% of the sentence (Bureau of Justice Statistics 1999, 2).

Life-without-parole. This institution cannot be understood without referring to capital punishment. Although the latter involves a tiny number of cases of the entire criminal justice system,[83] the notion that a person can be killed by the state has been symbolically relevant and has been working as a standard for other punishments. When it appears in the 1970s, life without parole was celebrated by some abolitionists as lenient in comparison with capital punishment – the lesser evil – (Zimring and Johnson 2001) and as a possible tool to undermine racial inequality.[84] However, life without parole has implied

---

83   Currently, capital punishment shows its lowest level in 24 years; the majority of U.S. citizens support life without parole; 93% of executions are concentrated in just four states – Texas, Missouri, Georgia, Florida; Nebraska has recently abolished the death penalty; the Connecticut Supreme Court declared it unconstitutional; and Pennsylvania imposed governmental moratoria on executions (Death Penalty Information Center 2015, 2). In the judicial sphere, more than a quarter of death sentences in 2015 were cases in which juries did not unanimously recommend death; 18 explains that sustain the death penalty did not impose death sentences in 2015; executions dropped by 20% compared to 2014 (4). When discussing capital sentences that have been already imposed, six former death row prisoners were exonerated in 2015, with an average of 19 years in prison as a result of their wrongful convictions (6); and two-thirds of the 28 people executed in 2015 exhibited severe mental illness, intellectual disability or effects of trauma and abuse (9). The purpose of capital punishment cannot be aimed at deterrence as the crimes that are punished with capital punishment are passion-based and not subject to calculating economic behavior. The justification is then that the death penalty is the expression of community desires that are expressed through the jury (Garland 2010). So the question is why the U.S. has not yet gotten rid of the death penalty when the Western world considers it as part of its barbaric past? Garland (2012) explains that the reasons are three-fold: 1. the federal structure of U.S. democracy that imposes limits on the national government to eliminate the death penalty nationwide, keeping it a state-by-state decision or subject to a Supreme Court ruling; 2. Short election cycles, primaries, weak political parties, and campaign finance needs that fasten lawmakers to public opinion; 3. the position of the Supreme Court that, though ruling in *Furman v. Georgia* that the death penalty, as then administered, was unconstitutional, then – in response to 35 states passing new legislation reinstating the death penalty, and the approval of capital punishment by U.S. citizens – stated that it is constitutionally permissible, so long as approved procedures are followed.

84   The race of the victim plays a major role in charging and sentencing decisions in capital cases. Those who victimize whites – and especially ethnic minorities who victimize whites – are more likely to be charged with capital crimes, to proceed to trial before death-qualified juries, and to be sentenced to death. Those who are young and male – pay a "punishment penalty" in both state and federal courts. Also, there is convincing

an expansion of the racialized and punitive criminal justice system: 12,453 people were serving time without parole in 1992, but the number increased up to 33,633 in 2003, while death row population grew by 31% in the same period. "Instead of saving lives, [life without parole] toughens the sentencing of criminals who would not have received the death penalty under the sentencing structure beforehand" (Ogletree and Sarat 2012). Moreover, far from being used for the most severe crimes or under racial equal terms, life-without-parole has been imposed for lower crimes as having a crack pipe, siphoning gasoline from a truck and shoplifting a $159 jacket. It has also been over-dimensionally applied against the Black-American population[85] (A.C.L.U. 2013).

Elimination of parole boards' discretion about when to release. This discretion was eliminated or restricted (Bureau of Justice Statistics 1999, 3). Even in those cases in which parole is still possible, discretionary parole releases have been decreasing: parole releases accounted for the 24% of the prison releases in 2000, in comparison with the 88% of 1977. This change has been particularly affected by the incorporation of the right of the victims to testify at parole hearings and request conditions for release (Petersilia, 2003, 13–14).

Three-strikes and-you-are-out laws. These laws established lifetime imprisonment as a response to the commission of three consecutive crimes (Porter 2013). A quick reading of original over-criminalization mechanisms shows us a remarkable parallel: in the 15th century, the *original* three-strikes-and-you-are-out imposed that the response to a triple repetition of trivial acts, such as panhandling or vagrancy, would be the most severe punishment (torture or capital punishment). The legally-disciplining social order introduced the elimination of the original three-strikes to seek proportionality between crime and punishment. This achievement disappeared in the bulimic social order.

Treatment of juveniles as adults. Juveniles are tried and sentenced as adults when their case is waived (removed) from the juvenile court to the adult court. These transfers occur at a rate of 250,000 per year. All states have transfer laws

---

evidence that Black-Americans and Latinos are more likely than similarly situated White-Americans to serve time in prison, and, among offenders prosecuted in federal courts, receive longer sentences than whites, especially for drug offenses (Charette and Koppen 2015).

85 Black-American prisoners "comprise 91.4% of the nonviolent LWOP [life-without-parole] prison population in Louisiana," despite the fact that "blacks make up only about one-third of the population in the state." Black-American defendants in Louisiana "were 23 times more likely than whites to be sentenced to LWOP for a nonviolent crime." (A.C.L.U. 2013). A July 2009 report by the Sentencing Project found that two-thirds of the people in the U.S. with life sentences are non-white. In New York, it is 83% (Quigley 2010).

that work by statutory exclusion, judicially control or prosecutorial discretion. The maximum age of juvenile court jurisdiction is 17 in 41 states, 16 in 7 states, and 15 in 2 states (N.Y. and N.C.). Among the harmful consequences of these transfer laws, we find that placing juveniles in adult jails make them face greater violence and sexual assault. To avoid this, correctional officers adopt an equally harmful solution: putting juveniles in solitary confinement. As a result, juveniles are 36 times more likely to commit suicide than in juvenile institutions. In terms of rehabilitation, because juveniles in the adult system must face the collateral consequences of convictions, they face harsher obstacles to get a job or housing when they are released. Here again, age and race play together, as there is a disproportionate impact on Black-Americans (Birckhead 2016).

Expansion of preventive detention. Since the 1970s, preventive detention of arrestees pending trial has been transformed. From being considered a possible violation of the constitutional right to bail, it has become a well-established power of the federal government and many state governments (Simon 2005–2006, 2139). Here again, class, race and gender worsen the situation of the detainees. Black-Americans suffer significantly higher odds of pretrial detention than whites (Spohn 2009, 898; Demuth and Steffensmeier 2004). Male offenders are more likely than female offenders to be held in custody before the sentencing hearing (Spohn 2009, 898). Class can be measured by the number of people that are granted bail but cannot pay it: in New York City in 2008, nearly 17,000 people accused of no more than a misdemeanor – such as possession of marijuana or jumping a subway turnstile – could not make bail of $1,000 or less (Human Right Watch 2010). Black-Americans from 18 to 29 years-old pay more to get out of jail than whites and Latinos, in a strict association with their socio-economic situation: people may have had difficulty getting a job due to their race, and thus, is rated as a higher flight-risk at the moment of settling bail (Pinto 2012).[86] Bail conditions further over-criminalization: pretrial

---

86   To bring some fairness to this situation, a few years ago the Bronx Defenders spun off a nonprofit called the Bronx Freedom Fund and started paying the bail of people that could not afford it. 93% of the fund's clients showed up for every single one of their subsequent court hearings – a return rate higher than that of defendants who post their bail or get commercial bail bonds. More than half of the fund's clients eventually saw their cases either completely dismissed or knocked down to some non-criminal disposition. Not a single one ever went back to jail on the charges for which they were bailed out. Without access to a bail fund, defendants in similar positions pleaded guilty to criminal charges 95% of the time (Pinto 2012).

detention has 'spillover effects' on the number of plea bargains and convictions, and the severity of the sentencing (Spohn 2014).[87]

Secondary Bulimic Over-Criminalization of the Social Dynamite. Social dynamite is the target of tougher secondary over-criminalization as a result of law enforcement profiling, courts' discretion and differential punishment.

Law Enforcement Profiling

Secondary over-criminalization of this sector starts with law enforcement profiling. Officials adjust their practices when they operate upon the social dynamite. This social sector suffers from higher levels of fragility and vulnerability as a result of the 'ontological crisis' within the process of inclusion – exclusion (Young 2007), which makes them more likely to be stalked by law enforcement. While this discretion of police officers has been referred to as 'racial profiling,' it is necessary to expand this meaning because biases also involve class, gender, age, ethnicity and religious features. It is then more appropriate to refer to 'law enforcement profiling.' The scope and severity of law enforcement profiling have been markedly more intense in the United States than in other Western countries. Even the United Kingdom, the most American of the European countries, introduced significant anti-poverty schemes to tackle crime during the periods of increased tough-on-crime rhetoric (Western 2013).

Law enforcement profiling has been particularly accentuated by the broken windows theory (Wilson and Kelling 1982). The logic of this policing model is to target the smallest acts of daily life and the most trivial behaviors with zero tolerance. Of course, the notion of 'zero tolerance' does not involve the strict application of all the laws (which would be impossible, not to say intolerable) but rather a highly discriminatory taxation against certain groups in certain

---

87 Offenders who were in custody at the time of the sentencing hearing received sentences that averaged eight months longer than those who were not detained before the hearing (Spohn 2014). People who are in the community are more likely to be able to help their defense lawyer to develop the facts that are needed to contest the case (Lewis 2013). The Bronx Freedom Fund' experience shows that more than half of the fund's clients eventually saw their cases either completely dismissed or knocked down to some non-criminal disposition. Not a single one ever went back to jail on the charges for which they were bailed out. Without access to a bail fund, defendants in similar positions pleaded guilty to criminal charges 95% of the time (Pinto 2012). According to Tim Murray, executive director of the Pretrial Justice Initiative, "studies going back as far as the 1960s show that defendants who are held pretrial are offered harsher plea offers than similarly situated defendants who are out on bail" (Walshe 2013).

areas (Wacquant 1999, 17).[88] The broken windows model does not necessary result in more convictions, but in over-enforcement. Consider the United States, 75% of criminal cases initiated respond to acts against property, while only 20% of convictions involves such offenses, i.e. criminal prosecution serves the purpose of control more than the effective judging of those acts, which are limited to cases of greater importance – crimes against life and sexual integrity to a greater extent – (Ferrajoli and Zolo 1994, 64). The figures show that in 2006, 49.3% of prisoners were incarcerated for nonviolent crimes, a figure that rose to 90.7% in 2008 (Sabol et al. 2008). Overall, violent crimes take up only 10% of the time of the officers, a phenomenon that is encouraged by the mechanisms of for-profit profiling (fines charged to finance municipal governments) and arrests quotas as a means of evaluating police performance (Karabel 2015). It is only upon the milder offenses that bulimic over-criminalization, both primary and secondary, fully operates, while the less severe crimes are kept at the level of policing.

Even worse, it is not necessary to commit an actual offense to be stopped by law enforcement because detention to verify criminal record or police searches without a warrant are available mechanisms. Since *Terry v. Ohio* (1968), police can conduct limited seizures and patdowns of a person based on a quantum of suspicion that is less than the 'probable cause' standard that is required for arresting (Thompson 1999, 962–963). Later on, in *Delaware v. Prouse* (1979) and *Whren v. US* (1996), the Supreme Court preserved the same temperament. Recently, in a dissent in the case *Utah v. Strieff*, Justice Sotomayor expressed:

> This case allows the police to stop you on the street, demand your identification, and check it for outstanding traffic warrants – even if you are doing nothing wrong [...] In many communities the tactics the court endorsed will allow the police to search people almost at will. It is no secret that people of color are disproportionate victims of this type of scrutiny.

Three days later, in another dissent in the case *Birchfield v. North Dakota*, Sotomayor stated:

> I fear that if the court continues down this road, the Fourth Amendment's warrant requirement will become nothing more than a suggestion

---

88 Wacquant (1999) wonders where is the 'zero tolerance' toward administrative crimes, commercial fraud, illegal pollution and violations against health and safety. He suggests that it would be more accurate to describe the so-called zero tolerance policies as strategies of 'selective intolerance.'

[...]For generations, black and brown parents have given their children 'the talk' – instructing them never to run down the street; always keep your hands where they can be seen; do not even think of talking back to a stranger – all out of fear of how an officer with a gun will react to them.

Becker (1962) had already identified this phenomenon as 'false accusations:' there is no deviant behavior but the personal characteristics of the individual are labeled as such. The authors of the broken windows theory themselves say that the actions that must be avoided are those that involve "beggars, drunks, addicts, rowdy teenagers, prostitutes, vagrants, mentally disturbed people" (Wilson and Kelling, 1982, 30). The granted discretion to police officers has been translated into an overuse of stop-and-frisk. In New York City alone, 600,000 persons were stopped and searched in 2010, and more than 685,000 in 2011 (Harcourt 2013, 256). From 2004 to 2012, the number of N.Y.C. stop-and-frisk rose to 4.4 million and, of these contacts, about one in nine resulted in an arrest or a citation, and about one in five lacked legal-ground (Fagan, 2013). D.W.B. has become a sadly-famous acronym to describe the large number of Black-Americans that are pulled over by police officers while driving: a black driver is about 31% more likely to be pulled over than a white driver, and about 23% more likely than a Hispanic driver (Langton and Durose 2013).[89]

Indeed, racial profiling is the core of law enforcement profiling, producing an over-representation of Black-Americans in crime statistics, despite the fact that weapons and drugs are more often found on whites (Shen 2013).[90]

---

89   White-Americans (50.1%) are more liable to get pulled over for speeding than Black-Americans (37.7%) or Latinos (39.2%). Black-Americans are more likely to get pulled over for vehicle defects or record checks. Black-Americans are nearly twice as likely not to be given any reason for the traffic stop. Once stopped, Black-American drivers are more than twice as likely to be subject to police searches as white drivers (Langton and Durose 2013). Black-Americans were also more likely to be handcuffed, even if they ultimately were not arrested. When officers report being able to identify the race of the person before stopping them, the person stopped is much more likely to be Black-American (62%) than when officers couldn't tell the race (48%). Black-American men were more likely to be handcuffed during a stop (1 out of 4 times) than whites (1 out of 15 times), excluding arrests. One of the researchers, Hetey, said: "We found a consistent and persistent pattern of racial disparity, even when we controlled for variables such as crime rate" (Sparq 2016). Also Goff (2016) found that police officers were more likely to use five categories of force (including Tasers and hand/body weapons) against Black-Americans than White-Americans.

90   The likelihood that a stop of a Black-American New Yorker yielded a weapon was half that of white New Yorkers stopped. The NYPD uncovered a weapon in one out every 49 stops of white New Yorkers. By contrast, it took the Department 71 stops of Latinos and 93 stops of Black-Americans to find a weapon. The N.Y.P.D. uncovered contraband in one out every

Or, as Wacquant (1999) claims, the formula 'Young + Black + Male' is now openly equated with 'probable cause' justifying the arrest, questioning, bodily search and detention of millions of Black-American and Latino males every year. Alexander analyzes police conduct operations in poor communities of color and finds that they are rewarded with cash for some people rounded up, and there is no meaningful check on their discretion, which taken together grant racial biases free reign (2010, 180). However, the Supreme Court has been silent about this topic and, in the cited references, it has enforced the image of a colorblind law enforcement activity: the court would not consider illicit racial motivation as a factor that can undermine the validity of a search, seizure, stop or frisk that rests on facts sufficient to satisfy the applicable quantum of suspicion. In *Terry*, the court rejected consideration of race because the Fourth Amendment could not provide a useful tool for combating racism by police officers. In *Whren*, the court invoked a doctrinal barrier, declaring illicit racial motivation categorically irrelevant to Fourth Amendment analysis and only within the province of the Equal Protection Clause (Thompson 1999, 981).[91]

The war on drugs is a central incentive of law enforcement profiling. In 2012, the F.B.I. stated that the maximum number of police arrests were for drug use: approximately 1,552,432 (Harcourt 2013, 256). When analyzing the interaction between war on drugs and over-criminalization of communities of color, the numbers show that in New York City alone and just during the first eight months of 2014, Black-American and Latino communities accounted for 86% of those arrested for marijuana possession (Goldstein 2014). Other important sources of law enforcement discretion are improper-entry prosecutions, which affect Latino communities in particular. The number of over-criminalized people for these crimes peaked at 54,175 in 2009 and 53,822 in 2013. The trend has been preserved and, in 2015, cases against immigrants for having illegally

---

43 stops of white New Yorkers. By contrast, it took the Department 57 stops of Latinos and 61 stops of Black-Americans to find contraband (Shen 2013).

91 As Thompson clarifies: "The Supreme Court's Fourth Amendment decisions treat race as a subject that can be antiseptically removed from a suppression hearing judge's review of whether a police officer had probable cause for an arrest or warrantless search or reasonable suspicion for a stop or frisk. The decisions imagine the world in which some officers are wholly unaffected by racial considerations and in which even biased officers may make objectively valid judgments that courts can sustain despite the underlying racial motivations of the officer" (1999, 983). In other words, it is not humanly possible for the police to leave their biased considerations aside to determine the quantum of suspicion that is necessary to proceed regarding the Fourth Amendment.

entered the United States (entry and re-entry) accounted for half of all cases in the federal court system (Feltz 2016).

The more extreme version of law enforcement profiling has to do with killings: in the United States, police kill more people and more police are killed by police, particularly Black-Americans. There are no official statistics: the F.B.I. annually issues a report that provides figures on 'justified police homicides,' but reporting from local police forces is voluntary and thousands of them turn in no information. Estimations by the *Washington Post* and *The Guardian* – drawn from two citizen-initiated sources, Killed by Police and Fatal Encounters – claim that there are 1,100 killings by police per year. From those, 95% are male; 50% are 34-years-old or younger; Black-Americans are heavily over-represented at about one in four – doubling their percentage of the population -; more than 250 victims suffer mental illness; 88% are killed by gunshot; and one-third were armed with non-gun weapons when they were killed (The Counted 2016).[92] Overall, Black-Americans are 2.5 times more likely to be killed by police than whites (Lowery 2016).[93]

This fatal aspect of bulimic over-criminalization is followed by bulimic under-criminalization: there is almost total impunity regarding police killings. Only 54 officers were charged in the past decade and this resulted in only 11 convictions with little prison time. No police officer received a sentence longer than ten years (Karabel 2015). This culture of impunity affected the limits of what is morally permissible in society, as it happened with lynching, capital punishment and mass incarceration.[94] Police killings as a central aspect of racial injustice was the trigger of the Black Lives Matter movement, which has recently mobilized the Black-American community to demand accountability

92 A recent report shows that more than a third of the people shot by L.A. police last year showed documented signs of mental illness. 21% of the killed people were Black-Americans, although they make up about 9% of Los Angeles population (Mather and Queally 2016).

93 White people make up roughly 62% of the U.S. population but only about 49% of those who are killed by police officers. Black-Americans, however, account for 24% of those fatally shot and killed by the police despite being just 13% of the U.S. population. These percentage mean that Black-Americans are 2.5 times as likely as white Americans to be shot and killed by police officers (Lowery 2016). These killings are connected to the fact that Black-Americans are over 20 times as likely as whites to be involved in a police interaction where an officer draws a weapon (Fryer 2016).

94 Police killings and lynching share the lack of accountability of their authors and the racial component of the victims. Also, both crimes tried to amalgamate the image of the young Black-American men and the one of the criminal, reinforcing discriminatory prejudices.

and a comprehensive reform of the biased criminal justice system.[95] Even though they did not have the same public dissemination, Native-Americans have also been a special target of police killings in correlation to their higher levels of unemployment and lower access to education and health care (Rice 2015).

Courts' Discretion

Although the selective functioning of the courts is commonly known as 'prosecutorial discretion,' it is necessary to expand this concept. Besides prosecutor, also judges, juries and even defense attorneys are plagued by explicit and implicit bias. It is then more accurate to refer to 'courts' discretion.' In the United States, courts' discretion is particularly affected by plea barging, the electoral character of prosecutors, the role of the Supreme Court' rulings in constraining defendants' guarantees, the racial composition of juries, the lack of funding of the public defender, and the homogenous racial composition of the courts. The result of this selective phenomena is that young males of color are more likely to get prison time (Mustard 2001, 285), to be convicted to longer sentences (Steffensmeier et al. 1998)[96] and to qualify for relief from

95 Black Lives Matter emerged as a response to police killings that went viral through the internet. They have transformed an overlooked problem into a major political issue, employing a variety of tactics (demonstrations, traffic blockages and disruptions of highly visible political events). They helped inspire a broader movement with concrete proposals (Campaign Zero and Building Momentum from the Ground Up). One of the central goals of the movement is to register police killings, identifying the race and gender of victims, and if he or she was armed (Karabel 2015). Paradoxically, while every step in the u.s. criminal justice system is registered in a criminal record that can be accessed by private and public actors, police killings are not registered in a national database and the civil movement has to develop tools from the ground up in order to detect and denounce them; a relevant aspect of under-criminalization.

96 Everett and Wojtkiewicz (2002) also find that Black-Americans, Latinos, and Native-Americans receive relatively harsher sentences than whites and that these differentials are only partly explained by offense-related characteristics. When discussing class, offenders who did not graduate from high school received longer sentences and offenders with college degrees received shorter sentences than high school graduates. Having no high school diploma resulted in an additional sentence of 1.2 months. Income had a significant impact on the prison time length.53 Offenders with incomes of less than $5,000 received harsher punishment. This group received sentences 6.2 months longer than people who had incomes between $25,000 and $35,000 (Mustard 2001, 300–301). Black-American males and offenders with low levels of education and income receive substantially longer sentences (285). This difference responds primarily generated by departures from the guidelines,

mandatory minimum penalties in drastically lower numbers than any other group (Sentencing Commission 2013).[97] Let us analyze the different factors that condition courts' discretion.

Plea bargaining. This is the outcome of most of the cases,[98] exponentially increasing the amount of convicted people serving time in prison, in comparison with the number that could be achieved through trials (which would take more money and time) (Stuntz 2011). At the federal level in 2014, 97.1% of sentenced defendants had pled guilty.[99] Pleading guilty seems more associated with the lack of sufficient legal defense than with a voluntary decision. The American Bar Association reviewed the u.s. public defender system in 2004 and concluded: "All too often, defendants plead guilty, even if they are innocent, without really understanding their legal rights or what is occurring [...] The fundamental right to a lawyer [...] does not exist in practice for countless people across the u.s." (Stohr and Walsh 2016, 23). Studies reveal that race and ethnicity affect the charge and plea bargaining decisions in both capital and noncapital cases (Walshe 2013). When analyzing race, Black-American defendants are more likely to be convicted of more charges and to receive more

---

rather than differential sentencing within the guidelines. The largest difference is in trafficking and bank robbery crimes (312).

97   Black-American offenders qualified for relief under the safety valve in 11.6% of cases in which a mandatory minimum penalty applied, compared to white offenders in 29% of cases, and Hispanic offenders in 42%. Because of this, though Black-American offenders in 2012 made up 26.3% of drug offenders convicted of an offense carrying a mandatory minimum penalty, they accounted for 35.2% of the drug offenders still subject to that mandatory minimum at sentencing (Sentencing Commission 2013).

98   By far the most common type of plea agreement is the charge bargain, where the prosecutor agrees to dismiss (or not to bring) certain charges in return for a plea of guilty to one charge. The sentence bargain allows the parties to agree to a particular sentence (or sentencing range) but it is very uncommon. There is also an agreement to recommend sentence but it is rarely practiced.

99   Mandatory minimums and severe guidelines' ranges facilitate the task of prosecutors to pursue plea bargaining. Judges' compliance, satisfaction of victims, defendants that do not want to expose themselves to a public audience, and decisions of resources allocations (prioritization of terrorism cases) are also key elements that discourage trials. Judge Gleeson (2016) stated: "As long as plea bargaining continues to happen against the backdrop created by that harsh regime, prosecutors will use the excessively strict guidelines to get people to plead guilty, and the federal criminal trial will remain on the endangered species list." *Fernandez v. u.s.*; u.s.d.j. 8, March 2016.

246   CHAPTER 4

severe sentences during plea barging (Penn Law Quattrone Center for the Fair Administration of Justice Plea).

Electoral character of prosecutors' designations. Because prosecutors are designated through an electoral process, they usually follow the thoughts of the community to ensure their vacancy. Indeed, there is a correlation between capital indictments – which is discretional – and electoral years (Garland 2016). This is complemented by a lack of accountability: there is low turnover and chief prosecutors rarely face challengers, the incumbent success rate when running for office is 95% and prosecutors run unopposed in 85% of all races (Wright 2009, 592–593).

The role of the Supreme Court' rulings. As shown in the precedents of stop-and-frisk, the Supreme Court has systematically reduced procedural protections over the past thirty years (e.g., weakening controls over police searches and seizures, limiting or eliminating habeas corpus protections, reducing jury trial rights and narrowing prisoners' ability to challenge prison conditions) (Tonry 2007). By disregarding race and class as key elements that condition the criminalization process, Supreme Court's rulings have operated as an instance of legitimization of the selective application of the law by the lower courts and law enforcement's actions.

The racial composition of juries. Juries' configuration affects the outcomes of trials, favoring the over-criminalization of people of color. While white jurors tend to credit police officers' testimony, jurors of color are more likely to approach them with skepticism or even mistrust (Taylor-Thompson 1999, 1313). However, juries of color have been systematically excluded from juries through the racially biased use of peremptory strikes and illegal racial discrimination in jury selection, particularly in serious criminal cases. Although the Supreme Court limited this discriminatory practice in *Batson v. Kentucky* (1968), the decision was not applied retroactively and the southern states have never granted a *Batson* relief in a criminal case (Alexander 2010, 189). In extreme cases, as it happens in Houston County, Alabama, 80% of Black-Americans qualified for jury service but they have been systematically struck by prosecutors in capital punishment cases (Equal Justice Initiative 2010, 5). Moreover, people of color continue to be underrepresented in the pools from which jurors are selected.[100]

---

100   The underrepresentation is an effect of the method of absolute disparity (if a group constitutes less than 10% of the population, the 10% absolute disparity requirement allows even the most blatant and intentional exclusion of members of that group). This method affects Black-Americans' possibility to challenge underrepresentation in 75% of counties in the United States (Equal Justice Initiative 2010, 36). As Taylor-Thompson correctly

The lack of funding of the public defender. Defense attorneys are under-funded in relation to their assigned workload. Criminal procedure regulations put them in a weak position in comparison with prosecutors, who have broader resources and power to gather evidence. Because of disclosure restrictions, defense attorneys are compelled to sign pleas without sufficient knowledge of the charges. Once again, racial minorities are particularly affected by the denial of meaningful legal representation and are pressured to plea guilty (Alexander 2010, 180–182).

The homogenous racial composition of the courts. 95% of elected prosecutors are white; 79% are white men; three in five states have no black elected prosecutor; 14 states have no elected prosecutors of color at all; and just 1% of elected prosecutors are minority women (Women Donors Network 2016). In short, the criminal justice system principally involves white decision-makers determining the fate of people of color (Taylor-Thompson 1998, 1316). Besides the racial composition of the courts, the vast majority of lawyers drag implicit bias: "automatic reactions that make associating white with good easier than associating white with bad." (Harvard University Project Implicit). Extensive explicit and implicit bias even affects defense attorneys: "[a] public defender may try harder for a client that he or she perceives as more educated or likely to be successful because of their race" (Adachi 2016).

The unfairness finds final expression in the fact that, when biased sentencing takes place, there is a lack of adverse consequences for the decision-makers (Equal Justice Initiative 2010, 7). This lack of accountability favors the (immune) perpetration of bulimic over-criminalization.

Differential Penalization
After law enforcement profiling and courts' discretion, bulimic over-criminalization is expressed in the activity of parole boards, the functioning of prisons, and the administration of criminal records.

Parole boards. They foster differential penalization because the risk assessments that they write are based not only on behavior during incarceration, medical concerns and the committed offense but also on socio-economic factors. As social status gets into consideration in the risk assessment, those offenders that have socio-economic advantages are better considered by the

---

clarifies "[o]f course, adding people of color to a jury will not necessarily reduce reliance on stereotypes [but] still, including Black-American jurors might expand the range of stereotypes in play and, in this way and others, enrich the conversation" (1998, 1315).

parole board, in what has been called the 'Mathew effect.' Parole boards also have to take into consideration the victim input: the Victim's Right Movement achieved the rights to be informed and to recommend the sentence and the parole board. In some U.S. states, parole boards are even conditioned by public feelings because they are elected and re-elected by the government (Subramanian and Shames 2013).

When parole[101] is granted, it includes obligations such as the prohibition of leaving the country, duty of informing residence, drugs testing, mandatory participation in rehabilitation programs, and the obligation of avoiding certain people or places. Parolees who violate one of the many rules governing their conditional release can be re-incarcerated, following an administrative revocation hearing at which there are no due process guarantees. In 2000, parole revocations constituted 34% of all prison admissions (Beckett and Murakawa 2012). This means that parole officers have become another mechanism of mass incarceration, instead of a path for rehabilitation. They stop developing social workers' functions to perform police ones: while a successful parole board used to be one with higher levels of rehabilitation, now a successful parole board is one that acts as a risk trigger that stops parolees as soon as they violate one of their obligations.

Functioning of prisons. The United States went from having less than 400,000 prisoners in 1975 to 750,000 in 1985, and 2,000,000 in 1998 (De Giorgi 2002, 17). By 2012, the total number of detainees reached 2,228,424 with an incarceration rate of 707 people per 100,000 citizens (International Centre for Prison Studies 2012),[102] which makes it the country with the highest number of detainees. The United States has less than 5% of the world's population and owns 24% of the

---

101   The meaning of 'parole' has to do with 'word' as, historically, people related to the offender gave his/her word that the offender will not commit another crime, for him/her to be released. Currently, 'parole' is supervised release.

102   There are, however, significant disparities among the different states: while Maine, Massachusetts, and Rhode Island have just twice the level of incarcerated population than European countries, Louisiana shows an outrageous difference. Overall, the rate of incarceration in state prison in the U.S. ranges from 147 per 100,000 residents in Maine to 865 per 100,000 residents in Louisiana. Meanwhile, in Germany, the rate is 79 per 100,000 residents and in the Netherlands, is 82 per 100,000 inhabitants (Subramanian and Shames 2013). China has 1,701,344 people in prison, despite having a dramatically higher population than the United States, and Russia has 671,400 individuals in prison (International Centre for Prison Studies 2012).

detained population.[103] Although there are recent policies aimed at reversing this process, it is still a difficult uphill battle.[104]

Besides the sheer numbers, the demographic of prisons shows that incarceration has become a likely part of the experience of a specific social sector:

---

103   It is relevant to highlight that, as Tonry (2007) clarifies, using only the rate of imprisonment (the number of people held in prison on an average day or an annual census count day per 100,000 population) it is not always enough to measure levels of punitiveness. The rate of incarceration obscures relations among convictions, prison admissions, and sentence lengths. An increasing incarceration rate can reflect a growing number of people convicted, rising chances that convicted offenders are sentenced to imprisonment, lengthening prison terms, changes in release policies, or combinations of some or all of these. It also obscures changes in sentencing patterns for different offenses (for example, it could be that mass incarceration rates respond to the underlined crimes, such as a high number of homicides). It may also be misleading because a slightly rising imprisonment rate during a period of rapidly rising crime rates might indicate not harsher but softer average punishments. Because of these difficulties, Tonry suggests that a better measure might include the probability of incarceration and average days served, in the aggregate or disaggregated by types of offense, about victimizations, recorded crimes, arrests, prosecutions, convictions, or (for sentence length) prison sentences. Moreover, comparisons of changes in penal policy need also to differentiate among their enactment, their implementation, and their practical use. Finally, it is necessary to introduce in the analysis both the risk factors (truancy and school failure, adolescent pregnancy and paternity, drug and alcohol abuse, delinquency, and characteristics of children and their environments) and the protective factors (good parenting, above-average household income, good schools, church participation).

104   Since 2011, the rate of incarceration has fallen, since twenty-six states, led by California, developed programs to combat prison overcrowding costs. However, federal prison populations continue to grow: an average of 6,100 prisoners have entered the system every year since 1980 (Porter 2013). Once again it is particularly important to reinforce that the war on drugs, though relevant to reduce racial profiling, is not the core of mass incarceration. Most of the incarcerated population is in state prisons, while federal incarceration involves only 10% of the incarcerated population (0.2 million people), though for lengthier periods. If political consensus resulted in the release of "everyone imprisoned for drugs tomorrow, the United States would still have 1.7 million people behind bars, and an incarceration rate four times that of many Western European nations" (Mauer and Cole 2015). The B.J.S. reports that 50% of the population is serving time for a violent crime, 20% for a drug crime, and 30% for nonviolent property crime or public order offenses (Petersilia, 2003, 13). Violent crimes – including assaults, robberies, homicides, rapes – are the central problem of mass incarceration. Another relevant factor to take into consideration with the aim of overturning mass-incarceration is that federal prisons only control the 10% of the prisoners, so the President by himself cannot change the shape of prisons, and needs the support of the states. If there are no further changes, it will take 89 years to go back to the number of prisoners in 1989 (Garland 2016).

young unemployed and under-educated Black and Latino males.[105] Indeed, imprisonment has become one of the social institutions that structure this group's experience (Garland 2016). In numbers, "the ethnic composition of the u.s. inmate population has *reversed*, turning over from 70% white at the mid-century point to nearly 70% Black and Latino today, although ethnic patterns of criminal activity have not been fundamentally altered during that period" (Wacquant 2001, 97). Today, the probability that a Black-American person ends up in prison is overwhelmingly higher than for whites (A.C.L.U. 2016).[106] Or, to say it clearer, more Black-Americans are under correctional control today than were enslaved in 1850, a decade before the civil war started (Alexander 2010, 175). The situation is so striking that young Black-American men are more likely to go to prison than to college. Just to give an example, while 992 Black-American men received a bachelor's degree from Illinois state universities in 1999, roughly 7,000 Black-American men were released from the state prison system the following year for drug offenses alone (184–185).

The biased demographic composition of prisons is invisible on the basis of actuarial criminology with its scientist-targeted interventions and its revival of the tenets of positivism of the second disciplining phase. Far from illuminating how criminal selectivity operates through ethnic, racial, social, cultural and economic criteria, actuarial criminology argues that the criminalized population represents the real and violent offenders. Thus, this theory argues, the overrepresentation of vulnerable groups in prisons is read as a real over-representation of them in the commission of crimes: the detainee – and, in particular, the immigrant or Black-American detainee – *is* the offender (Van Swaaningen 1997, 291). This is not accurate. Consider the war on drugs, even though Black young males are arrested for drug crimes at a rate ten times

---

105   Even though the female prison population is smaller than the male one, it has grown more emphatically: exactly, by 832% from 1977 to 2007, the male prison population grew 416% during the same period. Property and drug crimes – nonviolent offenses – make up nearly 2/3 of the population of women in prison (Heather and Sabol 2008, 11).

106   Previous statistics show the same pattern: by 1999, 6 out of 10 people in prison were Black-Americans or Latinos; less than 50% of them were full – employed at the time of their imprisonment, and two-thirds came from households with an income lower than half of the 'poverty line' (Wacquant 1999, 91). In 2002, one out of three Black-Americans, aged between 18 and 35 years, were imprisoned or subjected to an alternative measure (De Giorgi 2002, 17). In 2010, Hispanic and Black-Americans were incarcerated at a rate of 4,347 people per 100,000 US residents of the same race and gender, while white men were imprisoned at a rate of 678 prisoners per 100,000 inhabitants (Bureau of Justice Statistics 2010).

higher than that of whites, they are actually less likely to use drugs and less likely to develop substance use disorders, compared to whites, Native-Americans, Hispanics and people of mixed race (Szalavitz 2011).[107]

Migrants are the ones over-represented in European prison systems. Qualified non-Western immigrants, second generation immigrants and people of color are massively overrepresented in the prison population (Wacquant 1999, 112). Muslim and Caribbean people in Britain, Turks in Germany, Algerians or people from former French colonial territories in France, the Romanian Gypsies in Germany, Surinamese or Moroccan in the Netherlands, to name a few. They are often segregated in special wards of prisons according to ethnonational origins, such as in the case of La Santé prison in France, or expelled and confined in detention centers (116–117).

Other vulnerable targeted by over-criminalization all over the globe are the mentally ill. Even mental health institutions are absorbed by the punitive logic: in the United States, 52% of medical centers reported that their security personnel carried handguns, and 47% said they used tasers (Rosenthal 2016).

Administration of criminal records. Bulimic over-criminalization does not end upon completing the prison term. The collateral consequences of convictions show that offenders always have a 'life time sentence' (Jacobs 2015), an 'invisible punishment,' (Travis 2002, 17), an 'internal exile,' a 'civil death,' or a 'mark of Cain' (19) that transforms them into a new 'undercast' (Alexander, 2010, 13). In a vicious circle, punishment reinforces the concentration and exacerbation of inequality (Western 2006).

While this is a worldwide phenomenon, it is more drastic in the United States.[108] There, criminal records are used to deny the right to vote to prisoners and non-incarcerated felons, who comprise approximately three-quarters of the population of disenfranchised persons (Thompson 2011). The negative effects go beyond the right to vote to include drastic consequences as removal

---

107   Except for crack cocaine, white-Americans consume three to five times more drugs than Black-Americans. Thus, though whites consume more drugs and more often, and 80% of the population is white, 66% of people imprisoned for drug offenses are Black-Americans (Chambliss 1994, 182). By the end of the 20th century, while Black-Americans accounted for 13% of drug users (which corresponds to their demographic weight), they were three-quarters of those imprisoned for breaking drugs laws (Wacquant 1999, 101), a trend that is preserved today (Szalavitz 2011).

108   Demleitner (2009) explains that in Europe, the right to democratic governance is enshrined in the E.C.H.R., which includes the right of individuals to vote. Conversely, in the United States, even the language of Section 2 of the 14th Amendment that allows disenfranchisement for those convicted of "rebellion or other crimes."

from public housing, denial of social assistance and deportation.[109] Also in this aspect of bulimic over-criminalization, people of color are particularly affected: more Black-Americans are disfranchised today than in 1870, the year that the Fifteenth Amendment was ratified to prohibit laws that explicitly deny the right to vote on the basis of race (Alexander 2010, 175–176). More than one in seven Black-American men in the United States is disenfranchised because of his criminal record, raising fundamental questions about how we define (and redefine) citizenship (Gottschalk 2008, 243).[110] As Simon explains, it is the first time since the end of slavery that the descendants of those freed slaves are in a state of legal non-freedom either because of life-without-parole sentences, repeated incarcerations or collateral consequences of their convictions (2007, 6). In a symbolic reproduction of racial bias, while slavery defined Black-Americans as slaves, Jim Crow defined them as second-class citizens and mass incarceration categorizes them as [eternal] criminals (Alexander 2010, 192).[111]

---

109   Criminal records also allow to terminate parental rights (19 states), prohibit convicted people from becoming adoptive parents, limit the right to hold public office (25 states), as well as restrict the right to own guns (33 states) and to circulate in some locations (for example, schools). About felons, their conviction is an argument to ask for a divorce in 29 states. In drug-related crimes, convicted people cannot possess driving licenses, and they cannot receive loans for education, public assistant, and food stamps during their lifetime. The Immigration Reform and Control Act (1986) and the Illegal Immigration Reform and Immigrant Responsibility Act (1996) allow the deportation of immigrants with criminal records. Those with criminal records related to stalking, domestic violence, and sex offenses have the obligation to register with the police upon release, and they cannot ask for assisted housing (Jacobs 2015, 18–24). Because these collateral consequences are not part of the formal criminal justice system, they are not usually considered by judiciary committees, they are not part of the defense lawyers' counseling service, and they are not subjected to judicial review (Travis 2002, 15–17).

110   This phenomenon is even more complicated: the census' usual residence rule removes Black-Americans from urban districts and counts them in rural or suburban areas where they serve time, which tends to decrease the voting power of Black-Americans in their home communities.

111   While slavery and Jim Crow were explicitly race-based, mass incarceration is facially colorblind and enforced in a highly discriminatory fashion. This has a double effect: on the one hand, it contributes to the impunity of mass incarceration as a racial cast system; but, on the other hand, it makes available the possibility of a legal fight to demonstrate that the system has to be driven by racial bias, and overturn a sentencing or a police by legal advocacy and grounded-based activism.

In numbers, 25% of the U.S. adult population has criminal records (Jacobs 2015, 190–192 and 252). This outstanding number responds to the fact that not only convicted people are registered (as it happens in Europe). The United States uses 'rap sheets' (detention and acts performed by local police officers and centralized by the F.B.I.),[112] which expand the scope of registered population to arrestees, non-convicted people and wrongfully registered citizens. To examplify, one-third of criminal records in New York are mistaken (Legal Action Center Study 2016).[113] The 'informal' consequences of having criminal records are also different on different sides of the ocean because of the degree of confidentiality: criminal records are protected in Europe, while they become an innovative and convenient merchandise in the United States. U.S. private companies commercialize criminal records to every person that asks for them and pays the correspondent amount of money.[114] In this regard, "the [U.S.] criminal record is a kind of negative curriculum vitae or résumé" (Jacobs 2015, 202–203) that is available to everybody, including employers that want to screen out people who aspire to find a job (92). Despite the burden of having a record, race still outweighs criminality: studies prove that is easier to get a job being white with a criminal record than being black without one (Legal Action Center Study 2016).[115]

Having delved into the bulimic conflict – control in which bulimic criminal selectivity was deployed, it is possible to introduce the characterization of the social sectors addressed by it.

---

112 These acts take place in the very first moment of the criminal process without further subsequent clarification about whether or not the registered detention was erroneous, whether the charges were dismissed by the investigators, communicated to a judge or dismissed by a court.

113 The situation is so severe that several universities are developing 'Innocence Projects' which includes the support of vulnerable people who need to get rid of their wrongful and stigmatizing criminal records (Graham 2015).

114 This flexibility in the access to criminal record has a clear starting point: the resistance of firearms organizations protested about the long delays to obtain criminal records (criminal check was a prerequisite to buying guns) (Jacobs 2015, 63–75). These organizations promoted the creation of a system that could facilitate the immediate access to criminal record databases under the domain of police officers. After 9–11, the use of databases increased based on the argument that such access would allow the stopping of terrorist attacks. Jacobs warns that this "demonstrates the widely held belief that a criminal record is a valuable predictor of future unreliable and dangerous conduct" (273–274).

115 17% of white-job applicants with criminal records received call backs from employers while only 5% of Black-job applicants with criminal records received call backs (Pager 2013).

Who Were the Social Sectors Targeted by Bulimic Criminal Selectivity?

The recipients of the mechanisms of under-criminalization can be briefly named as monopolistic industrial bourgeoisie and international financial bourgeoisie (Boron 2001, 41). They have been mostly under-criminalized when acting through the growing symbiosis between crime and business, and when perpetrating crimes against terrorism. Importantly, it can be difficult to define these sectors in light of the complexities of the current social structure and lack of agreement on the relevant nomenclatures. Many Marxist theorists refer to these social actors as 'financial capital' (Houtart 2001, 27), 'financial powers' (Harvey 2005, 8), 'capitalist finance' (Duménil 2006, 182), 'global financial' (Formento and Merino 2011), 'global financial network' (Merino 2014). However, the concept of international financial bourgeoisie (Boron 2001, 41) helps obviate euphemisms such as its characterization as 'groups,' 'powers,' 'capital' or other supra-individual invisible instances. Then, the proposed notion clarifies that they are a class with a clear position in the production structure and they exercise political and criminal power.

Recipients of over-criminalization mechanisms have been characterized as 'underclass' in the Anglophone world, 'excluded' in the Francophone, and 'marginalized' in Latin-America (Pits Vasquez 1997). Regardless of the richness of these concepts, it is appropriate to preserve the category of 'pauperism,' deployed by Marx in Chapter 23 of *Capital*, and refer to the recipients of bulimic over-criminalization as 'modern pauperism.'

The notion of 'underclass' – extensively used in the 1980s and 1990s – was used as "an indicator element of the unfavorable conditions in social life [covering the] poor, unemployed, marginal, unaffiliated, etc." (Taylor 1999, 16). That means that it makes reference to a vague and relative notion such as 'the unfavorable situation.' This lack of intelligibility has led to the characterization of 'underclass' as a 'bizarre attachment' that links heterogeneous categories united only by the fact that they are perceived "as imposing a threat, inseparably physical, moral and fiscal, to the integrity of urban society" (Wacquant 1999, 43). The entry of this concept into the political language and the social sciences was a response to a boost of bureaucracies in the research field, eager to demonstrate its usefulness by clinging to the media and political issues of the moment (43). Wacquant proposes, instead of this, the term 'advanced marginality' which refers to a new regime of urban poverty characterized by precarious work and the sudden implosion of the Black-American ghettos. Regardless of its greater accuracy, it describes a particular socio-geographical situation, while dispensing a structural view of the link between this regime of poverty and the complexity of bulimic conflict-control within the framework of the capitalist system of production.

The same defects can be attributed to the francophone concept of 'exclusion' (Braga 2003, 57) because it only refers to the economic aspect and not to the complexity of the process of (cultural) inclusion – (economic) exclusion. As this book exposes, it is it not possible to qualify these masses as 'excluded' because that term would only be describing their material position in comparison with the 'included' sectors, ignoring the fact that, in cultural terms, they are firmly included.

The notion of 'marginality' – which was originated in 1950s Latin-America and then was expanded to Europe – reinforces the cultural aspect as well as the geographical and political spheres that these sectors do (and do not) occupy. It is then that 'marginality' can be defined as the lack of participation of individuals and groups in those areas in which, according to certain regulatory criteria, they should participate. 'Marginalization' describes this situation as transitional and susceptible of being overcome with economic development (Germani quoted in Retamal 1997). This notion was dismissed given the evidence that the suggested development never occurred. In the late 1970s, 'marginalization' was replaced by the concept of 'informality,' which referred to the absence of the inclusion of these masses within the official economy. When the informal sectors were involved in crimes, they were labeled as 'marginal inclusion' to point out that they were masses economically included but with incomes that did not correspond to the socially acceptable ones. With the persistence of informality, in the 1980s sociologists began referring to this social fringe in terms of 'poverty,' understood as a result of the implementation of neoliberal policies. This notion was criticized for overlooking the relational historical context and their blindness to the cultural dimensions of the problem i.e. it was a statement of a state of affairs without judging the mechanisms that produce it (Fassin quoted in Retamal 2007). Since the 1990s, the term 'exclusion' was assumed, reprising and expanding the francophone concept on a general scale, which is susceptible to the criticism already set forth.

The most recent theoretical contributions refer to 'disaffiliation,' which is an offshoot of the concept of 'marginality' that describes the process by which individuals find themselves dissociated from the social networks that allow their protection from the unforeseen (Castel 1995). The term 'social surplus' (Taylor 2001, 16) was also used to qualify the transition to post-Fordism in which disciplining technologies lost their role of social inclusion, and a subset of the population lost its place in the labor market (De Giorgi 2002). Bauman proposes to reassume the term 'underclass' that, in the context of a society that refuses to include all its members, "is a category of people below the classes, out of all hierarchy, without opportunities" (2004, 103). The only common feature of the 'underclass' is that modern society is not conducive to them; even worse, it would be better without them (106). Similarly, the notion of 'global informal working class' (Davis 2006) has been proposed, based on a conservative estimate of one billion people now living in slums and more than one billion people reduced to the status of informal workers struggling just to survive.

Although they are theoretically relevant, the mentioned proposals rest on a super-structural analysis, linked to the fragility and vulnerability of the over-criminalized sectors. Conversely, the concept of modern pauperism preserves a Marxist analysis that clarifies the structural nature of pauperism as an effect of the Law of Pauperization (Marx 1867). This structural analysis avoids linking the existence of these impoverished subsets to temporary factors or to unfortunate circumstances (with the additional risk of associating their condition to strictly voluntary decisions). It also helps preserve a material reading of the structural origins of these sectors under the capitalist production system, enabling a more enlightening reading of the systematic over-criminalization mechanisms deployed against paupers throughout capitalist history.

Within the category of modern pauperism, it is possible to differentiate an *ethnic-racial subset* identified within the Black-American population in the United States and the undocumented immigrants from former colonies in Europe. The notion of 'subset' shows that they constitute a markedly more vulnerable sector than their national peers. Immigrants are more economically excluded than their peers because of the impediments on migratory regularization. In this regard, bulimic mechanisms not only tend to divert the economic 'surplus' but also the geographical 'surplus,' preventing their free transit into the dominant countries. Under this logic, even when members of the subset are economically integrated, they enter into the most precarious jobs and obtain lower wages than their national peers. It has been noted that discrimination against real or imagined minorities also has the full approval of the monopolistic political economy. This is because minorities' wages and profits can be depressed below the current level and the favored sectors of the population can obtain important material compensation (Sweezy 1942, 341).

The more intensive economic exclusion of the *ethnic-racial subset* is combined with a cultural inclusion that is hampered by their distinctive customs. Rather than talking about biological death, we are facing 'biographical deaths' of those migrants who die in the confines of the European fortresses trying to exercise a denied 'right to flee,' of the 2 millions of prisoners held in u.s. prisons, and of those whose horizons tend to correspond with the boundary of the ghetto (De Giorgi 2002, 48). Even more economically excluded that the rest of the pauperism and immersed in a hindered cultural inclusion, these subsets suffer crime control in a more extreme manner.

Mixed Insertion in the Bulimic Social Order

A central aspect of the criminal immersion of the modern pauperism (and particularly of the social dynamite) is the combination of coarse crimes with intermittent legal work, in line with previous historical stages. Termed here as *mixed insertion*, this concept describes the hybrid processes of legal and illegal activities, ranging from employment in casual, sporadic and informal jobs to coarse crimes.

From the U.S. ghettos, Bourgois says it can easily be seen how on the same street there are some people repairing cars and others working informally in nightly demolition under the direction of unlicensed subcontractors. In the same space, others sell 'numbers' (the street name for illegal betting), bags with fake brands, or $5 or $10 pockets of illegal drugs (2010, 5). So most homes have unreported incomes or do not pay taxes to continue living. Drug trafficking constitues the primary source of their supplemental income (7). Likewise, Tonkonoff (1998) illustrates that within the crimes of urban youth, it is clear that the offender does not carry a radical (sociological or psychological) difference in comparison with the non-offender: the use of illegal practices is inserted into a set of mechanisms and behaviors that might be called 'youth reproductive strategies' (2001, 176). Also Kessler (2004) dealt with the 'amateur crime,' describing it as one which ignores the temporal projection, lacks planning and contrasts with criminal careers that understand crime as an exclusive profession. People combine legal and illegal activities, ranging from crime to occasional work, crossing the borders of legality and illegality without great personal conflict. These findings are consistent with the most sophisticated longitudinal studies, which show that only a fraction of those who commit crimes during their youth will engage in a future criminal career (2010, 25).

From these theoretical approaches, the concept of mixed insertion shows how immersion in crime under the bulimic social order takes place in conjunction with precarious employment. Mixed insertion does not only operate as a strategy of modern paupers to meet basic material needs (absolute deprivation) during temporary labor exclusion, or to supplement low incomes or insufficient social aid. As it has been stressed throughout the chapter, the criminal route, concomitantly to the discontinued legal activity, responds to the processes of supra-culturization and the eagerness for goods-acquisition as a form of framing their identities, other than mere vital reproduction. If we extend the concept of mixed insertion to incorporate not only the combination of coarse crimes and legal activities but also the combination between the latter and criminalized survival strategies, this phenomenon would be widespread, absorbing the entire modern paupers. This is because, in the course of their lives, these sectors are likely to be immersed in activities such as hawking, misuse of public space, occupation of public roads, encroachments, car care without legal authorization, prostitution, vagrancy, drinking alcohol in public, loitering, panhandling, playing loud music, marijuana possession or sleeping on the subway. Thus, against the social imagery of individuals doomed to an exclusive and volunteer crime life, the concept of mixed insertion allows us to demystify this stereotypical figure.

Having identified the social sectors that are subjected to bulimic criminal selectivity, the following analyzes the discourses surrounding punishment, and the latent functions behind them.

Punishment during Bulimic Criminal Selectivity

In the bulimic social order, legitimating discourses of punishment, grounded on the disciplining social order, are combined with theoretical approaches that delegitimize it. The following replicates the analytical structure of Chapters 2 and 3 to distinguish between those ideological discourses of punishment (manifest functions) and the implicit purposes of its material application (latent functions).

Manifest Functions

With the end of the welfare state, denounced as 'costly and useless' by conservatives,[116] and an 'apparatus of social control' by the most critical sectors, the 'correctional model of punishment,' exclusive to socio-disciplining criminal selectivity, collapsed. Although the existing international legislation (particularly A.C.H.R. and I.C.C.P.R.)[117] preserves rehabilitation as the

---

116 Saying that rehabilitation lost it central place because it did not work, is counterfactual thinking, because "[the] criminal law would have disappeared long ago if it had been judged in terms of its effectiveness. Obviously, there is more at stake [...] Before this fall, it was also not possible to hold back the 'theory of retribution,' as it lost legitimacy as fair when it was recognized that there has never been an original equality under the social contract" (Van Swaaningen 1997, 291).

117 The United States is the only signatory of the I.C.C.P.R., among the major human rights documents. Moreover, U.S. jurisprudence has developed the self-executing theory in U.S.S.C. *Missouri v. Holland,* which states that international treaties are not given domestic effect until Congress passes them into national law. Because Congress has not ratified the I.C.C.P.R., there is no official legal local effect. This constitutes the United States as an outlier for, although it still has several laws that preserve rehabilitation as the goal of punishment (e.g. 28 U.S. 994 (a) impose presumption of probation for first offenders), it also explicitly acknowledges incapacitation, retribution or deterrence as goals of punishment in the letter of its law. The 1984 Sentencing Reform Act remits to the 18 U.S.C. 3553(a)(2),

only permissible function of punishment, its implementation and theoretical framework have lost consistency. This niche of legitimating discourses was not occupied by an emancipatory project but by "an ideological vacuum which is replaced by the idea of multi-functionality" (Pavarini 1995, 88). It is no longer the religious discourse of the original criminal selectivity (late 15th to early of the 18th century), the legal speech of the legally-disciplining criminal selectivity (late 18th century), the medical discourse of the police-medically disciplining criminal selectivity (19th century) or the sociological discourse of the socio-disciplining criminal selectivity (early to late 20th century).

Rehabilitation discourses have been replaced by a multiplicity of different (and even contradictory) justifications that reframe old theories in eclectic compounds that juxtapose or present them in new declarative forms (Zaffaroni et al. 2000, 56). All of them have a common point: there is a resumption of the *original* emergency-based discourse that takes the shape of a 'war on crime and drugs' that, as any emergency, cannot accept delays or soft responses. This new emergency allowed an expansion of crime control to every space of the lives of the *others* (mostly Black-American and Latino unemployed young men in the United States and immigrants in Europe), transforming communities in areas of police control, according to the logic of broken windows theory. In other words, current discourses reassume the control pattern of the 15th to 18th centuries and apply it to the diverse theories of punishment that were developed during the 18th and 19th century in order to face a renew 'emergency' regarding crime and drugs. This new 'emergency' has been conceptualized by the actuarial criminology or new penology; the selective incapacitation theory; renewed versions of deterrence that link economy-based analysis with crime; renewed versions of retribution that are known as 'just desert' or 'commensurate desert;' renewed versions of general deterrence known as 'symbolic' or 'moral justice;' and renew versions of rehabilitation known as restorative justice. In contrast with the above, a delegitimizing theory has also been formulated.

These new perspectives, supposedly anchored in a purely managerial and politicized vision, are forged from a clear position: they legitimize the tight control of the impoverished, conceiving their control as a business and assuming that economic exclusion (read as isolation, ignoring their integration into the most complex inclusion – exclusion process) should be ascribed to the individual responsibility of the offender, who is perceived as a malicious,

---

which refers to general deterrence (2)(A), special deterrence (2)(B), incapacitation (2)(C), rehabilitation (2)(D); symptomatically, rehabilitation is the last one of the list. In the same line, the D.O.J. Memorandum (2010) explains that the "general purposes of criminal law enforcement [are] punishment, public safety, deterrence, and rehabilitation."

rational and calculating individual. In a return to the paradigm of the primitive accumulation and the first disciplining phase, the offender is seen as a person who 'voluntarily' perpetrates the crime, without considering the economic and social circumstances that condition him.

Actuarial Justice/New Penology

The new foundations of why we punish are not religious as in the late 15th to early 18th centuries; they are not legal as in the late 18th century; they are not medical as in the 19th century; and they are not sociological as they were at the end of the 20th century. They are purely economic or, more precisely, 'actuarial' because they focus on measuring risks through aggregate techniques and without considering external social factors. Their aim is to reduce every factor to a numerical risk through technocratic, administrative and managerial measures, in what Feely and Simon (1992) called the 'new penology.'

The most crucial change in the use of risk analysis has to do with their scope. Until the 1980s, risk assessments were primarily used to decide who to release from confinement. In the 1980s, their scope increased and they are used to extend detention or surveillance over persons either not yet convicted of a crime or who have already served their penal sentence (Simon 2005, 399). It is the revival of positivism – which believes that dangerous individuals can be identified by scientific methods (2005–2006). As it can be read in the classical text of conservative criminal analys, 'Crime Solutions: 18 Things We Can Now Do to Fight Back:'

> The guys who are now in jail are totally lost. The crack killed their mothers [...] they do not listen to anything or anyone, they have no respect or fear [...] Almost everyone in their lives have taught them by example to be extremely targeted only to the present and think only of themselves ... they are not morally or psychologically anchored by no future, no past, no love, no hate, no sorrow, no remorse. They are a new breed of criminals deadlier than any seen before.
> A.A.V.V. 1995

Technically, the clearest examples of this new penology are the incapacitation approaches (Feeley and Simon 1992), which are expressed in the forms of collective and selective incapacitation. Collective incapacitation appeared in the 1960s/70s when 'prediction criminology' started analyzing characteristics of offenders (age, arrests and convictions, social history) to determine which of those factors were most strongly associated with subsequent offending. These studies found out that criminal history, drug habits and history of unemployment were indicative of increased likelihood of recidivism (von Hirsch 1998, 158). However, from a practical perspective, these studies did not distinguish between serious and trivial recidivism, and did not promise crime rate reduction, which led to its abandonment in the 1970s (158–159).

Selective Incapacitation

In the 1980s, the technique of 'collective incapacitation' was adapted to target high-rate serious offenders, under a seven-factor predictive index, adopting the label of 'selective incapacitation' (Greenwoon 1982 quoted in von Hirsch 1998, 159). It explains that, for crime-reduction purposes, the most rational way to use the incapacitation potentiality of prisons was to do so *selectively*. Instead of imposing longer sentences for everyone, or according to their crime history or the seriousness of the offense, long sentences should be primarily reserved for those who, when free, commit the most crimes (1998, 152). Those have to be 'removed from circulation' for a specified period through imprisonment. The clearest example of this approach is the already mentioned U.S. law of three-strikes-and-you-are-out, which emerged as a popular initiative in California to establish lifetime imprisonment for the commission of three consecutive crimes (in a re-make of the ancient Poor Laws). The law was afterward passed in dozens of states and at the federal level.

Ignoring those critiques that claim that after long imprisonment offenders are more likely to commit crimes because of the iatrogenic conditions of prisons, defenders of the incapacitation theory pushed for longer sentences. The idea was to extend prison time until offenders were old enough to lose their criminogenic risk. Studies explain that "the older the offender at release, the lower the subsequent recidivism rate. There was substantial evidence that longer lengths of stay for the youngest offenders (18–24 years old) had the greatest impact on reducing high recidivism levels" (Kern 1995, 4).[118] However, there is counter – evidence that longer prison terms do not necessarily reduce recidivism, and that the aging of the prison population is causing disproportionate health care expenses (Ogletree and Sarat 2012). Moreover, this approach invites other critiques. First, official court' statistics in relation to recidivism are unreliable because it is tough to follow the path of the offenders to record recidivism rates. Second, the crime predictive index is built on the base of information provided by incarcerated (and, thus, already over-criminalized) people. Third, the association between crime-risk and ethnicity/economic/

---

118   Simon (2014) proposes to call this 'total incapacitation' because is an indiscriminate, long-term incarceration of both high – and low-risk individuals in facilities fundamentally driven by security and control logics.

racial factors hides the selective matrix that mediates them. This generates disproportionate punishments that are not coherent with the seriousness of the offenses but with predictive factors (socio-economic background, drug habits, criminal history) redoubling the selective application of punishment.[119]

The mentioned problems could be translated in the following queries: Are we ready to accept the 'deal' of accepting non-proportional punishments in exchange for (a largely broken) promise of avoiding recidivism? Do we acknowledge that the characteristics that are measured in the index are related to coarse crimes and ignore the harmfulness of white-collar crimes? What are the reasons that justify that the index does not measure features of public agents or businessmen? How would it be possible to control irregularities committed by the police, if they are authorized to perpetrate these biased-practices? Finally, 'selective incapacitation' opens the door to a dangerous slippery slope: would it be desirable and more efficient to imprison all the people who belong to certain socio-economic sectors without waiting them to commit a crime? Would this ensure public safety and prevent recidivism? Indeed, 'selective incapacitation' means going back to the legal framework prior to the 18th century: we are no longer equal under the law – not even in formal terms. This system labels and harshly criminalizes particular individuals of the population just because they are part of a problematic socio-economic sector that has to be controlled because of its disruptive potential. Treating people differently because of qualities that are beyond their control makes the entire criminal catalog a status-based regulation. It installs a system that stops focusing on a certain type of undesirable acts to start targeting a certain type of undesirable people. Even if public safety is invoked as a justification for this disparate treatment of offenders, it implicates an invitation to use supra-individual factors to restrict individual freedom and rights, in what deserves to be characterized as a pre-Kantian reasoning.

119　An example of the 'selective incapacitation' technique is the Virginia system. Facing a budget crisis as a result of tough-on-crime policies (mainly the abolish of parole and the establish of truth in sentencing), in 1994 the Virginia legislature asked the state sentencing commission to figure out which nonviolent offenders could be kept out of prison without risk of recidivism. The researchers found that unemployed single men in their 20's were a much higher risk and, from 2002 onwards, judges started to sentence offenders "the way insurance agents write policies, based on a short list of factors with a proven relationship to future risk: if a young, jobless man is convicted of shoplifting, the state is more likely to recommend prison time than when a middle aged, employed woman commits the same crime" (Bazelon 2005).

Renewed Versions of Deterrence: Economy and Crime

In combination with retribution, Van Den Haag (1975) proposes that, even though breaking the law is a sufficient argument to justify punishment, deterrence should always be the first goal. To achieve deterrence, he proposes to apply a *necessary punishment* for each type of person: the poor have to be separated to prevent them from doing harm; the innocent have to be protected; and the calculators, who constitute the vast majority of the population, have to be convinced, through criminal law, of the inconvenience of perpetrating crimes.

In a broader analysis of cost-benefit approaches, G. Becker's rational choice proposal (1968) consists of the application of economic reasoning to the study of crime. He argues that offenders make rational cost-benefit calculations that criminal law should discourage. This argument inspired the creation of the school of law and economics at the University of Chicago. Becker proposes to apply fines to anyone who could pay them and imprisonment as a supplement form of punishment.

Renewed Versions of Retribution: Just and Commensurate Desert

Combining retribution and victims' values, some positions advocate for a return to retribution but set upon a 'punitive populism' version; i.e. the justification is that punishment responds to social demands for harsher treatment for those who 'deserve' it.

Von Hirsch (1984) formulated the theory of commensurate desert as a double reaction. On the one hand, he rejects this new punitive version of retribution based on punitive populism. On the other, he is against the emphasis that rehabilitation places on the criminal history and demographic of the offenders because those elements sacrifice equity. Conversely, von Hirsch suggests then that the severity of punishment should be commensurate with the seriousness of the wrong (1998, 195–200). Yet, he fails to stipulate who is to determine the commensurate desert for a particular type of crime (Gibbs 1978).

Renewed Versions of General Deterrence: Symbolic or Moral Justice

With a higher degree of theoretical development, symbolic criminal law proposes a renewed version of the positive general deterrence or denunciation theory. Jakobs, its most prominent exponent, explains that the purpose of punishment is norm-affirmation as a social function. Punishment should advocate for sanctions that "restore equilibrium by balancing out only the harm attributable to a specific norm-violation" with the aim that, after the sentence, "[t]he normative order of society has been reaffirmed" (quoted in von Hirsch Andreas 2014, 27). The legitimacy of punishment does not rest on preventing future crimes or reforming offenders, but in avoiding social chaos (Alagia 2013,

248). Hence, reinforcing the relevance of values and the moral code that we expect people in society to adhere to, this theory is likely to be the theoretical foundation for having mandatory minimum sentences for certain offenses that attack basic social values.

Symbolic criminal law has been criticized for confirming conservative conceptions about deviation. Moreover, it has been said that Jakobs' contribution to the knowledge, construction and management of conflicts does not go beyond the traditional culture operating on the criminal justice system. Rather, his theory offers new support to that culture and reconfirms its primary function: the ideological and material reproduction of social relations (Baratta 1985, 21).

As part of the symbolic approach, some theoretical positions focus particularly on the reaffirmation of victims' rights (Zimring and Johnson 2001, 743). The supporters of this position recall that, in *Payne v. Tennessee*, 501 U.S. 808 (1991), the U.S. Supreme Court accepted a victim's testimony during the sentencing phase in order to decide the applicability of the death penalty. Since this ruling, the jurisprudence has been taken for granted that more punishment against the offender is better for the victims. Following this logic, several criminal laws were used as personal memorials: since 1993, 50 states have enacted laws with the names of the victims as a way of honor them (Megan's Law, Jessica's Law, and Amy's Law, among others).

This phenomenon of victims as symbolic representatives of the general public interests could not take place previous to 1970s because crime was something linked to poor or unlucky ones. Since the 1980s and 1990s, victims started to be everywhere because everyone could be victimized (Garland 2016). The Omnibus Crime Control and Safe Streets Act (1968) and the Violent Crime Control Act (1994) were the key pieces of legislations that expanded federal intervention in state and local criminal policies. Both of them sided with victims and law enforcement in a zero-sum game in which any gain for prisoners or criminals was experienced as a loss for the former (Simon 2007, 101).

Renewed Versions of Rehabilitation: Restorative Justice
Restorative justice relies on a triple relation between offender, victim and community. The traditional mechanisms of the criminal justice system in which restorative justice has been invoked are probation and mediation. As it has been pointed out throughout this chapter, although they are still formally presented under the restorative logic, probation and mediation have served to expand crime control and not to replace imprisonment.[120] Analyzing restorative jus-

---

120   Duff sustains that it is not incompatible to refer to restorative justice under a punitive approach. Conversely, he proposes the concept of "restoration through retribution" to think retribution as an essential element of restorative justice (2003, 82).

tice from the less eligibility principle shows that, under the bulimic social order, it is not possible for punishment to meet the ideal re-integration aim: to
the extent that modern pauperism experiences deteriorating conditions of life
(as shown through the processes of inclusion – exclusion), the situation of the
criminalized tends to deviate from the normative ideal. It is so that, although
the rehabilitation discourse is still preserved in the letter of some prison programs or problem solving courts, its impossibility is absolute. Correctional
postulates are doomed to perish on the level of discourse. There is no longer
a 'where' or 'how' to rehabilitate these individuals; prisoners come from previously suffering areas with social, economic, political and spatial exclusion, and
they go back there (Daroqui 2002, 11). They were social dynamite before imprisonment and cannot be anything else when they regain their freedom.

Delegitimizing Theory
The progressive agnostic theory (Zaffaroni et al. 2000) openly explains that
punishment is not useful for its proclaimed purposes:

> An agnostic theory of punitive power breaks the tradeoff between the
> ideologues of punishment as improvement, and the ideologies of pun-
> ishment as a deposit, because it does not impose the impossible task
> claimed by the first ones, nor it is pleased with the deterioration of the
> second one: it recognizes the operational reality of punitive power (se-
> lection by vulnerability) and proposes, as part of a general legal effort
> for their reduction and containment, the minimizing of the deleterious
> effect on the process of suffering and, if it is possible, it offers a possibility
> of elevating the levels invulnerability (175).[121]

This theory conceives punishment "as a phenomenon of reality that needs to
be contained (reductive teleology), because of its violent impulse (tendency
to excess)" (Carvalho 2013). It explains that legal operators should seek to apply criminal law progressively to minimize the damages. While this proposal is clear in its aim of orienting everyday judicial practice, this theory does
not provide a clear explanation about the latent functions of punishment.

---

121   Alagia proposes to enrich this position with the contributions of anthropology and psy-
      chology. He explains that we must stop dealing with punishment and the myth that it is
      necessary for the existence of society, and develop theoretical efforts to reduce irrational
      punitive treatment. He affirms that what remains unresolved is not if punishment is wor-
      thy, but why the illusion that producing suffering to another person can create a benefit
      persists (2013, 281).

Thus, it leaves too many questions unanswered. Some of these queries include: if punishment does not serve its manifest functions, what purposes does it serve? What explains the continuity of theories of punishment that have already been discredited? What are the social, economic, cultural and political interests behind this support? Is there a link between the functions assigned to punishment and the economic and social structure where it takes place? If we know that punishment does not work and that is harmful, are we satisfied only with minimizing damage? Could it be worth to advocating for a more structural solution?[122]

In short, though this theory implicates an advance in delegitimizing punishment, it fails to respond to questions of vital importance in finding out the genuine social function exercised by punishment, i.e., its material or latent functions, which are to be explored in the next section.

Latent Functions

Under the bulimic social order, characterized by its radical process of inclusion – exclusion, the hidden purposes of punishment follow the pattern of the previous forms of criminal selectivity. Latent functions have been oriented to incapacitating problematic social sectors; controlling the modern paupers; fragmenting the working class; and promoting a 'crime control industry' and the *omnipresent control* of the whole of society.

Incapacitating the Problematic Social Sectors

The primary function of punishment during the bulimic social order has been the disabling or incapacitation of the 'problematic' sectors. The goal has been making the universe of criminal marginality 'unproblematic' at any price (Pavarini 1995, 58). In this context, the dominant punitive mechanism of the disciplining criminal selectivity – the prison – is preserved, but converted to the needs of the bulimic logic. Prison is stripped of the disciplining guidelines that constitute its origins and survives as a 'terrorist' institute: for a political diversion, and for those individuals for which non-institutional control failed (57). Prison "lose[s] all ideological coverage, to be justified in

---

122 Zaffaroni's theory proposes an idealized vision of judicial agencies. He suggests that the legal actors are aware of the selective character of the penal system and operates in a permanent anti-selectivity mode, applying fundamental notions such as insignificance and vulnerability (Rafecas 2006, 82). However, that statement mixes two levels of analysis: the empirical dimension of police agency acting selectively, versus the ideal version of the judiciary applying the rule of the law, when it should be compared how both agencies effectively operate, and how they should act from an ideal perspective (85).

technocratic terms, depending on what it is: a supervisory authority for those that cannot be governed 'otherwise'" (2006, 43). Prison pursues exclusion and disqualification because the problem "is no longer how to manage poverty, but how to live with the exclusion" (Castel 1997). It is, therefore, organized on a basis of "neutralizing segregation [...] of those bodies that no longer need to be disciplined as labor, but simply managed as waste" (Daroqui et al. 2008, 12). Prison "collects and piles up the (sub) proletarians counted as useless, undesirable or dangerous, and so hidden misery and neutralizes its disruptive effects" (Wacquant 1999, 143). Prisons become a 'deposit' for those too poor to be financially punished and too marginal to be integrated (Scheerer quoted in Van Swaaningen 1997, 280); a 'factory of immobility' (Bauman 1998, 138); 'airtight containers' for social waste or in 'human dumps' for discarded, devalued and outcast minorities (2005, 113); a 'punitive swamp' where the movement thread lags removing from circulation risk sectors (Caimari 2004, 109); 'storehouses' or 'deposits' (Lewkowicz 2005); the 'final stop' for marginal communities (Stern 2006, 42).[123] Inside prisons, internal regulations reinforce the characterization of confinement as a non-right zone. To exemplify, U.S. regulations of sexual misbehaviors in prison include a statutory exception: they are not considered such if they are conducted by correctional officers. The result is that searches, strips and medical interventions are perpetrated everyday as part of the legal attributions of the prison staff, even though they are non-consensual and degrading for the prisoner (primary under-criminalization).[124] Conversely, sexual relationships between the imprisoned population are punished as felonies (primary over-criminalization) despite the existence of consent.[125]

---

123   The characterization of prisons as a mere 'deposit,' 'barn' or 'last stop' convey the message that they are passive accumulative places when, on the contrary, they are management institutions. It is also problematic to affirm that prisons are institutions that actively encourage the acquisition of criminal skills by those who are serving time in order to reinforce the illegal economy. It seems more accurate to say that this phenomenon constitutes an unwanted effect of punishment, as the main latent function of punishment in bulimic criminal selectivity is to incapacitate the problematic sectors, particularly the social dynamite, and transform them in non-problematic.

124   Sexual abuse includes "[...] any other *intentional* contact, either directly or through the clothing, of or with the genitalia, anus, groin, breast, inner thigh, or the buttocks, that is *unrelated to official duties* or where the staff member, contractor or volunteer has the intent to abuse, arouse, or gratify sexual desire" (emphasis added) (Prevention of Sexual Abuse and Sexual Harassment of Inmates at the Berkshire County Sheriff's Office).

125   The Berkshire County Sheriff's Office states that: "Engaging in sexual relations with an inmate is a FELONY under state law punishable by up to five years in state prison & $10,000 fine for each such act. M.G.L. c. 268, 21A."

The most radical form of bulimic prisons is the maximum security facility. Popularized as 'supermax,' they imply a martial criterion of order, a large number of restrictions on the rights of detainees, and a much more intensive and frequent monitoring than other prisons (Zysman 2011).[126] Supermax or 'waste management prison' (Simon 2007, 153) "provides the illusion of total security for the victim and complete deprivation for the offender" (164). In this type of facilities, prison guards do not have to focus on the rehabilitation of the imprisoned people; their concern is to avoid leaks.

With this emphasis on problematic sectors, punishment tends to render invisible the mechanisms of under-criminalization. As Manzanos Bilbao explains, the socio-political functions of punishment at the symbolically level serve to define what is considered crime and who are considered criminals. They also serve to legitimize the state as an alleged guarantor of public safety, and to make invisible those types of crime that are not the generally criminalized ones (such as white-collar crimes) (2002, 3). In the same vein, Baratta clarifies that punishing certain illegal behavior serves to cover a wider number of illegal actions that remain immune to the process of criminalization. Thus, the selective application of criminal law produces, as a collateral result, an ideological cover of the selectivity (1986, 173). The set of negative social behaviors linked to the expansion of capitalism remains under-criminalized while crime control preserves its attention on the acts perpetrated by the social junk and the social dynamite, through formally rehabilitative and materially disabling effects.

Controlling the Modern Pauperism

The second latent purpose of punishment has to do with controlling the modern pauperism, i.e., the social junk and social dynamite as a whole, outside of those effectively over-criminalized. The goal is to manage a problematic population that, because of its size, cannot be criminalized with the material and human resources available under *formal control*.[127] Based on actuarial

---

126 These limitations include total isolation in individual cells for 23 hours a day, prohibition of contact with other detainees, correctional officers and religious or medical personnel, elimination of work, regulation of visits through a particular regime (which includes intercoms and screens instead of personal contact), and restrictions on recreational activities. In some cases, furnishings and basic facilities are removed from the cells, including beds, sinks and toilets (Bauman 2000, 205–221 quoted in Zysman 2011).

127 If we assume the numbers provided by Davis (2006), slums in 2001 covered 921 million people worldwide, i.e. 78.2% of the urban population of the least developed countries and a third of the world's urban population. Facing the impossibility of imprisoning these masses, they are subjected to the control of the geographical areas where they live.

criminology, this latent purpose takes place through a change in the modality of criminal prosecution that now "points to groups rather than isolated criminals" (Wacquant 1999, 29). That means that there is "a passage of the individual subject as an object of control to the collective people characterized as hazardous as a whole" (De Giorgi 2002, 21). The latter "are institutionally treated as 'risk producer groups'" (16).[128] Based on a proactive control consisting of risk profiles, situational maps and scientific and technological tools, impoverished sectors are continuously monitored. As Van Swaaningen explains, police often use a metaphor arising from fishing: in the 'old days,' fishermen played and caught the fish that swam alongside their boat. Now, they first study what kind of fish swim in every place, project their movements on a map and only then they go there with specialized equipment to catch fish of particular species (1997, 278). The distinctive concept of this rationality is then that the 'risk' is not about jailing dangerous criminals – that is, to neutralize or incapacitate individual risk factors – but rather to manage the level of risk of entire populations that cannot be (and are not intended to be) effectively criminalized from an actuarial rationality (De Giorgi 2002, 21).

While it is possible to agree with this characterization as it pertains to renewed forms of control exercise, it is noted that, in practice, crime control has always been oriented to entire categories of individuals and not to mere individuals (although, theoretically, the discourses presented crime as an individual problem). The new feature of the bulimic criminal selectivity is that this orientation is made explicit and it serves to organize the activities of the law enforcement agencies. These agencies focus their efforts on entire areas explicitly described as problematic using risk assessments. In short, the greater control exercised over certain geographical regions inhabited by groups considered 'problematic' bears a historical continuity from the foundation of capitalist production, but now it is done in an explicit manner and based on the legitimacy emanating from the measurement of risk studies. Like a self-fulfilling prophecy, risk measures focus their attention on the geographical areas where

---

128   De Giorgi attributes the origins of this mutation to the process that Foucault describes in his later works (1977–8, 1978–9) as the emergence of bio-politics, i.e., that biopower is the political transformation of the community into a population that is subjected to health and biological controls. This process conditions the emergence of a new general technology of power, 'governmentality,' by which power abandons the surveillance and disciplining of bodies and starts to regulate populations, that can be described as the global masses that are affected by processes that are unique to life, such as birth, death, (re) production, disease (Foucault 1978–9, 433). Thus, these new techniques of power are characterized by an exercise of group control that takes the form of calculation and risk management, through actuarial criminology (De Giorgi 2002, 21).

the over-criminalized groups live. Then, they confirm that it is there where there are higher levels of risk. Later on, the confirming results legitimate a privileged control over all that space[129] that, thereby, becomes the target of a selective territorial control.

A parallel can be drawn with traditional criminal proceedings as a permanent threat to those who fail to accomplish the requirements of restorative justice mechanisms: in these territories, there is a generalized situation of potential or latent criminalization; i.e., law enforcement are not there all the time, but they can abruptly intervene at any moment to over-criminalize the local people. In moments of latency, these places are Erebus systems (Acuña Jimenez 2012)[130] where law enforcement is not there and individuals live without formal state protection. In this direction, the 'precarious everyday' turns the area into non-legal zones (Rodríguez 2008b, 121).

Finally, at the expense of the positions that underpin those territories as an absolute 'outside' (binary theory),[131] it is more desirable to argue that groups

---

129   These regions include the slums of the United States, the bustees of Kolkata, the chawls and zopadpattis of Mumbai, the abadis katchi of Karachi the kampung of Jakarta, the iskwaters of Manila, the shammasas Khartoum, the umjondolos of Durban, intra murios of Rabat, the slums of Abidjan, the baladis of Cairo, the gecekondus of Ankara, the tenements of Quito, the favelas of Brazil, the shantytowns of Buenos Aires, and the popular colonies of Mexico City (Davis 2006).

130   This concept is brought by Acuña Jimenez (2012), who proposes that the omnipresence of the state is nothing but a myth. Instead of it, it is enriching to use the concept 'systems in Erebus' to describe those systems where the state is less present, but that still operate under the presumption of the omnipresence of the state.

131   Wacquant (2006 and 2007) explains that ghetto, 'hyper-ghetto,' 'anti-ghetto,' and prison (judicial ghetto) are different configurations of a generic process of 'socio-spatial seclusion.' This process refers to the fencing of certain categories and social activities that are isolated in a quiet and restricted quadrant of physical and social space. The 'spatial confinement or containment' is then defined as a technique for controlling problematic categories and territories. Pavarini explains that ghettos constitute an atypical form of territorial segregation of marginalized individuals (1995, 56). Davis (2006) defines them as spaces in which the surplus of economic globalization is concentrated – the 'zero existential level' – and that they collaborate in the production of an implicit selection of humanity. However, as Young explains, these binary theories suggest barriers and divisions but incorrectly exaggerates their effectiveness and robustness: they confuse rhetoric with reality, they attempt to impose harsh lines in a city of late modernity confusing limits. Besides, they do not capture the intensity of the exclusion – the passionate resentment or resentment of the excluded – while they give a too calm and rational picture of the lucky citizen – the included ones (2007, 42). Young therefore rejects the thesis of the spatial exclusion of the ghetto (43) and explains that there is no dual city, but that the borders are regularly permeated, and that most of the employment as well as legal/illegal activities to

who inhabit those areas subjected to selective territorial control spend much of their days outside that perimeter. However, control follows them. Risk measurements do not only focus on certain areas but also in certain stereotypes – which are also constructed on the basis of the over-criminalized individuals -. The self-fulfilling prophecy conditions that, through the metonymic operation, the ones already over-criminalized are considered as physical representatives of the whole criminal population. Consequently, it is not necessary to be in the targeted neighborhood to be over-criminalized. Risk assessments justify and legitimize the permanent control of those who are 'alike' because they belong to the same neighborhood or because of their nationality, race, music taste, or type of clothing, among other features.

Fragmenting the Working Class

A third latent function of bulimic criminal selectivity is enforcing the separation of the working class, through making invisible the mechanism of over-criminalization and describing the over-criminalized as responsible of their situation. This idea is transmitted to the rest of the population, against which the situation of the over-criminalized appears as the exclusive result of his or her own actions. The over-criminalized are treated as people that 'voluntarily' decided to become criminals, as individuals who have traced their way by choice, as opposed to their hard working peers. This reasoning makes invisible the mechanism of over-criminalization, as well as its distant link to the actual commission of a crime and its closer relation to the demographic features of the over-criminalized. The similarities between the over-criminalized and the rest of the working class are erased and the differences are exacerbated. Even familiarities are perceived as 'otherness.' This process enables the rest of the working class not to feel intruded upon, not to assume the responsibility of being a silent witness of a criminal selectivity that targets the impoverished population. Meanwhile, it allows the middle and lower classes to deny the 'fear of falling' (Young 2007, 70), i.e., the fear of being in the situation of the over-criminalized.

The previously referenced metonymic operation transforms the over-criminalization of specific members of certain racial, religious, geographical or ethnic subsets into a perceived criminality of all the members of those subsets. Thus, the entire group of a certain geographical region, ethnic, cultural or national background is seen as contrary to the interests of those who are in a

---

obtain incomes take place outside the neighborhood (53). Following Young, it is possible to challenge the characterization of the ghetto as an insulation institution like prisons. By contrast, most of the inhabitants of the ghettos occupy much of their days outside them.

similar socioeconomic position but are not part of those stigmatized categories. This logic enforces intra-class fragmentations, which tend to re-legitimize the functionality of punishment in its bulimic form. Considering the peer as an 'other' seems the ideal way to avoid empathy, as this would render unbearable the validation of the system (Bauman 2004, 106).[132] Blalock (1967) identified that one of the leading causes of racial confrontation between white and black people in the United States is the 'symbolic threat,' which describes that whites perceive people of color as linked to crime.

Moral Entrepreneurs and Moral Panics

The three analyzed latent functions of punishment are deepened, here again, by moral panics encouraged by moral entrepreneurs. Even though moral panics have not been built in a vacuum (crime rates actually raised along bulimic social order), they have fueled over-dimensioned emotional responses in the public. Moreover, moral panics have been acting on the public without clarifying the consequences of a punitive and biased response to the existing crime rates.

A particularity of the bulimic social order has to do with the institutionalization of moral entrepreneurs through the figures of lobbyists and think tanks. Lobbyists work in private and official institutes – such as the American Enterprise Institute, the Cato Institute, the Heritage Foundation and the Manhattan Institute – and they decisively influence criminal politics and even communication strategies to carry them out. As an example, these institutions globally expanded the zero tolerance policies in a relatively short period. They did that through the intensive media exposure of the mayor of New York City Rudy Giuliani. He managed to divulge the success of zero tolerance policies to reduce crime, even though crime also drops at the national level, including those states where this type of policy was not applied. Moreover, even when this policing model had started to be criticized in the United States, lobbyists got to export it to the cities of Mexico, Buenos Aires, Brasilia, Cape Town, Frankfurt, and Toronto, as well as in France, Italy, England, Austria and New Zealand (Wacquant 1999, 33–35).

Moral panics have been exponentially multiplied through the spread of the media on a global scale, as well as through the incorporation of the internet, emails and social networks.[133] Such is the magnitude of this transformation

---

132 See *Down, Out, and Under Arrest. Policing and Everyday Life in Skid Row* (2016), recent book in which Forrest Stuart proved that the intensification of policing promotes conflicts among the most marginalized, and undermines relations in the community.

133 "All technologies can be used for both, oppression and liberation" (Castels 2009, 412). To exemplify, the internet promotes the communication and organization of their users, as

that it has been granted a particular field of study, the so-called 'media criminology' (Zaffaroni 2011).[134] This notion describes the "creation of reality through underreporting information and media disinformation in convergence with biases and beliefs, which is based on a simplistic criminal etiology seated in a magical causality" (365). It describes the discourses of media communicators that do not always have expertise in the topic they are transmitting, but still broadcast the news, statistics and police events, affecting public conceptions on crime and punishment.

Such are the dimensions of moral panics in the bulimic social order that they amplify the problem of crime and promote the sense that the 'other' awaits us everywhere, endorsing a continuous sense of risk, of being threatened. They foster a false conviction that all people who inhabit the neighborhood in which the criminal stereotype resides, as well as all individuals that wear a certain type of clothing or that have similar features, should be equally feared. Modern paupers became assimilated to the riskiest cases of social dynamite. The media has been particularly relevant in the dissemination of racial stereotypes: Black-Americans and Latinos are significantly more likely than whites to be portrayed as lawbreakers on television news, whereas whites are significantly more likely to be portrayed as defenders than as lawbreakers (Dixon and Linz 2000).

Following this logic, moral panics also reinforce intra-class fragmentation, by settling a fertile ground for the opposition between the 'good' worker and the over-criminalized, who is presented as an 'other' or an 'enemy.' News shows a break between the 'good' poor in contrast to the 'evil,' 'hard,' 'dangerous,' 'antisocial' one (Hoyos Vázquez 1997). Lea and Young pointed out that in England and the United States, the press and the television avoid showing the ethnicity of victims of crime, helping to feed the illusion that whites are the usual victims

---

well as a 'liquid monitoring' by agencies and state authorities (Bauman and Lyon 2013). Technologies are both a weapon of social control and a means of resistance (Rheingold 2004).

134 It is possible to trace the foundations of the concept of media criminology in the theoretical contributions of Angenot (2004, 2010) who rescues the value of social discourse as a creator of reality, as it produces legitimacies. In his words: "The social discourse, beyond the multiplicity of functions, built the social world, objectify and communicate these representations by allowing determine that good linguistic coexistence that is the essential factor of social cohesion. By doing this, it routinizes and naturalizes social processes" (2010, 67). Angenot differs from Marx to assert that hegemony is 'social' because it discursively produces society as a whole, but is not owned by a class. It just institutes preeminence, legitimacy, interests and values; that favors those best placed to take advantage of it (2010b).

of the offences committed by Black-Americans, even though most crimes are perpetuated among the same racial groups (1984, 132).

Moral panics also over-dimension the severity and the scope of the crime problem, regardless of the real level of crime rates (Chiricos 1996, 20). Mass media, especially television, press and websites spread news related to insecurity 24 hours a day. Even though deaths caused by traffic accidents or by abuse of medical products are higher than those that result from crime, the impact of the latter on the social imagination is tremendously greater than the other two. Thus, disconnected from the true dimensions of crime rates, a 'sense of collective insecurity' spread. This sense is nothing but the perception of external threats that disrupt routine (Kessler 2011, 11) or, in other words, the gap between social constructed expectations and the effective protective capabilities of a society to operate over them (66). Like the weather, the levels of crime can be low but moral panics – stimulated through media criminology – make us *feel* them even more. By this logic, moral panics artificially increased levels of anxiety convincing a 'silent majority' to support a 'more than usual' exercise of control (Hall et al. 1978, 221).

Furthermore, by bringing images of terrible crimes, media also brings legitimacy to the discourses that reject rehabilitation and propose that prison is there to produce suffering, and psychological and physical illnesses (Manzanos Bilbao quoted in Daroqui et al. 2008, 9).[135]

Finally, moral panics contribute to the legitimacy and invisibility of bulimic under-criminalization. The criminal stereotype that invokes the 'panic' is restricted to the over-criminalized, offering a mantle of 'immunity' for the specific acts committed by the non-stereotyped offender. Even in cases where illegal behaviors perpetrated by members of the upper classes are transmitted, they are reported as a 'scandal,' 'an exception,' an 'individual case.' Therefore, the

---

135   And why is prison a better tool to implement suffering? Because it keeps suffering 'behind the scenes,' away from the eyes of the public and the family of the imprisoned that cannot contest the conditions of imprisonment. It also serves to sustain a discourse of humanization that contrasts prison with physical punishment. In addition, prison can serve multiple purposes, regardless of whether they afterward materialize or not; judges and correctional officers can imagine purposes of rehabilitation to be more confident in pursuing their work. Prison also avoids the irreparable human error that can come with capital punishment. It is founded upon the widespread idea that mass incarceration works to reduce crime; even when crime goes up, it is possible to sustain that preventive ideal stating that it could be worse without mass incarceration. Finally, as Travis suggests, prisons are visible and, therefore, more suitable to respond to the punitive demands of the public, in contrast with community corrections and fines that are not as visible to the public (2002, 20–21).

systematic commission of those type of behaviors and its links with the origin and reproduction of the capitalist system are hidden. 'Popular' crimes, as publicized by the media, cover up the fact that the maintenance of our social order is based on a continuation of the primitive accumulation, always illegal, often violent, or at least based on relationships of power, domination and inequality (Pegoraro 2011, 80). Empirical research in various media shows the frequent use of complicated and specialized language in the transmission of news reports of illegal acts committed by the well-off. This type of news also omits relevant information (names, dates, places and activities) that could help to contextualize these crimes. Also, the suspects are not treated as criminals and are not publicly condemned before a sentence is confirmed (Ojeda Segovia 2013). To this is added that economic and war crimes are usually located in sections as Politics, Business, News, World, General Information or Technology but not in the criminal section, as has been shown by Sutherland (1949).

Promoting a 'Crime Control Industry' and the *Omnipresent Control* of the Social Whole

In the bulimic social order, moral panics also help develop a fourth latent function of punishment: the emergence of an 'industry' of crime control and the legitimation of an *omnipresent control* that concerns not only the problematic categories but the social whole. The fearful population seeks protection against feelings of insecurity, leading to the proliferation of products and services aimed at countering crime. Marx, in *Digression: (On Productive Labor)* (1861–3) ironically pointed out, that:

> A criminal produces crime. If we take a closer look at the connection between this latter branch of production and society as a whole, we shall rid ourselves of many prejudices. The criminal produces not only crimes but also criminal law, and with this also the professor who gives lectures on criminal law and in addition to this the inevitable compendium in which this same professor throws his lectures onto the general market as "commodities."

He adds that:

> The criminal moreover produces the whole of the police and criminal justice, constables, judges, hangmen, juries, etc; and all these different lines of business, which form just as many categories of the social division of labour, develop different capacities of the human mind, create new needs and new ways of satisfying them. Torture alone has given rise

to the most ingenious mechanical inventions and employed many honorable craftsmen in the production of its instruments.

In these passages, Marx shows how crime, overstressed by moral panics, is used as a *justifying element* for an overwhelming amount of services and products related to crime prevention. Making use of the notion of 'productivity' in a broad sense – and not specifically in relation to surplus value – Marx points out that "[c] rime, through its ever new methods of attack on property, constantly calls into being new methods of defense, and so is as productive as strikes for the invention of machines." i.e., what the most modern criminological literature called 'crime control as industry' (Christie 1993; Neuman 2005; Stern 2006). This 'industry' increasingly operates under the support of the actuarial logic that conceives crime control as a management of risk and fear as the primary motivator. With the possibility of increasing fear at very low costs through the spread of moral panics, the growth of the crime control industry seems to have a bright future. Let us analyze how it works a) 'inside' and b) 'outside' the borders of the criminal justice system itself.

a) Inside. In the 'inside,' this industry takes place through the expansion of the police and criminal apparatus that, as Marx observes, involves an enormous number of jobs. These positions are concentrated in the capital goods sector and prison services, strongly characterized by precarious instability (Wacquant 1999, 52). In the United States, it includes the privatization of prisons services; the privatization of the prison itself; along with pay to stay, monetary sanctions, victim restitution, legal, financial obligations and post-prison charges. All of them constitute strategies to ameliorate the high tax burden of confinement and they are growing as a new market (52–53).[136]

The privatization of prisons' services. Incarcerated people have to cover commissary purchases and a range of other charges, such as medical services or law library fees. Katzenstein and Waller offer the example of Florida, where the commissary sales and other transactions are managed through Department of Corrections' contracts with vendors awarded to businesses that will pay the highest commission to the state. Other striking example came from Texas, where Securus Technologies introduced video visitation in 2,600 correctional facilities, which costs about a dollar per minute and, in 70% of the contracts, replaces in-person visit (2015, 639–643). Other privatized services include telephone contracts: JPay, the large private company headquartered in Florida, guarantees by contract a commission of $2.50 to the Florida Department of

---

136   The first u.s. private prison was opened in 1983 (Christie 1993, 23). Since then, total detention in those facilities has tripled, reaching 5,000 nationwide (Wacquant 1999, 52).

Corrections for every phone call transaction. For every deposit made by family or friends to meet a court-ordered payment, JPay owes the Department of Corrections a percentage of the sum (643). Co-pay charges to see medical staff or to procure prescription drugs, to deposit money, to purchase food in vending machines and to deliver packages or gift orders are also common.

Prisons' privatization. This process became evident in 1977 when, for the first time in the U.S. history, more money was used in the private security industry than in the state (Christie 1993, 21). By 2010, 8% of all state and federal prisoners were in private facilities. In the federal system, 16% of detainees are in private facilities compared with 7% in public facilities. In 2011, nearly 50% of immigrant detention beds were in private facilities (Gottschalk 2015, 65).

Although the companies that own these prisons affirm that they save tax-money, independent studies show that it is untrue and that if there is any difference it is because they spend less on medical issues or require the government to pick up medical expenses. A particularly controversial form of privatization was developed by California and other states through the Lease Revenue Bonds: states create an agency to finance new prisons construction by using lease revenue bonds; this agency then would lease the prison back to the state, which becomes responsible for funding the lease payments that service the bond debt, without need of voters' approval for a general obligation bond (50–51).

Besides the cost analysis, private prisons tend to be more dangerous places because they have less paid, less numerous and less trained staff (65–71). Even more important, prison privatization, as part of the crime control industry, favors bulimic over-criminalization as a mean of social control and also for purely profit-driven motives. In 2013 the number of people in private prisons increased by 44% over the previous ten years, and, in those states in which this modality of imprisonment increased, the incarceration rates also augmented. For example, Louisiana has the highest incarceration rate in the world and most of the detainees are in private prisons.

The connection between private facilities and over-criminalization is strictly linked with the work of moral entrepreneurs. Companies that run prisons, such as the Corrections Corporation of America (C.C.A.) and the GEO Group, are collaborating in the American Legislative Exchange Council (A.L.E.C.) which advocates policies that increase incarceration. The contracts signed with the states stipulate that at least 90% of the beds (quotas lock) have to be guaranteed, or the state has to reimburse the company for the unused beds (Shapiro 2013). Bulimic over-criminalization is also promoted by the feeling of economic dependence created by private facilities in the counties where they install. Then, "counties with prisons, feeling the economic pinch of the

Great Recession of 2008, have begun vocally to oppose the closing of prisons merely because of the contributions prisons have made to the local economies" (Harcourt 2013, 269). However, this is not true, because most of the employees, goods and services came from outside the county. Conversely, prison towns experienced more unemployment and poverty (Gottschalk 2015, 50–51).

Room-and-board costs. One-third of the 3,000 county jails now charge prisoners to stay in them, regardless of their ability to pay. An arrest warrant might be issued if they have already been released and do not pay. As these procedures takes place in civil courts, prisoners lack due process protection (Beckett and Murakawa 2012). Monetary sanctions directed at individuals who have been convicted of felonies have ballooned over the last decades constituting what Katzenstein and Nagrecha term a "new regime of punishment." Post-prison charges include parole costs, accrued fines, fees and debts, and victim restitution. The Victim and Witness Protection Act of 1982, the Victims of Crime Act of 1984, the Comprehensive Crime Control Act of 1984 and the Federal Debt Collection Procedures Act of 1990 oblige law enforcement agencies to collect court-ordered financial obligations (Katzenstein and Waller 2005, 642). If they do not pay, offenders face the loss of motor vehicle licenses, wage garnishment or (re)confinement (641).

As prison workers earn no more than 40 cents an hour, and prisoners retain on average of only 20% of it, they cannot go far towards meeting the financial obligations or prison expenses, and turn to family members for financial support, shifting the burden to poor households (642). The state's Damocles sword of punishment has never been so close to the head of the offenders, and it even threatens the head of their families. This system inverts the welfare-poverty relationship altogether by taxing the poor to further their governance, polarizing class and racial groups (640–641).

This 'inside' of the development of crime control as industry has helped create a broad range of moral entrepreneurs that support the preservation and expansion of the prison complex. Among them, it is possible to mention correctional officers' unions, departments of corrections, private prison industry and segments of the financial sectors. These actors are currently pushing for the elimination of restrictions on the exploitation of penal labor and for the development of innovative financing mechanisms that help to keep the real fiscal costs of the prison boom out of the public eye (Gottschalk 2015, 48–49). Moreover, the victims' rights movements also play a central role in the preservation of the penal state in the United States. These movements have not become punitive only because of the influence of conservative politics but mainly because they did not find a welfare state able to insure and compensate them, which pushes them to look for punishment as a solution for their pain

(2006). Conversely, in Germany and the English-speaking world, the victims' rights movement has expressed itself in efforts to use mediation as a response to criminal behavior (Fletcher 2001, 280). U.S. Prosecutors have also expanded their power at the expense of other actors in the criminal justice system (Simon 2007). Finally, actuarial criminology legitimizes the system of mass penal control and the overrepresentation of vulnerable groups by affirming that they are an expression of the real scope of crime and a threat to public safety.

b) Outside. In the 'outside,' this crime industry calls the entire population through a variety of products that promise to ensure security. People from all social sectors became "eager consumers of public and private governmental tools against crime risk" (Simon 2007, 16). These devices include products such as panic buttons in taxis, insurances for burglary at ATMs, cell phones for children, property and car alarms, surveillance cameras, perimeter fences and photo-electric lights (Kessler 2011, 14). Private security is incorporated as a new 'amenity' in modern buildings; law enforcement is granted greater control to intervene in private spaces; access to personal information is provided to security-related software and apps (e.g. apps that wipe cell phones in case of theft or give personal information to/from taxi drivers/clients); surveillance cameras have access to the everyday life of those who circulate under them; private data and even the minutiae of daily circulation is provided to insurance companies, neighborhood networks and organizations against crime; and information of our changing locations is freely accessed through the use of GPS (which alerts us if we attempt to navigate a 'danger zone'). This industry even fosters the emergence of the gated community style of subdivision sport utility vehicles (SUVs) and their spread in the middle-class families (Simon 2007, 7). Particularly relevant is the use of social media and the data that people provide to it, which is ultimately send to intelligence agencies on a daily basis (Harcourt 2015).[137]

Under this logic, this industry is granted an *omnipresent control* over the fearful economically-included population that gives away its freedom for fear of losing its property. Paradoxically, this fear encourages the provision of

---

137 Harcourt (2016) explains that the Black Lives Matter demonstration of 2014 was posted as a Facebook event, for which that 50,000 people clicked "assist," bringing the N.Y.P.D. a list of individuals to investigate and control. Harcourt explains that this compulsion to publish our everyday movements and activities, even though this exposes us, has to do with the opposition between a material world of paper as a symbol of 'work' (paperwork), against a digital world where everything seems more like a game (digital-playing). Indeed, paperwork 'strips' individuals, while digital-playing gives a 'sense of freedom,' the possibility of escaping from the control of face-to-face environments.

personal data that is used to build databases that calculate risks and dangerous zones, which are later used to develop more products and services of the
industry that are eagerly acquired by the same population that once provided
their personal data, reinforcing the circle of fear – industry development. The
paradox is intensified by the fact that each new instrument or service of the industry carries the germ of fear of its failure: we live surrounded by systems that
provide security but they are complex and fragile constructions that take the
risk of failing in its objectives, frustrating expectations. Therefore, the search
for protection creates insecurity and to "be protected is also being threatened"
(Castel 2003, 13).

It is then that continuous inputs of new moral panics, enable, through a developing crime control industry, an omnipresent control that is condemned to
reinforce itself. In moments of bulimia, it is even more clear that crime control
is exercised not only over prisoners but also over those who are free because
it is a "power of surveillance, that justifies oversight mechanisms that we ordered and accept pleased, manipulated by fear as a *governance*" (Foucault 1975
quoted in Zaffaroni 2011, 506–507). In short, the crime control industry "hap-
pily hold the hands of the included to control their steps, while building gulags
for the excluded ones" (Van Swaaningen 1997, 382).

In conclusion, besides the three latent functions of punishment that have
been presented alongside the different modalities of criminal selectivity, bulimic criminal selectivity shows a fourth latent function, strictly connected
with the exponential increase of moral panics: the emergence of a crime control industry that allows an omnipresent control over the entire social space
with the consent of the controlled ones. In seeking the control of the modern
paupers, all of us are controlled in an omnipresent manner.

Brief Reflections

This Chapter delved into the analysis of the *bulimic social order*. Notwithstanding that, for chronological reasons, it was not possible to account for this process through the texts of Marx and Engels, it was shown how, through their
theoretical contributions, it is feasible to find seeds of the elements that characterize the functioning of criminal selectivity in the context of globalization.
Marx's concepts of 'general intellect' and the 'Tendency of the Rate of Profit
to Fall' help to show that criminal selectivity acquired a new shape in the late
20th century, that has been called *bulimic criminal selectivity*.

This mode of criminal selectivity operates as the last resort of a complex mechanism of (cultural) inclusion – (economic) exclusion. The over-criminalized sectors are not entirely excluded because, in spite of their economic segregation, they are intensively included in cultural terms. They overwhelmingly incorporate the demands of consumption in a process of supra-culturization that confuses the acquisition of goods with the possibility of (re)structuring personal narratives. Excessive cultural inclusion, extreme economic exclusion: the bulimic social order culturally swallowed the modern pauperism only to economically 'vomit' it. While this process might condition the incursion of the paupers into crime, more attention should be paid to the application of crime control deployed over them in the bulimic social order, which exceeds the motivation of reducing crime.

On the contrary, the response to modern pauperism through the massive increase of crime control finds its axis in the pursuit of social control, as a replacement of the insufficient economic constraints. Crime control has expanded until swallowing social assistance itself (which can be called *punitive welfare*), leading the assisted into the criminal orbit if they fail to accomplish administrative requirements. Also those behaviors that during the disciplining social order were approached through social, administrative or therapeutic agencies, become absorbed by crime control.

This chapter re-assesses the category of 'pauperism' through its division into social junk and social dynamite because, despite these nomenclatures being crude, they enable the clarification of the treatment that these sectors received in the bulimic social order. Work availability and assistance flared up, while reasons to arrest, processes and condemn the modern pauperism increased, sentences became more severe and prisons adopted the model of maximum security.

In contrast, bulimic under-criminalization covered negative social behaviors that cause higher levels of social harm, such as occupations of countries accused of perpetrating or facilitating acts of terrorism, or the symbiosis between crime and business. Moral entrepreneurs hide these facts and overstress the acts perpetrated by modern paupers. Crime control not only operates as the last post of exclusion of the over-criminalized but also encourages an omnipresent control of the whole population. The entire population is mired in moral panics that condition it to give its privacy away. After all, we are all preyed upon by these 'panics' and deprived of a sustainable securitarian organizing project.

CHAPTER 5

Final Reflections

The followed historical path allowed us to explore the continuity of unfairness in crime and punishment in the different configurations of a capitalist society. Criminal selectivity was the proposed theoretical tool to analyze this unfairness because it captures the historical and socio-economic conditions underpinning unequal legal treatment, law enforcement profiling, courts' discretion, and differential penalization of peoples based on criteria such as class, race, ethnic, religion, gender, and age.

Nourishing the contributions of Marx and Engels with a complex interdisciplinary perspective, the book has challenged the abstract legal standpoint of criminal selectivity and has proposed to read it through the lens of its historical character. This analysis has demonstrated that, far from being a contemporary and cyclical phenomenon, criminal selectivity is rooted in the very origins of capitalist production. Moreover, the book has shown how criminal selectivity has been an element of utmost relevance for the purpose of establishing and reproducing the current system of production. Mainly through over-criminalization, in its various configurations, it seems to be an essential tool of social control. Through under-criminalization, criminal selectivity appears to have facilitated the invisibility of those individual and collective behaviors that were necessary for the preservation and expansion of capital.

Table 4 clarifies the various features involved in each of the three predominant and successive modes of criminal selectivity.

As the table shows, there have been relevant continuities and ruptures in the characteristics of each modality. Particularly relevant is to focus our attention on (a) the evolution of the behaviors that have been over-criminalized and under-criminalized through the capitalist society; (b) their geographical distribution; (c) the required criminal procedures to impose punishment; (d) the interaction between primary and secondary criminalization; (e) the characteristics of punishment; (f) the argumentative basis for punishment; (g) the features of the principle of less eligibility; (h) the characteristics of the over-criminalized social sectors; and (i) the pursuit of territorial control.

a. This first striking aspect of the evolution of criminal selectivity shows that over-criminalization of offenses against property perpetrated by subjugated sectors (coarse crime) spanned all temporal and geographical contexts. Since primitive accumulation, in a pattern that crossed the disciplining social order and is preserved until today, regulations have consistently been intended to

TABLE 4   *The different modalities of criminal selectivity*

Characteristics		Chapter 2 Original criminal selectivity	Chapter 3 Disciplining criminal selectivity			Chapter 4 Bulimic criminal selectivity
			Legally-disciplining criminal selectivity	Police-medically disciplining criminal selectivity	Socio-disciplining criminal selectivity	
Section 1 Contextual settings: Where, When and How		Primitive Accumulation – Late 15th Century to Early 18th Century	First Disciplining Phase (Late 18th Century)	Second Disciplining Phase (Late 20th to 21th Century)	Third Disciplining Phase (Early to Late 20th Century)	Bulimic Social Order (Late 20th to 21th Century)
Section 2 Conflict-Control	Under-Criminalization	Acts of conquest (death, enslavement, fire, torture) and illegal expropriations in European rural lands.	Legal expropriations in European country-side. Crimes linked to religion, moral, slander or defamation	Colonial plunder (death, enslavement, torture) and workers' subjugation in European factories.	Gangsterism (organized crime) and white-collar crimes	illegal occupations, extermination, robbery and complex business-crime.
	Over-Criminalization	Criminalized survival strategies (vagrancy, begging, prostitution), coarse crime (rough crimes against property), religious crimes (heresy, witchcraft, contraception, infanticide), and resistance to land expropriation.	Criminalized survival strategies (vagrancy, begging, prostitution), coarse crime (mainly, petty crimes against property) and peasant resistance to expropriation.	Criminalized survival strategies (vagrancy, begging, prostitution), coarse crime (mainly petty crimes against property) and union-political activities	Coarse crimes, 'deviations,' and anti-capitalist activities	Criminalized survival strategies (vagrancy, begging), coarse crime (mainly petty crimes against property and drug-related offenses)

TABLE 4   *The different modalities of criminal selectivity* (cont.)

Characteristics		Chapter 2 Original criminal selectivity	Chapter 3 Disciplining criminal selectivity			Chapter 4 Bulimic criminal selectivity
			Legally-disciplining criminal selectivity	Police-medically disciplining criminal selectivity	Socio-disciplining criminal selectivity	
Section 3 Who Were Prosecuted?	Under-Criminalized Social Sectors	Monarchy, feudal lords, and mercantile bourgeoisie.	mercantile bourgeoisie, monarchies, and feudal remnants	emerging industrial bourgeoisie and financial bourgeoisie	monopolistic industrial bourgeoisie and emerging international financial bourgeoisie	Monopolistic industrial bourgeoisie and international financial bourgeoisie
	Over-Criminalized Social Sectors	Proto-Lumpen-proletariat and proto-proletariat.	Urban pauperism	Pauperism and organized dissident	Pauperism and organized dissident	Modern Pauperism (social junk and social dynamite)
Section 4 Punishment	Manifest Functions	Emergency Discourses (witchcraft, leisure, peasant rebellion, games, begging as threatens).	Retribution, Incapacitation, Deterrence, Social re-integration			Delegitimising theory of punishment and new versions of the theories of social order disciplinary

defend private property. Since the advent of legally-disciplining criminal selectivity, the bourgeoisie has vigorously enforced the message of absolute respect for private property, banishing any vestiges of communal property: it was the moment of transformation of customary rights into crimes, which was done through violence, correlating with the abruptness of the change needed to be imposed. The most emblematic historic example is discussed by Marx (1842) when he describes the criminal prohibition of collecting firewood in the Prussian forests. The use of common pasture, the hunt of loose animals and the occupation of free land – practiced for centuries by impoverished people – were also turned into crimes that received relentless persecution.

There has also been historical continuity in the over-criminalization of survival strategies to ensure revenue outside of formal employment (panhandling and vagrancy being the clearest examples). During primitive accumulation, repression had an exceptional importance, as the central social conflict was to create a working class, and criminalized survival strategies challenged wage labor. Within the disciplining social order, criminalized survival strategies were contained by the expansion of employment that covered large masses of workers who, though still sporting a high degree of pauperization, were likely to be included in the formal labor market. Since the bulimic social order, over-criminalization grew to include different behaviors such as violence against animals during waste collection, misusing public areas, occupation of public roads, encroachments, car care without legal authorization, and sex in public, among others. Witchcraft and heresy have been mostly targeted by over-criminalization during the primitive accumulation. The disciplining social order established, at least in the formal letter of the law, the separation of law and moral/religious components, forbidding the criminalization of such acts, in a pattern that lasts until today.

Over-criminalization of unions and activities surrounding political organization was particularly enhanced during disciplining criminal selectivity. This occurred in line with the purpose of settling the bourgeois order (legally-disciplining criminal selectivity), enforcing discipline in the factories and the social whole (police-medically disciplining criminal selectivity), and combating communist militants, challengers to the Vietnam war, and Black-American activists against racial injustice, in the context of the two World Wars and the Cold War (socio-disciplining criminal selectivity). While various regulations continue over-criminalizing political dissidence today (particularly anti-terrorism laws), it is also valid to say that coarse crimes and criminalized survival strategies have consolidated as the core of crime control.

Concerning under-criminalization, peasants' dispossession was protected during the primitive accumulation and the first disciplining phase. During the primitive accumulation (particularly in the 15th and 16th centuries), expropriations were carried out violently and illegally, i.e. against monarchical regulatory provisions that, unsuccessfully, sought to stop them. Conversely, during the first disciplining phase, disciplining regulations legitimated and fostered enclosures. The first wave of enclosures made it evident that policies (in this case, the monarchical limitation of enclosures) are futile when they contradict prevailing economic and social needs (in this case, the need of land for sheep feeding, and the need to force peasants' migration to cities). The second wave of enclosures, which pursued the introduction of agricultural technique in the fields, showed how, since the end of the 18th century, legal regulations fostered upper-classes' impunity. Thus, while dispossession occurred in both cases, the legal component was essential to ensure that the first wave of enclosures was not prosecuted, even by existing regulations. Meanwhile, the second wave was not only not persecuted but encouraged by existing rules that guaranteed that these negative social behaviors (expropriation, dispossession, forced migration) would be allowed.

Opprobrious work conditions have been part of a logic of under-criminalization throughout capitalism – from the harsh conditions in work-houses during the primitive accumulation and the first disciplining phase to the terrible conditions of factories in the second disciplining phase (including physical and sexual assault). Nevertheless, those acts were barely registered as crimes: they were mostly qualified as mere violations of civil or administrative law, while in the few cases that were primarily criminalized, regulations were poorly enforced due to executive and judicial agencies' tolerance or connivance with factory owners. Finally, on the rare occasions in which convictions took place, they resulted in lenient punishments. This logic was broken in the socio-disciplining criminal selectivity with the increasing standardization of labor rights. It emerged again during bulimic criminal selectivity, through the dismemberment of welfare policies and the growth of job insecurity. However, generally speaking, working conditions did not return to the ignominious situation that was dominant up to the second disciplining phase.

Under-criminalization of profit through illegal means was a permanent feature since the 15th century. However, it was during socio-disciplining criminal selectivity that those acts became visualized in the form of white-collar crimes and organized crime. The former preserved most of the features of the economic crimes presented in the police-medically disciplining criminal selectivity: it was performed in an individual manner (they were committed by private individuals under a decentralized organization) and only to facilitate a lawful primary activity (and thus their authors did not respond to the marginal stereotype, but to the average professional). Conversely, organized crime was a collective crime, it rested solely on illegal activities, and it deepened the networks between public and private sectors, based on widespread corruption. Its highest expressions were the U.S. mafias that emerged in the heat of Prohibition. Despite the extension of white-collar crimes and the rawness and social harm of organized crime, they were mostly under-criminalized. Even in the case of the mafias, the paradoxical situation was that, while the great organizers were not criminally persecuted, minor violations of the Prohibition, such as drinking alcohol, were prolifically over-criminalized. During bulimic criminal selectivity, economic crimes became widely linked to global financial activity. The line between legal/illegal business was diluted, both forms of business assumed a corporate nature, and the networks between public and private sectors grew. Far from provoking a clarification of its criminogenic nature, the new features reinforced the intertwining of economic crimes with legitimate businesses.

Historically, the most harmful behaviors took place in the colonies and during significant military conflicts. During original criminal selectivity, the colonial territories were the scenes of death, torture, enslavement, arson and plunder, all carried out systematically by individuals under state control that acted for the benefit of the European governments. The prosecution of those actions was extremely limited as they relied on the legitimizing discourse that included them as part of a 'civilizing' process that was necessary to achieve global progress. During disciplining criminal selectivity, and particularly police-medically disciplining criminal selectivity, there was a breaking point as slavery was normatively prohibited and a widespread recognition of the character of persons occurred. In spite of this, acts of extreme violence (mainly in Africa and India) continued to be under-criminalized. Positivism legitimized the limited persecution of these harmful acts by characterizing the colonized as 'savage' and 'primitive,' and therefore worthy of subjugation. This medical discourse was tied to the emergence and growth of police forces aimed at disciplining the inhabitants of the colonies. After the two World Wars and global massacres during socio-disciplining selectivity, bulimic criminal selectivity fostered illegal occupations based on combating terrorism in the Middle East. Despite advances in international law, these occupations have been under-criminalized both because of the low standards applicable to these acts (mainly the constraints of the international definition of 'genocide') and because of the limited enforcement of international law. The legitimizing discourse for the perpetration of these acts has been resting on a Manichean division between 'citizens' and 'enemies.' The inhabitants of the occupied territories are treated as 'terrorists' in a metonymic operation that enables the indiscriminate use of force against entire populations, based on accusations against specific individuals. Notice how, in a line of historical continuity, these conquests and occupations are essential preconditions for the settlement and reproduction of capital, both by ensuring the domain of new or captive markets and by guaranteeing raw materials at low or no cost for the global powers, strengthening their position in the world market. Under-criminalization of counter-terrorist acts has paradoxically been accompanied by the over-criminalization of those individuals who tried to confront and resist the occupations.

b. A second striking aspect of the historical development of under-criminalization and over-criminalization mechanisms is linked to their geographical distribution. Over-criminalization had an over-dimensioned deployment in rural areas during original and legally-disciplining criminal selectivity. This was performed mainly through the persecution of peasants who resisted the waves of enclosures, or who did not respect private property, imposed without qualms by the rising bourgeoisie. On the contrary, during police-medically disciplining criminal selectivity, over-criminalization was mainly urban, as an effect of town expansion to the detriment of the fields. A geographical analysis also shows that the crudest acts were further under-criminalized when they took place in the colonies. Massacres committed in developed countries (e.g. the two World Wars) were matched by some level of legal response, and led to a breakthrough regarding enactment of international legislation and the creation of international organizations and courts. Without entering into the discussion on the content of these instruments and institutions, it is relevant to highlight the dissimilar response of crime control to events of similar levels of violence (in terms of loss of lives and material values) depending on the fact that they occurred in colonial/occupied territories or Western Europe/United States, that is, within global centers of economic and political power.

c. A third relevant breaking point that can be detected in the historical evolution of over-criminalization and under-criminalization mechanisms refers to the applicable criminal procedure. Original criminal selectivity involved differential treatment of individuals, depending on their social position even to judge the same facts; i.e., selectivity was redoubled according to the class status of the offender. By contrast, legally-disciplining criminal selectivity involved the construction of a large bureaucratic regulatory framework that treated all citizens as formally equal, and demanded certain criminal proceedings as a pre-requisite to convict someone. This was not an obstacle for the establishment of privileged jurisdictions that favored the bourgeoisie by imposing lenient punishments, while corruption transformed the division of powers into an illusion. However, the principle of equal treatment under the law – at least in formal terms – was a breaking point with the primitive accumulation, and it has not been overturned until today.

d. Over-criminalization mechanisms have been differently conjugated in a primary and secondary level. During primitive accumulation, primary over-criminalization transformed the 'able-bodied poor' (the ones that were not authorized to beg but could not find a job) into 'offenders' through the sanction of criminalized survival strategies (basically, panhandling or loitering without authorization). Secondary over-criminalization transformed the 'offenders' into potential employees through the introduction of work patterns in the workhouses where they were confined. During disciplining criminal selectivity, the urban poor continued to be considered delinquents because of primary over-criminalization, while secondary over-criminalization – through the prison-factory device – transformed them into disciplined workers. Finally, during bulimic criminal selectivity, while primary over-criminalization has not changed its mechanism of turning the poor into 'offenders,' secondary over-criminalization lost its disciplinarian goal and now transforms offenders into outcasts with even fewer chances of recovering a place in the market than before being criminalized.

e. A fifth relevant aspect refers to the continuity in the functioning and features of crime control from the 15th century to the present. Since primitive accumulation, crime control organized itself through a bureaucratic structure at the core of the nascent states, and with a very particular characteristic: over-criminalization became a sword of Damocles hanging over the oppressed social sectors and applying atrocious penalties even for minor acts. Despite its disproportion and brutality, punishment was not conceived as a crime because it was part of the legal matrix: it decriminalized itself. This logic has remained in force ever since.

With disciplining criminal selectivity, this Damocles' sword stopped operating through corporal punishment, and deprivation of freedom was established as the hegemonic mechanism of reprimand. However, the break was not as abrupt as it appears: discipline, essential to the application of crime control, was already present in the workhouses that had emerged during original criminal selectivity. The qualitative difference lies in the fact that in the primitive accumulation, discipline – through confinement and forced labor in the workhouses – lawfully co-functioned with flogging and the death penalty. Within legally-disciplining criminal selectivity, imprisonment was imposed as the main lawful punishment. Torture and death are still present in prisons, but they are not legally recognized.

Regardless of its continuity, imprisonment has shown different forms since its imposition. It was connected with forced labor in its first mode in the workhouses during original criminal selectivity. It was afterward linked to disciplining work during legally-disciplining criminal selectivity. Prison became a terrifying punishment during police-medically disciplining criminal selectivity. It oriented towards social rehabilitation with improvements in prisons during socio-disciplining criminal selectivity. Prison finally converted into a mode of expelling undesirables during bulimic criminal selectivity.

f. A religion-based discourse dominated original criminal selectivity. A legal and philosophical-based discourse was imposed during the legally-disciplining criminal selectivity. A medical one reigned during police-medically disciplining criminal selectivity. A sociological discourse ruled during socio-disciplining criminal selectivity. Finally, an actuarial or simply administrative-type discourse has been the hegemonic one during bulimic criminal selectivity. Each of these discourses has been sustained by moral entrepreneurs who gained strength through the dissemination of moral panics among the general population, reinforcing a socially constructed perception about conflict-control.

The implicit functions of punishment responded to the specific socio-economic needs of each historical context. Nevertheless, they can be systematized in a triple purpose: (a) modeling, disciplining or incapacitating the subsets of the problematic social sectors that perpetrate (or are accused of perpetrating) offenses; (b) modeling, disciplining or controlling the whole problematic sector of which the formers are part; (c) fragmenting the working class between 'criminals' and 'good workers.' Specifically, in the bulimic criminal selectivity, the latent functions delve into a fourth one which resulted in promoting 'crime control as industry,' and the omnipresent control of the society as a whole, enabling an extension of the networks of control with the approval of the controlled population.

g. Another relevant aspect of interest that caters specifically to the evolution of over-criminalization mechanisms is linked to the principle of less eligibility. Punishment has tended to offer worse conditions than social policies, which compelled the marginalized to accept welfare assistance instead of taking the risk of being apprehended when committing a crime. In turn, social policies have tended to offer worse conditions than the jobs offered to the most disadvantaged sectors of the working class, forcing them to accept those jobs when available. Following this logic, during primitive accumulation, punishment acquired fearsome characteristics that configured it as 'less eligible' than welfare, which was designated for the 'non-working' poor. In turn, welfare marked the level of less eligibility for workers who could perform in the labor market. The worst conditions offered by social policies had to do with the fact that charity was meager and required multiple pre-requisites (registration, authorization, not having family resources, remaining in the town of origin) and with the fact that avoiding work when capable of doing it could result in criminal sanctions.

As a consequence, even though employment conditions were extremely hostile, they proved to be a better scenario than social assistance.

During legally-disciplining criminal selectivity, even though the progressive incorporation of the masses into the labor market improved workers' conditions in comparison with primitive accumulation, they remained at a level of extreme pauperization. Applying the less eligibility principle, social assistance (already fully regulated by secular institutions) remained tied to the institution of workhouses, under harsh conditions of oppression. During police-medically disciplining criminal selectivity, welfare became worse in comparison with the dismal conditions suffered by the employed population. Social policies developed through workhouses and became the last option for the pauperized population before starvation. As 'less eligible' than workhouses, prison conditions were 'houses of terror,' both through a productive work profile in the United States and as mere confinement in Europe. During socio-disciplining criminal selectivity, improvements in the conditions of the working class, income distribution policies and social inclusion of the most disadvantaged resulted in the improvement of public assistance. These social policies, in turn, were accompanied by a more lenient criminal policy, which prioritized more flexible forms of crime control.

During bulimic criminal selectivity, along with the increasing precariousness of the labor market, welfare reassumed the original fragmentation among the poor entitled to the assistance (the 'good' poor) and the growing number of those who – accused of fraud or wrongdoing – are referred to the criminal sphere (the 'bad' poor) through the so-called punitive welfare. Thus, welfare remains 'less eligible' than the precarious jobs that would hardly be taken if the welfare system were preserved. As even 'less eligible' than punitive welfare, punishment became harsher and prisons adopted the model of maximum security.

h. The book proposed the concept of mixed insertion and demonstrated that the combination of legal and illegal work by the over-criminalized population, noted in recent sociological research, is far from being an exclusive feature of late modernity. It is a historical constant that was already present at the dawn of the capitalist system. This analysis problematizes the perception of offenders as a differentiated category of individuals because of their inferior biological constitution (as advocated during the second disciplining phase) or their weak integration ability (as promoted during the third disciplining phase). Even if we acknowledge that the over-criminalized populations effectively commit crimes, over-criminalization is still not defensible because it imposes punishments that are not proportional to the social harm produced by the targeted behavior, and because its purpose is resolving social conflicts that exceed the crime conflict. The objective here was not to identify the over-criminalized and under-criminalized social sectors from an ethical or moral perspective. The aim was rather to study the socio-economic implications of mechanisms that put human beings on either side of that line, not because their acts are more or less harmful, but because they produce more or less social unrest in the framework of an unequal social order. Various sections of the book showed how crimes committed by the most disadvantaged sectors tended to harm others in a similarly deprived situation. However, the under-criminalized acts have produced even more severe social harm throughout modern history, without receiving the same response by crime control.

i. Over-criminalization also shows a historical pattern in its compulsion to territorially ingrain the 'problematic' social sectors. During the primitive accumulation, there was an obligation to be registered in one's place of residence for the purpose of being able to beg. Confinement in workhouses and the first prisons were imposed during disciplining criminal selectivity, as well as the requirement of reporting an address before being released – a logic that continues today. Bulimic criminal selectivity introduced a spatial control of society as a whole. As it was already intuited by Foucault with the notion of 'biopolitics' (1978/9), today we can see how various technological innovations (biometric identification, GPS, interactive maps with satellite location) perpetuate and expand the possibility of locating any individual at any time, in what has been called 'liquid surveillance' (Bauman and Lyon 2013).

How are we now? Having made this long historical journey and pointing out relevant remarks of the evolution of criminal selectivity, it is possible to analyze more precisely the current situation and visualize more sharply the continuities and ruptures in the exercise of crime control since the primitive accumulation. Today, under-criminalization continues along the same historical pattern that has been sustained since the 15th century. It covers the most harmful acts committed in the under-developed countries (now presented in terms of counter-terrorism measures), including murder, plunder and torture. Over-criminalization also follows its historical patterns: it operates on the criminalized survival strategies of those who are not included in the formal economy, regardless of the low or non-existent harm of those behaviors. The turning point introduced by legally-disciplining criminal selectivity (formal proclamations of equal rights and guarantees) is still alive, and it has even been expanded with the incorporation of cultural, social and economic rights in Constitutions and general legislation. Legally-disciplining criminal selectivity additionally introduced progressive legal standards that have been preserved, such as the codification of offenses. Furthermore, specific procedural requirements have been accepted as a prerequisite for implementing punishment. Despite these innovations, it has not been possible then, nor now, to ensure the full exercise of rights for all individuals as material inequity prevents them from effectuating the rights assigned to them as abstract right-holders. Conversely, mainly as a result of legally-disciplining criminal selectivity, we still tend to think that the law is equally applicable to all members of society, even though – as it has been demonstrated in this book – the law is often used as a tool to oppress the marginalized sectors.

Deprivation of freedom as the accepted legal punishment and the hegemonic global tendency to prohibit corporal punishment and the death penalty have also been inaugurated in the context of the legally-disciplining criminal selectivity and preserved until now. Several innovations that have been developed within police-medically disciplining criminal selectivity have also been maintained until today. Among them, it is possible to identify the decisive value of forensic examinations, the biased consideration of people with mental health issues or the youth whose rights are restricted 'for their own sake' under a paternalistic paradigm, and the discriminatory remnants that legitimize physical stereotypes of offenders based on race or socio-economic status. The most relevant and risky feature that has been preserved since Lombroso's studies in prisons has been the amalgamation between those effectively over-criminalized and the real offenders, without considering the selectivity of the criminal justice system. Notwithstanding that there are current theoretical positions that insist on the return to a positivist perspective, the socio-disciplining approach was an inflection point regarding the impossibility of circumventing social issues when analyzing a criminal case.

Indeed, the sociological perspective that is used today to analyze crime and punishment is undoubtedly indebted to the third disciplining phase. This stage also marked the emergence of restorative justice mechanisms and the introduction of qualitative, empirical and pragmatic research in the criminal field. These sociologic-based approaches are used today to challenge a system of mass penal control. However, the reversal of mass incarceration will not necessarily bring a fairer system.

Far from witnessing the uprising of a more equal and human right-based criminal justice system, it seems that we are observing a rebirth of the disciplining modality of criminal selectivity. This resurgence does not emulate the inclusive forms of the 18th to 20th centuries because it is built upon the inherence of bulimic criminal selectivity. The result is a forthcoming modality of criminal selectivity that seeks to discipline those that are not needed in the capitalist system of production; that is, the disciplining of the culturally included and economically excluded. Innovative mechanisms in the criminal justice system (problem-solving courts, restorative justice mechanisms, G.P.S. control of offenders) suggest a return to the paternalistic spirit of the disciplining modality of criminal selectivity that now pursues the discipline of the left-overs. This upcoming approach helps reduce the political and economic costs of the criminal justice system, while poor families and communities become in charge of controlling the over-criminalized individuals. Once again, these mechanisms operate under the coverage of the latent penal control: if the community-based control does not work, the prison system will be waiting. The alternative for the over-criminalized individuals would be to accept the (cheaper) community-based disciplining mechanisms by hook or to be subjected to the traditional punitive mechanisms by crook.

It seems undisputable that is preferable to be controlled in the community rather than in inhuman prison facilities. However, more important than the *how* is the *who*. We need to think further and take advantage of this critical moment of criminal justice systems to seek new mechanisms to approach crime conflict that bring an alternative to the prison-centered system. But we also need to consider who are the ones that will be targeted by this alternative system and who will not. In short, we need to discuss if it is possible to dismantle a long-term history of poor and racially-disadvantaged over-criminalized and rich and racially-advantaged under-criminalized.

Our misconceived understanding of the law as neutral and evenly applicable to all partly emanates from a long-established legal research tradition that studies legal issues in a vacuum – isolated from the various socio-economic factors that impact real lives. As Marx has repeatedly reminded us, this kind of thinking only creates a myth of equality, while the various injustices continue to be perpetrated against the poor and racially marginalized groups. If the law has a meaningful impact in ensuring social outcomes, it is imperative that we take stock of the various interests represented in the legal decision-making process and build decisions that are sensitive to historical injustices that are closely tied to the capitalist form of production. It is time to think which model of criminology we need in order to foster a courageous analysis of crime and crime control that makes it clear who are the targets of the criminal justice system and how can we challenge that situation.

Pursuing this goal, it seems desirable to reject the model of the 'wise criminologist' that, pursuing a corporate interest, defends the hegemonic discourses on punishment as the correct ones, and denounces fraternity among human beings as a utopia (Zaffaroni 2005, 6–9). We should also reject the 'naive criminologist,' who critically analyzes and denounces the ideological content of the hegemonic discourses and does not discard fraternity as a possible future, but fails to explain how to achieve that goal and does not propose an alternative discourse. It seems necessary to offer a more radical model that we can call 'transformative criminologist.' The ones following this approach would support a certain model of criminal justice and defend it on an explanatory basis. They would permanently question their theoretical positions and expose themselves to praxis. The transformative criminologist-model would object to the 'wise criminologists' for being functional to the preservation of the existing social-economic structure and would encourage the 'naive criminologists' to remember Marx's critique of Feuerbach Thesis 11, inviting them to transform the world (Marx 1845, 45).

As a global aim, the abolition of crime is tantamount to the abolition of a criminogenic system of domination and control (Taylor et al. 1973, 231). This necessarily requires the realization of a revolutionary praxis that involves us all. The success of researchers should not be judged regarding static description, but in relation to their ability to feed back their research with interventions within the targeted population (1974, 448). This is important to enable us to develop an imperative that weighs on the consciences of those who have chosen to work as legal operators. It is a vital condition of our actions in this field: be aware that our work is intrinsically linked to punishment, and that the latter is capable of inflicting significant and biased pain, particularly given the selectivity with which it operates. Paraphrasing Marx (1895, 45), I hope this book creates awareness of the selective operation of the criminal justice system so that we can work to overthrow it and to create something new, something fairer.

Afterword

Critical Theory of the Carceral State: Its Hour Come Again

In the 1970s, as global prison populations declined, concern for prisoners' rights grew, and debates about the end of the death penalty as a punishment for murder widespread, criminology as well as punishment and society scholarship were infused with new readings from the Marxist tradition. Not that there were not important earlier precedents there already, including Evgeny Pashukanis in the Soviet Union in the 1920s and Georg Rusche in Germany and the United States in the 1930s. However, the outbreak of Marxist analysis of penality that began in the 1970s was different. It was international; it was particularly concerned with the origins of the penitentiary project, and it was less tethered to the text of *Capital* and the ideas about penality contained there. In the United Kingdom, E.P. Thompson (1963) and students working with him (Hay et al. 1975) were producing a new Marxist historiography of English criminal law and its role in forging a working class in the course of the 18th and 19th centuries. In France, Michel Foucault (1975) was reading Thompson's book, *The Making of the English Working Class*, and producing a new kind of Marxist reading of the rise of the prison, one informed by an analysis of disciplinary forms of social control that Marx had only alluded to. In Italy, Dario Melossi and Massimo Pavarini (1980) were drawing together the very same links. In the same time but less anchored on the prison, critical criminologists in the United Kingdom (Taylor, Walton, Young 1973; Cohen 1974; Hall et al. 1979) and in the United States (Platt 1969) were reintroducing Marx into discussions of primary criminalization, policing, and the media response to deviance. Rather than simply rethinking Marx's thoughts on punishment, this stream of scholarship opened up the field of punishment and society based on a common perspective that linked the analysis of punishment with class struggle (Garland 1990).

Elsewhere, I have written on this critical juncture, its social and political context, and its consequences for the academic and public discussion of punishment (Simon and Sparks 2013; Simon 2013). Here, I want to note that we seem to be in the midst of a new Marxist conjuncture. It has arguably begun some time ago with new and explicitly political-economic analyses of global penal trends (De Giorgi 2006; Harcourt 2011). With the publication of *Marxism and Criminology. A History of Criminal Selectivity* by Valeria Vegh Weis, this conjuncture now has its own systematic rereading of the Marxist criminology tradition, with a lot of care attention not only to Marx but also to the critical juncture of the 1960s and 1970s. More than past criminological interventions of this sort (but see the Foucault revealed by the lectures being translated and published, see Elden 2016), Vegh Weis critiques substantive criminal law theory, the rationalizations of punishment that legitimate modern criminal law authority, and the mechanisms that make possible a comprehensive coercive control over a once emerging working class, and over today's more globalized 'dangerous' class. Students of the evolution of modern punishment will be rewarded by the effort to theorize the role of penality at very different moments of capitalist economic development.

With its precise focus on the work of *under-* and *over-criminalization* as the two mechanisms of *criminal selectivity* in the political economic logic of penality, this is Marxist criminology, and punishment and society for an age of austerity and economic crisis (as opposed to Neoliberal ascendancy). As with the 1970s, the ability of the privilege to enjoy valuable spheres of immunity are examined as closely as the ways in which the bodies of the poor are disciplined. While the last Marxist wave, a biblical generation ago, responded to increasing militarization of the state and to the upwelling of revolutionary movements among the most criminalized segments of the community, Vegh Weis' millennial Marxism is well selected and read for the new logics of permanent unemployment, financial risk taking, mass migration and terrorism. It comes at a timely moment when new profound problems that arise with the global economy have subjected the carceral state to more intense economic scrutiny than in the past, and when a growing social movement of people of color and others excluded by forms of normality are challenging the role of punishment in maintaining racial hierarchies as a threat to their dignity, and even survival. With growing pressure from both ends to reform the carceral state in the United States and elsewhere (as in the 1960s and 1970s), Critical Theory – with a generationally sharpened edge – is vital. This book delivers just that.

Jonathan Simon
Adrian A. Kragen Professor of Law
Director of the Center for the Study of Law & Society
University of California, Berkeley.

References

Cohen, Stanley (1974) Folk devils and moral panics. London: Routledge, 2004.
De Giorgi (2006) Re-Thinking the Political Economy of Punishment: Perspectives on Post-Fordism and Penal Politics (Aldine).

Elden, Stuart (2016) Foucault's Last Decade (Wiley).

Foucault, Michel (1975) Discipline and Punish. The Birth of the Prison. New York: Vintage Books.

Garland, David (1990) Punishment and Modern Society (Clarenton Press).

Harcourt, Bernard (2011) The Illusion of Free Markets: Punishment and the Myth of Natural Order (Harvard University Press).

Hay, Douglas, Linebaugh, Peter and Thompson, Edward (1975) Albion's Fatal Tree. Crime and Society in Eighteenth-Century England (Penguin).

Melossi, Dario and Pavarini, Massimo (1980) The Prison and The Factory: Origins of the Penitentiary System (Macmillan).

Platt, Anthony (1969) The Child Savers: The Invention of Delinquency. Chicago: University of Chicago Press, 1977.

Simon, Jonathan (2013) Punishment and the Political Technologies of the Body, in Handbook of Punishment & Society, Simon Jonathan and Sparks Richard eds. (Sage).

Simon, Jonathan and Sparks Richard (2013) "Introduction- Punishment & Society: The Emergence of an Academic Field," in Handbook of Punishment & Society, Simon Jonathan and Sparks Richard eds. (Sage); 1–19.

Taylor, Ian; Walton, Paul and Young, Jock (1973) The New Criminology. For a Social Theory of Deviance (Routledge).

Thompson, Edward (1963) The Making of the English Working Class. New York: Phanteon Books, 1964.

References

"13th," directed by Ava Du Vernay (2016; Netflix).

A.A.V.V. (1995) "Crime Solutions, 18 Things We Can Now Do to Fight Back." *The American Enterprise.* Translated by Delito y Sociedad no. 15 (2001).

Ackerman, Spencer (2015) "Torture by Another Name: C.I.A. Used 'Water Dousing' on at Least 12 Detainees," *The Guardian,* October 16, 2015. http://www.theguardian.com/law/2015/oct/16/cia-torture-water-dousing-waterboard-like-technique.

A.C.L.U. v. Clapper (2013) 785 F.3d 787.

A.C.L.U. (2013) "A Living Death: Life Without Parole for Nonviolent Offenses," A.C.L.U. Website, November 2013. https://www.aclu.org/files/assets/111813-lwop-complete-report.pdf#page=4.

A.C.L.U. (2014), "C.P.D. Traffic Stops and Resulting Searches in 2013," A.C.L.U. Website, December 2014. http://www.aclu-il.org/cpd-traffic-stops-and-resulting-searches-in-2013/.

A.C.L.U (2016), "Mass incarceration," A.C.L.U. Website. https://www.aclu.org/issues/mass-incarceration.

Acuña Jiménez, Víctor Hugo Lenin (2012) *¿Cómo se comporta el orden social en aquellos espacios sociales en que el estado, en este caso chileno, se encuentra menos presente.* Santiago: Universidad Academia de Humanismo Cristiano.

Adachi, Jeff (2016) "Public defenders can be biased, too, and it hurts their non-white clients," *The Washington Post,* June 7, 2016. https://www.washingtonpost.com/posteverything/wp/2016/06/07/public-defenders-can-be-biased-too-and-it-hurts-their-non-white-clients/.

Agamben, Giorgio (1995) *Homo Sacer. Sovereign Power and Bare Life.* California: Stanford University Press, 1998.

Agamben, Giorgio, (2003) *State of exception.* Chicago-London: The University of Chicago Press, 2005.

Alagia, Alejandro (2012) "Conferencia" (lecture, *Jornadas cuestión criminal y marxismo,* Facultad de Derecho de la Universidad de Buenos Aires, August 13, 2012).

Alagia, Alejandro, (2013) *Hacer sufrir.* Bs. As.: Ediar, 2013.

Al Baker (2015) "Beyond the Chokehold: The Path to Eric Garner's Death," *N.Y. Times,* June 13, 2015. http://www.nytimes.com/2015/06/14/nyregion/eric-garner-police-chokehold-staten-island.html?_r=0.

Alexander, Michelle (2010) *The New Jim Crow: Mass Incarceration in the Age of Colorblindness.* New York: The New Press.

Allen-Bell, Angela (2014) "Activism Unshackled & Justice Unchained: A Call to Make a Human Right Out of One of the Most Calamitous Human Wrongs to Have Taken Place on American Soil." *LSD Journal* no. 7.

Alston, Philip and Goodman, Ryan, (2013) *International Human Rights.* Oxford: Oxford University Press.

Althusser, Louis (1968) *Ideology and Ideological State Apparatuses*. Marxists Internet Archive, accessed April 7, 2016. https://www.marxists.org/reference/archive/al thusser/1970/ideology.htm.

Anderson, Perry, (1979) *Lineages of the Absolutist State*. London-New York: Verso, 2013.

Andrew, Donna and McGowen, Randall (2001) *The Perreaus and Mrs Rudd: Forgery and Betrayal in Eighteenth-Century London*. Berkeley: California Press.

Angenot, Marc (2004) "Social Discourse Analysis: Outlines of a Research Project." *The Yale Journal of Criticism* 17, no. 2 (2004): 199–215.

Angenot, Marc, (2010) "Una era de hegemonías dinámicas," *Página/12*, October 2, 2010.

Anitua, Gabriel Ignacio (2005) *Historia de los Pensamientos Criminológicos*. Bs. As.: Del Puerto, 2006.

Anitua, Gabriel Ignacio and Tedesco, Ignacio (2009) *La cultura penal. Homenaje al Prof. Dr. Edmundo Samuel Hendler*. Bs. As.: Del Puerto.

Anitua, Gabriel Ignacio and Zysman Bernaldo de Quirós Diego (2014) *La tortura. Una práctica estructural del sistema penal, el delito más grave*. Bs. As.: Didot.

Aniyar de Castro, Lola (1988) "Notas para el análisis de las relaciones entre democracia y justicia penal." *Capítulo Criminológico* no. 16.

Antunes, Ricardo (2003) *¿Adiós al trabajo? Ensayo sobre las metamorfosis y el rol central del mundo del trabajo*. Bs. As.: Herramienta.

Arendt, Hanna (1963) *Eichmann in Jerusalem: A Report on the Banality of Evil*. London: Penguin Books, 2016.

Arrighi, Giovanni, (1970) *Sviluppo económico sovrastruttura in África*. Milano: Einaudi.

Arrighi, Giovanni (1994) *The Long Twentieth Century*. London- New York: Verso.

Asbridge, Mark and Weerasinghe, Swarna (2008) "Homicide in Chicago from 1890 to 1930: Prohibition and its Impact on Alcohol- and Non-Alcohol-Related Homicides." *Addiction History* no. 104 (3) (2009): 355–364.

Ashworth, A. (1998) "Principled Sentencing: Readings on Theory and Policy." *Northwestern University Press*.

Astarita, Carlos (1992) *Desarrollo desigual en los orígenes del capitalismo*. Bs. As.: Tesis 11.

Astarita, Carlos, (1998) "Dinámica del sistema feudal, marginalidad y transición al capitalismo." In *Disidentes, heterodoxos y marginados en la Historia*, edited by Universidad de Salamanca, 21–50. Salamanca: Ediciones Universidad de Salamanca.

Astarita, Carlos, (2003–5) "Prácticas del conde y formación del feudalismo. Siglos VIII a XI." *Anales de la Universidad de Alicante. Historia Medieval* no. 14: 21–52.

Astarita, Carlos, (2005) *Del feudalismo al capitalismo. Cambio social y político en Castilla y Europa Occidental, 1250–1520*. Valencia: Universidad de Valencia.

Astarita, Carlos, (2014) *Revolución en el burgo* (unpublished paper).

Aston, Trevor (1998) *The Brenner Debate*. Cambridge: Press Syndicate of the University of Cambridge.

Auerhahn, Kathleen (1999) "The Split Labor Market and the Origins of Antidrug Legislation in the United States." *Law & Social Inquiry* 24, no. 2: 411–440.

Ayala, Manuel José de (1945) *Notas a la recopilación de Indias: origen e historia ilustrada de las Leyes de Indias*. Madrid: Cultura Hispánica.

Balbachan, Mauricio (2011) "La selectividad como mecanismo necesario para la subsistencia y consenso sobre el libre mercado." *Instituto de Investigaciones Ambrosio L. Gioja* V, no. Especial.

Balbus, Isaac (1977) "Commodity Form and Legal Form." *Law & Society Review* 11: 871–88.

Bales, Kevin (1984) "The Dual Labor Market of the Criminal Economy." *Sociological Theory* 2: 140–164.

Ballester Brage, Lluis and Colom Cañellas, Antonio (2005) "El concepto de explicación en las ciencias sociales." *Papers* 77.

Baptist Edward E. (2014) "The Half Has Never Been Told." New York: Basic Books.

Baratta, Alessandro (1974) "Derecho y justicia en Marx." In *Im Kreuzverhor der Wissenschaften*. Zurich-Munich: Artemis.

Baratta, Alessandro, (1985) "Integración-Prevención: una 'nueva' fundamentación de la pena dentro de la teoría sistémica." *Doctrina Penal* 8, no. 29: 9–26.

Baratta, Alessandro, (1986) *Criminología Crítica y Crítica del Derecho Penal*. Bs. As.: Siglo XXI, 2001.

Baratta, Alessandro, (1995) "Viejas y nuevas estrategias en la legitimación del derecho penal." In *Prevención y Teoría de la Pena*, 77–93. Santiago de Chile: Conosur.

Barker Vanessa (2009), "The Politics of Imprisonment: How the Democratic Process Shapes the Way America Punishes Offenders." Oxford-New York: Oxford University Press.

Barral, María (2007) *De sotanas por la Pampa. Religión y Sociedad en el Bs. As. rural tardo-colonial*. Bs. As.: Prometeo.

Bauman, Zygmunt (2000) "Social Issues of Law and Order." *British Journal of Criminology* 40: 205–221.

Bauman, Zygmunt, (2004) *Vidas desperdiciadas, la modernidad y sus parias*. Bs. As.: Paidós, 2005.

Bauman, Zygmum and Lyon, David (2013) *Liquid Surveilance*. Cambridge: Polity Press, 2013.

Bazelon, E. (2005) "Sentencing by the Numbers," *N.Y. Times*, January 2, 2005.

Beccaria, Cesar (Cesare) (1764) *On Crime and Punishment*. The Federalist Papers Project, accessed April 7, 2016. http://www.thefederalistpapers.org/wp-content/uploads/2013/01/Cesare-Beccaria-On-Crimes-and-Punishment.pdf.

Becker, Howard (1962) *Outsiders: Studies in the Sociology of Deviance*. New York: The Free Press, 1966.

Becker, Howard, (1964) *The Other Side. Perspectives on Deviance*. Nueva York: Free Press of Glencoe.

Becker, Howard, (1967) "Whose Side Are We On?" *Social Problems* no. 14: 239–247.

Becker, Gary (1968) "Crime and Punishment: An Economic Approach." *Journal of Political Economy* 76.

Becker, Howard, (1986) *Manual de escritura para científicos sociales*. Bs. As.: Siglo XXI, 2011.

Beckett Katherine and Western Bruce (2001) "Governing Social Marginality: Welfare, Incarceration and the Transformation of State Policy." *Punishment & Society* 3, no. 1: 43–55.

Beckett Katherine and Murakawa Naomi (2012) "Mapping the Shadow Carceral State: Toward an Institutionally Capacious Approach to Punishment." *Theoretical Criminology* 16, no. 2: 221–244.

Beirne, Piers (1979) "Empiricism and Critique of Marxism on Law and Crime." *Social Problems* 26, no. 4: 373/385.

Beirne, Piers, (1980) "Some More on Empiricism in the Study of Law: A Reply to Jacobs." *Social Problems* 27, no. 4: 471–475.

Beirne, Piers and Quinney, Richad (1982) *Marxism and Law*. Nueva York: Wiley.

Bensaid, Daniel (2007) "Marx y el robo de leña. Del derecho consuetudinario de los pobres al bien común de la humanidad." *Los debates de la dieta renana*. Barcelona: Gedisa.

Bensoussan, Georges (2008) "Editorial." *Revue d´ historie de la Shoah* no. 189.

Bergalli, Roberto (1980) "La ideología del control social tradicional." *Doctrina Penal* 3, no. 12: 805–818.

Bergalli, Roberto, (1982) *Crítica de la Criminología*. Bogotá: Temis.

Bergalli, Roberto, (1987) "Una intervención equidistante pero a favor de la sociología del control penal." *Doctrina Penal* 10, no. 36: 777–785.

Bergalli, Roberto, (1996) *Control social punitivo. Sistema penal e instancias de aplicación (Policía, Jurisdicción y Cárcel*. Barcelona: M.J. Bosch.

Bergalli, Roberto, (1997) "La caída de los mitos." *Secuestro Institucionales. Derechos Humanos*, edited by en Rivera Beiras, Iñaki and Dobon, Juan. Barcelona: M.J. Bosch.

Bergalli, Roberto, (2003) *Sistema penal y problemas sociales*. Valencia: Tirant Lo Blanch.

Bergalli, Roberto, (2008) "Violencia y sistema penal. Fundamentos ideológicos de la política criminal de exclusión social." *Violencia y sistema penal*, edited by Bergalli, Roberto and Rivera Beiras, Iñaki. Bs. As.: Del Puerto, 2008.

Bergalli, Roberto, (2012) (lecture, Facultad de Derecho de la Universidad de Buenos Aires, May 21, 2012).

Berman, Marshall (1981) *Todo lo sólido se desvanece en el aire. La experiencia de la modernidad*. Bs. As.: Siglo XXI, 1991.

Bermúdez, Emilia (2001) "Consumo cultural y representación de identidades juveniles" (lecture, Congreso LASA, Washington, September 6–8, 2001).

Bethell, Leslie (1984) *The Cambridge History of Latin America* II. Cambridge: Cambridge University Press.

Betran, Raúl Susin (2000) "Los discursos sobre la pobreza." *Brocar* no. 24: 105–135.

Binns, Peter (1980) "Law and Marxism. A critique of 'The General Theory of Law and Marxism.'" *Capital and Class* no. 10: 100–113.

Birckhead Tamar (2016) "Treating Juveniles as Adults" (lecture. Rev Law Conference, New Heaven, Yale University, February 19, 2016).

Black, Donald (1983) "Crime as Social Control." *American Sociology Review* 48, no. 1: 34–45.

Blalock, Hubert (1967) *Toward A Theory of Minority-Group Relations*. New York: John Wiley and Sons.

Boes, María (1969) "Public Appearance and Criminal Judicial Practices in Early Modern." *Social Science History* 20, no. 2: 259–279.

Bohm, Robert (1984) "Beyond Employment, Toward a Radical Solution to the Crime Problem." *Crime and Social Justice* no. 21–22: 213–222.

Bondeson, Jan (2002) *The London Monster: A Sanguinary Tale*. Cambridge: Mass.

Bonefeld, Werner (2010) "Abstract labour: Against its Nature and on Its Time." Capital & Class no. 34: 257–277.

Bonger, William Adrian (1905) *Criminality and Economic Conditions*. Boston: Little, Brown and Company, 1916.

Boron, Atilio (2000) *La filosofía política moderna. De Hobbes a Marx*, Bs. As.: Consejo Latinoamericano de Ciencias Sociales.

Boron, Atilio, (2004) *El nuevo orden imperial y cómo desmontarlo*. Bs. As.: Consejo Latinoamericano de Ciencias Sociales Editorial. http://biblioteca.clacso.edu.ar/gsdl/collect/clacso/index/assoc/D1684.dir/3boron.pdf.

Boron, Atilio, (2004) "Hegemonía e imperialismo en el sistema internacional." In *Nueva Hegemonía Mundial. Alternativas de cambio y movimientos sociales*. Bs. As.: Consejo Latinoamericano de Ciencias Sociales.

Boron, Atilio, (2006) "Por el necesario (y demorado) retorno al marxismo." In *Teoría Marxista hoy*. Bs. As: Consejo Latinoamericano de Ciencias Sociales.

Boron, Atilio, (2008) *Socialismo del siglo XXI ¿Hay vida después del neoliberalismo?*. Bs. As.: Luxemburg.

Boron, Atilio and Lizárraga, Fernando (comps.) (2014) *El liberalismo en su laberinto: renovación y límites en la obra de John Rawls*. Bs. As.: Luxemburg.

Boumediene v. Bush (2008) 553 U.S. 723.

Bourdieu, Pierre (2000) *Language and Symbolic Power*. Cambridge: Polity Press, 1991.

Bourgois, Phillipe (2010) *In search of Respect, Selling Crack in EL Barrio*. Cambridge Cambridge: University Press.

Box, Steven and Hale, Chris (1982) "Economic Crisis and the Rising Prisoner Population in England and Wales." *Crime and Social Justice* no. 17: 20–35.

Braga, Raquel Willadino (2003) *Procesos de exclusión e inclusión social de Jóvenes en el contexto urbano brasileño, un análisis de trayectorias de violencia y estrategias de resistencia*. Madrid: Universidad Complutense de Madrid.

Braithwaite, John (2002) *Restorative Justice and Responsive Regulation*. Oxford: Oxford University Press.

Braudel, Fernand (1949) *The Mediterranean and the Mediterranean World in the Age of Phillip II*. Berkeley: University of California Press, 1995.

Braudel, Fernand (1958) "La larga duración." *Revista Académica de Relaciones Internacionales* no. 5 (2006).

Brewster, Alice Rollins (1894) "Early Experiments with the Unemployed." *The Quarterly Journal of Economics* 9, no. 1: 88–95.

Brown, Ames (1915) "Prohibition." *The North American Review* 202, no. 720: 702–729.

Brown, Widney (2015) "The Shamefully Unfinished Story of the C.I.A. Torture Program," A.C.L.U. Website, December 9, 2015. https://www.aclu.org/blog/speak-freely/shamefully-unfinished-story-cia-torture-program.

Building a Grad Nation Report (2016) "Report," Americas Promise Website, accessed August 13, 2016. http://www.americaspromise.org/building-grad-nation-report.

Buncombe, Andrew (2016) "Hijab Wearing Is 'Passive Terrorism', Says U.S. Military Publication," *The Independent*, February 24, 2016. http://www.independent.co.uk/news/world/americas/hijab-wearing-is-passive-terrorism-says-us-military-publication-a6893931.html.

Bureau of Justice Statistics (1999) "Truth in Sentencing in State Prisons," January 1999, accessed April 20, 2016. http://bjs.gov/content/pub/pdf/tssp.pdf.

Bureau of Justice Statistics, (2010) "Prisoners in 2010," June 23, 2010, accessed April 19, 2016. http://www.bjs.gov/content/pub/press/pim09stpy09acpr.cfm.

Burn, Richard (1764) *The History of the Poor Laws, With Observations*. London: Woodfall.

Bustos Ramírez, Juan (1982) *Bases Críticas de un Nuevo Derecho Penal*. Bogotá: Temis.

Bustos Ramírez, Juan, (1983) *El pensamiento criminológico*. Bogotá: Temis.

Caimari, Lila (2004) *Apenas un delincuente. Crimen castigo y cultura en la Argentina, 1880–1955*. Bs. As.: Siglo XXI.

Cacciola, Scott (2014) "At Nets' Game, a Plan for a Simple Statement Is Carried Out to a T," *N.Y. Times*, December 9, 2014. http://www.nytimes.com/2014/12/10/sports/basketball/i-cant-breathe-tshirts-in-the-nba-how-jayz-lebron-james-and-others-made-them-happen.html?_r=0.

Calavita, Kitty, Tillman, Robert and Pontell, Henry (1997) "The Savings and Loan Debacle, Financial Crime, and the State." *Annual Review of Sociology* 23: 19–38.

Campagne, Fabián (2005) *Feudalismo tardío y revolución. Campesinado y transformaciones agrarias en Francia e Inglaterra (siglos XVI–XVIII)*. Bs. As.: Prometeo.

Campbell Michael C. and Schoenfeld Heather (2013) "The Transformation of America's Penal Order: A Historicized Political Sociology of Punishment." *American Journal of Sociology* 118/5: 1375–1423.

Capella, Juan Ramón (1969) "Introducción." In *Marx, El derecho y el Estado*. Barcelona: Oikos- Tau, 1979.

Cardoso, Fernando and Faletto, Enzo (1977) *Dependencia y desarrollo en América Latina*. Bs. As.: Siglo XXI.

Carvalho, Salo (2013) "Sobre as possibilidades de uma penologia crítica." *Polis e Psique*, no. 3: 143–164.

Casagrande, Agustín (2012) *Los vagabundos y la justicia de Bs. As. durante el período tardo colonial (1785- 1810)*. Bs. As.: Dunken.

Castel, Robert (1995) *Transformation of the Social Question*. New Brunswick-London: Transaction Publishers.

Castel, Robert, (2003) *La inseguridad social. ¿Qué es estar protegido?* Bs. As.: Manantial, 2013.

Castells, Manuel (2009) *Communication Power*. Oxford: Oxford University Press.

Cerroni, Umberto (1965) *Marx y el derecho moderno*. Barcelona: Jorge Álvarez.

Cerroni, Umberto, (1972) *La libertad de los modernos*. Barcelona: Martínez Roca, 1994.

Cerroni, Umberto, (1973) *Teoría política y socialismo*. México: ERA, 1976.

Cerroni, Umberto, (1974) "El problema de la teorización de la interpretación de clase del Derecho burgués." In *Luso alternativo dil diritto* 1. Roma: Laterza.

Cerroni, Umberto, (1975) *La teoría de las crisis sociales en Marx*. Madrid: Alberto Corazón.

Cervantes Martínez, Rafael, Másicon Gil Chamizo, Felipe, Másicon Regalado Alvarez, Roberto, and Másicon Regalado Alvarez, Roberto (2000) *Transnacionalización y desnacionalización: ensayos sobre el capitalismo contemporáneo*. Bs. As.: Tribuna Latino Americana.

Chambliss, William (1964) "A Sociological Analysis of the Law of Vagrancy." *Social Problems* 12, no. 1: 67–77.

Chambliss, William, (1975) "Toward a Political Economy of Crime." *Theory and Society* 2, no. 2: 149–170.

Chambliss, William, (1976) "Functional and Conflict Theories of Crime. The Heritage of Emilie Durkheim and Karl Marx." In *Whose law what order?* 1–28. Nueva York: Wiley.

Chambliss, William, (1978) *On the Take, from Petty Crooks to Presidents*. Indiana: Indiana University Press, 1988.

Chambliss, William, (1994) "Policing the Ghetto. Underclass, the Politics of Law and Law enforcement." *Social Problems* 41, no. 2: 177–194.

Chetty, Raj (2016) "Childhood Environment and Gender Gaps in Adulthood." *NBER Working Paper Series*, January 2016, http://www.equality-of-opportunity.org/.

Chile (2008) "Report to United Nation." In U.N. Compilation Prepared by the Office of the High Commissioner for Human Rights. http://ap.ohchr.org/documents/alldocs.aspx?doc_id=14940.

Chiricos, Theodore (1996) "Moral Panic as Ideology, Drugs, Violence, Race and Punishment in America." In *Justice with Prejudice, Race and Criminal Justice in America*, 19–48. Nueva York: Harrow and Heston.

Chiricos, Theodore and Delone, Miriam (1992) "Labor Surplus and Punishment, a Review and Assessment of Theory and Evidence." *Social Problems* no. 39: 421–446.

Chomsky, Noam (1992) *Year 501, the Conquest Continues.* New York: South End Press. http://library.uniteddiversity.coop/More_Books_and_Reports/Noam_Chomsky-5_books.pdf.

Chomsky, Noam, (2001) "Interview 5, Global Policy Website, accessed September 26, 2016. https://www.globalpolicy.org/component/content/article/154/26538.html.

Christie, Nils (1993) *Crime Control as Industry.* London-New York: Routledge.

Ciafardini, Mariano (2011) *Globalización tercera y última etapa del capitalismo. Un análisis desde el materialismo histórico.* Bs. As.: Luxemburg.

Ciafardini, Mariano, (2012) "Prólogo." In *El vértigo de la modernidad tardía.* Bs. As.: Didot.

Ciafardini, Mariano, (2012b) "Criminología" (lectures, Universidad Nacional de Quilmes, Aug/Dec).

Clapham, Andrew (2010) *Human Rights Obligations of Non-State Actors.* Oxford: Oxford University Press.

Cloward Richard (1960) *Delinquency and Opportunity, a Theory of Delinquent Gangs.* Nueva York: Free Press.

CNN (2016) "Iraq Prison Abuse Scandal Fast Fact," CNN Website. http://www.cnn.com/2013/10/30/world/meast/iraq-prison-abuse-scandal-fast-facts/.

Codino, Rodrigo (2010) "Presentación." In Prins, Adolphe, *La defense social y las transformaciones del derecho penal.* Buenos Aires: Ediar.

Cohen, Stanley (1974) *Folk Devils and Moral Panics.* London: Routledge, 2004.

Cohen, Gerald (1978) *Karl Marx's Theory of History.* Oxford: Clarendon Press.

Cohen, Gerald, (1982) "Reply to Elster on 'Marxism, Functionalism, and Game Theory.'" *Theory and Society* no 11: 483–495.

Cohen, Stanley, (1985) *Visiones de control social.* Barcelona: Ediciones PPU, 1988.

Cohen, Gerald, (1988) *History, Labor and Freedom. Themes from Marx.* Oxford: Clarendom Press.

Cohen, Gerald, (1995) *Self-Ownership, Freedom and Equality.* Cambridge: Cambridge University Press.

Cohen, Gerald, (2014) *Por una vuelta al socialismo. O cómo el capitalismo nos hace menos libres.* Bs. As.: Siglo XXI.

Colombres, Adolfo (1989) *A los 500 años del choque de dos mundos.* Bs. As.: Ediciones del Sol, Serie Antropológica, 1991.

Colvin, Mark and Pauly, John (1983) "A Critique of Criminology. Toward an Integrated Structural-Marxist Theory of Delinquency." *American Journal of Sociology* 89, no. 3: 513–551.

Council on Foreign Relations (2012) "Enemy Combatants," December 12, 2002. http://www.cfr.org/international-law/enemy-combatants/p5312.

Coser, Lewis (1956) *The Functions of Social Conflict*. Nueva York: The Free Press.

Cullen James (2016) "Ending New York's Stop-and-Frisk Did Not Increase Crime," *Brennan Center for Justice*, April 11, 2016. https://www.brennancenter.org/blog/ending-new-yorks-stop-and-frisk-did-not-increase-crime.

Daroqui, Alcira (2002) "La cárcel del Presente, su 'sentido' como práctica de secuestro institucional" (lecture, Universidad Nacional General Sarmiento, Bs. As., October 4, 2002).

Daroqui, Alcira (2011) "Marginaciones sociales y violencia" (lecture, Universidad de Buenos Aires, Bs As., November 3, 2011).

Daroqui, Alcira, Guemureman, Silvia, Pasin, Julia, López, Ana Laura and Bouilly Ma. del Rosario (2008) "Administración punitiva de la exclusión. La funcionalidad de la cárcel del siglo XXI" (lecture, Universidad Nacional de Rosario, School of Law, Rosario, 2008).

Davis, Mike (1990) *City of Quartz, Imagining the Future in Los Angeles*. London: Verso.

Davis, Mike, (2006) *Planet of Slums*. Nueva York: Verso.

De Giorgi, Raffaele (1997) "Riesgo, malestar y desviación, reflexiones sobre la violencia y los menores." *Delito y Sociedad* 6, no. 9/10: 15–17.

De Giorgi, Alessandro (2002) *El gobierno de la excedencia – Postfordismo y gobierno de la multitud*. Barcelona: Virus, 2006.

De Giorgi, Alessandro, (2005) *Tolerancia cero. Estrategias y prácticas de la sociedad de control*. Barcelona: Virus.

De Sousa Santos, Boaventura (1998) *La globalización del Derecho. Los nuevos caminos de regulación y la emancipación*. Bogotá: ILSA.

Death Penalty Information Center (2015) "The Death Penalty in 2015: Year End Report," Death Penalty Information Center Website. http://deathpenaltyinfo.org/documents/2015YrEnd.pdf.

Debandi, Natalia, (2013) "Retorno forzado. Prácticas y políticas de expulsión de migrantes en Francia" (Ph.D. Dissertation, Universidad Sorbona and Universidad de Buenos Aires).

Deleuze, Gilles (1995) "Post-scriptum sobre las sociedades de control." In *Conversaciones*: 277–281. Valencia: Pretextos, 1999.

Delgado, Richard (2009) "The Law of the Noose: A History of Latino Lynching." *Harv. C.R.- C.L. L. Review* 44.

Demleitner, Nora V. (2009) "US Felon Disenfranchisement: Parting Ways with Western Europe." In *Criminal Disenfranchisement in an International Perspective*, edited by A. Ewald and B Rottinghaus, 79–108. New York: Cambridge University Press.

Demuth, Stephen, and Steffensmeier, Darrell (2004) "Ethnicity Effects on Sentencing Outcomes in Large Urban Courts: Comparisons among White, Black, and Hispanic Defendants." *Social Science Quarterly* 85: 991–1011.

Derrida, Jaques (1989) *Fuerza de ley. El 'fundamento místico de la autoridad'.* Madrid: Tecnos, 1997.

Devah Pager (2003) "The Mark of a Criminal Record." *American Journal of Sociology* 108, no. 5: 937–975.

Devoto, Fernando and Madero, Marta (1999) *Historia de la vida privada en la Argentina,* Bs. As.: Taurus.

Dixon Travis L. and Linz, Daniel (2000) "Overrepresentation and Underrepresentation of Black-American and Latinos as Lawbreakers on Television News." *J. Comm.* 50, no. 2: 131–154.

Dobb, Maurice (1969) *Studies in the Development of Capitalism.* London: Routledge & Kegan Paul Ltd., 1971.

Downes David and Hansen Kirstine (2005) "Welfare and Punishment in Comparative Perspective." In *Perspectives on Punishment,* edited by S. Armstrong and L. McAra, 133–154. Oxford: Oxford University Press.

Drones Watch (2013) Codepink Peace Delegation to Yemen to Meet with Drone Strike Victims' Families of Guantanamo Prisoners, accessed June 5, 2016. http://drone swatch.org/2013/06/06/codepink-peace-delegation-to-yemen-to-meet-with-drone -strike-victims-families-of-guantanamo-prisoners/.

Duff, Antony (2000) *Punishment, Communication and Community.* Oxford: Oxford University Press.

Duff, Antony, (2003) "Probation, Punishment and Restorative Justice: Should Altruism Be Engaged in Punishment?" *The Howard Journal* 42, no. 2 (May 2003): 181–197.

Duff, Robin (2010) "Towards a Theory of Criminal Law?" *The Aristotelian Society* no. 84: 1–28.

Dujardin, Philippe (1978) *Pour une critique du droit.* París: PGU- Masperó.

Duménil, Lévy (2006) "Les trois champs de la théorie des relations financières de Marx. Le Capital financier d' Hilferding et Lénine." In *Séminaire d'Études Marxistes, La finance capitaliste,* 181–219. Paris: Presses Universitaires de France.

Durkheim, Émile (1895) *The Rules of Sociological Method.* New York-London-Toronto-Sydney: The Free Press.

Durkheim, Émile, (1897) *Suicide.* London-New York: Routledge Classics.

Durkheim, Émile, (1917) "Criminalidad y salud social." In *Delito y Sociedad* 16, no. 24 (2007): 121–132.

Eastern State Penitentiary accessed July 22, 2016, http://www.easternstate.org/.

Echart, Enara (2005) *Origen protestas y propuestas del movimiento antiglobalización.* Madrid: Los libros de la catarata.

Edin, Kathryn J. and Shaefer H. Luke (2015) *$2.00 a Day. Living on Almost Nothing in America.* Boston-New York: Houghton Mifflin.

Ellet, Wade (2004), "The Death of Dueling." *Historia* 13 (2004): 59–67.

Elster, Jon (1980) "Review of G. Cohen: Karl Marx's Theory of History." *Political Studies* 28: 121–128.

Elster, Jon, (1982) "Marxism, Functionalism, and Game Theory. The Case of Methodological Individualism." *Theory and Society* 11, no. 4: 453–482.

Elster, Jon, (1985) *Making Sense of* Marx. Cambridge: Cambridge University Press, 1987.

Emsley, Clive (2007) *Crime, Police & Penal Policy. European Experiences 1750–1940.* Oxford: Oxford University Press.

Engels, Friedrich (1845) *The Condition of the Working Class in England.* London: Project Gutenberg eBook, 1943.

Engels, Friedrich, (1847) "Principles of Communism." In *Selected Works* 1: 81–97. Moscow: Progress Publishers, 1969.

Engels, Friedrich, (1848) "The Latest Heroic Deed of the House of Bourbon." In Karl Marx and Friedrich Engels, *Collected Works* 7. Lawrence & Wishart Electric Book, 2010. http://www.koorosh-modaresi.com/MarxEngels/V7.pdf.

Engels, Friedrich, (1848b) "Origin of the Family, Private Property, and the State." Marxists Internet Archive, accessed April 15, 2016. https://www.marxists.org/archive/marx/works/download/pdf/origin_family.pdf.

Engels, Friedrich, (1850) *The Peasants War in Germany.* New York: International Publishers, 1926.

Engels, Friedrich, (1852) "El reciente proceso de Colonia." Marxists Internet Archive, accessed April 15, 2016. www.marxists.org/espanol/m-e/1850s/1852-colonia.htm.

Engels, Friedrich, (1870) "Preface to the Second Edition of 'The Peasant War in Germany.'" Marxists Internet Archive, accessed April 15, 2016. https://www.marxists.org/archive/marx/works/download/Engels.

Engels, Friedrich, (1878) "General." Marxists Internet Archive, accessed April 15, 2016. https://www.marxists.org/archive/marx/works/download/Engels_Anti_Duhring.pdf.

Engels, Friedrich, (1880) *Socialism: Utopian and Scientific.* Marxists Internet Archive, accessed April 15, 2016. https://www.marxists.org/archive/marx/works/download/Engels_Socialism_Utopian_and_Scientific.pdf.

Engels, Friedrich, (1884) "Marx and The Neue Rheinische Zeitung (1848–9)." Marxists Internet Archive, accessed April 15, 2016. https://marxists.anu.edu.au/archive/marx/works/1884/03/13.htm.

Engels, Friedrich, (1888) "On the Question of Free Trade." Marxists Internet Archive, accessed April 15, 2016. https://www.marxists.org/archive/marx/works/1888/free-trade/.

Engels, Friedrich, (1890) "Letter to J. Bloch." Marxists Internet Archive, accessed April 15, 2016. https://www.marxists.org/archive/marx/works/1890/letters/90_09_21.htm.

Enns, Peter K. (2004) "The Public's Increasing Punitiveness and Its Influence on Mass Incarceration in the United States." *American Journal of Political Science* 58, no. 4: 857–872.

Enzensberger, Hans Magnus (1974) *Conversaciones con Marx y Engels*. Barcelona: Anagrama, 2009.

Epp, Charles and Maynard-Moody, Steven (2014) "Driving While Black." *Washington Monthly*, January/February 2014. http://washingtonmonthly.com/magazine/janfeb-2014/driving-while-black/.

Equal Justice Initiative (2010) *Illegal Racial Discrimination in Jury Selection: A Continuing Legacy*. Alabama: EJI.

Equal Justice Initiative, (2013) *Slavery in America: The Montgomery Slave Trade*. Alabama: EJI.

Escohotado, Antonio (1983) *Historia general de las drogas*. Madrid: Espasa Calpe, 2008.

Everett, Ronald S. and Wojtkiewicz, Roger A. (2002). "Difference, Disparity, and Race/Ethnic Bias in Federal Sentencing." *Journal of Quantitative Criminology* 18, no. 2: 189–211.

Fagan, Jeffrey (2013) "Testimony." In David Floyd et al. v. The City of New York, Case 1:08-cv-01034-SAS-HBP. https://www.justice.gov/sites/default/files/crt/legacy/2013/06/13/floyd_soi_6-12-13.pdf.

Fassin, Didier (1996) "Marginalidad et marginados. La construction de la pauvreté urbaine en Amérique Latine." In *L'exclusion, l'état des savoirs*. París: Éditions La Découverte, 2014.

Federal Bureau of Investigations (2009) "Crime in the United States, 2008," September 2009.

Federal Bureau of Investigation (2012) "Persons Arrested," accessed April 19, 2016. http://www.fbi.gov/about-us/cjis/ucr/crime-in-the-u.s/2012/crime-in-the-u.s.-2012/persons-arrested/persons-arrested.

Federal Sentencing Statistics, U.S.S.C. Website (2014), accessed April 8, 2016. http://www.ussc.gov/sites/default/files/pdf/research-and-publications/federalsentencing-statistics/state-district-circuit/2014/1c14.pdf.

Federici, Silvia (2004) *Caliban and the Witch. Women, the Body and Primitive ccumulation*. New York: Autonomedia, 2009.

Feeley, Malcolm and Simon, Jonathan (1992) "The New Penology; Notes on the Emerging Strategy of Corrections and Its Implications." *Criminology* 30, no 4: 449–474.

Feierstein, Daniel (2007) *El Genocidio como Práctica Social*. Bs. As.: Fondo de Cultura Económica, 2011.

Feltz, Renee (2016) "Prosecutions of Illegal Entry a Driving Force in Mass Incarceration in U.S. – report," *The Guardian*. July 14, 2016. https://www.theguardian.com/us-news/2016/jul/14/immigrants-illegal-entry-us-mexico-prosecution-prisons-report.

Ferrajoli, Luigi (1999) *Derecho y Razón*. Madrid: Trotta, 2001.

Ferrajoli, Luigi and Zolo, Daniel (1977) "Marxismo y cuestión criminal." *Delito y Sociedad* no. 4 (1994): 66–67.

Ferrell, Jeff; Hayward, Keith and Young, Jock (2008) *Cultural Criminology. An Invitation.* London: Sage.

Fletcher George P. (2001) "Criminal Theory in the Twentieth Century." *Theoretical Inquiries in Law* 2, no. 12: 265–286.

Fletcher Michael (2013) "Fifty Years after March on Washington, Economic Gap Between Blacks, Whites Persists," *The Washington Post*, August 28, 2013. https://www .washingtonpost.com/business/economy/50-years-after-the-march-the-economic -racial-gap-persists/2013/08/27/9081f012-0e66-11e3-8cdd-bcdc09410972_story.html.

Forman James Jr. (2012) "Racial Critiques of Mass Incarceration: Beyond the New Jim Crow." *Faculty Scholarship Series*, paper 3599.

Formento Walter and Merino Gabriel (2011) *Crisis Financiera Global. La lucha por la configuración del orden mundial*. Bs. As.: Continente.

Foster, John Bellamy and McChesney, Robert (2009) "A New Deal under Obama." *Monthly Review* 60, no. 9: 2–3.

Foucault, Michel (1964) *Nietzsche, Marx, Freud*. Bs. As.: El cielo por asalto, 1995.

Foucault, Michel, (1964b) *History of Madness*. London: Routledge, 2006

Foucault, Michel, (1970) "The Order of Discourse." In *Untying the Text*, 51–78. Boston-London-Henley: Routledge & Kegan Paul.

Foucault, Michel, (1972) *Power/Knowledge: Selected Interviews and Other Writings, 1972–1977*. New York: Pantheon Books.

Foucault, Michel, (1975) *Discipline and Punish. The Birth of the Prison*. New York: Vintage Books.

Foucault, Michel, (1977/8) *Security, Territory, Population*. New York: Palgrave Macmillan.

Foucault, Michel, (1978) *Truth and Juridical Forms*. New York: Routledge.

Foucault, Michel, (1978/9) *The Birth of Biopolitics*. Thing. http://www.thing.net/~rdom/ ucsd/biopolitics/NeoliberalGovermentality.pdf.

Frégier, Honoré (1840) *Des classes dangereuses de la population dans les grandes villes et des moyens de les rendre meilleures*. París: Bailliere.

Freud, Sigmund (1905) "Three Essays on the Theory of Sexuality." Sigmund Freud. http://www.sigmundfreud.net/three-essays-on-the-theory-of-sexuality-pdf-ebook .jsp.

Gacto, Enrique (1989) "Aproximación al Derecho Penal de la Inquisición." In *Perfiles jurídicos de la Inquisición española*, 175–193. Madrid: Instituto de Historia de la Inquisición, Universidad Complutense de Madrid.

Galbraith, John K (1958) *The Affluent Society*. Boston- New York: Houghton Mifflin Company.

Galeano, Eduardo (2005) "The Empire of Consumption." *StreetVisuals.* https://street visuals.wordpress.com/2010/05/17/eduardo-galeano-the-empire-of-consumption -meditation-for-an-article/.

Galeano, Diego (2007) "En nombre de la seguridad: Lecturas sobre policía y formación estatal." In *Cuestiones de Sociología* no. 4: 102/125.

García Marín, José María (1989) "Magia e Inquisición, Derecho Penal y proceso inquisitorial en el siglo XVII." In *Perfiles jurídicos de la Inquisición española*: 205–275. Madrid: Instituto de Historia de la Inquisición de la Universidad Complutense.

García Ramírez, José Carlos (2009) "Siete tesis sobre la descolonización de los derechos humanos en Karl Marx. Un diagnóstico popular para evaluar la calidad de la democracia en América Latina." *Tabula Rasa* no. 11 (2009): 253–285.

García Méndez, Emilio (2006) "Epílogo." In Rusche, George and Kirchheimer, Otto (1930) *Pena y Estructura Social.* Bogota: Temis.

Gargarella, Roberto (1995) "Marxismo Analítico, el marxismo claro." *Doxa* no. 17–18: 231–256.

Gargarella, Roberto, (1997) "Political Liberalism, una brevísima aproximación." *Revista jurídica de la Universidad de Palermo* 2, no. 1–2.

Gargarella, Roberto (2005) *El derecho a la protesta. El primer derecho.* Bs. As.: Ad-Hoc.

Gargarella, Roberto, (2007) "Mano dura sobre el castigo. Autogobierno y comunidad." *Revista jurídica de la Universidad de Palermo* 8, no. 1.

Gargarella, Roberto, (2007b) "'Neopunitivismo' y (re)educación republicana. Respuesta a Diego Freedman." *Revista jurídica de la Universidad de Palermo* 8, no. 1.

Gargarella, Roberto, (2007c) "El derecho de resistencia en situaciones de carencia extrema." *Astrolabio: revista internacional de filosofía* no. 4: 1–29.

Gargarella, Roberto, (2011) "Jon Elster: El camino del descreimiento." *Claves de razón práctica*, Madrid no. 211: 42–49.

Gargarella, Roberto, (2011b) "Penal Coercion in Contexts of Social Injustice." *Criminal Law and Philosophy* 5, no. 1: 21–38.

Gargarella, Roberto, (2014) "Notas sobre marxismo, justicia y derecho penal." *Ideas de izquierda* no. 9.

Gargarella, Roberto and Queralt Jahel (2014) "Introducción. Por una vuelta a Cohen." In *Por una vuelta al socialismo. O cómo el capitalismo nos hace menos libres*, 7–25. Bs. As.: Siglo XXI.

Garland, David (1990) *Punishment and Modern Society.* Oxford: Clarenton Press, 1990.

Garland, David, (2001) *The Culture of Control Crime and Social Order in Contemporary Society.* Chicago: The University of Chicago Press.

Garland, David, (2001b) "Introduction: The Meaning of Mass Imprisonment." In *Mass Imprisonment: Social Causes and Consequences*, edited by David Garland: 1–3. London- Thousand Oaks-New Delhi: SAGE.

Garland, David, (2010) *Peculiar Institution: America's Death Penalty in an Age of Aboli-tion.* Cambridge-Massachusetts: The Belknap Press of Harvard University Press.

Garland, David, (2012) "Why Does the U.S. Have Capital Punishment?" *Embassy of the United States of America,* May 2012. http://photos.state.gov/libraries/amgov/133183/english/P_You_Asked_WhyCapitalPunishment_English.pdf.

Garland, David, (2016) "The American Penal State' (lectures, New York University Law School, Jan-May).

Garófalo, Raffaele (1891) *Criminología. Estudio sobre el delito y sobre la teoría de la repre-sión.* Montevideo- Buenos Aires: BdF, 2005.

Garófalo, Raffaele, (1895) *La superstizione socialista.* Torino: Roux Frassati.

Garzón López, Pedro (2012) "Pluralismo jurídico y derecho alternativo, dos modelos de análisis." *Universitas* no. 16: 215–244.

Gee, Taylor (2016) "Something Is Rotten in the State of Minnesota." Politico.com, July 16, 2016. http://www.politico.com/magazine/story/2016/07/minnesota-race-inequality-philando-castile-214053.

Geremek, Bronislaw (1986) *La piedad y la horca. Historia de la miseria y de la caridad en Europa.* Madrid: Alianza, 1989.

Germani, Gino (1980) *El concepto de marginalidad.* Bs. As.: Nueva Visión.

Gerstein, Josh (2014) "Obama: 'We tortured some folks'," *Politico,* August 1, 2014. http://www.politico.com/story/2014/08/john-brennan-torture-cia-109654.

Gibbs, J. (1978) "The Death Penalty: Retribution and Penal Policy." *The Journal of Crimi-nal Law, Criminology and Police Science* 69.

Gil Claros, Mario Germán (2009) "Para una biopolítica y una fenomenología de la ex-clusión y del Derecho" (lecture, Biblioteca Departamental Jorge Garcés Borrero, Cali, August 4, 2009).

Gill, T.D. and van Sliedregt, E. (2005). "Guantánamo Bay: A Reflection on the Legal Status and Rights of 'Unlawful Enemy Combatants," *Utrecht Law Review.* 1 no. 1: 28–54.

Gleeson, J. (2016) "Sentencing Seminar" (lectures, New York University Law School, Jan-May).

Goff, Phillip Atiba (2016) "The Science of Justice: Race, Arrests, and Police Use of Force." U.C.L.A. *Center for Policing Equity,* August 2016. http://policingequity.org/wp-content/uploads/2016/07/CPE_SoJ_Race-Arrests-UoF_2016-07-08-1130.pdf.

Goffman, Erving (1961) *Asylums: Essays on the Social Situations of Mental Patients and other Inmates.* Oxford: Doubleday.

Goldhagen, Daniel (1996) *Hitler's Willing Executioners.* New York: Vintage Books, 1997.

Goldhagen, Daniel, (2009) *Worse Than War, Genocide, Eliminationism and the Ongoing Assault of Humanity.* Nueva York: Public Affairs.

Goldstein, Joseph (2014) "Marijuana May Mean Ticket, Not Arrest, in New York City," *N.Y. Times*, November 9, 2014.

Gómez Crespo, Santiago (2012) "Prólogo, explicación y anotaciones." In *El Manifiesto Comunista* 3, no. 6.

Gordon, David (1976) "Class and the Economics of Crime." In *Whose Law What Order*. Nueva York: Wiley.

Marie Gottschalk (2006) "The Prison and the Gallows: The Politics of Mass Incarceration in America." Cambridge-New York-Melbourne-Madrid-Cape Town-Singapore: Cambridge University Press.

Gottschalk Marie, (2008) "Hiding in Plain Sight: American Politics and the Carceral State." *Annual Review of Political Science*: 235–260.

Gottschalk Marie, (2015) "Caught: The Prison State and the Lockdown of American Politics." Princeton-Oxford: Princeton University Press.

Gouldner, Alvin (1973) *For Sociology: Renewal and Critique in Sociology Today*. Harmondsworth: Penguin.

Graham Ruth (2015) "How Criminal Records Hold Americans Back," *Globe Correspondent*, March 8, 2015.

Gramsci, Antonio (1930) *Prison Notebooks* III. New York: Columbia University Press.

Gramsci, Antonio, (1948) *El materialismo histórico y la filosofía de Benedetto Croce*. México: Juan Pablos Editor, 1986.

Gramsci, Antonio, (1949) "Brief Notes on Machiavelli's Politics." In *Prison Notebooks*, 316–330. London: Elecbook.

Green Stuart (2011) "Just deserts in Unjust Societies. A Case Specific Approach." In *Philosophical Foundations of Criminal Law*, edited by Green, Stuart and Duff, Antony, 352–376. Oxford: Oxford University Press.

Greenberg, David (1976) "One-dimensional Marxist Criminology." *Theory and Society* 3, no. 4: 611–621.

Greenberg, David and Anderson, Nancy (1981) "Recent Marxist Books on Law. A Review Essay." *Contemporary Crises* no. 5: 293–322.

Grüner, Eduardo (2006) "Lecturas culpables. Marx(ismos) y la praxis del conocimiento." In *La teoría marxista hoy. Problemas y perspectivas*, edited by Boron, Atilio, Amadeo, Javier and González, Sabrina, 105–147. Bs. As.: CLACSO.

Grüner, Eduardo, (2012) "Conferencia" (lecture, *Jornadas cuestión criminal y marxismo*, Facultad de Derecho de la Universidad de Buenos Aires, 13 de agosto de 2012).

Gustafson, Kaaryn (2009) "The Criminalization of Poverty." *The Journal of Criminal Law and Criminology* 99, no. 3: 643–716.

Guy Bois, Georges (1989) *La revolución del año mil*. Barcelona: Crítica, 2000.

Hall, Stuart, (1980) *Drifting into a Law and Order Society*. London: Cobden Trust.

Hall, Stuart, (1997) "Visceral Cultures and Criminal Practices." In *Theoretical Criminology* no. 1: 453–478.

Hall, Wayne (2010) "What are the policy lessons of National Alcohol Prohibition in the United States, 1920–1933." In *Addiction History* no. 105: 1164–1173.

Hall, Stuart, Critcher, Charles, Jefferson, Tony, Clarke, John and Roberts, Brian (1978) *Policing the Crisis, Mugging the State, and Law and Order.* London: Macmillan.

Hamdan v. Rumsfeld (2006) 548 U.S. 557. https://supreme.justia.com/cases/federal/us/548/557/.

Harcourt Bernard E. (2013) "Punitive Preventive Justice: A Critique." In *Prevention and the Limits of the Criminal Law*, edited by Ashworth, Andrew, Zedner, Lucia and Tomlin, Patrick. Oxford: Oxford University Press.

Harcourt Bernard E., (2015) *Exposed: Desire and Disobedience in the Digital Age.* Cambridge, Massachusetts, London: Harvard University Press.

Harcourt Bernard E., (2016) "Conference" (lecture: New York University Law School, February 22, 2016).

"Harvard University Project Implicit" (2016), accessed June 30, 2016. https://implicit.harvard.edu/implicit/selectatest.html.

Harvey, David (2003) *The New Imperialism.* Oxford: Oxford University Press.

Harvey, David, (2005) *A Brief History of Neoliberalism.* Oxford: Oxford University Press.

Hay, Douglas, Linebaugh, Peter and Thompson, Edward (1975) *Albion's Fatal Tree. Crime and Society in Eighteenth-Century England.* London: Penguin.

Hayward, Keith (2004) *City Limits: Crime, Consumer Culture and the Urban Experience.* London: Glasshouse Press.

Heather, West and Sabol, William (2008) "Prisoners in 2007." *Bureau of Justice Statistics*, December 2008.

Heather, West and Sabol, William (2009) "Prison Inmates at Midyear 2008 – Statistical Tables." *Bureau of Justice Statistics*, March 2009.

Hegel, Georg (1808) "Who Thinks Abstractly?" In *Hegel, Texts and Commentary*, edited by Kaufmann, Walter, 113–118. Nueva York: Anchor Books, 1966.

Hegel, Georg, (1821) *Philosophy of Right.* Kitchener: Batoche Books, 2001.

Herrnstein, Richard and Murray, Charles (1994) *The Bell Curve.* Nueva York: The Free Press.

Hilferding, Rudolf (1910) *Finance Capital.* London-Boston-Henley: Routledge & Kegan Paul, 1981.

Hillyard, Paddy and Tombs, Steve (2004) "Beyond Criminology?" In *Beyond Criminology: Taking Harm Seriously,* edited by Hillyard, P., Pantazis, C.; Tombs, S. and Gordon, D., 10–29. London: Pluto Press.

Hinkelammert, Franz (2006) "La globalidad de la tierra y la estrategia de globalización." In *La teoría marxista hoy. Problemas y perspectivas*, edited by Boron, Atilio, Amadeo, Javier and González, Sabrina. Bs. As.: CLACSO.

Hirst, Paul (1975) "Radical Deviancy Theory and Marxism: A Reply to Taylor and Walton." In *Critical Criminology*, 238–245. New York: Routledge, 1975.

Hirst, Paul, (1975b) "Marx and Engels on Law, Crime and Morality." In *Critical Criminology*, 203–233. New York: Routledge, 1975.

Hirst, Paul, (1979) *On Law and Ideology* New Jersey: Humanities.

Hirst, Paul, (1980) "Law, Socialism and Rights." In *Radical Issues in Criminology*, 58–108. Oxford: Carlen M. Collison.

Hobsbawm, Eric (1962) *The Age of Revolution 1789–1848*. New York: Vintage Books, 1996.

Hobsbawm, Eric, (1969) *Bandits*. New York: Pantheon Books, 2000.

Hobsbawm, Eric, (1971) *En torno a los orígenes de la revolución industrial*. Madrid: Siglo XXI, 1988.

Hobsbawm, Eric, (1975) *The Age of Capital 1848–1875*. Great Britain: Weidenfeld. https://libcom.org/files/Eric%20Hobsbawm%20-%20Age%20Of%20Capital%20-%201848-1875.pdf.

Hobsbawm, Eric, (1977) *Industry and Empire*. New York: The New Press.

Hobsbawm, Eric, (1992) *Nations and Nationalism since 1780*. Cambridge: Cambridge University Press.

Hobsbawm, Eric, (2011) *How to Change the World, Reflection on Marx and Marxism*. New Heaven: Yale University Press.

Holder, Eric (2012) "Attorney General Eric Holder Speaks at Northwestern University School of Law," U.S. Department of Justice Website, March 5, 2012. https://www.justice.gov/opa/speech/attorney-general-eric-holder-speaks-northwestern-university-school-law.

Holder v. Humanitarian Law Project (2010), 561 U.S. 1.

Holland, Barbara (2004) *Gentlemen's Blood: A History of Dueling*. London-New York: Bloomsbury.

Holloway, John (2002) *Change the World Without Taking Power*. London: Pluto Press.

Horkheimer, Max and Adorno, Theodor (1944) *Dialectic of Enlightenment*. Stanford: Stanford University Press, 2002.

Horton, John and Platt, Tony (1986) "Crime and criminal justice under capitalism and socialism: Towards a marxist perspective." *Crime and Social Justice* no. 25: 115–135.

Houtart, Francois (2001) "Hacia una sociedad civil globalizada: la de abajo o la de arriba." In *Alternatives sud*. La Haya: Centre Tricontinental louvain-la neuve.

Hulsman, Louk (1991) "The abolitionist Case: Alternative Crime Policies." *Israel Law Review* no. 25: 681–709.

Human Right Watch (2010) "The Price of Freedom. Bail and Pretrial Detention of Low Income Non-Felony Defendants in New York City." Human Right Watch Website, accessed July 2, 2016. https://www.hrw.org/sites/default/files/reports/us1210webwcover_0.pdf.

Human Right Watch (2014) "Illusion of Justice." Human Right Watch Website, accessed July 21, 2014. https://www.hrw.org/report/2014/07/21/illusion-justice/human-rights-abuses-us-terrorism-prosecutions.

Huws, Ursula (2003) *The Making of a Cybertariat (Virtual Work in a Real World)*. New York-London: Monthly Review Press/The Merlin Press.

Iadicola, Peter (2009/10) "Controlling Crimes of Empire." *Social Justice* 36, no. 3: 98–110.

Ignatieff, Michael (1978) *A Just Measure of Pain, The Penitentiary in the Industrial Revolution*. London Macmillan.

INCITE-NATIONAL (2016) "Police Violence & Domestic Violence," accessed September 1, 2016. http://www.incite-national.org/.

International Centre for Prison Studies (2012) "Highest to Lowest – Prison Population Total," accessed April 19, 2016. http://www.prisonstudies.org/highest-to-lowest/prison-population-total?field_region_taxonomy_tid=All&=Apply.

International Committee of the Red Cross (2016), "Terrorism," accessed September 1, 2016. https://www.icrc.org/eng/resources/documents/faq/terrorism-faq-050504|.htm.

Iñigo Carrera, Nicolás (2003) "El concepto de clase obrera." *International Institute of Social History*, accessed April 19, 2016. http://www.iisg.nl/labouragain/documents/inigocarrera.pdf.

Jacobs James B. (2015) *The Eternal Criminal Record*. Cambridge-Massachusetts-London: Harvard University Press.

Jacobs James B. (2015b) "European Employment Discrimination based on Criminal Records II- Discretionary Bars." In *Resource Center*, January 13, 2015.

Jakobs, Günter and Meliá Cancio, Manuel (2003) *Derecho penal del enemigo*. Madrid: Civitas.

Jankovic, Ivan (1980) "Labor Market and Imprisonment." In *Punishment and Penal Discipline*, edited by Platt, Tony and Takagi, Paul, 93–104. Berkeley: Crime and Social Justice Associates.

Juliano, Mario (2012) "Los paralelismos entre el hurto de leña y la legislación contravencional argentina" (lecture, Facultad de Derecho de la Universidad de Buenos Aires, August 13, 2012).

Kaleem Jaweed (2012) "Police Spying Leaves New York Muslim Students 'Violated'," *Huffington Post*, February 24, 2012. http://www.huffingtonpost.com/2012/02/24/police-spying-new-york-muslim_n_1300379.html.

Kant, Immanuel (1785) *Groundwork of the Metaphysics of Morals*. New Haven and London: Yale University Press.

Karabel, Jerome (2015) "Police Killings Surpass the Worst Years of Lynching, Capital Punishment," *Huffpost Politics*, April 11, 2015.

Katz, Claudio (2000) "Una interpretación contemporánea de la ley de la tendencia decreciente de la tasa de ganancia." *Herramienta* no. 13.

Katzenstein, Mary and Waller, Maureen R. (2015) "Taxing the Poor: Incarceration, Poverty Governance, and the Seizure of Family Resources." *Perspectives on Politics* 13: 638–656.

Kelsen, Hans (1934) *Teoría pura del derecho. Introducción a los problemas de la ciencia jurídica.* Madrid: Trotta, 2011.

Kern, R. (1995) "Sentence Reform in Virginia." *Vera Institute 1 Federal Sentencing Reporter* 8, 2 Sep./Oct.

Kessler, Gabriel (2004) *Sociología del delito amateur.* Bs. As.: Paidós.

Kessler, Gabriel, (2010) "Delito, sentimiento de inseguridad y políticas públicas" (lecture, Facultad de Humanidades y Ciencias de la Educación de la Universidad Nacional de La Plata).

Kessler, Gabriel, (2011) *El sentimiento de inseguridad.* Bs. As.: Siglo XXI.

King, Peter (1987) "Newspaper Reporting, Prosecution Practice and Perceptions of Urban Crime: The Colchester Crime Wave of 1765." *Continuity and Change* no. 2: 423–454.

Kinsey, Richard (1978) "Marxism and the Law, Preliminary Analyses." *Br. J. Law & Society* no. 5: 202–227.

Kinsey, Richard, Lea, John, Picciotto, Sol and Young, Jock (1979) *Capitalism and the Rule of Law.* London: Hutchinson.

Klein, Naomi (2000) *No Logo. Taking Aim at the Brands Bullies.* Toronto: Vintage Canada.

Kohan, Néstor (2006) *Marxismo para principiantes.* Bs. As.: PierBitro.

Kohen, Alberto (1972) *Marxismo, Estado y Derecho.* Bs. As.: Ediciones Centro de Estudios.

Kohler-Hausmann, Julilly (2010) "'The Attila the Hun Law': New York's Rockefeller Drug Laws and the Making of a Punitive State." *Journal of Social History* 44, no. 1: 71–95.

Kohler-Hausmann, Julilly (2016) "Guns and Butter: The Welfare State, the Carceral State and the Politics of Exclusion." *Journal of American History* 102, no. 1: 87–99, 2015. http://jah.oxfordjournals.org/content/102/1/87.full.pdf+html.

Kramer, Heinrich and Sprenger, Jacobus (1486) *El martillo de las brujas para golpear a las brujas con poderosa masa.* Valladolid: Felmar, 1976.

LaFree, Gary (2002) "Too Much Democracy or Too Much Crime." *Law & Social Inquiry* 27, no. 4: 875–902.

La Ganga, Maria (2016) "C.I.A. Torture Program: Victims' Lawsuit Can Move Forward, Judge Says," *The Guardian*, April 22, 2016.

Langton, Lynn and Durose, Matthew (2013) "Police Behavior during Traffic and Street Stops, 2011. Special Report." *Bureau of Justice Statistics*, September 2013, http://www.bjs.gov/content/pub/pdf/pbtss11.pdf.

Laplanche, Jean and Pontalis, Jean-Bertrand (1996) *The Language of Psychoanalysis.* London: The Hogarth Press and the Institute of Psycho-Analysis.

Lappi-Seppälä Tapio, "American Exceptionalism in a Comparative Perspective" (unpublished paper).

Larrauri, Elena (1991) *La herencia de la criminología crítica.* Madrid: Siglo XXI, 2000.

Larrauri Elena and James Jacobs (2015) "Retention of DNA Profiles and Fingerprints – Europe and the U.S." In *Collateral Consequences Resource Center*, February 4, 2015.

Las Casas, Bartolomé de (1537) *Del único modo de atraer a todos los pueblos a la verdadera religión*. México: Fondo de Cultura Económica, 1972.

Laschi, Rudolfo and Lombroso, Cesare (1890) *Il delitto políttico e la revoluzioni*. París: Félix Alcan, 1892.

Lascoumes, Pierre and Weinberger, Jean-Claude (1978) "Delinquenza d'affaristi e problemi d' affari." *La Questione Crimínale* no. 1.

Lascoumes, Pierre and Zander, Hartwig (1984) *Marx, du "bol de vois" à la critique du droit*. París: Les Presses Universitaires de France.

Lea, John and Young, Jock (1984) *What is to Be Done about Law and Order?* Harmondsworth: Penguin.

Le Bon, Gustave (1895) *The Psychology of Peoples*. New York: The Macmillan Co., 1895.

LeBron James (2014), "'I Can't Breathe' T-shirt the Latest Display of Politics on the Playing Field," *The Washington Times*, December 4, 2014. http://www.washingtontimes.com/news/2014/dec/4/politics-playing-field/.

Lecourt, Dominique (1980) "¿Cómo defender el materialismo histórico? (a propósito de un libro de G A Cohen)." *Revue philosophique de la France et de l'étranger* no. 2.

Legal Action Center Study (2016) "Challenges to Re-Entry for Formerly Incarcerated" (lecture: Rev Law Conference, Yale University, February 19, 2016).

Lemmer, Edwin (1951) *Social Pathology. A Systematic Approach to the Theory of Sociopathic Behavior*. Nueva York: McGraw-Hill.

Lenin, Vladimir Ilich (1916) *Imperialism. The Highest Stage of Capitalism*. Sidney: Resistance Book, 1999.

Lenin, Vladimir Ilich, (1917) *The State and Revolution*. Pekin: The Foreign Language Institute, 1976.

Lenton, Diana, "El Estado se construyó sobre un genocidio," *Página/12*, October 10, 2011.

Lerman Amy E. and Weaver Vesla (2014) "The Carceral State and American Political Development 2015." In *The Oxford Handbook of American Political Development*, edited by Lieberman, Robert, Mettler, Suzanne and Richard Valelly. New York: Oxford, University Press.

Levene, Ricardo (1924) *Introducción a la historia del derecho indiano*. Bs. As.: Valerio Abeledo.

Levi Strauss, Claude (1955) *Tristes Tropiques*. New York: Criterion Books.

Levrero, Renato (1979) "Marx, Engels y la cuestión nacional." In *Imperio y colonia. Escritos sobre Irlanda*. México: Cuadernos de Pasado y Presente no. 72.

Lewis, Robert (2013) "No Bail Money Keeps Poor People Behind Bars." *WNYC*, September 19, 2013. http://www.wnyc.org/story/bail-keeps-poor-people-behind-bars/.

Lewkowicz, Ignacio (2005) *Los prisioneros de la expulsión, de la normalización al depósito* en *Pensar sin Estado. La subjetividad en la era de la fluidez*. Bs. As.: Paidós.

Leyret, Henry (1909) *Las sentencias del magistrado Magnaud. Reunidas y comentadas.* Madrid: Hijos de Reus Editores.

Linebaigh, Peter (1976) "Karl Marx, the theft of Wood and Working Class Composition. A Contribution to the Current Debate." *Crime and Social Justice* no. 5: 5–16.

Lizarraga, Fernando (2006) *La justicia en el pensamiento de Ernesto Che Guevara.* La Habana: Editorial de Ciencias Sociales.

Lizarraga, Fernando, (2012) "Estudio introductorio. Pérdida y recuperación de la utopía" In *Del socialismo utópico al socialismo científico.* Bs. As.: Luxemburg.

LoBianco, Tom (2016) "Report: Aide Says Nixon's War on Drugs Targeted Blacks, Hippies." *CNN*, March 24, 2016. http://edition.cnn.com/2016/03/23/politics/john -ehrlichman-richard-nixon-drug-war-blacks-hippie/.

Lombroso, Cesare (1887) *L'uomo delinquiente in rapporto all'antropologia, alla giuris- prudenza ed alla psiquiatría,* Torino: Fratelli Bocca.

Lombroso, Cesare, (1894) *Los anarquistas.* Barcelona: Jucar, 1978.

Lombroso, Cesare and Ferrerro, Guglielmo (1915) *Criminal Woman, the Prostitute, and the Normal Woman.* Durham, NC: Duke University Press, 2004.

López Castellano, Fernando (2004) *Las raíces históricas del tercer sector.* Granada: Fun- dación Once.

Lowery, Wesley (2016) "Aren't More White People than Black People Killed by Police? Yes, But No," *The Washington Post,* July 11 2016. https://www.washingtonpost.com/ news/post-nation/wp/2016/07/11/arent-more-white-people-than-black-people -killed-by-police-yes-but-no/?utm_term=.a1ef4cc5c749.

Lowery, Wesley (2016) "Korryn Gaines, Cradling Child and Dhotgun Is Fatally Shot by Police," *The Washington Post,* August 2 2016. https://www.washingtonpost.com/ news/post-nation/wp/2016/08/02/korryn-gaines-is-the-ninth-black-woman-shot -and-killed-by-police-this-year/?utm_term=.1f43f880a014.

Luchía, Corina (2004) "Aportes teóricos sobre el rol de la propiedad comunal en la transición al capitalismo." *Mundo Agrario* 5, no. 9.

Luxemburgo, Rosa (1925) *Introducción a la economía política.* Madrid: Siglo XXI, 1974.

Macaskill Ewen and Dance Gabriel (2013) "NSA Filed: Decoded. What the Rev- elations Mean for You," *The Guardian,* November 1 2013. http://www.theguardian .com/world/interactive/2013/nov/01/snowden-nsa-files-surveillance-revelations -decoded#section/1.

Maclachlan, Colin (1974) *Criminal Justice in the Eighteenth Century. Mexico: A study of the Tribunal of the Acordada.* Berkeley-Los Angeles-London: University of California Press.

Mandel, Ernest (1967) *The Formation of the Economic Thought of Karl Marx.* London- New York: Verso.

Mansilla, Anastasio (1965) *Comentarios a la sección séptima del tomo I de 'El Capital'.* La Habana: Publicaciones Económicas.

Manzanos Bilbao, César (2002) "Funciones y objetivos de las prisiones. La cárcel contra el Estado de Derecho." *Hika* no. 133.

Marat, Jean Paul (1780) *Plan de Legislation Criminelle*. Kessinger Publishing, 2010.

Marcuse, Herbert (1954) *El hombre unidimensional*, Bs. As., Planeta, 1993.

Mari, Eduardo (1983) *La Problemática del castigo: el discurso de Jeremy Bentham y Michel Foucault*. Bs. As.: Hachette.

Markowitz, Eric (2006) "The FBI Now Has the Largest Biometric Database in the World. Will it Lead to More Surveillance?" IBT, 5 April 2006. http://www.ibtimes.com/fbi-now-has-largest-biometric-database-world-will-it-lead-more-surveillance-2345062.

Marx, Karl (1835) "Reflections of a Young Man on the Choice of Profession." Marxists Internet Archive, accessed April 15, 2016. https://www.marxists.org/archive/marx/works/download/Marx_Young_Marx.pdf.

Marx, Karl, (1842) "Debates on the Law on the Theft of Wood," Marxists Internet Archive, accessed April 15, 2016. https://www.marxists.org/archive/marx/works/download/Marx_Rheinishe_Zeitung.pdf.

Marx, Karl, (1843) "From the Mosel." Marxists Internet Archive, accessed April 15, 2016. https://marxists.anu.edu.au/archive/marx/works/1843/01/15.htm.

Marx, Karl, (1844) "On the Jewish Question." Marxists Internet Archive, accessed April 15, 2016. https://www.marxists.org/archive/marx/works/1844/jewish-question/.

Marx, Karl, (1844b) *Critique of Hegel's Philosophy of Right'*. Cambridge-London-New York-New Rochelle-Melbourne-Sidney: Cambridge University Press, 1982.

Marx, Karl, (1844c) *Economic and Philosophic Manuscripts of 1844.*, First Start Publishing eBook, 2012.

Marx, Karl, (1845) *Theses on Feuerbach*. Peking: Foreign Languages Press, 1976.

Marx, Karl, (1847) *The Poverty of Philosophy*. Moscow: Foreign Langiages Publishing House, 1876. https://www.marxists.org/archive/marx/works/download/pdf/Poverty-Philosophy.pdf.

Marx, Karl, (1848) *"The Revolutions of 1848."* Marxists Internet Archive, accessed April 15, 2016. https://www.marxists.org/archive/marx/works/sw/penguin/revolutions-1848.htm.

Marx, Karl, (1848) *The Communist Manifesto*, accessed July 7, 2016. https://www.marxists.org/archive/marx/works/download/pdf/Manifesto.pdf

Marx, Karl, (1848b) *The Holy Family or Critique of Critical Critique*. Morcow: Foreign Languages Publishing House.

Marx, Karl, (1848/49) "Articles from the Neue Rheinische Zeitung." Marxists Internet Archive, accessed April 15, 2016 https://www.marxists.org/archive/marx/works/subject/newspapers/neue-rheinische-zeitung.htm.

Marx, Karl, (1849) "Speech in Defense." In *Marx and Engels Collected Works*, VI, 232–245. Moscú: Progress Publishers.

Marx, Karl, (1849b) "A Bourgeois Document." Marxists Internet Archive, accessed April 15, 2016. https://www.marxists.org/archive/marx/works/1849/01/04.htm.

Marx, Karl, (1850) *The Class Struggles in France*. Cambridge: The Electric Book Company Ltd., 2001.

Marx, Karl, (1852) *The Eighteenth Brumaire of Louis Bonaparte*. Mountain View: Socialist Labor Party of America, 2003.

Marx, Karl, (1852b) "Revelations Concerning the Communist Trial in Cologne." Marxists Internet Archive, accessed April 15, 2016. https://marxists.anu.edu.au/archive/marx/works/1853/revelations/index.htm.

Marx, Karl, (1853) "Capital Punishment – Mr. Cobden's Pamphelt – Regulation of the Bank of England." Marxists Internet Archive, accessed April 15, 2016. https://www.marxists.org/archive/marx/works/1853/02/18.htm.

Marx, Karl, (1853b) "The East India Company – Its History and Results." Marxists Internet Archive, accessed April 15, 2016. https://www.marxists.org/archive/marx/works/1853/07/11.htm.

Marx, Karl, (1855) "Ireland's Revenge." Marxists Internet Archive, accessed April 15, 2016. https://www.marxists.org/archive/marx/works/1855/03/16.htm.

Marx, Karl, (1857) "Investigation of Tortures in India." Marxists Internet Archive, accessed April 15, 2016. https://www.marxists.org/archive/marx/works/1857/09/17.htm.

Marx, Karl, (1857b) "The Revolt in India." Marxists Internet Archive, accessed April 15, 2016. https://www.marxists.org/archive/marx/works/1858/10/01.htm.

Marx, Karl, (1857c) "Whose Atrocities?" Marxists Internet Archive, accessed April 15, 2016. https://www.marxists.org/archive/marx/works/1857/04/10.htm.

Marx, Karl, (1858) "Imprisonment of Lady Bulwer-Lytton." Marx Engels Public Archive Net. accessed April 15, 2016. http://marxengels.public-archive.net/en/ME1074en.html.

Marx, Karl, (1858b) "The British Government and the Slave-Trade." Marxists Internet Archive, accessed April 15, 2016. https://www.marxists.org/archive/marx/works/1858/07/02.htm.

Marx, Karl, (1858c) "Taxation in India." Marxists Internet Archive, accessed April 15, 2016. https://www.marxists.org/archive/marx/works/1858/07/23.htm.

Marx, Karl, (1858d) "Free Trade and Monopoly." Marxists Internet Archive, accessed April 15, 2016. https://www.marxists.org/archive/marx/works/1858/09/25.htm.

Marx, Karl, (1859) "From Population, Crime and Pauperism." Marxists Internet Archive, accessed April 15, 2016. www.marxists.org/archive/marx/works/1859/09/16.htm.

Marx, Karl, (1859b) *A Contribution to The Critique of Political Economy*. Moscow: Progress Publishers, 1993.

Marx, Karl, (1861) "The Intervention in Mexico." Marxists Internet Archive, accessed April 15, 2016. https://www.marxists.org/archive/marx/works/1861/11/23.htm.

Marx, Karl, (1861–3) "Digression: (On Productive Labour)." Marxists Internet Archive, accessed April 15, 2016. https://marxists.anu.edu.au/archive/marx/works/1861/eco nomic/ch33.htm.

Marx, Karl, (1867) *Capital. A Critique of Political Economy I.* Chicago: Charles H. Kerr & Company, 1909.

Marx, Karl, (1867b) *Teorías sobre la plusvalía (v. IV of Capital)*, accessed April 4, 2016. http://ecopol.sociales.uba.ar/files/2013/09/Marx_Teor%C3%ADas-sobre-la-plus val%C3%ADa-I.pdf.

Marx, Karl, (1867c) *Capital. A Critique of Political Economy III.* New York, Cosmo Classics, 2007.

Marx, Karl, (1871) *The Civil War in France.* Peking: Foreign Language Press, 1977.

Marx, Karl, (1875) *Critique of the Gotha Program.* Cambridge: The Electric Book, 2001.

Marx, Karl and Engels, Friedrich (1845) *La Ideología Alemana.* Bs. As.: Rueda de Editores, 2005.

Mather, Kate and Queally, James (2016) "More than a Third of People Shot by L.A. Police Last Year Were Mentally Ill, LAPD Report Finds," *L.A. Times*, March 1 2016.

Mathiesen, Thomas (1987) *Prison on Trial.* Winchester: Waterside Press, 2000.

Mauer, Marc and Cole, David (2015) "How to Lock up Fewer People," *N.Y. Times*, May 24, 2015.

Mayer Jane (2009) "The Predator War. What Are the Risks of the C.I.A.'s Covert Drone Program?" *The New Yorker*, October 26, 2009. http://www.newyorker.com/ magazine/2009/10/26/the-predator-war.

McManus, Jane (1978) "The Emergence and Non-Emergence of Legislation," *Br. J. Law & Society* no. 5: 185–201.

McKernan, Mary Ratcliffe, Caroline and Cellini, Stephanie (2009) "Transitioning In and Out of Poverty." *Urban Institute*, September 10, 2009. http://www.urban.org/ research/publication/transitioning-and-out-poverty.

Meillassoux, Claude (1991) *Les espectres de Malthus.* Orstom: EDI Ceped.

Melossi, Dario (1980) "Cárcel y trabajo en Europa y en Italia en el período de la formación del modo de producción capitalista." In *The Prison and The Factory: Origins of the Penitentiary System*, 27–132. London: Macmillan, 1981.

Melossi, Dario, (1980b) "The Penal Question in Capital." In *Punishment and Penal Discipline*, edited by Platt, Tony and Takagi, Paul. Berkeley: Center for Research on Criminal Justice.

Melossi, Dario, (1984) "¿Está en crisis la criminología crítica?." *Nuevo Foro Penal* no. 26: 511–521.

Melossi, Dario, (1990) *El Estado del control social.* Madrid: Siglo XXI, 1992.

Melossi, Dario, (1991) "Weak Leviathan and Strong Democracy; or Two Styles of Social Control." (lecture, Law and Society Conference, June 26–29).

Melossi, Dario, (1997) "La radicación ('radicamento'- 'embeddness') cultural del control social (o de la imposibilidad de la traducción) reflexiones a partir de la comparación de la cultura italiano y norteamericana con respecto al control social." *Delito y Sociedad* 6, no. 9/10: 12–14.

Merino, Gabriel (2014) *Crisis del Orden Mundial y encrucijada Nacional-Latinoamericana. Aportes para el análisis de la situación actual de crisis y oportunidad histórica.* Paraná: Ediciones Universitarias Nacional de Misiones.

Merriman, John (2006) *Police Stories: Building the French State, 1815–1851.* Oxford: Oxford University Press.

Merton, Robert (1949) *Teoría y estructura social.* México: Fondo de Cultura Económica, 1992.

Meszaros, Istvan (2002) *Para alem do capital,* San Pablo, Boitempo.

Michael, Javen Fortner (2015) "Black Silent Majority: The Rockefeller Drug Laws and the Politics of Punishment." *Harvard University Press.*

Michalowski, Raymond (1977) "Repression and Criminal Justice in Capitalist America." *Sociological Inquiry* no. 46: 95–106.

Miliband, Ralph (1969) *Marx and the State.* Marxists Internet Archive, accessed April 17, 2016. https://www.marxists.org/archive/miliband/1965/xx/state.htm.

Miller, Jaques-Alain (2010) *Extimidad.* Bs. As.: Paidós.

Miller, Lisa L. (2015) "What's Violence Got to Do with It? Inequality, Punishment and State Failure in U.S. Politics." *Punishment & Society* 17, no. 2: 184–210. http://pun.sagepub.com/content/17/2/184.abstract.

Mir Puig, Santiago (2008) *Derecho Penal. Parte General.* Montevideo: B de f.

Mishra, Ramesh (1975) "Marx and Welfare." *Sociological Review* no. 23: 287–313.

Mitrani, Sam (2013) *The Rise of the Chicago Police Department: Class and Conflict, 1850–1894.* Illinois: University of Illinois Press.

Moore, Robert Ian (1987) *La formación de una sociedad represora. Poder y disidencia en la Europa occidental, 950–1250.* Barcelona: Crítica, 1989.

Moore, Nina M. (2015) *The Political Roots of Racial Tracking in American Criminal Justice.* New York: Cambridge University Press.

Morell, Antonio (2002) *La legitimación social de la pobreza.* Barcelona: Anthropos.

Moro, Tomas (1516) *Utopia* Project Gutenberg, accessed April 16, 2016. http://www.gutenberg.org/files/2130/2130-h/2130-h.htm.

Morrison, Wayne (2006) *Criminology, Civilization and the New World Order.* London: Routledge-Cavendish.

Moulier- Boutang, Yann (1998) *From slavery to Wage Labour.* Rome: Manifestolibri, 2002.

Muñoz Gómez, Jesús (1992) *El concepto de pena. Un análisis desde la criminología crítica.* Bogotá: Forum Pacis.

Murphy, Jeffrie (1973) "Marxism and Retribution." *Philosophy & Public Affairs* 2, no. 3: 217–243.

Mustard, David Racial (2011) "Ethnic, and Gender Disparities in Sentencing: Evidence From the U.S. Federal Courts." Journal of *Law & Economy 44*.

Navarrete, Calderón Caridad (1984) *La prevención de las transgresiones de la ley entre los menores de edad*. La Habana: Departamento de Evaluación de la Dirección de Menores.

Nelken, David (2009) "Comparative Criminal Justice: Beyond Ethnocentrism and Relativism." *European Journal of Criminology* 6, no.4: 291–311

Neuman, Elias (1997) *Los que viven del delito y los otros, la delincuencia como industria*. Bogotá: Temis, 2005.

Nightingale, Carl (1993) *On the Edge*. Nueva York: Basic Books.

Novak, Daniel A. (1978) *The Wheel of Servitude: Black Forced Labor after Slavery*. Lexington: University Press of Kentuky.

Nun, José, (1969) "Superoblación relativa, ejercito industrial de reserva y masa marginal." *Revista Latinoamericana de Sociología* 5, no. 2: 180–225.

Nun, José, (1999) "El futuro del empleo y la tesis de la masa marginal." *Desarrollo Económico* 38, no. 152: 985–1004.

Nun, José, (2001) *Marginalidad y exclusión social*. Bs. As.: Fondo de Cultura Económica.

Nun, José; Murmis, Miguel and Marin Juan Carlos (1968) *La marginalidad en América Latina*. Bs. As.: Instituto Torcuato Di Tella.

O' Brien, Patricia (1978) "Crime and Punishment as Historical Problems." *Journal of Social History* 11, no. 4: 508–520.

O' Connor, James (1973) *The Fiscal Crisis of the State*. Nueva York: St. Martin's Press.

Ogletree, Charles J. and Sarat, Agustin (2012) "Introduction: Lives on the Line: From Capital Punishment to Life without Parole." In *Life Without Parole: America's New Death Penalty*, 1–24. New York-London: New York University Press.

Ojeda, Segovia Lautaro (2013) "Tratamiento mediático de los delitos de cuello blanco o del poder." *Chasqui. Revista latinoamericana de comunicación* no. 122: 31–38.

Parenti, Christian (2008) *Lockdown America: Police and Prisons in the Age of Crisis*. New York: Verso.

Pashukanis, Evgeny (1924) "'Law and Violation of Law', The General Theory of Law and Marxism." Marxists Internet Archive, accessed April 17, 2016. https://www.marxists .org/archive/pashukanis/1924/law/cho7.htm.

Pavarini, Massimo (1975) "Ricerca in tema di criminalita económica." *La cuestione criminale* no. 3: 537–545.

Pavarini, Massimo, (1980) "La invención penitenciaria: la experiencia de los Estados Unidos de América en la primera mitad del siglo XIX." In *Cárcel y fábrica, los orígenes del sistema penitenciario (siglos XVI–XIX)*, 133–233. México: Siglo XXI.

Pavarini, Massimo, (1980) *Control y dominación. Teorías criminológicas burguesas y proyecto hegemónico*. Bs. As.: Siglo XXI, 2003.

Pavarini, Massimo, (1995) *Los confines de la cárcel*. Montevideo: Instituto Iberoamericano de Estudios Criminales.

Pavarini, Massimo, (2006) *Un arte abyecto. Ensayo sobre el gobierno de la penalidad*. Bs. As.: Ad-Hoc.

P.B.S (2016) "Hoover and the F.B.I," accessed August 1, 2016. http://www.pbs.org/ hueypnewton/people/people_hoover.html.

Pearce, Frank (1976) *Crimes of the Powerful: Marxism, Crime and Deviance*. London: Pluto Press.

Pegoraro, Juan (2002) "Teoría sociológica y Delito Organizado. El eslabón perdido" *Encrucijadas* no. 19 (2002).

Pegoraro, Juan, (2008) "Las paradojas del control social punitivo." *Delito y Sociedad* no. 25: 7–34.

Pegoraro, Juan, (2010) "La excepcionalidad del pensamiento de Karl Marx acerca del delito y la política penal." *Revista Electrónica del Instituto de Investigaciones Ambrosio L. Gioja* IV, no. 5, accessed April 17, 2016. http://www.derecho.uba.ar/revistagioja/ articulos/R0005A004_0007_investigacion.pdf.

Pegoraro, Juan, (2011) "El lazo social del delito económico, un enfoque sociológico del orden social." *Delito y Sociedad* no. 31: 7–8.

Pegoraro, Juan, (2012) "Marx y el delito económico organizado." (lecture, Facultad de Derecho de la Universidad de Buenos Aires, May 21, 2012).

"Penn Law Quattrone Center for the Fair Administration of Justice Plea," accessed June 30, 2016. https://www.law.upenn.edu/institutes/quattronecenter/.

Petersilia, Joan (2003) "Introduction and Overview. The Emerging Importance of Prisoner Reentry to Crime and Community." In *When Prisoners Come Home. Parole and Prisoner Reentry*, 3–20. Oxford-New York: Oxford University Press.

Piketty, Thomas (2013) *Capital in the 21st century*. Cambridge: Harvard University Press, 2014.

Pinto, Nick (2012) "Bail is Busted: How Jail Really Works." *The Voice*, April 25, 2012. http://www.villagevoice.com/news/bail-is-busted-how-jail-really-works-6434704.

Pirenne, Jacques (1961) *Historia Universal* II. Barcelona: Éxito.

Pitch, Tamar (1989) *Responsabilità limitate. Attori, conflitti, giustizia penale*. Milano: Feltrinelli.

Piven, France and Cloward, Richard (1969) *Regulating the Poor. The Functions of Public Welfare*. Nueva York: Vintage, 1993.

Platt, Anthony (1969) *The Child Savers: The Invention of Delinquency*. Chicago: University of Chicago Press, 1977.

Polanyi, Karl (1944) *The Great Transformation. The Political and Economic Origins of Our Time*. Boston: Beacon Press, 1957.

Polischuk, Sebastian (2015) "El intento de aplicar la Ley Antiterrorista sobre el pueblo mapuche en Argentina." *Resumen Latinoamericano*, April 25, 2015. http://www .resumenlatinoamericano.org/2015/04/25/el-intento-de-aplicar-la-ley-antiter rorista-sobre-el-pueblo-mapuche-en-argentina-el-caso-de-la-comunera-relmu -namku/.

Portero, Ashley (2013) "Drug Offenses, Not Violent Crime, Filling Up Federal Prisons." *International Business Times* no. 30.

Poulantzas, Nicos (1969) "Marxist Examination of the Contemporary State and Law and the Question of the Alternative." In *The Poulantzas Reader. Marxism, Law and the State*. 25–46. London- New York: Verso, 2008.

Pound, John (1971) *Poverty and Vagrancy in Tudor England*. Hong Kong: Longman, 1978.

Poynter, Ralph (2016) "Political Prisoners" (lecture: Rev Law Conference, NH, Yale University, February 2016).

Prado, Carolina (2004) "Dos concepciones del castigo en torno a Marx." In *Mitologías y Discursos sobre el Castigo. Historia del presente y posibles escenarios*, edited by Rivera, Iñaki, 113–130. Barcelona: Anthropos.

Prins, Adolphe (1886) *Criminalité et repression*, Bruselas: Librairie Europeenne Muaquardt.

Quigley, Bill "Fourteen Examples of Racism in Criminal Justice System," *Huffington Post*, May 25, 2011. http://www.huffingtonpost.com/bill-quigley/fourteen-examples -of-raci_b_658947.html.

Quinney Richard "Crime Control in Capitalist Society: A Critical Philosophy of Legal Order." In *Critical Criminology*, 181–203. New York: Routledge, 1975.

Raffin, Marcelo (2012) "Conference" (lecture, *Jornadas cuestión criminal y marxismo*, Facultad de Derecho de la Universidad de Buenos Aires, August 13, 2012).

Rasul v. Bush (2004) 542 U.S. 466 (2004).

Rau, Victor (2007) "En los orígenes de la teoría marxista." In *Los debates de la Dieta Renana*. Barcelona: Gedisa.

Real Academia de la Historia (1807) *Las Siete Partidas del Rey Don Alfonso X El Sabio cotejado con varios códices antiguos* III. Madrid: Imprenta Real.

Real Academia de la Historia (1861) *Cortes de los Antiguos Reinos de León y de Castilla, 1863–1882* V. Madrid: Imprenta y Estereotipia de M. Rivadeneyra.

Recopilación de las Leyes de los Reynos de las Indias (1680). Gabriel Bernat Website, accessed April 16, 2016. http://www.gabrielbernat.es/espana/leyes/rldi/indice/in-dice.html.

Rekers, Romina Frontalini (2012) "Populismo y castigo penal." *Pensamiento Penal*, accessed April 17, 2016. http://www.pensamientopenal.com.ar/system/files/2012/10/doctrina34815.pdf.

Renner, Karl (1949) *The Institutions of Private Law and Their Social Functions*. Boston: Kahn-Freund.

Retamal, Christian (1997) "Ciudades soñadas, ciudades temidas, elementos sobre marginalidad y modernidad." In *Congreso Latinoamericano sobre Filosofía y Democracia*, edited by Giannini, Humberto and Bonzi, Patricia. Santiago de Chile: LOM.

Reyes, Roman (1983) *Cien años después de Marx*. Madrid: Akal.

Rheingold, Howard (2004) *Smart Mobs: The Next Social Revolution*. Cambridge: Basic Books.

Rice, Zak (2015) "The Police Are Killing One Group at a Staggering Rate, and Nobody Is Talking About It." *Indentities Mic*, February 5, 2015. https://mic.com/articles/109894/the-police-are-killing-one-group-at-a-staggering-rate-and-nobody-is-talking-about-it#.BJaOI8bix.

Rochefort, David (1981) "Progressive and Social Control Perspectives on Social Welfare." *Social Service Review* 55, no. 4: 568–592.

Rodríguez, Esteban (2008) *Vida lumpen bestiario de la multitud*. Bs. As.: Edulo.

Rodríguez, Esteban, (2008b) "Las estrategias securitarias de los grupos desaventajados." *Delito y Sociedad* 17, no. 26: 117–136.

Rodríguez Giles, Ana (2010) "Aportes al estudio de la marginalidad socioeconómica en la temprana modernidad." *Trabajos y Comunicaciones* no. 36: 333–342.

Rodríguez, Esteban, (2012) "Circuitos carcelarios, el encarcelamiento masivo-selectivo, Preventivo y rotativo en la argentina." *Question* 1 no. 36: 81–96.

Rodríguez Giles, Ana, (2011) "La estigmatización de los mendigos en el siglo de oro. Análisis de Guzmán de Alfarache (1599)." *Anales de historia antigua, medieval y moderna* no. 43: 191–210.

Rodríguez Giles, Ana (2013) "La socialización marginal entre los criados. Análisis de una relación a través de algunos ejemplos presentes en el 'Guzmán de Alfarache.'" *Cuadernos de historia moderna* no. 38: 121–137.

Roland G. Fryer (2016) "An Empirical Analysis of Racial Differences in Police Use of Force." *National Bureau of Economic Research*, July 2016. http://www.nber.org/papers/w22399.pdf.

Rosdolsky, Roman (1968) *Génesis y Estructura de El Capital de Marx*. Bs. As.: Siglo XXI, 2004.

Rosenthal Elisabeth (2016) "When the Hospital Fires the Bullet," *N.Y. Times*, February 12, 2016.

Roth Randolph (2009 *American Homicide*. Cambridge-Massachusetts-London: The Belknap Press of Harvard University Press.

Rothe, Dawn and Friedrichs, David (2006) "The State of the Criminology of Crimes of the State." *Social Justice* 33, no. 1: 147–161.

Rovere, Richard (1959) *Senator Joe McCarthy*. Berkeley: University of California Press.

Rudé, George (1964) *The Crowd in History: A Study of Popular Disturbances in France and England, 1730–1848*. London: Serif, 1995.

Rusche, George (1930) "Labor Market and Penal Sanction: Thoughts on the Sociology of Punishment." *Social Justice* no. 10 (1978): 2–8.

Rusche, George, (1933) "Prison Revolts or Social Policy: Lessons from America." *Social Justice* no. 13, (1980): 41–44.

Rusche, George and Kirchheimer, Otto (1938) *Punishment and Social Structure*. New Brunswick-London: Transaction Publishers, 2009.

Rusconi, Maximiliano (2009) *Derecho Penal. Parte General*. Bs. As.: Ad hoc.

Russell, Jeffrey B. (1980) *A History of Witchcraft: Sorcerers, Heretics, Pagans*. London: Thames and Hudson.

Sacks, Ethan (2016) "Eric Garner's Dister and Brother Release Song, 'I Can't Breathe' on Two-Year Anniversary of His Death at Hands of Police," *N.Y. Daily News*, July 11, 2016. http://www.nydailynews.com/entertainment/music/eric-garner-sister-broth er-release-song-breathe-article-1.2707421.

Said, Edward (1996) *Cultura e Imperialismo*. Barcelona: Anagrama.

Salas, Minor (2006) "Interdisciplinariedad de las Ciencias Sociales y Jurídicas: ¿im- postura intelectual o aspiración científica?" *Revista de Ciencias Sociales* III-IV, no. 113–114: 55–69.

Salles, Vania (2005) "Dos estudios agrarios de Max Weber." *Sociológica* no. 59: 233–248.

Sánchez Ascona, Jorge (1976) *Derecho, poder y marxismo*. México: Porrúa.

Sanz Rozalén, Vicente (2000) *Propiedad y desposesión campesina*. Valencia: UNED.

Savage, Charlie (2014) *"Judge Dismisses Suit Against Administration Officials Over Drone Strikes," N.Y. Times*, April 4, 2014. http://www.nytimes.com/2014/04/05/world/judge -dismisses-suit-against-administration-officials-over-drone-strikes.html?_r=0.

Scaron, Pedro (1972) "Karl Marx Friedrich Engels. Materiales para la historia de Améri- ca Latina." *Cuadernos de Pasado y Presente* no. 30.

Schafer, Stephen (1969) *Theories in Criminology*. Nueva York: Random House.

Schur, Edwin (1971) *Labeling Deviant Behavior*. London: Harper y Row.

Schwendinger, Herman and Schwendinger, Julia (1970) "Defenders of Order or Guard- ians of Human Rights." *Issues in Criminology* 5, no. 2 123–157.

Sedeillán, Gisela, "Las leyes sobre vagancia, Control policial y práctica judicial en el ocaso de la frontera (Tandil 1872–1881)." *Trabajos y Comunicaciones 2006–2007* no. 32–33: 141–166.

Sellin, Johan Thorsten (1944) *Pioneering in Penology, The Amsterdam Houses of Correc- tion in the Sixteenth and Seventeenth Centuries*. Philadelphia: Pennsylvania Press.

Semelin, Jaques (2010) "De la matanza al proceso genocida." *Investigaciones I*: 45–57.

Sentencing Commission (2013), "Suggestions of the Sentencing Commission to the Congress," November 26, 2013, accessed April 13, 2016. http://www.ussc.gov/sites/de fault/files/pdf/news/congressional-testimony-and-reports/submissions/20130918 _SJC_Mandatory_Minimums.pdf.

Severin, Carlos (1976) "Las Cifras Doradas de la Delincuencia" (lecture, European Con- sortium for Research, Lovaina, 1976).

Sewel, William (1980) *Work & Revolution in France. The Language of Labor from the Old Regime to 1848*. Cambridge: Cambridge University Press.

Sgubbi, Filippo (1975) "La tutela penale di 'interessi difusi.'" *La Questione Criminale* 3: 439–484.

Shamas, Diala and Arastu, Nermeen (2014) "Mapping Muslims. NYP Spying and its Impact on American Mulims," *CUNY.*

Shapiro, David (2013) "Banking on Bondage: Private Prisons and Mass Incarceration." A.C.L.U. Website, accessed April 17. https://www.aclu.org/files/assets/bankingonbondage_20111102.pdf.

Shen, Aviva (2013) "White People Stopped By New York Police Are More Likely To Have Guns Or Drugs Than Minorities." *Think Progress*, May 22, 2013, http://thinkprogress .org/justice/2013/05/22/2046451/white-people-stopped-by-new-york-police-are -more-likely-to-have-guns-or-drugs-than-minorities/.

Sigmann, Jean (1848) *1848: The Romantic and Democratic Revolutions in Europe.* London: Harper & Row, 1973.

Simon, Jonathan (1998) "Refugees in a Carceral Age. The Rebirth of Immigration Prisons in the United States." *Public Culture* lo, no. 3: 577–607.

Simon, Jonathan, (2000) "The 'Society of Captives' in the Era of Hyper-Incarceration." *Theoretical Criminology* 4, no. 3: 285–308.

Simon, Jonathan, (2002) "Governing Through Crime: Criminal Law and the Reshaping of American Governance, 1965–2000" (Oct. 7, 2002) (unpublished manuscript, on file with author).

Simon, Jonathan, (2005) "Reversal of Fortune: The Resurgence of Individual Risk Assessment in Criminal Justice." *Annual Review of Law Social Sciences* 1:397–421.

Simon, Jonathan, (2005–2006) "Positively Punitive- How the Inventor of Scientific Criminology Who Died at the Beginning of the Twentieth Century Continues to Haunt American Crime Control." *Texas Law Review* 84: 2135–2172.

Simon, Jonathan, (2007) *Governing through Crime. How the War on Crime Transformed American Democracy and Created a Culture of Fear.* Oxford: Oxford University Press, 2009.

Simon, Jonathan, (2014) *Mass Incarceration on Trial: A Remarkable Court Decision and the Future of Prisons in America.* New York: The New Press.

Smith, Larry (2012), *The Moment: Wild, Poignant, Life-Changing Stories from 125 Writers and Artists Famous & Obscure.* New York: Smith Magazine.

Soboul, Albert (1987) *Los sans-culottes. Movimiento popular y gobierno revolucionario.* Madrid: Alianza.

Sorel, Georges (1908) *Reflections on Violence.* Cambridge: Cambridge University Press, 1999.

Sparks, Richard (1980) "A Critique of Marxist Criminology." *Crime and Justice* 2: 159–210.

SPARQ (2016) "Scientists Release Oakland Police Findings," accessed May 31, 2016. https://sparq.stanford.edu/opd-reports.

Spitzer, Steven (1975) "Toward a Marxian Theory of Deviance." *Social Problems* 22, no. 5: 638–651.

Spohn, Cassia (2009) "Race, Sex, and Pretrial Detention in Federal Courts: Indirect Effects and Cumulative Disadvantage." *University of Kansas Law Review* 57:879–902.

Spohn Cassia (2014) "Racial Disparities in Prosecution, Sentencing, and Punishment." In *The Oxford Handbook of Ethnicity, Crime, and Immigration*, edited by Bucerius, Sandra and Tonry, Michael. Oxford: Oxford University Press.

Spohn, Cassia and Stacey, Ann Martin (2006) "Gender and the Social Costs of Sentencing: An Analysis of Sentences Imposed on Male and Female Offenders in Three U.S. District Courts" *Berkeley J. Crim. L.* no. 11.

Spohn, Cassia and Sample, Lisa L. (2008) "The Dangerous Drug Offender in Federal Court: Intersections of Race, Ethnicity, and Culpability." *Crime & Delinquency.*

Spohn, Cassia, and Robert Fornango (2009) "US Attorneys and Substantial Assistance Departures: Testing for Inter-Prosecutor Disparity." *Criminology* 47:813–42.

Stallybrass, Peter (1990) "Marx and Heterogeneity. Thinking the Lumpen-proletariat Representations." *The Margins of Identity in Nineteenth-Century* no. 31: 69–95.

Stedman Jones, Gareth (1973) "Engels and the End of Classical German Philosophy." *New Left Review* 1, no. 79 (1973).

Steffensmeier, Darrell, Ulmer, Jeffery and Kramer, John (1998) "The Interaction of Race, Gender, and Age in Criminal Sentencing: The Punishment Cost Oo Being Young, Black, And Male." *Criminology*, 36, no. 4, November 1998.

Stern, Vivien (2006) *Creating Criminals. Prisions and People in a Market Society.* London-New Zeland: Zed Books, 2006.

Stohr, Mary and Walsh, Anthony (2016), *Corrections: The Essentials.* Washington D.C.: Sage.

Strange, Susan (1986) *Casino Capitalism*, Manchester: Manchester University Press, 1997.

Subramanian, Ram and Shames, Alison (2013) "Sentencing and Prison Practice in Germany and the Netherlands: Implication for the United States." *VERA Institute* (2013).

Sueiro, Carlos Christian (2008) "Los requisitos típicos del crimen de lesa humanidad y su efecto de imprescriptibilidad. Los peligros que entraña desdibujar los principios generales del derecho penal a la luz de su 'internacionalización'." *Revista de Derecho Penal y Procesal Penal* no. 8: 1335–1347.

Star-Ledger (2012) "Leaked Secret Report Details How NYPD Kept Tabs on Newark's Muslim Community," *NewJersey.com*, February 22, 2012. http://www.nj.com/news/index.ssf/2012/02/leaked_secret_report_details_h.html.

Sumner, Colin (1979) *Reading Ideologies. An Investigation into the Marxist Theory of Ideology and Law.* London: Academic.

Sumner, Colin, (1983) "Law, Legitimation and the Advanced Capitalist State. The Jurisprudence and Social Theory of Jürgen Habermas" *Legality, Ideology and the State*, edited by Sugarman, David, 110–158. London-New York: Academic Press.

Sutherland, Edwin (1940) "White-Collar Criminality." *American Sociological Review* 5, no. 1 (1940).

Sutherland, Edwin, (1949) White-Collar *Crime*. New York: Dryden Press, 1949.

Stuart, Forrest (2016) *Out, and Under Arrest. Policing and Everyday Life in Skid Row*. Chicago: The University of Chicago Press.

Sweezy, Paul (1942) *The Theory of Capitalist Development*. London: Dennis Dobson Limited.

Sykes, Gresham, and Matza, David (1957) "Techniques of Neutralisation: A Theory of Delinquency." *American Sociological Review* 22: 664–670.

Szalavitz, Maia Study (2011) "Whites More Likely to Abuse Drugs Than Blacks." *TIM*, November 7, 2011. http://healthland.time.com/2011/11/07/study-whites-more-likely -to-abuse-drugs-than-blacks/.

Tadic, Ljubomir (1979) "Kelsen y Marx. Contribución al problema de la ideología en la 'teoría pura del derecho' y en el marxismo." In *Marx, El derecho y el Estado*. Barcelona: Oikos- Tau.

Tadros, Victor (2009) "Poverty and Criminal Responsibility." *The Journal of Value Inquiry* 43, no. 3: 391–413.

Tannenbaum, Frank (1938) *Crime and the Community*. Nueva York: Grinn and Co.

Taylor, Ian, (1974) "Advances towards a Critical Criminology." *Theory and Society* 1, no. 4: 441–476.

Taylor, Ian (1982) "Against Crime and for Socialism." *Crime and Social Justice* 18 (1982): 4–15.

Taylor, Ian, (1999) "Crime and Social Criticism." *Social Justice* 26, no. 2: 150–167.

Taylor, Ian; Walton, Paul and Young, Jock (1973) *The New Criminology. For a Social Theory of Deviance*. New York: Routledge, 1973. http://samples.sainsburysebooks .co.uk/9781135006877_sample_524363.pdf.

Taylor, Ian and Walton, Paul (1975) "Radical Deviancy Theory and Marxism: a reply to Paul Q. Hirst's 'Marx and Engels on Law, Crime and Morality." In *Critical Criminology*: 233–238. New York: Routledge, 1975.

Taylor-Thompson, Kim (1998) "The Politics of Common Ground." *Harvard Law Review* 111 no. 5 (March, 1998): 1306–1321.

Ternon, Yves (2007) *Guerres et génocides au XX siecle. Architectures de la violence de masse*. París: Odile Jacob.

The Economist (2014) "Stuffed," August 2, 2014, accessed April 19, 2016. http://www .economist.com/news/leaders/21610265-britains-prisons-are-shameful-state -solution-simple-takes-courage-stuffed?fsrc=scn/tw/te/pe/stuffed.

Thompson, Edward (1963) *The Making of the English Working Class*. New York: Phanteon Books, 1964.

Thompson, Edward, (1971) "Mode de domination et revolution en Anleterre." *Actes de la Recherche en Sciences Sociales* no. 2/3: 128–142.

Thompson, Edward, (1975) *Whigs and Hunters: The Origin of the Black Act.* London: Allen Lane, 1975.

Thompson, Edward, (1984) *Tradición, revuelta y conciencia de clase,* Barcelona: Crítica-Grijalbo.

Thompson, Edward, (1991) *Customs in Common: Studies in Traditional Popular Culture.* London: Merlin Press.

Thompson, Anthony C., (1999) "Stopping the Usual Suspects: Race and the Fourth Amendment." *NYU Law Review* 74, no. 4: 956–1013.

Thompson, Anthony C., (2011) "Unlocking Democracy: Examining the Collateral Consequences of Mass Incarceration on Black Political Power." *Howard Law Journal* 54.

Tiedemann, Klaus (1975) "El concepto de delito económico y de derecho penal económico." *Nuevo Pensamiento Penal:* 461–475.

Tittle, Charles (1983) "Social Class and Criminal Behavior, A Critique of the Theoretical Foundation." *Social Forces* 62, no. 2: 334–358.

Todorov, Tzvetan (1982) *La Conquista de América. El problema del otro.* México: Siglo XXI, 2007.

Tomás y Valiente, Francisco (1969) *El derecho penal de la monarquía absoluta (siglos XVI–XVII–XVII).* Madrid: Tecnos.

Tonkonoff, Sergio (1998) "Desviación, diversidad e ilegalismos. Comportamientos juveniles en el Gran Bs. As." *Delito y Sociedad,* no. 11/12: 139–168.

Tonkonoff, Sergio, (2001) "'Meter caño'. Jóvenes populares urbanos, entre la exclusión y el delito." *Delito y Sociedad* 10, no. 15/16: 171–182.

Tonkonoff, Sergio, (2007) "Juventud, exclusión y delito. Notas para la reconstrucción de un problema." *Alegatos* no. 65: 33–46.

Tonry Michael (2007) "Determinants of Penal Policies." *Crime and Justice* 36, no. 1: 1–48.

Tonry Michael, (2012) "Race, Ethnicity and Punishment." In *The Oxford Handbook of Sentencing and Corrections,* edited by Petersilia, Joan and Reitz, Kevin R., 53–82. Oxford-New York: Oxford University Press.

Trasher, Frederic (1927) *The Gang: A Study of 1313 Gangs in Chicago.* Chicago: University of Chicago Press.

Travis Jeremy (2002) "Invisible Punishment: An Instrument of Social Exclusion." In *Invisible Punishment: The Collateral Consequences of Mass Imprisonment,* edited by Mauer, M. and Chesney-Lind, M., 15–36. New York: New Press.

"USA Freedom Act: What's in, what's out," *Washington Post,* June 2, 2015. https://www.washingtonpost.com/graphics/politics/usa-freedom-act/.

Van den Haag, Ernest (1975) *Punishing Criminals: Concerning a Very Old and Painful Question.* New York: Basic Books, 1975.

Van Swaaningen René (1997) *Perspectivas europeas para una criminología crítica.* Montevideo: B de F, 2011.

Vassberg, David (1986) *Tierra y sociedad en Castilla*. Barcelona: Crítica.

Vattimo, Gianni (2013) "Los desafíos de la izquierda," *La Nación*, January 11, 2013.

Veblen, Thorstein (1899) *Teoría de la clase ociosa*. Bs. As.: Fondo de Cultura Economica, 2010.

Vedantam, Shankar (2016) "Research: Black Judges Are Reversed On Appeal More Than White Judges" *WNYC*, July 12, 2016. http://www.wnyc.org/story/research -black-judges-are-more-likely-to-be-reversed-on-appeal-than-white-judges/?utm _source=sharedUrl&utm_medium=metatag&utm_campaign=sharedUrl.

Vegh Weis, Valeria (2011) "El hurto de leña en Marx y las usurpaciones de terrenos en Buenos Aires hoy" (lecture, Instituto Gino Germani, Bs. As., November 10, 2011).

Vegh Weis, Valeria, (2013) "Sobre la cuestión judía de K. Marx y un debate necesario sobre la naturaleza de los derechos." *Razón y Revolución* no. 24: 123–146.

Vercellone, Carlo (2007) "Subsunción formal, subsunción real y general intellect: una perspectiva histórica de las transformaciones de la división del trabajo" en *Materialismo histórico* no. 15: 13–36.

Vercellone, Carlo, (2011) *Capitalismo cognitivo, renta, saber y valor en la época posfordista*, Bs. As.: Prometeo.

Vilar, Pierre (1964) *Crecimiento y desarrollo. Economía e historia. Reflexiones sobre el caso español*. Barcelona: Crítica.

Vilar, Pierre, (1975) "Marxist History, a History in the Making: Toward a Dialogue with Althusser." *New Left Review* no. 80 (1973): 65–106.

Vilar, Pierre, (1982) *Iniciación al vocabulario del análisis histórico*. Barcelona: Crítica.

Virno, Paolo (2001) "General Intellect." In *Lessico Postfordista*. Milano: Feltrinelli, 2001.

Virgolini, Julio (2005) *La razón ausente: Ensayo sobre criminología y crítica política*. Bs. As.: Del Puerto.

Vitagliano, Miguel (2013) "La condición lumpen," *Página/12*, January 27, 2013.

von Hirsch, A. (1984) "The Ethics of Selective Incapacitation: Observations on the Contemporary Debate" *Crime & Delinquency*: 175–194.

von Hirsch, A. (1998) "Proportionate Sentences: A Desert Perspective / Andrew von Hirsch in von Hirsch, Andrew and Ashworth, Andrew. Principled sentencing: readings on theory and policy." *Northwestern University Press*, 1998.

von Hirsch, A. (2005) "Selective Incapacitation: Some Doubts." Stanford Law Review 58, no. 1 (Oct., 2005): 67–83.

Von Hirsch, Andreas (2014) *Liberal Criminal Theory*. Oregon: Hart Publishing, 2014.

Wacquant, Loïc (1999) *Prisons of Poverty*. Mineapolis-London: University of Minnesota Press, 2009.

Wacquant, Loïc, (2001) "Deadly Symbiosis: When Ghetto and Prison Meet and Merge" *Punishment & Society* 3 no. 1: pp. 95–133.

Wacquant, Loïc, (2002) "From Slavery to Incarceration: Rethinking Incarceration in the U.S." *New Left Review* 13.

Wacquant, Loïc, (2006) *The Two Faces of the Ghetto and Other Essays*. New York-Oxford: University Press, 2012.

Wacquant, Loïc, (2007) *Urban Outcasts: A Comparative Sociology of Advanced Marginality*. Cambridge: Polity Press, 2008.

Wacquant, Loïc, (2009) *Punishing the Poor, The Neoliberal Government of Social Insecurity*, Durham-London: Duke University Press.

Wacquant, Loïc, (2011) "The Wedding of Workfare and Prisonfare Revisited." *Social Justice*, no. 38: 203–221.

Wacquant, Loïc, (2013) "Foreword, Probing the Meta-Prison" *The Globalization of Supermax Prisons*, ix–xiv. New Brunswick: Rutgers University Press.

Wacquant, Loïc and Standing, Guy (2011) *The Precariat, The New Dangerous Class*, London: Bloomsbury Academic.

Walker, Samuel and Katz, Charles M., (1996) *The Police in America: An Introduction*. Boston: McGraw-Hill.

WallMart1Percent (2016), accessed June 1, 2016. http://walmart1percent.org/how-rich-are-the-waltons.

Walshe, Sadhbh (2013) "America's Bail System: One Law for The Rich, Another for Poor," *The Guardian*, February 14, 2013. https://www.theguardian.com/commentis free/2013/feb/14/america-bail-system-law-rich-poor.

Weber, Max (1904) *The Protestant Ethic and the Spirit of Capitalism*. Mineola-New York: Dover Publications, 2003.

Weber, Max, (1906) "Capitalism and Rural Society in Germany." In *From Max Weber: Essays in Sociology*, edited by Gerth, H. and Wright Mills, C., 366–470. Nueva York: Galaxy Books, 1968.

Weber, Max, (1918) *El político y el científico*. Bs. As.: Prometeo, 2003.

Weber, Max, (1922) *Economy and Society*. Berkeley-Los Angeles-London: University of California Press, 1992.

Weichselbaum, Simone (2016) "The End of the Bratton Era." *The Marshall Project*, August 2, 2016.

Werkentin, Falco, Hofferbert, Michael and Bauermann, Michael (1974) "Criminology as Police Science or How Old Is the New Criminology?" *Crime and Social Justice* no. 2: 24–41.

Western, Bruce (2013) "Poverty Politics and Crime Control in Europe and America." *Contemporary Sociology* 40, no. 3: 283–286.

Wichmann, Clara (1912) *Beschouwingen over de historische grondslagen der tegenwoordige omvormin van het strafbegrip*. Leiden: Brill.

William, Stuntz (2011) "The Rise and Fall of Crime; the Rise and Fall of Punishment." In *The Collapse of American Criminal Justice*, 244–281. Cambridge-Massachusetts-London: The Belknap Press of Harvard University Press.

Wilson, James and Kelling, George (1982) "Broken Windows. The Police and neighborhood safety." *The Atlantic Monthly* 249, no. 3: 29–38.

Wolf, Paul (1995) "Esplendor y miseria de las teorías preventivas de la pena." In *Prevención y Teoría de la Pena*. Santiago de Chile: Conosur.

Women Donors Network (2016), "Who Leads Us?" accessed September 3, 2016. http://wholeads.us/justice/#.

Wonders, Nancy (2007) "Beyond Transnational Crime. Globalization, Border Reconstruction Projects, and Transnational Crime." *Social Justice* 34, no. 2: 33–46.

Wright Ronlad (2009) "How Prosecutor Elections Fail Us." *Ohio State Journal of Criminal Law* 6: 581–610.

Yanick, Charette and Vere van, Koppen (2015) "A Capture-Recapture Model to Estimate the Effects of Extra-Legal Disparities on Crime Funnel Selectivity and Punishment Avoidance." *Security Journal* 2, November 2015.

Young, Jock (1975) "Working Class Criminology." In *Critical Criminology*, 238–245. New York: Routledge.

Young, Jock, (1980) "Foreword." In *Crimes of the Powerful: Marxism, Crime and Deviance*, edited by Pearce, Frank. London: Pluto Press.

Young, Jock, (1999) *The Exclusive Society, Social Exclusion, Crime and Difference in Late Modernity*. London: Sage.

Young, Jock, (1999b) "Cannibalism and Bulimia: Patterns of Social Control in Late Modernity." *Theoretical Criminology* 3, no. 4: 387–407.

Young, Jock, (2007) *The Vertigo of Late Modernity*. London: SAGE Publications Ltd.

Young, Jock, (2008) "Merton with Energy, Katz with Structure: The sociology of Vindictiveness and the Criminology of Transgression." *Theoretical Criminology* 7, no. 3: 388–414.

Young, Jock, (2012) "Entrevista." *Delito y Sociedad* 33, no. 21: 13–14.

Zaffaroni, Raúl (1982) *Política Criminal Latinoamericana, Perspectivas- disyuntivas*, Bs. As.: Hammurabi.

Zaffaroni, Raúl, (1988) *Criminología. Aproximación desde un margen*. Bogotá: Temis.

Zaffaroni, Raúl, (1995) "El crimen organizado, una categoría frustrada." *Cuadernos del Departamento de Derecho Penal y Criminología*. Universidad Nacional de Córdoba.

Zaffaroni, Raúl, (2005) *En torno a la cuestión penal*. Bs. As.: Euros Editores.

Zaffaroni, Raúl, (2011) *Las palabras de los muertos*. Bs. As.: Ediar.

Zaffaroni, Raúl, (2011b) *La cuestión criminal*. Bs. As.: Planeta.

Zaffaroni, Raúl, (2012) *Congreso de Derecho Penal* (lecture, Facultad de Derecho de la Universidad de Buenos Aires, September 5, 2012).

Zaffaroni, Raúl, Alagia, Alejandro and Slokar, Alejandro (2000) *Derecho Penal. Parte general*. Bs. As.: Ediar, 2002.

Zambrana Moral, Patricia (2005) "Rasgos generales de la evolución histórica de la tipología de las penas corporales." *Estudios Histórico-Jurídicos* XXVII: 197–229.

Zimring, Franklin E. and Johnson, David T. (2001) "The Dark at the Top of the Stairs: Four Destructive Influences of Capital Punishment on American Criminal Justice." In *The Oxford Handbook of Sentencing and Corrections* 737–752. Oxford-New York: Oxford University Press.

Zizek, Slajov (1997) "Multiculturalism, or, the Cultural Logic of Multinational Capitalism." *New Left Review* I/225: 28–51.

Zysman Bernaldo de Quirós, Diego (2011) "Las Federal Sentencing Guidelines de los Estados Unidos de América (U.S.S.G.) y la justificación del castigo. Un estudio socio- jurídico sobre la determinación de la pena" (Ph.D. dissertation, Universidad de Barcelona).

Zysman Bernaldo de Quirós, Diego, (2013) *Sociología del castigo: genealogía de la determinación de la pena.* Bs. As.: Didot.

Zysman Bernaldo de Quirós, Diego, (2013b) *Castigo y determinación de la pena en los Estados Unidos. Un estudio sobre las United States Sentencing Guidelines.* Madrid: Marcial Pons.

Index